If you liked Bill Bennett's Book of Virtues, you will love this book by the Briscoes. Every family that reads it will greatly benefit.

> ~ Ben Haden, speaker
> Changed Lives TV & Radio

This book affords encouragement that people can relate to. The stories and illustrations bring the message into your life.

> ~ Bill and Lyndi McCartney, Promise Keepers

This priceless collection of short, fascinating Christian classics should be in every home. It's perfect for personal or family devotions. . . . Thank you, Stuart and Jill, for this wonderful contribution.

> ~ Bill Bright, Campus Crusade for Christ

Stu and Jill Briscoe have put together a book that challenges us [parents] to reach much deeper than we do on days when we juggle tuba lessons, PTA meetings, and soccer practice. I smiled when reading some of these selections; I was inspired by others.

> ~ Dr. Mary Manz Simon, mother of three teenagers and
> author of How to Parent Your 'Tweenager'

A balanced blend of healthy truth that can help families discover and develop Christian virtues and values. Desperately needed—wisely selected—these stories will build moral muscle.

> ~ Warren W. Wiersbe, author and conference speaker

Wonderful stories with insight for the family. I recommend this helpful volume for teaching your children what's eternally important—Christian values.

> ~ John Maxwell, pastor, national speaker, and
> founder of INJOY, Inc.

Godly values come from the Scriptures, . . . story-telling, and our Christian heritage. Stuart and Jill Briscoe combine these elements beautifully for the benefit of us all. May the families of America be encouraged and edified by The Family Book of Christian Values.

> ~ Art Gay, President
> World Relief

❧ The Family Book of Christian Values ❧

A wonderful collection of stories and verse, ancient and contemporary, with wisdom and entertainment for today's Christian family. Full of classic excerpts from the famous and inspiring insights from the not-so-famous, introduced by two of my favorite authors. . . .

> ~ Robertson McQuilkin, President Emeritus
> Columbia International University

A majority of youth—churched youth—can no longer determine right from wrong, and I firmly believe that these crumbling foundations must be rebuilt in our homes. The Family Book of Christian Values is an excellent resource that will help parents pass on a Bible-based value system to their children.

> ~ Josh McDowell, author and speaker

A wonderful treasury of classic stories, delightful poems, and inspiring Scriptures that will appeal to young and old alike. This comprehensive resource will encourage families to rediscover the value of reading aloud together.

> ~ Dr. Charles F. Stanley, Senior Pastor
> First Baptist Church, Atlanta

This book is destined to become a family treasure.

> ~ Bill Hybels, Senior Pastor
> Willow Creek Community Church

In a day when family values are eroding all around us, it is wonderful to have this rich resource made available to us from authors whom we respect greatly. . . .

> ~ Paul Cedar, President
> Evangelical Free Church of America

A precise, much-needed approach to establishing values that make a difference in lives. Beautifully written, easily understood, and clearly directed—it convinces us in various ways that we must BE before we can do . . . it's a book that uniquely establishes the importance of Christian values and, ultimately, what they will mean in our lives. Must reading for the Christian and secular community.

> ~ Zig Ziglar, author and motivational teacher

THE FAMILY BOOK OF CHRISTIAN VALUES

THE FAMILY BOOK OF CHRISTIAN VALUES

TIMELESS STORIES FOR TODAY'S FAMILY

STUART & JILL BRISCOE

Christian
Parenting
BOOKS

In memory of our late parents

STANLEY AND MARY BRISCOE
AND
BILL AND PEGGY RYDER

from whom we first learned
about values that count

Chariot Family Publishing
Cook Communications, Colorado Springs, CO 80918
Cook Communications, Paris, Ontario
Kingsway Communications, Eastbourne, England

THE FAMILY BOOK OF CHRISTIAN VALUES
© 1995 Briscoe Ministries

Cover design by Larry Smith & Associates, Inc.
Cover illustration by Clint Hansen
First printing, 1995
Printed in the United States of America
99 98 97 96 95   5 4 3

ISBN 0-7814-0245-X

Acknowledgements begin on page 499.

Library of Congress Cataloging-In-Publication Data
Briscoe, D. Stuart.
        The family book of christian values : timeless stories for today's family / Stuart
and Jill Briscoe.
                    p.   cm.
        Includes index.
        ISBN 0-7814-0245-X (hardcover). —ISBN 0-7814-0270-0 (audio)
        1. Literature—Collections. 2. Christian life—Literary collections.
        3. Conduct of life—Literary collections.
        I. Briscoe, Jill. II. Title.
        PN6014.B7317 1995
        808.8—dc20
                                                                        95-30477
                                                                           CIP

Published in association with the literary agency of Alive Communications, Inc.,
P. O. Box 49068, Colorado Springs, Colorado, 80949.

✦ Spiritual Values ✦

Contents

✦ Relational Values ✦

Foreword

When I was asked to write a foreword for this book, I agreed even before seeing the manuscript; the outline furnished me was enough for me to see its great significance. *The Family Book of Christian Values* encourages Christians to rethink their values, which have been degraded by movies and TV. Popular sitcoms and talk shows usually appeal to our baser instincts. Evils whispered about twenty years ago are now shouted from the housetops. This shift in worldly culture during the last few years has hardened the hearts of Christians, too.

Even we who are believers have become desensitized to violence and abuse. Our hearts' beliefs have been eroded by the snickers and scorn and godless urgings of the media. Sacred things are retained in our heads rather than eagerly sought after and felt with our hearts. Our values need to be refreshed, and our thoughts about God need to be re-inspired. *The Family Book of Christian Values* does this in a wonderful way. I have been encouraged while reading it, and have been fortified in turning toward God's values by observing what the characters in this collection of stories and essays have thought and done.

A hearty word of thanks to Stuart and Jill Briscoe, the compilers of this volume. They have gleaned some of the best of the

harvest, written by inspirational writers who tell us about heroic
actions and about tenacity in holding to the age-old values of the
Ten Commandments and the Sermon on the Mount. The Briscoes'
introductions and comments have directed me, as a reader, to the
application of these extracts to my own life.

I hope you will enjoy and profit from this book as much as
I have.

Kenneth N. Taylor
Children's author, publisher,
translator of *The Living Bible*

A Word from the Briscoes

Why do we need *The Family Book of Christian Values?*
"One child lost to the faith usually becomes a family lost to the faith, and not many generations later a whole community of unbelievers is set in motion because of some earlier neglect of parental duties."

It is out of concern for the spiritual decline in our nation, so starkly described above by theologian Dr. Carl F. H. Henry, that we gladly accepted the invitation to work on this book. As the parents of three grown children, grandparents of eight (at last count) lively youngsters, and pastor of a great community of believers in the Milwaukee area, we look at our world with a mixture of delight and disappointment. The delight comes from the many families we know who are committed to nurturing their marriages and caring for the physical, emotional, intellectual, social, and spiritual well-being of their children; the disappointment from the obvious erosion of standards and the resultant dysfunction, disorientation, and despair that are encroaching on the lives of young and old, rich and poor.

We are convinced that the recovery of Christian values is imperative for the well-being of society in general and families in particular. And if Dr. Henry is correct, as we believe he is, part of the problem is that parents wittingly or unwittingly are guilty of the "neglect of parental duties" in this area.

What do you mean by "Christian values"?
In former days people used to have ideals and talk about virtues; now "values" is the buzzword. Because it is currently in vogue and communicates more readily than the older, less familiar terms, we have chosen to use it. In *A Question of Values* Hunter Lewis writes, "Although the term values is often used loosely, it should be synonymous with personal beliefs . . . that propel us to action, to a particular kind of behavior and life." We regard Christian values as those authoritative principles taught by Scripture that require us to live in a certain way in the power of the indwelling Spirit to the glory of God.

What's the difference between a book of Christian values and a book outlining traditional virtues? The uniqueness of Christian teaching is not to be found in its moral principles—those same principles can be found in other religions and from pre-Christian times. But much moral teaching, good as it is, can lead good people to self-righteousness. Christian teaching does the opposite. "By the law is the knowledge of sin," says the apostle Paul, and this knowledge leads us to repentance and forgiveness through Christ's sacrifice. The uniqueness of Christianity is that when we look at moral teaching, we are confronted with our own failure—and in Christ we have somewhere to turn for help. When we ask His forgiveness, Christ Himself comes into our hearts to strengthen us "with might by His Spirit in the inner man," thus enabling us to live out the moral principles He taught.

What's in *The Family Book of Christian Values*?
It may seem odd to some of our readers that in a book purportedly promoting Christian values we should utilize some material from non-Christian sources. We feel that it is perfectly appropriate to do this, not only because all truth is God's truth, but also because even the most fallen of individuals was created in the image of God and

through common grace is gifted by God to have insights and skills that redound to His glory. Pastor and author A. W. Tozer said, "Every true work of art praises God apart from the composer's intentions, because it could not have been written without the gifts which God gave His creation." Remember, God was not at all reticent on one occasion to speak through a donkey when He had a message to get across!

We have seen even as we have talked about the project that many people are intrigued to discover the spiritual truths to be found in unexpected literary places and are then stimulated to read further. This does not mean, of course, that because we have quoted a particular title we endorse the book in its entirety or that we regard the author as being a model of Christian behavior.

The introductory comments about each value are intended to set the stage for the readings that illustrate the point being made, while the brief comments before most selections are designed to give context to the reading or to provoke further thinking and possible discussion. There should be something under each value to appeal to young, old, and in between (each section begins with material for younger children), and there should be enough material of wide interest to make it possible for families to read and enjoy this book together. We encourage families to turn off their televisions for a while and rediscover the old-fashioned art of reading aloud, and we hope that some young people will be encouraged to step out of the isolated world of Walkman and join the rest of the world in the pleasure of reading and thinking together.

Stuart and Jill Briscoe

Special Thanks

You may be interested in learning how this project came into being. We were approached by the people at Chariot Family Publishing through the good graces of our friend and agent Rick Christian. Would we be interested in putting together a selection of literature based on the values they had used for many years as the basis of their balanced curriculum of Sunday school material and other publications? We were immediately intrigued at the possibilities, not only because of our aforementioned concerns, but also because of our love of books and good reading. An animated conversation over Swedish pancakes with Karl Schaller and Julie Smith was enough to convince us that this was something we would be pleased to be a part of.

So armed with Chariot's list of values and a stack of cuttings from their archives, we began the task of reading, selecting, and writing commentary. We scoured the dusty cobwebs of our memories for recollections of books long forgotten and literature learned long ago and far away. (This accounts for what some American readers may feel is a preponderance of British material. Sorry! We learned to read in Britain!)

The task of clipping and copying was performed with admirable patience and precision by Kappie Grissell, a gifted servant if ever there was one, and a lady who knows not the meaning of retirement. An appeal to Iva Danielson, former director of English literature curriculum in the Milwaukee public school system, brought to our attention all kinds of material we did not know and also the sources of things we did know but didn't know how we knew them or where they were! A chance remark to our good friend Sarah Knott of Raleigh, North Carolina (mother of six, including quadruplets), led to the discovery that she was a walking encyclopedia of children's material. Her contributions were invaluable. Two staff colleagues also deserve special thanks: Dr. Doug Schoen for sending many pithy quotes my way, and Alice Hamilton for helpful research assistance.

After amassing a pile of material enough for half a dozen books, we handed everything over to the tender mercies of our gifted editor Lora Beth Norton, who wielded her blue pencil with grace and skill. Along with Joy Sherfey, who efficiently orchestrated the details of scheduling, obtaining permissions, typing, designing, and proofreading, she shaped the finished product while we flew off to South Africa (not to escape reading the galleys, but to minister to the people of that wonderful country).

Thank you to all these people and many more unsung, without whom *The Family Book of Christian Values* would still be just a breakfast-table idea.

—SB

⤙PERSONAL⤚
VALUES

The Mice in Council
AESOP

Talk is cheap—action requires courage.

Once upon a time all the Mice met together in Council and discussed the best means of securing themselves against the attacks of the cat. After several suggestions had been debated, a Mouse of some standing and experience got up and said, "I think I have hit upon a plan which ensures our safety in the future, provided you approve and carry it out. It is that we should fasten a bell around the neck of our enemy the cat, which will by its tinkling warn us of her approach."

This proposal was warmly applauded, and it had been already decided to adopt it, when an old Mouse finally got upon his feet and said, "I agree with you all that the plan before us is an admirable one: but I ask, who is going to bell the cat?" &

The King's Champion
PAULINE ROTHRAUFF

It takes courage to do what God says is right. Rob's action is a good lesson for young and old alike, because for every opportunity to "do right" there is a chance to "go wrong"—and often the latter seems easier than the former.

It was the year 1189, more than 800 years ago. From the window of his father's inn, Rob watched the travelers go by. He thought of the great celebration that would take place tomorrow in Westminster Abbey, in London.

"I want to see the Coronation procession," thought Rob. He had heard many stories of Richard the Lionhearted, who would be crowned king tomorrow.

His father was busy with early morning chores when Rob

approached him. "Father," he said, "I want very much to go to Westminster to see the new king."

His father looked doubtful. "It's no place for a lad of fifteen," he replied. "There'll be all sorts of people there—beggars and thieves, as well as good people. And yet . . . when I was your age, I, too, would have wanted to go.

"Very well, Rob," his father finally said. "Go if you wish, but you must be careful. Ask your mother to fix some food for you. And here are a couple of coins to spend."

"Thank you, Father," replied Rob. "I will be careful. God will take care of me."

Soon he was on his way, a big package of food under his arm. "I'll try to get to the edge of London by night," he planned as he walked along. "Then tomorrow at daybreak I'll go straight to Westminster."

At noon Rob decided to find a shady spot and have his lunch. When he came to a forest, he left the road and walked until he came to a clear spring. He drank some of the delicious, cool water, then opened his package of food. Then Rob bowed his head and thanked God for his food.

While sitting there eating and trying to imagine what the coronation procession would be like, Rob heard the sound of a horse's hoofs. In a few minutes a horse and its rider, a tall man with red-gold hair, appeared and rode up to Rob.

"How about something to eat for a weary traveler?" he asked, with a merry smile. He dismounted and led his horse to a patch of grass.

When the stranger returned, Rob spread his food package open before him. "Help yourself, sir," he invited. "You're welcome to whatever I have."

While the man ate, Rob mentioned that he was on his way to the Coronation. "I can hardly wait," he said. "I'll be in London by nightfall, won't I?"

"Easily," replied the stranger. "You are only a few miles away now. I would offer to let you ride with me, but I have a visit to make before I go into the city."

"Are you going to the Coronation, too?" Rob asked.

"Yes, I'll be there for all of it," the man said with a smile. "I must be on my way now. Thank you for the food, lad, and here is a coin with which to buy a pie in London."

He held out a gold piece, but Rob shook his head. "No, I want no money. I was glad to share my food with you."

"Good lad," said the man as he went to get his horse. But when he rode past Rob, he tossed the gold coin down on the grass. After Rob watched the man ride away, he picked up the coin and put it in his pouch. He had never owned a gold piece before. It was a lot of money.

Shortly after he had wrapped up the little food that was left and started through the forest, Rob again heard the sound of horses' hoofs. Soon five riders rode out from among the trees.

"Stop there, boy," commanded the leader, riding his horse in front of Rob to block his way. The man who spoke was ugly and had an evil look about him. "Tell me," he ordered Rob, "have you seen a tall, red-haired man pass by here?"

Because Rob was almost certain that these men meant to harm his friend, he replied, "I have been busy with my own affairs, sir. I wasn't looking for anyone."

The man glared at Rob but continued on with his men through the forest. As Rob watched them go, he said to himself, "I wonder what they want with my kind friend? I hope they don't find him."

It was getting dark when Rob arrived at the edge of London, but he soon found a quiet place where he could rest. It had been a long day, and he slept soundly.

When Rob opened his eyes, it was nearly daylight. He got up and started through London to find the road that led to

Westminster. Although it was still very early in the morning, and the procession wouldn't be starting for some time yet, there was a large crowd around the Abbey. Rob had to push and shove his way through to get in front of many taller people who blocked his view. But he finally found an opening where there was no one between him and the road.

He would be almost close enough to reach out and touch King Richard, Rob thought happily.

While he waited, Rob glanced around at some of the people standing near him. Suddenly he gasped, and a chill ran down his back. Just a few steps away from him stood the evil-looking horseman who had asked about Rob's red-haired friend. A case of arrows hung at the man's side, and he held a bow in his hand.

Rob felt sure the man meant to cause trouble. He wished he could leave, but if he wanted to see the procession, there was nothing he could do but stay calm and wait.

"I'll pretend I haven't seen him," decided Rob, trying to act natural as he listened to the noise of the parade beginning in the distance.

The procession soon came near, and the crowd happily watched the colorful scene.

First came a great number of people in elaborate costumes, carrying gaily decorated flags. Next came beautifully dressed noblemen, four of whom carried the clothes the newly crowned king would wear. They were followed by the man who carried the crown itself. He walked directly in front of the canopy that was being held over the king. Behind the king marched another richly dressed group of royal persons.

But it was toward the king that everyone looked, and Rob, too, leaned out into the road to get a good look.

It was then that Rob's eyes almost popped out of his head. King Richard was none other than his red-haired friend, the man with whom Rob had shared his lunch the day before!

After his surprise at seeing that his friend was the king, Rob's next thought was for the ugly man standing nearby. Rob began to pray that God would help him do what was right.

Rob turned to look at the man just in time to see him raise his bow and arrow and aim straight at the king. Because everyone else in the crowd was watching the procession, no one but Rob saw that the man intended to kill the king.

Without hesitating, Rob raced toward the canopy and flung himself in front of the king just as the arrow came whizzing toward him.

Rob felt the sharp point pierce his shoulder and heard the cries of the crowd, as well as the king's exclamation of surprise and alarm. Then everything went black.

When Rob opened his eyes, he was lying on a couch in a large, beautifully furnished room. A doctor was bandaging his shoulder while several of the king's men stood nearby.

"There," said the doctor as he finished, "it will soon be better. Now drink this medicine and sleep for a while."

Rob drank from the cup which the doctor handed him. Then he lay back again, weak and tired.

"That was a splendid thing you did," said one of the guards. "Our king will not forget it."

"Where is the evil man who shot the arrow?" asked Rob.

"He was soon caught and is now in prison," replied one of the king's men. "The man was a leader of some troublemakers who were trying to keep Richard from the throne. But now, thanks to you, young sir, our king is safe and at this moment is being crowned king in the Abbey." ❧

First Lady of Flight
FRANCIS AND KATHARINE DRAKE

Amelia Earhart is to this day a symbol of extraordinary courage and adventure. The comfort and ease of modern air travel tend to obscure the fact that pioneer aviation was extremely dangerous—no place for a woman, many said. Amelia Earhart thought otherwise.

Mr. George Putnam sat at his desk waiting. He had a crazy job to do: to find a young American woman willing to risk her life on a hair-raising adventure. She was to be modest and dignified, ready to face death calmly, and able to keep a secret.

There was a knock on the door. And into Mr. Putnam's office stepped a smiling towheaded girl with freckles and steady gray eyes. Her name was Amelia Earhart. Occupation: social-service worker. Hobby: flying.

For George Putnam, well-known publisher and author, the search was over. He had found his candidate for the dangerous feat of becoming the first woman to fly the Atlantic.

Amelia Earhart was born in Kansas in 1898. Her early life was much like that of other children in the Middle West. But she would rather use the hayloft in her grandfather's barn as a break-neck roller coaster than play with dolls. She also liked to fish, to ride astride, and to belly-flop.

In 1920 her father took her to her first air meet, in California. Many who came to the air meet that day had never seen a plane before. Amelia talked her father into letting her take a "joy ride." And her heart filled with gladness as the field dropped away.

"I knew then," she said, "that I must fly."

It was a Sunday when the *Friendship*, with Amelia Earhart on board, clawed its way out of Trepassey harbor in Newfoundland and pressed its nose eastward against the heavy fog.

For eighteen hours, Pilot Wilmer Stultz fought his way through blinding storms and bandages of fog. Sometimes he dropped to shake ice from the plane's wings. Sometimes he climbed to escape the waves. The motor coughed all the time. The mechanic, Louis Gordon, paid out fuel faster and still faster as the *Friendship* bucked heavy headwinds. The radio died, and he struggled in vain to restore it to life.

With fuel for sixty minutes in the tanks, and rain dripping icily down her neck, Amelia spent what might have been her last hours scribbling in her logbook. She filled it with bits of poetry, gay drawings, and word pictures of the flight. "The clouds," she wrote, "are like fantastic gobs of mashed potatoes."

The *Friendship* made a safe landing at Burry Port, Wales—the eleventh heavier-than-air machine to complete the North Atlantic crossing.

During the next four years, Amelia flew for distance records, tested experimental planes and engines, gave lessons, and boosted air travel with lectures and articles. Men admired her good sportsmanship. Women liked her modesty. And George Putnam married her.

But always there was that prodding spirit of adventure. True, Amelia had flown the Atlantic—but as "cargo." Now she began to study navigation, radio, and instrument flying. More than 1000 air hours later, she felt that she was ready.

On the evening of May 20, 1932, Amelia climbed into the cockpit of her single-engine Lockheed-Vega at Harbour Grace, Newfoundland. Her heart was set on doing what no one but Charles Lindbergh had ever done: a transatlantic solo.

When she was four hours out of Newfoundland, flames began spurting from the engine. The engine might fail at any moment.

Should she turn back? To land at night at unfamiliar Harbour Grace with a full load of gasoline could only mean disaster. Should she go on? Amelia weighed the evils and kept going. With lightning stabbing the darkness ahead, and solid fog below, the altimeter broke. From then on she had to guess how far she was above the sea.

Amelia climbed until ice formed on the wings. The little plane shuddered and went into a spin, but she regained control. For five hours she flew through violent storms. Then the tachometer—the vital instrument that measures revolutions per minute—failed. A leaking fuel gauge near the blazing engine filled the ship with gas fumes. Though she had enough fuel to reach Paris, she decided to land at the first place she could find.

Thus it was that, fourteen hours and fifty-six minutes after leaving Newfoundland, she came down in a pasture near Londonderry, Ireland. Some astonished cows bolted for safety as the alarming red machine, belching blue flame and smoke, sat down among them. Amelia had established a new world record under conditions that are hard to believe.

The transatlantic solo made Amelia famous. She was showered with honors and decorations, feted by royalty, and mobbed wherever she went. But success did not turn her head.

Amelia wanted to take just one flight around the world. After that she planned to give up long-distance flying.

On the first leg of that flight the new twin-engine Lockheed Electra, overloaded with gasoline to take it from Honolulu to distant Howland Island, north of Samoa, ground-looped and cracked up at the take-off. Repairs caused delay. Then the weather changed, forcing the flyers to reverse their plan and fly eastward around the world. This left to the home stretch the most dangerous part of the whole flight—picking tiny Howland Island, only two square miles in size, out of the vast Pacific Ocean.

The thought of Howland Island must have haunted Amelia and Fred Noonan, her navigator, as they winged their way around three-quarters of the globe. On July 2, 1937, Amelia and Noonan took off from New Guinea. Ahead, more than 2500 miles across the water, lay Howland Island. Hours later, a lookout Coast Guard cutter picked up a familiar voice: "Head winds . . . half an hour's gas . . . circling."

Judging by the signals, the lost plane was only a hundred miles from Howland. Somewhere near journey's end, the needle of the gas gauge must have sunk against the stop. In the distant and empty sea, Amelia's luck ran out. . . .

What made this adventure-loving girl risk her life on such a gamble? The answer may be found in a letter she wrote to her husband, George Putnam, before she took off. She had marked it to be read only if she did not return.

"Please know that I am quite aware of the hazards," the letter read. "I want to do it—because I want to do it. Women must try to do things as men have tried. When they fail, then failure must be but a challenge to others." &

Courage
KARLE WILSON BAKER

The last two lines of this six-line poem give the best definition of courage I know.

Courage is armor
    A blind man wears;
The calloused scar
    Of outlived despairs:
Courage is Fear
    That has said its prayers. &

The Storm
THE ACTS OF THE APOSTLES 27:13-44, NIV

Though he was sailing as a prisoner to an uncertain future before Caesar in Rome, Paul didn't seem to be afraid. Even when confronted by shipwreck, sword, and snakes all in one day, his courage was so impressive that the soldiers guarding him and the sailors threatening mutiny acknowledged his leadership. His secret, of course, was that he knew his Lord.

When a gentle south wind began to blow, they thought they had obtained what they wanted; so they weighted anchor and sailed along the shore of Crete. Before very long, a wind of hurricane force, called the "Northeaster," swept down from the island. The ship was caught by the storm and could not head into the wind; so we gave way to it and were driven along. As we passed to the lee of a small island called Cauda, we were hardly able to make the lifeboat secure. When the men had hoisted it aboard, they passed ropes under the ship itself to hold it together. Fearing that they would run aground on the sandbars of Syrtis, they lowered the sea anchor and let the ship be driven along. We took such a violent battering from the storm that the next day they began to throw the cargo overboard. On the third day, they threw the ship's tackle overboard with their own hands. When neither sun nor stars appeared for many days and the storm continued raging, we finally gave up all hope of being saved.

After the men had gone a long time without food, Paul stood up before them and said: "Men, you should have taken my advice not to sail from Crete; then you would have spared yourselves this damage and loss. But now I urge you to keep up your courage, because not one of you will be lost; only the ship will be destroyed. Last night an angel of the God whose I am and whom I serve stood beside me and said, 'Do not be afraid, Paul. You must stand trial before Caesar; and God has graciously given you the lives of all who said with you.' So keep up your courage, men, for I have faith in God that it will happen just as he told me. Nevertheless, we must run aground on some island."

On the fourteenth night we were still being driven across the Adriatic Sea, when about midnight the sailors sensed they were approaching land. They took soundings and found that the water was a hundred and twenty feet deep. A short time after they took soundings again and found it was ninety feet deep. Fearing that we would be dashed against the rocks, they dropped four anchors from the stern and prayed for daylight. In an attempt to escape from the ship, the sailors let the lifeboat down into the sea, pretending they were going to lower some anchors from the bow. Then Paul said to the centurion and the soldiers, "Unless these men stay with the ship, you cannot be saved." So the soldiers cut the ropes that held the lifeboat and let it fall away.

Just before dawn Paul urged them all to eat. "For the last fourteen days," he said, "you have been in constant suspense and have gone without food—you haven't eaten anything. Now I urge you to take some food. You need it to survive. Not one of you will lose a single hair from his head." After he said this, he took some bread and gave thanks to God in front of them all. Then he broke it and began to eat. They were all encouraged and ate some food themselves. Altogether there were 276 of us on board. When they had eaten as much as they wanted, they lightened the ship by throwing the grain into the sea.

When daylight came, they did not recognize the land, but they saw a bay with a sandy beach, where they decided to run the ship aground if they could. Cutting loose the anchors, they left them in the sea and at the same time untied the ropes that held the rudders. Then they hoisted the foresail to the wind and made for the beach. But the ship struck a sandbar and ran aground. The bow stuck fast and would not move, and the stern was broken to pieces by the pounding of the surf.

The soldiers planned to kill the prisoners to prevent any of them from swimming away and escaping. But the centurion wanted to spare Paul's life and kept them from carrying out their plan. He ordered those who could swim to jump overboard first and get to land. The rest were to get there on planks or on pieces of the ship. In this way everyone reached land in safety. ♣

A Courageous Preacher
John Pollock

George Whitefield (1714-1770), one of the world's most courageous evangelists, was by nature a timid man. This excerpt from Pollock's biography, George Whitefield, *paints a vivid picture of the man at work in the midst of violent and dangerous opposition.*

Every Easter week the London poor gave themselves over to fun. Strolling players, bear-leaders with bears taught to dance by cruelty; clowns and "merry-andrews," and a whole host of conjurers and troupers would converge on the capital. Every freak and mountebank came to Moorfields or Marylebone Fields or Kennington Common; every trickster, thief and pickpocket, gamester and gin seller knew where to find the crowds.

For weeks beforehand in the spring of 1742 George Whitefield had been summoning his courage to "lift up a standard amongst them in the name of Jesus of Nazareth," since thousands who never would come to an open air sermon would be there.

Easter Monday fair began at sunrise. George determined to outflank the devil. In the early hours a large group of his friends met him at the Tabernacle and prayed that Easter might become a Pentecost and that they would be given grace to lift up their voices against the enemy. As they prayed they could hear the tramp of people converging on the fairground, sober and quiet so far, but pliable material for the powers of darkness—or the powers of light.

As dawn broke, Whitefield and his friend proceeded the short

16

distance to Moorfields and erected the portable pulpit in the middle of a good-humored crowd eager for fun. Not a booth or sideshow had opened, the clowns were still dressing up and the gin sellers trundled their barrows of jars and jugs and cups, so that the portable pulpit looked like the first entertainment of the day; others recognized Mr. Whitefield and knew that anyway he could tell a rattling good story. A few, shamed at the vices they had come to enjoy, drew near because, at heart, they hungered.

He began to speak on the Serpent in the Wilderness, bringing before their very eyes the murmuring Israelites, the poisonous snakes, the cry for healing and safety. Then Moses makes a serpent of brass and lifts it up and by a look of faith the people are healed. The crowd listened awestruck as George applied the story to their own sins, their own need of healing and salvation. His voice boomed out: "As Moses lifted up the serpent in the wilderness, even so must the Son of man be lifted up, that whosoever believeth in him should not perish—but have eternal life."

When he finished preaching he knew by the stillness, except for weeping, that here grew a field white to harvest indeed. He resolved to go out again at noon.

At noon, the fair rollicked in full swing. George had the pulpit pitched on the far side from the sideshows. He could see dancing bears, and the wild beasts in cages; the puppets and the leaping acrobats, the bearded woman paraded by the freak-master, followed by dwarfs. He trembled a little at the noise of drums and trumpets, of laughter, and fights breaking out here and there; and almost everybody in sight had their backs to him.

He boomed out his text and began to describe the riot at Ephesus, in his usual graphic terms. The voice reached across, the people turned to leave the shows by the score. This was too much for several showmen. They promptly showered Whitefield with dirt and rotten eggs and pieces of dead cat, even a few jagged stones: he laughed aside a few cuts. The showmen gave up. The congregation swelled, became quieter, and for an hour the fair and George Whitefield continued independently.

George returned to "Vanity Fair" at dusk. His friends erected the pulpit right beside a "merry-andrew" or jester in bright motley dancing about on a torchlit stage, who promptly lost most of his audience to the parson in black robes. The merry-andrew was furious, so were the other showmen, since many converts from the morning and afternoon had deserted them, to go home or to spend the rest of the holiday with Whitefield's Christians to learn the rudiments of prayer and Scripture. . . .

Liquor stalls or sideshows, takings had dropped. Therefore, when George's enormous voice rang out across the fairground for the third time and people ran to him, frustrated showmen decided things had gone far enough. George heard "a kind of roaring" a little distance away as they bellowed in chorus to drown him. The yelling drew nearer. George stopped preaching and led his people in a hymn, for no words could be heard above the din.

The merry-andrew had armed himself with a carter's long, heavy whip. He now climbed onto the shoulders of his friends and in a peculiar phalanx they trotted round behind the pulpit. Here the listeners stood more thinly, being behind the preacher, and the shock of the phalanx broke the ranks a little. The man then slashed at George with the whip, found him just out of range, lost his balance and fell off. He remounted the shoulders, slashed again and fell. George had looked round at the crack of the whip and could hardly restrain his laughter; but the audience were deadly serious and a little afraid, and he started to preach again.

After a few more attempts the man withdrew. George Whitefield held the field. Not for long. He heard a drumming draw nearer and louder: his opponents had found one of the Army recruiting parties in scarlet and pipe clay who always frequented a fair, and had bribed the sergeant to drum the preacher off the ground. The sergeant marched, the drummer boy drummed with all his strength. George stopped preaching and called out to the crowd, "Make way for His Majesty's officer!" They parted. The sergeant could hardly demean His Majesty's uniform by not marching on through the gap—and away out of earshot.

. . . At about 9 p.m. George left Moorfields and returned to the Tabernacle "with my pockets full of notes from persons under concern." He read them out, one by one, to a building which rang with praises "that so many sinners had been snatched in such an unexpected, unlikely place out of the very jaws of the devil." &

Death, Be Not Proud
JOHN DONNE

John Donne (1572-1631) was an Anglican clergyman and one of the most gifted poets in English literature. His challenge in this sonnet shows in a startling way the unique blessings to which death introduces the believer. This helps us conquer the fear of death, allowing us to live courageously.

Death be not proud, though some have called thee
    Mighty and dreadful, for thou art not so;
For those whom thou think'st thou dost overthrow
    Die not, poor death, nor yet canst thou kill me.
From rest and sleep, which but thy pictures be,
    Much pleasure; then from thee much more must flow,
And soonest our best men with thee do go,
    Rest of their bones, and soul's delivery.
Thou art slave to fate, chance, kings, and desperate men,
    And dost with poison, war, and sickness dwell;
And poppy or charms can make us sleep as well,
    And better than thy stroke; why swell'st thou then?
One short sleep past, we wake eternally,
    And death shall be no more; death, thou shalt die. &

The Pilgrim

JOHN BUNYAN

John Bunyan (1628-1688) lived in England in a time of religious turmoil and civil war. Ignoring the magistrate's order to stop preaching, he was imprisoned over a period of twelve years. In prison he wrote these stirring words of courage.

Who would true valour see,
    Let him come hither;
One here will constant be,
    Come wind, come weather;
There's no discouragement
Shall make him once relent
His first avowed intent
    To be a Pilgrim.

Whoso beset him round
    With dismal stories
Do but themselves confound;
    His strength the more is.
No lion can him fright,
He'll with a giant fight,
But he will have a right
    To be a Pilgrim.

Hobgoblin nor foul fiend
    Can daunt his spirit;
He knows he at the end
    Shall life inherit.
Then fancies fly away,
He'll fear not what men say;
He'll labour night and day
    To be a Pilgrim.

Gladys Aylward:
The Small Woman
RUTH TUCKER

"The small woman" was tiny! But when we met her we discovered she had a big voice, a big heart, and a very big God!

Gladys Aylward was born in London in 1902 into a working-class family. She became a parlormaid—a position that included heavy chores, long hours, and low pay. Although she had attended church off and on and was familiar with the gospel message, she did not identify with Christ personally until one night at the close of a church service, when she was confronted by a stranger concerning her spiritual need.

With her conversion, Gladys's life changed. She began dreaming about serving the Lord as a foreign missionary. It was this dream that brought her to the China Inland Mission headquarters in 1929, and it was that same dream that would not die when she was not invited to continue her training after her probationary term was over. She was convinced that God was calling her, and if she could not obtain a mission's sponsorship she would go on her own. She began saving every penny she earned and depositing it with the ticket agent at the railway station. She also began reading and inquiring about China every opportunity she had, which brought her in contact with Jeannie Lawson, an elderly widowed China missionary who was anxious that someone come out to assist her.

If Gladys needed a direct sign from God, that was it, and on October 15, 1932, tickets in hand, she departed from the Liverpool Street Station en route to China. Besides her bedroll Gladys carried two suitcases (one stocked with food) and a bag clanking with a small stove and pots and pans. Russia was in the midst of an undeclared border war with China, and after passing through

Moscow, Gladys's train was packed with Russian troops. At every stop the validity of her tickets and passport was questioned, and it was only by the grace of God that the non-English-speaking authorities allowed her to continue. Alone with hundreds of soldiers, crossing the stark Siberian landscape, Gladys had second thoughts about her decision, but it was too late to turn back. Then, almost without warning, she was told that she had gone as far as she would be allowed to travel. Only soldiers were allowed to stay on the train. But Gladys refused to get off. She insisted that she be allowed to go on until the train stopped, thinking that every mile was bringing her closer to China. The train continued on several miles down the track, and then it stopped. The sound of gunfire could be heard in the distance as the soldiers and supplies were unloaded, and Gladys found herself all alone in a deserted train only hundreds of yards away from the war zone. She had no choice but to trudge back on the snow-covered tracks to the closest town.

Once in China, Gladys began the arduous trek across the mountains to Yangcheng, where Jeannie Lawson was faithfully continuing the work she and her husband had begun so many years earlier. Gladys was shown around and then, without any celebration, got settled into the work of being a missionary. The work was not what Gladys had expected. Her first assignment consisted of operating an inn for muleteers who passed through Yangcheng on their route west. For Jeannie it was an opportunity to share the gospel with the muleteers each evening, but for Gladys it was hard work—making her housework back in London seem like a genteel profession.

Despite the hard work and few rewards, Gladys was making progress. What she never could have learned in formal language training, she was readily picking up as she dealt with the muleteers. The Chinese tongue was not just a language of complex written characters, but a language of emotion and feeling, and it was through this facet of the language that she learned to communcate.

With the eventual death of Mrs. Lawson, Gladys no longer had the financial support she needed to operate the inn, but a new opportunity opened up—one that gave her a far wider influence than the inn had. She was asked by the Chinese magistrate of Yangcheng to become the local foot inspector. It became her job to go from house to house, making sure the new laws against female footbinding were being complied with. It was an exciting opportunity for her to improve her language skills, to get to know the people, and to share the gospel.

As Gladys traveled around, her ministry blossomed. Wherever she went people came out to see her and to listen to her Bible stories. As she visited and revisited villages, her prestige grew and the people began to view her as an authority figure—so much so that on one occasion she was called on to use her prowess to put down a prison riot.

During the years that Gladys spent traveling from village to village, she made friends and converts, and the future for her ministry seemed bright. But outside her little world around Yangcheng in the Shansi Province, massive plots and military maneuvers were taking place. It was a period of time when the yet-obscure guerrilla leader, Mao Tse Tung, was building his revolutionary force, and when Japan was amassing thousands of troops on the Manchurian border. But life went on in Yangcheng as usual until the summer of 1937. The once peaceful mountain villages of Shansi suddenly became targets of Japanese bombing raids. Gladys, who had recently become a Chinese citizen, stayed on; and in the spring of 1938, when Yangcheng itself was bombed, she refused to leave until the last casualties were accounted for.

The war brought Gladys courage and physical endurance that even amazed herself. She moved behind enemy lines, bringing supplies and assistance to villagers, and served so effectively as a spy for the Chinese military that she had a high price on her head.

Ninepence was her first child—a tiny abandoned girl she had

purchased for that amount. And as the years passed she "adopted" more, and besides her own there were dozens of war orphans that depended on her for sustenance. It was this overwhelming responsibility that loomed above all else, impelling Gladys to leave Shansi with her brood of nearly one hundred children in the spring of 1940 and to cross the mountains and the Yellow River into safety in Sian.

The journey was a harrowing one. Enemy troops were never far away, and moving unnoticed with nearly one hundred noisy children was a constant emotional strain. When at last they reached their destination, Gladys collapsed from mental and physical exhaustion, and the children were scattered around in refugee housing. They had made it out safely. ☙

Courage consists not in hazarding without fear,
but being resolutely minded in a just cause.
PLUTARCH

Be strong and courageous. Do not be terrified; do not be discouraged, for
the Lord your God will be with you wherever you go.
JOSHUA 1:9

Faithfulness

"LIKE A BAD TOOTH OR A LAME FOOT is reliance on the unfaithful in times of trouble." Proverbs 25:19

Ouch! That hurts! It's bad enough when trouble comes, but it's much worse if the people you're relying on to help let you down. The hurt is like toothache. The letdown is like jumping on a sprained ankle that gives way.

Jesus must have felt like this in the garden of Gethsemane. He was deeply troubled by the thought of what lay ahead for Him. He asked His inner circle of disciples to join Him in the quiet place to wait on God for His strength and encouragement. But while Jesus prayed, they fell asleep. They let Him down, and it hurt.

Faithfulness is doing what you say you will do, delivering what you promise to deliver. Being faithful means being reliable, turning up on time, finishing the job, being there when you need to be there.

Life operates on the basis of faith and trust. And faith, to be secure, needs a faithful object. Trust, to be safe, requires a trustworthy point of reference. Every bank note is a promise to pay, and you trust it. But the bank better come through! Every marriage is a commitment to love that the married embrace, but the spouse must deliver. Every traffic light negotiated is an exercise in faith. You believe if you've got a green, they've got a red, and if they've got a red, they'll stop. And you don't even know who "they" are!

One of the most oft-mentioned attributes of God throughout Scripture is His faithfulness. The Old Testament is a testimonial to His total reliability and unchanging commitment to His fractious people, Israel. They grumbled and rebelled, cheated and connived, tested God and questioned Him. But He remained the same— committed to their well-being and unrelenting in His intentions and purpose.

In the New Testament we are shown the incredible faithfulness of Jesus to the Father: His fixed intent on doing the Father's will, His unswerving obedience, His face set as a flint, His resolve to go through with all that was necessary for mankind's redemption, even to the point of death, even death on a cross. And Jesus made it clear that, unlike the Marines, He was not looking for "a few good men"—He sought a host of reliable, committed men and women who would follow Him and follow through on their commitments.

But faithfulness has its own peculiar challenges. We live in an environment in which faithfulness is not always highly regarded, where it is even seen as hopelessly out of date. Times change, we are told, and people change. Commitments must be tentative and options kept open. To be faithful can be seen at best as odd; at times it can be downright dangerous, as martyrs down through the ages have shown. But they and we always bear in mind the thought that one day we may hear the biggest accolade of all, from the One who knows—"Well done, good and faithful servant." ❧

The Animal Ark Hotel

When Noah built the "Animal Ark Hotel" (see Genesis 6–9) because God told him to, the people laughed. But when the floods came, nobody laughed. Being faithful isn't easy—but it's always right.

God was very sad. The world He had made was beautiful, but the people He had created did not obey Him. They wanted to do evil things.

"Why should we work?" they said. "We'll steal what we want from our neighbors."

"The sun makes our crops grow," they said. "So let's worship the sun instead of God."

Finally God said, "I will destroy all of the people, the animals, and the birds. I am sorry that I made them."

But there was one good family that God did not want to destroy—Noah's family. One day God said to Noah, "I will send a flood to cover the earth. You must make a boat. It will keep you and your family safe."

So Noah began to build the ark. He followed God's plan exactly.

The wicked people laughed at Noah. "Poor Noah thinks he can float a boat on dry land," they said.

But Noah went right on doing what God told him to do. At last the ark was finished. Again God spoke to Noah, "Go into the ark. Take seven pairs of animals and birds that are good to eat. Take one pair of each kind that is not good to eat."

It was a big job getting all the animals into the ark. Elephants, giraffes, zebras, hippos—every one had a special spot to eat and sleep. The ark was one BIG animal hotel! When all were inside, God shut the door.

It began to rain. It rained for forty days and forty nights. Water covered the whole earth. But everyone in the ark was safe.

At last the rain stopped. The water went down. God told Noah that his family and the animals could come out of the ark. The birds stretched their wings and flew. The animals pushed and ran to reach the new green grass.

Noah and his family built an altar to worship God for keeping them safe.

God was pleased with Noah. "I will never again send water to cover the earth," God said. Then God put a beautiful rainbow in the sky. "When you see a rainbow, remember My promise," God said. And God has never broken His promise. ❧

A Little Light
M. BENTHAM EDWARDS

A little light shines a long way on a dark night.

God make my life a little light,
    Within the world to glow;
A little flame that burneth bright
    Wherever I may go. ❧

The Faithful Servant
E. B. R. HIRSH

God fills all of our lives with opportunities to do what He wants us to do. Everybody is different, but all of us are expected to do one thing—to faithfully use what we have been given. Here is a story Jesus told to illustrate this point (Matthew 25:14-30).

Jesus continued speaking to his disciples, saying: "The kingdom of heaven will be like a man who called his servants to trust them with his property: to one servant he gave five gold coins, called

talents; to another he gave two gold coins, to the third he gave one. Each was given according to his ability.

"The man who received the five traded with them and made five more. The man who had two did the same thing and made two more. The man who received only one made a hole in the ground and buried the coin.

"After a time the master came to settle accounts with his servants. The one who had been given the five coins came to his master, bringing five more.

"The master said: 'Well done, good and faithful servant. You have been faithful over the little I gave you; now I will put you in charge of much. You have brought joy to your master.'

"The man who had been given two coins, brought the two and the two he had made. To him the master said the same thing: 'Well done, good and faithful servant. You have been faithful over a little; now I will put you over much. You have brought joy to your master.'

"The third man came forward with the one gold coin, saying: 'I know you are a hard man, reaping where you do not plant and harvesting where you do not work, so I hid your coin. Here, this is yours.'

"The master answered: 'You are a wicked and lazy man. You should have invested my money so I would have received it with interest. The coin shall be taken from you and given to the man who has ten.'"

Then Jesus said: "To everyone who has and uses what he has wisely, more will be given and he will have much. But from the man who has little and does not use it wisely, even what little he has shall be taken away. So the worthless servant shall be cast out into the darkness."

The Faithless Ranger
DAVID & KAREN MAINS

Having escaped the clutches of the evil Enchanter, Hero flees Enchanted City and takes refuge in Great Park, where the King lives in exile. Out exploring his new home, he meets a young girl named Amanda, who explains to him the ways of Great Park. This story is excerpted from Tales of the Kingdom, *the first book in David and Karen Mains's "Tales Trilogy."*

"The Rangers keep watch," Amanda explained to Hero. "They guard the park against Burners and Naysayers. They also look for lame things and fire in the forest, and they protect the outcasts. Their hearts are brave and full of courage."

Suddenly a loud horn blew in the forest. It was answered by another and another. *Croi-e-e-e-e-e-e! Croi-e-e-e-e-e-e!*

Amanda's body tensed with action. The smile left her eyes. "Danger!" she cried. "Ranger horns. Sounding warning."

The horns wailed again. Then three short blasts. *Croie! Croie! Croie!*

"Fire! Fire in the forest!" Amanda shouted. "Come! We must help. The horns are calling for help!"

Amanda and Hero hurried to a large lodge built on the edge of Deepest Forest. Hundreds of Rangers were gathering, men and women wearing long, blue cloaks, with the silver clasp at their shoulders. Some grabbed buckets, some shovels and brooms; then they all rushed into the sprawling building.

Hero and Amanda were pushed along by the crowd to the front of the large hall. On the platform a tall and powerful-looking man was examining maps, barking commands, sending off small groups of Rangers this way and that.

Amanda answered Hero's unasked question. "No, this is not the King. This is Ranger Commander."

"Fire in the forest," announced the Commander. He pointed to the maps spread on the large boards. "Two fires begun at distant

points within a short space of time. Here and here."

A low murmur spread through the hall. That could mean only one thing. Someone was deliberately burning the trees and planning to set fire to the entire forest.

"These fires are in the third and fourth forest quad, thirteenth and fifteenth fighting districts. First-alarm response crews are already in positions."

Ranger Commander faced his maps and explained strategy. "Mobilize at once. Spade and hatchet crews on this side and this. Bucket gangs waiting behind. Be ready to set backfires, but wait until the horn blasts signal you to begin. Remember, no more fire than absolutely necessary."

He faced the waiting hall. "Work hard," he called. "Pray for calm winds. Call on the rain."

Then he shouted, "To the King! To the Restoration!"

The hall reverberated as each Ranger lifted a hatchet and replied, "To the King! To the Restoration!" Then commotion. The tramp of feet. A flurry of pushing as fire fighters raced to their assignments.

In an instant Ranger Commander was standing beside Amanda and Hero. "Come with me," he said to the little girl. "Your gifts of seeing are of value to me. And you, boy, come, too. You can help on a support crew. Amanda will show you what to do when we are finished." The man turned and rushed out of the hall.

Confused, relieved, and strangely disappointed, Hero followed. He wanted both to be a part of the drama and not to be.

The powerful man hurried to a nearby watchtower and vaulted up the outside ladder, two rungs at a time. Amanda and Hero did their best to keep pace.

At the top, Hero looked out over all of Great Park. The Ranger on duty soon came over to them and pointed to two faint columns of smoke rising out of Deepest Forest.

"Small, early fires," he reported. "Two miles apart. The hand-pump-and-hose team at Lake Marmo can siphon water up to the first position if that fire gets bad. The second is going to be tougher. A backfire ring is probably the best strategy."

Suddenly Amanda pointed. "Look! Over there to the left." All four squinted. Before Hero could see anything, the duty Ranger pulled a large, curled horn from its place on the watchtower wall. He stepped out onto a narrow balcony circling the structure and blew three short blasts, *Croie! Croie! Croie!*

In a fraction of an instant, the blast was answered from a neighboring watchtower, then the next and the next, then others more distant, and on and on deep into the forest.

"A new fire," Ranger Commander explained to Hero in a grim voice. The man pointed. "See the second swirl of smoke? Now look to the north. The new fire's in the twenty-first district."

Now Ranger Commander turned to Amanda. "What do you see?"

The princess stared out into Deepest Forest. Then, to Hero's surprise, she closed her eyes. A silent moment passed as the girl seemed to lose all awareness of her surroundings. Hero had a feeling she was looking deeply inward at things other people could never see. She answered. "A blue cloak . . . a running man . . . a lit torch. . . ."

She opened her eyes. They were wide with horror. Ranger Commander glanced at the Ranger; each of them was shocked to learn that the offender wore a Ranger's cloak. "We are more in danger than we know," the Commander said in a voice thick with concern.

That afternoon three more fires flamed in Deepest Forest, six in all. Hero followed after Amanda, carrying barrels of drinking water to the parched fire fighters who battled ring after ring.

Finally the last fire was put out, and all the Rangers, dripping and exhausted, were assembled once more.

Ranger Commander walked to the middle of the platform and

motioned for quiet. "Divisions!" he ordered.

Everyone in the hall shuffled into order; scrambled crews found each other. Wounded Rangers limped to join their proper teams.

"All present!" called Ranger Commander.

Counting began: "Division One, present or accounted for, sir." "Division two, present or accounted for, sir." On and on came the cries. Miraculously, not one Ranger was missing.

Then the Commander, with blazing eyes, called, "Amanda! Stand forth!" The princess took two steps forward.

"Ordeal by passage," ordered the Commander.

Scarcely missing a step, the community of Rangers marched one by one into a bare circle outlined on the floor of the lodge— the viewing center—to stand before Ranger Commander and Amanda, who looked deep into each heart. Those who were pure bore it without shirking, marching into the center and out again. But those who had a shadow on their souls dreaded the time their turn would come.

About midway through the column of Rangers, Amanda made a motion with her hands. The Ranger who was in the viewing center paused. His hand slipped beneath his cloak. Ranger Commander looked at Amanda, a question in his eyes.

She nodded.

At that the faithless Ranger uttered an anguished cry, "No-o-o-o!" He pulled his hatchet from beneath his cloak. Holding it out in both hands, he turned and turned in a wide circle. "Stay away! Stay!"

When the Ranger had cleared a swatch around him, he stopped, raised his hatchet, and aimed to throw it at Ranger Commander.

"Who are you?" asked the Commander, absolutely calm, as though his life was not in mortal danger. "And why has your heart turned faithless?"

"I am a King's man!" shouted the Ranger. "I have taken the King's vow! I am part of the watch of the protectors! You have not judged me rightly. You are mistaken."

"Repent," said Ranger Commander, his voice rough. "Repent and do penance. The Kingdom will open to you again."

"I repent not!" The faithless Ranger held the hatchet above his head. "I grovel not! One move and you'll regret it!" He swung his weapon around in warning.

Undaunted, Amanda swiftly grabbed Caretaker's hatchet from the silver belt that girded Ranger Commander's waist. "Let fly and *you'll* regret it!" she shouted. Hero watched as the bold girl pointed the blade toward the center of the empty circle. Carefully, she sighted aim. She swung her hatchet round and round over her head.

The girl took one step forward and released the weapon. It tumbled end, over end, over end, and latched, neck to neck, around the hatchet in the faithless Ranger's hand. Circling still, it lifted the other hatchet out the man's grasp and carried it *thrum* into the wall far away.

The room was absolutely still.

Ranger Commander spoke. "You have loved the power of fire too much. It controls you. For the sake of Great Park, banishment into Enchanted City will be your punishment. There you will find enough fire . . . Pray that it will not burn your soul."

Footsteps echoed through the room, timed and in order. A band of blue cloaked Rangers surrounded the man in the middle. One tore off his silver shoulder clasp. One removed the long, blue cloak. Another demanded the silver buckle and belt. Finally, another gathered the garments of the faithless Ranger together and placed them in the hands of Ranger Commander.

The Rangers closed ranks around the traitor, and marched him from the hall. A terrible and heavy silence surrounded the weary men and women in the lodge after the faithless Ranger left.

For the first time that day, Hero saw the proud head of Ranger Commander droop with weariness. "Pray," he whispered, "that the faithless ones may again desire to follow the King."

What would happen to the faithless Ranger in Enchanted City? Hero wondered. He had not met the King, but the boy knew at that moment that he would rather be among these people who used the King's name than among any others. If need be, he would give his life to Great Park.

And the boy learned that a kingdom is a place where it is not enough to say the King's name. One must do the King's will in the King's way or lose the Kingdom altogether. &

Vanity Fair
JOHN BUNYAN

Faithfulness has its own costs, but promises great rewards. Nobody has shown this more vividly than John Bunyan in The Pilgrim's Progress, *one of the most widely read works of Western literature.*

This great allegory is told as if it were a dream. Christian, the hero, is seen as he leaves the City of Destruction to journey to the Celestial City. He carries a heavy burden of sin on his back and the Scriptures in his hand. One of his earliest difficulties is getting through the famous Slough of Despond. Further obstacles are encountered in the Hill of Difficulty, the Valley of Humiliation, the Valley of the Shadow, and the imprisonment at Doubting Castle by the Giant Despair. Through the first few of these adventures Christian is accompanied by Faithful, who suffers martyrdom at Vanity Fair.

Then I saw in my dream, that when they were got out of the wilderness, they presently saw a town before them, and the name of that town is Vanity. And at the town there is a fair kept, called Vanity Fair. . . .

This fair is no new-erected business, but a thing of ancient standing . . . a fair wherein should be sold all sorts of vanity, and that it should last all the year long; therefore at this fair are all such merchandise sold. . . . And moreover, at this fair there is at all times to be seen jugglings, cheats, games, plays, fools, apes, knaves, and rogues, and that of all sorts. Here are to be seen too, and that for nothing, thefts, murders, false swearers, and that of a blood-red color.

The arrival of the pilgrims Christian and Faithful creates a great commotion, which is attributed to three causes: their strange clothing, their foreign language of Heaven, and their failure to be impressed by the wares at Vanity Fair.

One chanced mockingly, beholding the carriages of Christian and Faithful, to say unto them, "What will ye buy?" But they, looking gravely upon him, answered, "We buy the Truth." At that there was an occasion taken to despise the men the more; some mocking, some taunting, some speaking reproachfully, and some calling upon others to smite them. At last things came to a hubbub and great stir in the fair, insomuch that all order was confounded.

Now was word presently brought to the Great One of the fair, who quickly came down and deputed some of his most trusty friends to take those men into examination, about whom the fair was almost overturned. So the men were brought to examination; and they that sat upon them, asked them whence they came, whither they went, and what they did there in such an unusual garb. The men told them that they were pilgrims and strangers in the world, and that they were going to their own country, which was the heavenly Jerusalem; and that they had given no occasion to the men of the town, nor yet to the merchandisers, thus to abuse them, and to let them in their journey, except it was for that, when one asked them what they would buy, they said they would buy the Truth. But they that were appointed to examine them did not believe them to be any other than bedlams and mad, or else such as came to put all things into a confusion in the fair. Therefore they took them and beat them, and besmeared them with dirt, and then put them into the cage, that they might be made a spectacle to all the men of the fair. There, therefore, they lay for some time, and were made the objects of any man's sport, or malice, or revenge, the Great One of the fair laughing still at all that befell them.

But the men being patient, and not rendering railing for railing, but contrariwise blessing, and giving good words for bad, and kindness for injuries done, some men in the fair that were more observing, and less prejudiced than the rest, began to check and blame the baser sort for their continual abuses done by them to the men; they, therefore, in angry manner let fly at them again, counting them as bad as the men in the cage, and telling them that they seemed confederates, and should be made partakers of their misfortunes. The others replied, that for aught they could see, the men were quiet, and sober, and intended nobody any harm; and that there were many that traded in their fair that were more worthy to be put into the cage, yea, and pillory too, than were the men that they had abused. Thus, after divers words had passed on both sides (the men behaving themselves all the while very wisely and soberly before them), they fell to some blows among themselves, and did harm one to another.

Then were these two poor men brought before their examiners again, and there charged as being guilty of the late hubbub that had been in the fair. So they beat them pitifully and hung irons upon them, and led them in chains up and down the fair, for an example and a terror to others, lest any should speak in their behalf, or join themselves unto them. But Christian and Faithful behaved themselves yet more wisely, and received the ignominy and shame that was cast upon them, with so much meekness and patience, that it won to their side (though but few in comparison of the rest) several of the men in the fair. This put the other party yet into a greater rage, insomuch that they concluded the death of these two men. Wherefore they threatened, that the cage nor irons should serve their turn, but that they should die, for the abuse they had done, and for deluding the men of the fair.

Then were they remanded to the cage again, until further order should be taken with them. So they put them in, and made their feet fast in the stocks. . . .

Then a convenient time being appointed, they brought them forth to their trial, in order to their condemnation. When the time was come, they were brought before their enemies, and arraigned. The judge's name was Lord Hategood. Their indictment was one and the same in substance, though somewhat varying in form, the contents whereof was this:

"That they were enemies to and disturbers of their trade; that they had made commotions and divisions in the town, and had won a party to their own most dangerous opinions, in contempt of the law of their prince."

Then Faithful began to answer, that he had only set himself against that which had set itself against Him that is higher than the highest. And said he, "As for disturbance, I make none, being myself a man of peace; the parties that were won to us, were won by beholding our truth and innocence, and they are only turned from the worse to the better. And as to the king you talk of, since he is Beelzebub, the enemy of our Lord, I defy him and all his angels."

Then proclamation was made, that they had aught to say for their Lord the King against the prison at the bar, should forthwith appear and give in their evidence. So there came in . . . witnesses, to wit, Envy [and] Superstition. . . . They were then asked if they knew the prisoner at the bar; and what they had to say for their Lord and King against him.

Then stood forth Envy, and said to this effect: "My Lord, I have known this man a long time, and will attest upon my oath before this honorable Bench, that he is—"

Judge. "Hold! Give him his oath."

So they sware him. Then he said, "My Lord, this man,

notwithstanding his plausible name, is one of the vilest men in our country. He neither regardeth prince nor people, law nor custom; but doth all that he can to possess all men with certain of his disloyal notions, which he in the general calls principles of faith and holiness. And in particular, I heard him once myself affirm that Christianity and the customs of our town of Vanity were diametrically opposite, and could not be reconciled. By which saying, my lord, he doth at once not only condemn all our laudable doings, but us in the doing of them."

. . . Then they called Superstition, and bid him look upon the prisoner. They also asked what he could say for their Lord the King against him. Then they sware him; so he began:

Superstition. "My Lord, I have no great acquaintance with this man, nor do I desire to have further knowledge of him; however, this I know, that he is a very pestilent fellow, from some discourse that the other day I had with him in this town; for then talking with him, I heard him say that our religion was naught, and such by which a man could by no means please God. Which sayings of his, my Lord, your Lordship very well knows what necessarily thence will follow, to wit, that we still do worship in vain, are yet in our sins, and finally shall be damned; and this is that which I have to say."

. . . Then the Judge called to the jury (who all this while stood by, to hear and observe), "Gentlemen of the Jury, you see this man about whom so great an uproar hath been made in this town; you have also heard what these worthy gentlemen have witnessed against him; also you have heard this reply and confession. It lieth now in your breasts to hang him, or save his life; but yet I think meet to instruct you into our Law. . . ."

Then went the jury out, whose names were, Mr. Blind-man, Mr. No-good, Mr. Malice, Mr. Love-lust, Mr. Live-loose, Mr. Heady, Mr. High-mind, Mr. Enmity, Mr. Liar, Mr. Cruelty, Mr. Hate-light, and Mr. Implacable; who every one gave in his private verdict against him among themselves, and afterwards unanimously concluded to bring him in guilty before the Judge. And first Mr. Blind-man the foreman, said, "I see clearly that this man is an heretic." Then said Mr. No-good, "Away with such a fellow from the earth." "Ay," said Mr. Malice, "for I hate the very looks of him." Then said Mr. Love-lust, "I could never endure him." "Nor I," said Mr. Live-loose, "for he would always be condemning my way." "Hang him, hang him," said Mr. Heady. "A sorry scrub," said Mr. High-mind. "My heart riseth against him," said Mr. Enmity. "He is a rogue," said Mr. Liar. "Hanging is too good for him," said Mr. Cruelty. "Let us dispatch him out of the way," said Mr. Hate-light. Then said Mr. Implacable, "Might I have all the world given me, I could not be reconciled to him; therefore let us forthwith bring him in guilty of death." And so they did; therefore he was presently condemned to be had from the place where he was, to the place from whence he came, and there to be put to the most cruel death that could be invented.

They therefore brought him out, to do with him according to their Law; and first they scourged him, then they buffeted him, then they lanced his flesh with knives; after that they stoned him with stones, then pricked him with their swords; and last of all they burned him to ashes at the stake. Thus came Faithful to his end.

The description of Faithful's execution is no great exaggeration of the kind of torture common in Europe during religious persecutions. 🍂

*Faith is the means by which the infirmity of man
lays hold on the infinity of God.*
JOHN BLANCHARD

Yet If His Majesty, Our Sovereign Lord
SIXTEENTH CENTURY

"It is required of stewards that a man be found faithful." I Corinthians 4:2

Yet if his majesty, our sovereign lord,
  Should of his own accord
Friendly himself invite,
  And say, "I'll be your guest tomorrow night,"
How should we stir ourselves, call and command
  All hands to work! "Let no man idle stand.
Set me fine Spanish tables in the hall,
  See they be fitted all;
Let there be room to eat,
  And order taken that there want no meat.
See every sconce and candlestick made bright,
  That without tapers they may give a light.
Look to the presence: are the carpets spread,
  The dais o'er the head,
The cushions in the chair,
  And all the candles lighted on the stair?
Perfume the chambers, and in any case
  Let each man give attendance in his place."
Thus, if the king were coming would we do,
  And 'twere good reason too;
For 'tis a duteous thing
  To show all honor to an earthly king,
And, after all our travail and our cost,
  So he be pleased, to think no labor cost.
But at the coming of the King of Heaven
  All's set at six and seven:

We wallow in our sin;
>Christ cannot find a chamber in the inn.
We entertain him always like a stranger,
>And, as at first, still lodge him in the manger. ❧

Living by Vows
ROBERTSON McQUILKIN

After his wife was diagnosed with Alzheimer's disease, Columbia Bible College and Seminary President Robertson McQuilkin found himself torn between two commitments, two divine callings—his wife and the school. His decision to resign in order to care for Muriel is a simple and moving example of faithfulness. He had promised "for better, for worse." This was "worse," but he kept his promise.

It has been a decade since that day, during a Florida vacation, when Muriel, my wife, repeated to the couple we were visiting the story she had told just five minutes earlier. *Funny*, I thought, *that's never happened before*. But it began to happen occasionally.

Three years later, when Muriel was hospitalized for tests on her heart, a young doctor called me aside. "You may need to think about the possibility of Alzheimer's," he said. I was incredulous. *These young doctors are so presumptuous and insensitive*. Muriel was doing the same things she had always done, for the most part. True, we had stopped entertaining in our home—no small loss for the president of a thriving seminary and Bible college. She was a great cook and hostess, but she was having increasing trouble planning menus. And, yes, she was having uncommon difficulty painting a portrait of me, which the college and seminary board—impressed by her earlier splendid portrait of my predecessor—had requested. But Alzheimer's? While I had barely heard of the disease, a dread began to lurk around the fringes of my consciousness.

When her memory deteriorated further, we went to Joe Tabor, a neurologist friend, who gave her the full battery of tests and, by elimination, confirmed that she had Alzheimer's. But because she had none of the typical physical deterioration, there was some question. We went to the Duke University Medical Center, believing we should get the best available second opinion. My heart sank as the doctor asked her to name the Gospels and she looked pleadingly at me for help. . . .

This time I accepted the verdict.

Muriel never knew what was happening to her, though occasionally when there was a reference to Alzheimer's on TV she would muse aloud, "I wonder if I'll ever have that?" It did not seem painful for her, but it was a slow dying for me to watch the vibrant, creative, articulate person I knew and loved gradually dimming out.

I approached the college board of trustees with the need to begin the search for my successor. I told them that when the day came that Muriel needed me full-time, she would have me. I hoped that would not be necessary till I reached retirement, but at fifty-seven it seemed unlikely I could hold on till sixty-five. They should begin to make plans. But they intended for me to stay on forever, I guess, and made no move. *That's not realistic, and probably not very responsible*, I thought, though I appreciated the affirmation.

So began years of struggle with the question of what should be sacrificed: ministry or caring for Muriel. Should I put the kingdom of God first, "hate" my wife and, for the sake of Christ and the kingdom, arrange for institutionalization? Trusted, lifelong friends—wise and godly—urged me to do this.

"Muriel would become accustomed to the new environment quickly." Would she? Would anyone love her at all, let alone love her as I do? I had often seen the empty, listless faces of those lined up in wheelchairs along the corridors of such places, waiting, waiting for the fleeting visit of some loved one. In such an environment, Muriel would be tamed only with drugs or bodily restraints, of that I was confident.

In 1988 we planned our first family reunion since the six children had left home, a week in a mountain retreat. Muriel delighted in her children and grandchildren, and they in her. Banqueting with all those gourmet cooks, making a quilt that pictured our life, scene by scene, playing games, singing, picking wild mountain blueberries was marvelous. We planned it as the celebration of our "fortieth" anniversary, although it was actually the thirty-ninth. We feared that by the fortieth she would no longer know us.

But she still knows us—three years later. She cannot comprehend much, nor express many thoughts, and those not for sure. But she knows whom she loves, and lives in happy oblivion to almost everything else.

She is such a delight to me. I don't *have* to care for her, I *get* to. . . . Muriel cannot speak in sentences now, only in phrases and words, and often words that make little sense: "no" when she means "yes," for example. But she can say one sentence, and she says it often: "I love you."

She not only says it, she acts it. The board arranged for a companion to stay in our home so I could go daily to the office. During those two years it became increasingly difficult to keep Muriel home. As soon as I left, she would take out after me. With me she was content; without me, she was distressed, sometimes terror stricken. The walk to school is a mile round trip. She would make that trip as many as ten times a day. Sometimes at night, when I helped her undress, I found bloody feet. When I told our family doctor, he choked up. "Such love," he said simply. Then after a moment, "I have a theory that the characteristics developed across the years come out at times like these."

I wish I loved God like that—desperate to be near him at all times. Thus she teaches me, day by day.

As she needed more and more of me, I wrestled daily with the question of who gets me full-time—Muriel or Columbia Bible

College and Seminary? Dr. Tabor advised me not to make my decision based on my desire to see Muriel stay contented. "Make your
plans apart from that question. Whether or not you can be successful in your dreams for the college and seminary or not, I cannot
judge, but I can tell you now, you will not be successful with
Muriel."

When the time came, the decision was firm. It took no great
calculation. It was a matter of integrity. Had I not promised, forty-
two years before, "in sickness and in health, till death do us part"?

This was no grim duty to which I was stoically resigned, however. It was only fair. She had, after all, cared for me for almost four
decades with marvelous devotion; now it was my turn. And such a
partner she was! If I took care of her for forty years, I would never
be out of her debt.

But how could I walk away from the responsibility of a ministry God had blessed so remarkably during our twenty-two years at
Columbia Bible College and Seminary?

Not easily. True, many dreams had been fulfilled. But so many
dreams were yet on the drawing board. And the peerless team God
had brought together—a team not just of top professionals, but of
dear friends—how could I bear to leave them? Resignation was
painful; but the right path was not difficult to discern. Whatever
Columbia needed, it did not need a part-time, distracted leader. It
is better to move out and let God designate a leader to step in
while the momentum surges.

. . . I have been startled by the response to the announcement
of my resignation. Husbands and wives renew marriage vows, pas-
tors tell the story to their congregations. It was a mystery to me,
until a distinguished oncologist who lives constantly with dying
people told me, "Almost all women stand by their men; very few
men stand by their women." Perhaps people sensed this contemporary tragedy and somehow were helped by a simple choice I
considered the only option.

It is all more than keeping promises and being fair, however. As I watch her brave descent into oblivion, Muriel is the joy of my life. Daily I discern new manifestations of the kind of person she is, the wife I always loved. I also see fresh manifestations of God's love—the God I long to love more fully. ❧

A Short Time Faithfully Spent
RICHARD BAXTER

On December 11, 1655, a group of clergymen gathered to hear an address by Richard Baxter, Vicar of Kidderminster. Unfortunately for them, he was taken ill and was unable to attend. Fortunately for us, his talk was published and three hundred years later is still in print. He pulled no punches; in fact, some of his ministerial brethren thought the text should have been in Latin so that the "vulgar people" wouldn't hear how the ministers were being challenged to faithfulness.

What comfort will it be to you at death, that you lengthened your life by shortening your work? He that worketh much, liveth much. Our life is to be esteemed according to the ends and works of it, and not according to the mere duration . . . Will it not comfort us more at death, to review a short time faithfully spent, than a long life spent unfaithfully? ❧

Faith that saves has one distinguishing quality; saving faith is a faith that produces obedience, it is a faith that brings about a way of life.
BILLY GRAHAM

Humility

THE ANCIENT GREEKS, who had much of great value to say about virtues, were not enthusiastic about "humility." They regarded it as a servile attitude, appropriate only to those of low estate. To them it was illogical to regard highly the lowly; instead the lowly were disparaged and so were their attitudes.

The Hebrews knew better, and for good reason. They saw mankind as created by the Eternal Creator and therefore of lowly estate compared to Him. Accordingly, a humble attitude before the Lord was not only appropriate but imperative.

After all, we are not capable of bringing ourselves into existence. We cannot keep ourselves alive. We are not able to live according to God's standards; we cannot forgive our own sin or make ourselves fit for heaven. All our achievements are made possible only through God's gifts of energy, time, and skills. As Winston Churchill remarked about a political opponent, "Clement Attlee is a very humble man. Of course, he has a lot to be humble about!" Exactly. So do we all!

The opposite of humility, of course, is pride. And God, we are told, hates pride—presumably because it is a denial of all the fundamental things that He has shown us about our humanity. But therein lies a problem for us. On the one hand we are told that humility is a virtue to be prized, while on the other hand we are encouraged to take pride in our appearance, to be proud of our achievements, to push ourselves forward, and generally to promote ourselves to best possible advantage. What is a poor mortal to do?

One of the mistakes we sometimes make in this regard is to indulge in false humility, like the pastor whose admiring parishioner said that his sermon had changed her life. He responded humbly, "Madam, it wasn't me, it was the Lord." To which she retorted, "Oh, it wasn't *that* good." The pastor's problem is a problem for all—to understand the balance between what is possible only because of the Lord and our dependence on Him, and what is attributable to our ability to utilize His gifts and exercise our will in His direction.

Corrie ten Boom, a remarkable Dutch woman who survived the Nazi death camps, received a great amount of praise and adoration and yet remained remarkably unspoiled by it. When asked how she managed to stay so humble amidst all the accolades, she replied, "I accept every compliment as a flower, say 'thank you,' and each evening I put them in a bunch and lay them at Jesus' feet where the praise belongs."

We all need to learn that lesson, because God has promised that if we don't humble ourselves, He will do it for us—and that is not a smart way to go. 🐾

Vanity and Vexation of Spirit
L. M. MONTGOMERY

Anne Shirley, heroine of Lucy Maud Montgomery's Anne of Green Gables, *has a great ability to learn lessons the hard way. In this selection we read how her pride went to her head and cost her her hair! That's humbling!*

Marilla, walking home one late April evening from an Aid meeting, realized that the winter was over and gone with the thrill of delight that spring never fails to bring to the oldest and saddest as well as to the youngest and merriest. . . .

Her eyes dwelt affectionately on Green Gables, peering through its network of trees and reflecting the sunlight back from its windows in several little coruscations of glory. Marilla, as she picked her steps along the damp lane, thought that it was really a satisfaction to know that she was going home to a briskly snapping wood fire and a table nicely spread for tea, instead of to the cold comfort of old Aid meetings before Anne had come to Green Gables.

Consequently, when Marilla entered her kitchen and found the fire black out, with no sign of Anne anywhere, she felt justly disappointed and irritated. She had told Anne to be sure and have tea ready at five o'clock, but now she must hurry to take off her second-best dress and prepare the meal herself against Matthew's return from plowing.

"I'll settle Miss Anne when she comes home," said Marilla grimly, as she shaved up kindlings with a carving knife and more vim than was strictly necessary. Matthew had come in and was waiting patiently for his tea in his corner. "She's gadding off somewhere with Diana, writing stories or practicing dialogues or some such tomfoolery, and never thinking once about time or her duties. She's just got to be pulled up short and sudden on this sort of thing. I don't care if Mrs. Allan does say she's the brightest and sweetest child she ever knew. She may be bright and sweet enough, but her head is full of nonsense and there's never any knowing what shape it'll break out in next. Just as soon as she grows out of one freak she takes up with another. But there! Here I am saying the very thing I was so riled with Rachel Lynde for saying at the Aid today. I was real glad when Mrs. Allan spoke up for Anne, for if she hadn't I know I'd have said something too sharp to Rachel before everybody. Anne's got plenty of faults, goodness knows, and far be it from me to deny it. But I'm bringing her up and not Rachel Lynde, who'd pick faults in the Angel Gabriel himself if he lived in Avonlea. Just the same, Anne has no business to leave the house like this when I told her she was to stay home this afternoon and look after things. I must say, with all her faults, I never found her disobedient or untrustworthy before and I'm real sorry to find her so now."

"Well now, I dunno," said Matthew, who, being patient and wise and, above all, hungry, had deemed it best to let Marilla talk her wrath out unhindered, having learned by experience that she got through with whatever work was on hand much quicker if not delayed by untimely argument. "Perhaps you're judging her too hasty, Marilla. Don't call her untrustworthy until you're sure she has disobeyed you. Mebbe it can all be explained—Anne's a great hand at explaining."

"She's not here when I told her to stay," retorted Marilla. "I reckon she'll find it hard to explain that to my satisfaction. Of course I knew you'd take her part, Matthew. But I'm bringing her up, not you."

It was dark when supper was ready, and still no sign of Anne, coming hurriedly over the log bridge or up Lovers' Lane, breathless and repentant with a sense of neglected duties. Marilla washed and put away the dishes grimly. Then, wanting a candle to light her down cellar, she went up to the east gable for the one that generally stood on Anne's table. Lighting it, she turned around to see

Anne herself lying on the bed, face downward among the pillows.

"Mercy on us," said astonished Marilla, "have you been asleep, Anne?"

"No," was the muffled reply.

"Are you sick then?" demanded Marilla anxiously, going over to the bed.

Anne cowered deeper into her pillows as if desirous of hiding herself for ever from mortal eyes.

"No. But please, Marilla, go away and don't look at me. I'm in the depths of despair and I don't care who gets head in class or writes the best composition or sings in the Sunday school choir any more. Little things like that are of no importance now because I don't suppose I'll ever be able to go anywhere again. My career is closed. Please, Marilla, go away and don't look at me."

"Did any one ever hear the like?" the mystified Marilla wanted to know. "Anne Shirley, whatever is the matter with you? What have you done? Get right up this minute and tell me. This minute, I say. There now, what is it?"

Anne had slid to the floor in despairing obedience.

"Look at my hair, Marilla," she whispered.

Accordingly, Marilla lifted her candle and looked scrutinizingly at Anne's hair, flowing in heavy masses down her back. It certainly had a very strange appearance.

"Anne Shirley, what have you done to your hair? Why, it's *green!*"

Green it might be called, if it were any earthly color—a queer, dull, bronzy green with streaks here and there of the original red to heighten the ghastly effect. Never in all her life had Marilla seen anything so grotesque as Anne's hair at that moment.

"Yes, it's green," moaned Anne. "I thought nothing could be as bad as red hair. But now I know it's ten times worse to have green hair. Oh, Marilla, you little know how utterly wretched I am."

"I little know how you got into this fix, but I mean to find out," said Marilla. "Come right down to the kitchen—it's too cold up here—and tell me just what you've done. I've been expecting something queer for some time. You haven't got into any scrape for over two months, and I was sure another one was due. Now, then, what did you do to your hair?"

"I dyed it."

"Dyed it! Dyed your hair! Anne Shirley, didn't you know it was a wicked thing to do?"

"Yes, I knew it was a little wicked," admitted Anne. "But I thought it was worth while to be a little wicked to get rid of red hair. I counted the cost, Marilla. Besides, I meant to be extra good in other ways to make up for it."

"Well," said Marilla sarcastically, "if I'd decided it was worth while to dye my hair I'd have dyed it a decent color at least. I wouldn't have dyed it green."

"But I didn't mean to dye it green, Marilla," protested Anne dejectedly. "If I was wicked I meant to be wicked to some purpose. He said it would turn my hair a beautiful raven black—he positively assured me that it would. How could I doubt his word, Marilla? I know what it feels like to have your word doubted. And Mrs. Allan says we should never suspect any one of not telling us the truth unless we have proof that they're not. I have proof now—green hair is proof enough for anybody. But I hadn't then and I believed every word he said *implicitly*."

"Who said? Who are you talking about?"

"The peddler that was here this afternoon. I bought the dye from him."

"Anne Shirley, how often have I told you never to let one of those peddlers in the house! I don't believe in encouraging them to come around at all."

"Oh, I didn't let him in the house. I remembered what you told me, and I went out, carefully shut the door, and looked at his things on the step. . . . He had a big box full of very interesting things and he told me he was working hard to make enough money to bring his wife and children out from Germany. He spoke so feelingly about them that it touched my heart. I wanted to buy something from him to help him in such a worthy object. Then all at once I saw the bottle of hair dye. The peddler said it was warranted to dye any hair a beautiful raven black and wouldn't wash off. In a trice I saw myself with beautiful raven black hair and the temptation was irresistible. But the price of the bottle was seventy-five cents and I had only fifty cents left out of my chicken money. I think the peddler had a very kind heart, for he said that seeing it was me, he'd sell it for fifty cents and that he was just giving it away. So I bought it, and as soon as he had gone I came up here and applied it with an old hairbrush as the directions said. I used up the whole bottle, and oh, Marilla, when I saw the dreadful color it turned my hair I repented of being wicked, I can tell you. And I've been repenting ever since."

"Well, I hope you'll repent to good purpose," said Marilla severely, "and that you've got your eyes opened to where your vanity has led you, Anne. Goodness knows what's to be done. I suppose the first thing is to give your hair a good washing and see if that will do any good."

Accordingly, Anne washed her hair, scrubbing it vigorously with soap and water, but for all the difference it made she might as well have been scouring its original red. The peddler had certainly spoken the truth when he declared that the dye wouldn't wash off, however his veracity might be impeached in other respects.

"Oh, Marilla, what shall I do?" questioned Anne in tears. "I can never live this down. People have pretty well forgotten my other mistakes—the liniment cake and setting Diana drunk and flying into a temper with Mrs. Lynde. But they'll never forget this. They will think I am not respectable. Oh, Marilla, 'what a tangled web we weave when first we practice to deceive.' That is poetry, but it is true. And oh, how Josie Pye will laugh! Marilla, I *cannot* face Josie Pye. I am the unhappiest girl in Prince Edward Island."

Anne's unhappiness continued for a week. During that time she went nowhere and shampooed her hair every day. Diana alone of outsiders knew the fatal secret, but she promised solemnly never to tell, and it may be stated here and now that she kept her word. At the end of the week Marilla said decidedly:

"It's no use, Anne. That is fast dye if ever there was any. Your hair must be cut off; there is no other way. You can't go out with it looking like that."

Anne's lips quivered, but she realized the bitter truth of Marilla's remarks. With a dismal sigh she went for the scissors.

"Please cut it off at once, Marilla, and have it over. Oh, I feel that my heart is broken. This is such an unromantic affliction. The girls in books lose their hair in fevers or sell it to get money for some good deed, and I'm sure I wouldn't mind losing my hair in some such fashion half so much. But there is nothing comforting in having your hair cut off because you've dyed it a dreadful color, is there? I'm going to weep all the time you're cutting it off, if it won't interfere. It seems such a tragic thing."

Anne wept then, but later on, when she went upstairs and looked in the glass, she was calm with despair. Marilla had done her work thoroughly and it had been necessary to shingle the hair as closely as possible. The result was not becoming, to state the case as mildly as may be. Anne promptly turned her glass to the wall.

"I'll never, never look at myself again until my hair grows," she exclaimed passionately.

Then she suddenly righted the glass.

"Yes, I will, too. I'll do penance for being wicked that way. I'll look at myself every time I come to my room and see how ugly I am. And I won't try to imagine it away, either. I never thought I was vain about my hair, of all things, but now I know I was, in spite of its being red, because it was so long and thick and curly. I expect something will happen to my nose next."

Anne's clipped head made a sensation in school on the following Monday, but to her relief nobody guessed the real reason for it, not even Josie Pye, who, however, did not fail to inform Anne that she looked like a perfect scarecrow.

"I didn't say anything when Josie said that to me," Anne confided that evening to Marilla, who was lying on the sofa after one of her headaches, "because I thought it was part of my punishment and I ought to bear it patiently. It's hard to be told you look like a scarecrow and I wanted to say something back. But I didn't. I just swept her one scornful look and then I forgave her. It makes you feel very virtuous when you forgive people, doesn't it? I mean to devote all my energies to being good after this and I shall never try to be beautiful again. Of course it's better to be good. I know it is, but it's sometimes so hard to believe a thing even when you know it. I do really want to be good, Marilla, like you and Mrs. Allan and Miss Stacy, and grow up to be a credit to you. Diana says when my hair begins to grow to tie a black velvet ribbon around my head with a bow at one side. She says she thinks it will be very becoming. I will call it a snood—that sounds so romantic. But am I talking too much, Marilla? Does it hurt your head?"

"My head is better now. It was terrible bad this afternoon, though. These headaches of mine are getting worse and worse. I'll have to see a doctor about them. As for your chatter, I don't know that I mind it—I've got so used to it." Which was Marilla's way of saying that she liked to hear it. ❧

The True Princess
ANGELA ELWELL HUNT

Jesus told His disciples, "Whoever wants to become great among you must be your ser-
vant, and whoever wants to be first must be your slave—just as the Son of Man did
not come to be served, but to serve, and to give his life as a ransom for many"
(Matthew 20:26-28). This may be difficult for us to believe, but this simple story illus-
trates the principle beautifully.

Once upon a time, in a faraway land, there lived a generous king
who had one lovely little daughter. She was always beautifully
dressed in silk dresses and jewels. Poets wrote poems to praise her
sweet smile and musicians sang songs about her beautiful golden
hair.

Whatever she needed was provided. Whatever she wanted
was given to her. There were maids to dress her, singers to sing for
her, and jokers to make her laugh. But best of all, there was Nana,
who took care of her, and her father the king, who loved her.

One day, however, the king heard news of trouble in another
kingdom. "I must go away on a long journey to help a friend, he
told his daughter. "You must remain here with Nana."

The king and Nana knew the princess must be kept safe.
Some people in the land would want to protect her, but others
might want to put her out of the kingdom.

The king instructed Nana to put away the royal robes and
crown of the princess and hide her away from the palace.
"Remember," he said, "no one would expect a child of the king to
be living as a servant."

When the time came to say good-bye, the princess was worried. "Father," she asked, "how can I live outside the palace? Who
will feed me? Who will dress me? Who will sing for me? Who will
make me laugh?"

The king smiled. "One day you will help me rule this kingdom," he told her, "but now you have much to learn."

He placed his gentle hand on her head. "Nana will be with you," he promised. "She is following my wishes so you will never be out of my care."

The people of the kingdom searched everywhere, but no one could find a beautiful princess with long golden hair and lovely royal robes.

While the people searched, Nana and the princess settled in the center of town over a little bakery shop where they worked together. "If we want to eat, we must bake," Nana said simply. "We will bake cakes, pies, and breads to eat and sell."

On their first morning in the little bakery house, the princess woke and murmured, "Dress me, please, Nana."

"My dear girl, I simply don't have time," replied Nana, slipping into her baking dress and apron. "But if you will be kind enough to tie my apron, I promise I'll tie yours."

So the princess learned to dress herself.

After several weeks of baking, the princess was exhausted. "Nana, there is no time to listen to music," she complained. "Why can't we stop working and call in the singers?"

"My dear girl," said Nana, "songs from your own heart would be more refreshing."

So the princess learned to sing while she worked.

Another day the princess put too much yeast in a loaf of bread and the dough exploded—POP—all over the room. She looked at the mess and sighed. She called to Nana in the next room: "Nana, can't we call in the jokers? I need to laugh again."

When Nana looked in and saw the mess, she burst into a fit of giggles. "Who needs jokers?" she said. "Take a look in the mirror."

The princess did—and she learned to laugh at herself.

Now when the princess could not be found, many girls in the kingdom thought they could take her place when the king returned. They spent hours designing and sewing lovely royal robes and grew their hair long and stood in the sun for hours so that it reflected the sun's golden rays.

They made fun of the girl from the bakery because she was too busy working to try to look like them. "Poor little muffin-maker," they called as she ran by making deliveries. "You don't have what it takes to be a princess."

But the bakery girl just laughed and hummed a little song to herself as she hurried by.

After many, many months the king returned. His guards and servants escorted him immediately to his palace and announced that the king would receive his daughter the next morning.

The next morning when the palace guards announced, "The princess is here!", the king was surprised to see twenty-five young ladies waiting for him. They all had long golden hair and were wearing royal robes. A twenty-sixth girl stood quietly in a patched dress at the back of the room.

The king smiled at the crowd of beauties. "So many prin-cesses?" he asked. He paused in front of the first girl. "Would you mind helping my servant put on his cloak?"

The girl frowned. "A true princess," she sniffed, "does not dress *anyone*. She has maids to do that."

The king stopped in front of the second girl. "Would you mind singing a song or two for the kitchen helpers? They would enjoy it so much."

The second girl smiled a little smile. "Princesses do not sing for cooks," she murmured. "They hire singers to sing for *them*."

The king paused in front of a third girl. "Would you tell my soldiers a funny story?" he asked. "They are tired from our long trip."

"Call the royal jokers," she suggested. "That is what a *real* princess would do."

The king looked at the young ladies before him. "Is there anyone who would sing for me? Tell a joke? Serve me in any way?"

The quiet girl in the patched dress spoke up. "I'd be happy to, Sire," she whispered. "Because I love you."

"My darling child," said the king, hugging his daughter close. "It is love that marks a true daughter of the king."

So the king and his princess were reunited, and it has been said that no princess ever was kinder, more loving, or a wiser ruler than she was.

And no one in the world could bake a better pie. ❧

The Last Supper
KEN TAYLOR

Washing the guests' feet was work for servants in Jesus' day. When no one appeared on the scene to do the unpleasant job, and none of the disciples volunteered, Jesus embarrassed everyone by doing it Himself. But that demonstration of humility was only a foretaste of His supreme humiliation on the cross. We are told in John 13:1-17 to learn from His example.

In the evening Jesus arrived with His other apostles and they all sat down for the supper. "I have wanted very much to eat this Passover supper with you before I die," He told them, "for I will not again eat a lamb that has been sacrificed until I Myself am sacrificed for the sins of the people."

But the apostles didn't understand Him. They didn't know what he was talking about. They still thought He was going to become king of the Jews, and that the time for this was very near.

They began arguing among themselves, as they had before, as to which of them would be greatest in the kingdom. Then Jesus told them, "Here in this world the rulers and the wealthy are the greatest, but with you it is different. For whichever of you is the humblest will be the greatest. The one who wants to be the leader must be the servant of all!"

Then Jesus asked them which was greater, the master who ate

at the table, or the servant who waited on him as he ate? They said it was the master. Then Jesus pointed out to them that He was their servant, even though He was their master, and they should serve each other as He served them. Then He demonstrated what He meant:

He got up from the table, wrapped a towel around his waist, poured water into a basin, and began to wash their feet and to wipe them with the towel. When He came to Peter, Peter didn't want Him to do it, for he didn't want Jesus to act like his servant. Jesus told him, "You don't understand now why I am doing it, but you will later."

"No," Peter told Him. "You shall never wash my feet."

Jesus replied, "If I don't, you can't be My disciple!"

"Then, Lord, don't wash just my feet, but my hands and my head too!" Peter exclaimed.

But Jesus told him, "When you have had a bath, it is only necessary to rewash the feet!"

After He had washed their feet and returned to the table again, He said to them, "Do you know what I have done to you? You call Me Master and Lord, and that is correct, for I am. If I, then, your Lord and Master, have washed your feet, you ought to wash each other's feet, for you should follow My example; you should do as I have done to you." He meant that we should help each other at all times.

The Christian virtue of humility affects relationships with others as well as reflects personal dependence on God. The humble person is not concerned with his or her prestige.

REVELL BIBLE DICTIONARY

The Suffering Servant
ISAIAH 53:1-7, NIV

None of Isaiah's eighth-century prophecies is more poignant and powerful than his description of the Messiah's humble self-offering for the sins of the world.

Who has believed our message
    and to whom has the arm of the Lord been revealed?
He grew up before him like a tender shoot,
    and like a root out of dry ground.
He had no beauty or majesty to attract us to him,
    nothing in his appearance that we should desire him,
He was despised and rejected by men,
    a man of sorrows, and familiar with suffering.
Like one from whom men hide their faces
    he was despised, and we esteemed him not.
Surely he took up our infirmities
    and carried our sorrows,
yet we considered him stricken by God,
    smitten by him, and afflicted.
But he was pierced for our transgressions,
    he was crushed for our iniquities;
the punishment that brought us peace was upon him,
    and by his wounds we are healed.
We all, like sheep, have gone astray,
    each of us has turned to his own way;
and the Lord has laid on him
    the iniquity of us all.
He was oppressed and afflicted,
    yet he did not open his mouth,
he was led like a lamb to the slaughter,
    and as a sheep before her shearers is silent,
    so he did not open his mouth.

The Sweeper of the Floor
GEORGE MACDONALD

The Christ who modeled humility commends His servants who exhibit the same virtue.

Methought that in a solemn church I stood.
    Its marble acres, worn with knees and feet,
Lay spread from door to door, from street to street.
    Midway the form hung high upon the rood
Of Him who gave His life to be our good;
    Beyond, priests flitted, bowed, murmured meet
Among the candles shining still and sweet.
    Men came and went, and worshipped as they could;
And still their dust a woman with her broom,
    Bowed to her work, kept sweeping to the door.
Then saw I slow through all the pillared gloom
    Across the church a silent figure come.
"Daughter," it said, "Thou sweepest well my floor!"
    "It is the Lord!" I cried, and saw no more. ❧

Freedom from a sense of one's own importance, with honest concern for others and personal dependence on God, makes humility one of the most mentioned and encouraged of Christian virtues.
REVELL BIBLE DICTIONARY

Humility
THOMAS À KEMPIS

Written in the late fourteenth century, The Imitation of Christ *is probably the second most read book in the world, after the Bible. This spiritual diary holds many treasures, none more beautiful than this meditation on humility.*

Be not troubled about those who are with you or against you, but take care that God be with you in everything you do. Keep your conscience clear and God will protect you, for the malice of man cannot harm one whom God wishes to help. If you know how to suffer in silence, you will undoubtedly experience God's help. He knows when and how to deliver you; therefore, place yourself in His hands, for it is a divine prerogative to help men and free them from all distress.

It is often good for us to have others know our faults and rebuke them, for it gives us greater humility. When a man humbles himself because of his faults, he easily placates those about him and readily appeases those who are angry with him.

It is the humble man whom God protects and liberates; it is the humble whom He loves and consoles. To the humble He turns and upon them bestows great grace, that after their humiliation He may raise them up to glory. He reveals His secrets to the humble, and with kind invitation bids them come to Him. Thus, the humble man enjoys peace in the midst of many vexations, because his trust is in God, not in the world. Hence, you must not think that you have made any progress until you look upon yourself as inferior to all others. 🐾

A Greater Wonder
JOHN DONNE

In this sonnet, Donne muses on the amazing submissiveness of powerful animals to puny humans and then contemplates the submission of the Creator of all things to death on our behalf. It seems that humility abounds where not called for, and is in short supply where clearly necessary.

Why are we by all creatures waited on?
 Why do the prodigal elements supply
Life and food to me, being more pure than I,
 Simple, and further from corruption?
Why brook'st thou, ignorant horse, subjection?
 Why dost thou, bull and boar, so sillily
Dissemble weakness, and by one man's stroke die,
 Whose whole kind you might swallow and feed upon?
Weaker I am, woe is me, and worse than you,
 You have not sinned, nor need be timorous.
But wonder at a greater wonder, for to us
 Created nature doth these things subdue,
But their Creator, whom sin nor nature tied,
 For us, His creatures, and his foes, hath died. ❧

The Hebrew term for humility originally described persons who were economically and socially powerless. The poor call upon God because He is their only hope. The wealthy and powerful become arrogant, and depend not on God but on their social status.
REVELL BIBLE DICTIONARY

The Fool's Prayer

EDWARD ROWLAND SILL

The royal feast was done; the King
    Sought some new sport to banish care,
And to his jester cried: "Sir Fool,
    Kneel now, and make for us a prayer!"

The jester doffed his cap and bells,
    And stood the mocking court before;
They could not see the bitter smile
    Behind the painted grin he wore.

He bowed his head, and bent his knee
    Upon the monarch's silken stool;
His pleading voice arose: "O Lord,
    Be merciful to me, a fool!

" 'Tis not by guilt the onward sweep
    Of truth and right, O Lord, we stay;
'Tis by our follies that so long
    We hold the earth from heaven away.

"These clumsy feet, still in the mire,
    Go crushing blossoms without end;
These hard, well-meaning hands we thrust
    Among the heart-strings of a friend.

"The ill-timed truth we might have kept—
    Who knows how sharp it pierced and stung?
The word we had not sense to say—
    Who knows how grandly it had rung?

"Our faults no tenderness should ask
    The chastening stripes must cleanse them all;
But for our blunders—oh, in shame
    Before the eyes of heaven we fall.

"Earth bears no balms for mistakes;
    Men crown the knave, and scourge the tool
That did his will; but Thou, O Lord,
    Be merciful to me, a fool!"

The room was hushed; in silence rose
    The King, and sought his gardens cool,
And walked apart and murmured low,
    "Be merciful to me, a fool!" 🦎

The Apologist's Evening Prayer
C. S. LEWIS

*An apologist is one who can argue and reason a point of view with exceptional skill.
There have been few better Christian apologists than the British professor and writer
C. S. Lewis (1898-1963), but behind the brilliant mind and quick tongue lay a
humble spirit.*

From all my lame defeats and oh! much more
    From all the victories that I seemed to score;
From cleverness shot forth on Thy behalf
    At which, while angels weep, the audience laugh;
From all my proofs of Thy divinity,
    Thou, who wouldst give no sign, deliver me.

Thoughts are but coins. Let me not trust, instead
    Of Thee, their thin-worn image of Thy head.
From all my thoughts, even from my thoughts of Thee,

O thou fair Silence, fall, and set me free.
Lord of the narrow gate and the needle's eye,
    Take from me all my trumpery least I die. ❧

Fling Away Ambition
WILLIAM SHAKESPEARE

Thomas Wolsey rose to dizzy heights under Henry VIII, but when he stood against the king's intention to divorce his queen and remarry, the king stripped him of everything. Only then did he realize his slavery to ambition and his addiction to power. Then, and only then, he was humbled. The incomparable Shakespeare (1564-1616) captures Wolsey's sentiments in unforgettable language in this speech from Henry VIII, Act III, Scene 2.

Cromwell, I charge thee, fling away ambition:
    By that sin fell the angels; how can man, then,
The image of his Maker, hope to win by 't?
    Love thyself last; cherish those hearts that hate thee:
Corruption wins not more than honesty.
    Still in thy right hand carry gentle peace,
To silence envious tongues. Be just; and fear not:
    Let all the ends thou aim'st at be thy country's,
Thy God's, and truth's; then if thou fall'st, O Cromwell!
    Thou fall'st a blessed martyr.
Serve the king; and—pr'ythee, lead me in:
    There take an inventory of all I have,
To the last penny; 'tis the king's: my robe,
    And my integrity to heaven, is all
I dare now call mine own. O Cromwell, Cromwell!
    Had I but served my God with half the zeal
I served my king, he would not in mine age
    Have left me naked to mine enemies! ❧

God of Humble Hearts

BLAISE PASCAL

It is worth noting that the seventeenth century French philosopher Pascal, who wrote about humility and intellect, was not only a brilliant thinker and writer on spiritual matters but was also a trailblazing physicist and inventor.

Instead of complaining that God had hidden Himself, you will give Him thanks for not having revealed so much of Himself; and you will also give Him thanks for not having revealed Himself to haughty sages, unworthy to know so holy a God.

Two kinds of persons know Him: those who have a humble heart, and who love lowliness, whatever kind of intellect they may have, high or low; and those who have sufficient understanding to see the truth, whatever opposition they may have to it. ❧

The Lord sustains the humble but casts the wicked to the ground.
PSALM 147:6

*Humility is the mother of giants. One sees great things
from the valley; only small things from the peak.*
G. K. CHESTERTON

Perseverance

LET ME TELL YOU about an unfortunate young man. When he was twenty-two years of age, he was fired from his job. Then he went into business with a partner, but the business lasted less than a year. He tried politics, but was defeated twice before he gained a seat—which he promptly lost. At the same time his girlfriend turned him down. Subsequently he was passed over for an appointment by his political party and, not surprisingly, suffered a nervous breakdown. Three more ventures into politics led to three more defeats. Then at the age of fifty-one, after a history of memorable failures, he became President of the United States. His name? Abraham Lincoln—a model of perseverance if ever there was one!

Robert the Bruce, King of Scotland, was hiding from his enemies in a cave. He was deeply discouraged, but as he sat there he noticed a spider trying to weave its web. Time after time it attempted to climb the silvery thread, only to fall back to where it had started. Fascinated, the king watched as the tiny creature refused to give up, and eventually succeeded in attaining its objective. Assuming that he had at least the determination of a spider, Robert returned with renewed vigor to his task. From a lowly spider, no less, he had learned,

" 'Tis a lesson you should heed,
Try, try again.
If at first you don't succeed,
Try, try again."

Winston Churchill, whose wartime speeches we remember listening to when we were children during World War II, was another man who refused to be dissuaded from his task. Asked to speak at his alma mater, he surprised and delighted the students by giving the shortest speech on record. He stood before them and said, "Never give up. Never give up. Never, never give up!" And sat down!

Florence Nightingale was born to luxury. The carefree life awaited her, but to the horror of her family she chose instead to be a nurse—a profession that in those days was regarded as undesirable for young ladies. She persevered through training, then offered herself to work in the church—and was devastated when she was not wanted. When she heard of the deplorable conditions in which the soldiers wounded in the Crimean War were living, she and a group of women she organized headed for the front. They were told they were neither needed nor wanted, but Florence insisted and was given permission to scrub the blood from the floor. Eventually she made herself indispensable and became much beloved by the soldiers, who called her "The Lady with the Lamp." She changed the lot of those wounded and dying men, and on returning to England was hailed and feted. She changed the face of nursing and became the inspiration for the founding of the Red Cross.

Jesus clearly expected the same kind of perseverance from His disciples. He told them in no uncertain terms, "In this world you will have trouble. But take heart! I have overcome the world." Down through the centuries, followers of Jesus have found this to be true. They've had trouble, but they've had enough encouragement in Christ to "keep on keeping on." ❧

W-a-t-e-r
STEWART AND POLLY ANNE GRAFF

Helen Keller lost her hearing and her sight before she was two years old. Living as a small child in this black isolation, she became "wild and unruly," until a remarkable woman named Anne Mansfield Sullivan lovingly took over Helen's care. The following excerpt from Helen Keller shows Annie Sullivan's incredible patience and perseverance.

The next weeks were an adventure for Helen. She liked the sewing cards and the kindergarten beads that Annie gave her. She liked their long walks through the cool woods. They rode horseback together. Annie led Helen's pony.

Whatever they did Annie spelled letters into Helen's hand. When they petted the cat Annie spelled "C-A-T." Helen quickly learned to imitate Annie's fingers. She could make the letters for "C-A-K-E" when she wanted a treat, and "M-I-L-K" when she was thirsty.

"Helen is like a clever little monkey," Annie wrote. "She has learned the *signs* to ask for what she wants but she has no idea that she is spelling *words*."

Helen enjoyed the adventures with Annie. But she did not know that the stranger was her teacher. She was very unhappy when Annie tried to make her obey.

Annie did not believe that Helen's parents were right to let Helen always do exactly as she pleased. At mealtimes Helen walked around the table. She dipped her fingers into everyone's plates and gobbled whatever she wanted.

Annie make Helen sit in her own chair and eat from her own plate. Helen was furious. When Annie gave her a spoon, Helen threw it on the floor and kicked the table. They spent a whole afternoon fighting while Annie insisted that Helen fold her napkin.

Mrs. Keller was upset. "I cannot bear to have Helen punished," she said.

71

Annie was firm. "We must make Helen know we love her," she said. "But we must not let her think she is different because she is blind and deaf. She must behave like other children."

Helen's bad tempers went on. Once she locked Annie in her room and hid the key. Captain Keller had to put a ladder up to Annie's window and help her down.

One morning during her lesson Helen was especially bad. She slammed her new doll on the floor and broke it. Annie was too tired to go on with the lesson. Her eyes ached. She took Helen by the hand and led her outdoors. They stopped at the pump for a drink.

Then something happened that changed Helen's whole life.

Helen held her hand under the spout while Annie pumped. As cold water poured over Helen's hand, Annie spelled in her other hand "W-A-T-E-R." A new expression came into Helen's face. She spelled *water* several times herself. Then she pointed to the ground. Annie quickly spelled "G-R-O-U-N-D."

Helen jumped up. She suddenly realized that she was understanding *words*. She pointed to Annie, and Annie spelled "T-E-A-C-H-E-R." Helen never called Annie by any other name.

Then Helen pointed to herself and Annie slowly spelled out "H-E-L-E-N K-E-L-L-E-R."

Helen's face broke into a wide smile. It was the first time she knew that she had a name.

Helen and Annie were both excited. They raced to the house to find Mrs. Keller. Helen threw herself in her mother's arms while Annie spelled "M-O-T-H-E-R" into her hand. When Helen nodded to show that she understood there were tears of happiness in Mrs. Keller's eyes.

All the rest of the day Helen ran about touching things and Annie spelled the names. When she touched her little sister, Annie spelled "B-A-B-Y."

At supper Annie rubbed her fingers. "No wonder my hand is

numb from spelling," she said, smiling at Captain Keller. "Helen is trying to make up in one day what other children have taken six years to learn."

When Helen want to bed that night she kissed her teacher for the first time. Annie wrote, "I thought my heart would burst with joy."

Helen herself said many years later, "I was born again that day. I had been a little ghost in a *no-world*. Now I knew my name. I was a person. I could understand people and make them understand me." ❧

The Hare and the Tortoise
AESOP

A hare was one day making fun of a tortoise for being so slow upon his feet. "Wait a bit," said the tortoise; "I'll run a race with you, and I'll wager that I win." "Oh, well," replied the hare, who was much amused at the idea. Let's try and see." It was soon agreed that the Fox should set a course for them and be the judge. When the time came both started off together, but the hare was soon so far ahead that he thought he might as well have a rest; so down he lay and fell fast asleep. Meanwhile the tortoise kept plodding on, and in time reached the goal. At last the hare woke up with a start, and dashed on at his fastest, but only to find that the tortoise had already won the race.

Slow and steady wins the race. ❧

The Surprise Birthday Present
ARLETA RICHARDSON

Everybody finds waiting difficult, especially children. In this incident from Still More Stories from Grandma's Attic, *Mabel discovers that patience and perseverance can only be learned slowly but surely.*

Pa's birthday was in May, but we started thinking about it right after Christmas. We had attended a service at the church on New Year's Eve, and Ma remarked about the state of Pa's good suit.

"Your work overalls look better than your Sunday suit," she said to him. "The seat of those pants is so thin I don't think you're going to be able to wear them much longer."

"I agree that they aren't in the best of shape," Pa replied. "But I can't afford another suit this year. Maybe if the crops are good, I can get one next winter. In the meantime, I'll just sit easy."

Ma shook her head. "That one will never last. But I don't know what we can do about it."

Nothing further was said, but Ma didn't forget about Pa's worn suit. One morning in January she mentioned it again before we left for school.

"The new Sears catalog is here," she said. "We could get a good suit for your father for twenty-five dollars. The question is, where will we get twenty-five dollars?"

"Twenty-five dollars!" I gasped. It might as well have been twenty-five thousand, as far as we were concerned.

"It would sure be nice to get that suit for his birthday," Ma continued. "I'm going to start thinking about how I can earn some money."

"We will, too," Reuben offered. "Roy and I can go in with you and buy it."

"I want to help, too," I put in. "I can earn money if you can."

Ma looked at me kindly. "There's not much a little girl can do for pay. But it's nice of you to offer. We'll see what we can do."

. . . [In school] I was only half listening as Miss Gibson read the Scripture for the morning.

"Trust in the Lord . . . wait patiently for Him . . . and He will give you the desires of your heart."

There was the answer! Trust in the Lord. I knew all about doing that. We had been taught that God takes care of His children and gives them everything that is necessary. A new suit for Pa was necessary, wasn't it?

But wait patiently? That would be the hard part. I wasn't very long on patience. I usually wanted things to happen right away—or sooner. . . .

All of January went by, and I had not earned a single penny. Reuben brought home ten cents he had earned helping a neighbor mend harnesses. Roy got five cents for sweeping out Mr. Clapp's store.

"He wanted to give me candy," Roy reported. "But I told him I needed the money."

Ma had sold some eggs, and made a dress for the minister's wife. Altogether she had a dollar and a half.

"$1.65," Reuben counted. "We're not getting there very fast, are we?"

"It's $1.65 more than we had at the beginning of the month," Ma reminded him. "We'll keep working and praying about it."

In February Mrs. Carter gave me a nickel for going to the store for her. I had to make three trips to get everything she wanted, but it was worth it. Joyfully I handed it over to Ma.

"That's good, Mabel. Every little bit helps. We have almost three dollars now. You mustn't be too disappointed if we can't earn it all. We'll do the best we can."

"But, Ma," I protested, "the Bible says if we trust in the Lord, He'll give us the desires of our heart. We're trusting Him, aren't we?"

"Yes, of course," Ma replied. "But remember, God doesn't

always answer our prayers the way we expect Him to. He gives us what is best for us. Money may not be His best."

I couldn't think of anything that would be better, but I didn't say that to Ma. . . .

March passed slowly, and then April arrived with heavy spring rains. I complained to Ma.

"How can I go out and find errands to do in this kind of weather? It isn't good for anything."

"Except to help the gardens and fields to grow," Ma reminded me. "Nothing that God sends is useless."

The next week a rainstorm did help solve our problem. Sarah Jane and I were spending the afternoon at her house. Just as we had gathered all our things together to go to the creek to play, it began to rain.

"Oh, bother!" Sarah Jane exclaimed. "Now what shall we do?"

"Why don't you play in the attic?" her mother said. "You can use the clothes in the old trunk to play dress-up, if you like."

. . . After routing through some dresses and shoes, I lifted out something heavy. It was made of a woolen material.

"That was a great coat of my grandfather's," said Sarah Jane.

"My, it's big," I marveled. "I never saw so much cloth in one coat."

"My grandpa was big," Sarah Jane informed me. "My mother said he would make two of anyone she ever saw. No one else has ever been able to wear his coat."

I could hardly get my breath for excitement. "Oh, Sarah Jane, do you think your mother would sell it to us?"

"Sell it to you? Whatever for? Your Pa could wrap it around him three times. He would sure look silly in it."

"No, no. He wouldn't wear it like that. Ma could make him a whole suit out of it! She can do anything with a needle and thread."

"We'll have to ask. Ma might want to sell it."

But she didn't. "Oh, my. I couldn't take money for an old coat like that. I can't imagine what anyone would want it for. But if you think your mother could use it, you may have it.

"Oh, thank you!" I cried. "I just know we can use it. I'll take it home right now."

When I finally arrived at our yard, Pa was starting toward the house. Quickly I detoured around to the barn and went in. The coat would be safe under some hay until after supper.

As soon as Ma and I were alone doing the dishes, I whispered to her, "There's something in the barn you have to see, Ma. It's an answer to our prayer!"

Ma looked surprised, but she didn't question me. As soon as we were finished, we hurried out to the barn. I laid the big coat out on the straw for her to inspect.

"Sarah Jane and I found this in a trunk, Ma. Her mother said we could have it. You can make a suit for Pa out of it, can't you?"

Ma was so astonished that she couldn't speak for a moment. "Why, Mabel, I believe I can! Isn't this wonderful? We can get buttons for it with the money we've saved. We'll even have enough money left over to buy a fine linen handkerchief."

Ma hugged me, and together we took the coat to the house.

"Monday we'll start taking the seams out," she said. "I'll brush the pieces good and air them. When they are pressed neatly, they'll be as fine as any yard goods. I do believe we can have it ready for Pa's birthday."

And it was. On the third Sunday in May, Pa proudly left for church in his new suit.

"I don't know where you got enough money to buy anything as nice as this," he said to us. "I didn't see one this fine in the catalog. You didn't sell one of the cows, did you?" he teased.

"Never you mind, Pa," I said. "That's our secret. I can tell you this much, though. We trusted in the Lord, and waited patiently for Him. Then He gave us the desires of our heart!" ❧

Job's Troubles

VIRGINIA MUIR

It is hard to imagine the trials suffered by Job, whose story is told in the Old Testament book of that name. He was not helped by his wife or his friends, but he held on to his faith and came through the experience trusting the Lord as never before. We call that perseverance.

Job was a very rich man who lived in Uz. He had a wife and a large family—seven grown-up sons and three daughters. He worshiped God and tried to please him every day. His flocks and herds were huge, with thousands of animals.

. . . One day, God was talking to Satan the evil tempter. Satan told God he thought Job obeyed God only because he was rich and had a lovely family. God said, "You may test him by taking away those things."

So Satan sent terrible trouble to Job. First his oxen and donkeys were stolen by enemies. Then fire burned up his sheep and their shepherds. Next, another tribe took his camels and killed their herdsmen. Worst of all, a terrible windstorm collapsed his oldest son's home, where all the brothers and sisters had gathered. All ten of them were killed when the roof caved in.

Job was heartbroken. But all he said was, "God gave them and now God has taken them away. I still love him and praise him."

Then Satan said to God, "Well, Job is still faithful to you because he is healthy." So God gave Satan permission to make Job ill. Job felt terrible because he had big sores all over his body.

When Job became sick, his wife asked him, "Why don't you curse God for letting all this happen to you?"

Job said, "That's a foolish thing to say! God has given me many blessings. Why shouldn't I have trouble, too? Even if he killed me, I wouldn't curse him."

. . . At last Job got tired of suffering so long, and he complained that God was being unfair to him.

Finally God said, "Job, let me ask you some questions, and you answer if you can. Where were you when I made the world? Can you possibly understand how wonderful my creation is—the lightning, the snow, the hail, the beautiful stars?" And he described the animals and told how he takes care of them, giving them food and protecting them. He said, "Do you think you are wise enough to do all those things? You forget you are just a man, and I'm the great God of the universe!"

Then Job told God he was sorry for being so impatient and not understanding God's ways. He said, "Lord, I've heard about you all my life, but now I really know you. I've seen how wonderful you are, and now I despise myself. I am so sorry I acted like that."

. . . Then the Lord gave Job back his health and more riches than before. He even gave him and his wife ten more children—seven sons and three daughters, the same number as before. Job lived 140 more years and was very happy with his children, grandchildren, and great-grandchildren. &

Rise and Walk
DENNIS BYRD WITH MICHAEL D'ORSO

On November 29, 1992, Dennis Byrd, a defensive lineman for the New York Jets, collided headfirst with a teammate while trying to make a tackle. Just like that, Dennis's neck was broken, and he was paralyzed from the neck down. Doctors said he would probably never walk again. But he did. The story of his gritty perseverance, told in his book Rise and Walk, *makes for compelling reading.*

Now I know exactly how fragile life is and how close to the edge we live. In an instant, our lives can change forever.

I remember lying there and looking up at the sky, the tingling in my body slowly subsiding, my eyes and mind gradually regaining their focus on the gray New Jersey sky above me.

The buzzing inside my body gradually slipped away, replaced by a new, more terrifying feeling—nothing. I had to get to my feet, to stand upright, to prove to myself that everything was all right. All I needed to do was push myself off the turf, as I had a thousand times before.

I tried to get up. My head raised off the ground just enough for its weight to dislodge the bone chips randomly filling the space that had been my C-5 vertebra. I felt something give way. I heard it, too, a grinding and crunching at the top of my spine. And I knew then. I'd broken my neck.

I had no idea what lay ahead of me, but I knew this was going to be a test, a trial for which I would need God's help and a strong faith. And I believed I had both those things. I had spent much of my life reading the Bible, learning about God and Jesus Christ. I understood that the Lord has plans for people and their lives that we sometimes have no way of comprehending. There had been plenty of times in my life when I'd had the opportunity to bail out, to say, "Hey, God, why did you do this? Why did you do that?" But I never had bailed out before. And I wasn't about to now.

Which is not to say that I didn't feel fear at that moment and that I wouldn't continue to feel it again and again in the coming days and weeks. This was going to be tough, no question. Tortuous feelings and emotions were going to flood through me for a long time. Questions without answers were going to beat at my brain, frustrating me, filling me with anger at times. . . .

It was so hard lying there *after* the surgery. The doctors had taken their shot, they'd stabilized me, gotten me pretty much out of harm's way. But I was still paralyzed, still as helpless as I'd been the day before. It was deflating, depressing. I was totally dependent, which is a nightmare for an outgoing personality like mine. I had to ask for *everything*, from whichever nurse or attendant happened to be in the room: *Could you prop that pillow under my shoulder? Could you wipe my nose? May I have a drink of water? Could you turn me a little this way? Could you turn me a little that way? Can I have something to eat?*

Two days later, I could feel the impulses inside the toes of my right foot. I couldn't move anything, but I could *feel* the nerves firing. Something was happening down there! There was no doubt about it.

The next morning, Dr. O'Leary was asking me the usual questions, pushing and poking me in the usual places, telling me to try to move this, try to move that. Finally, he came to my right foot. He asked me to try to move the toes. And suddenly, almost imperceptibly, the big toe . . . moved. You could hardly see it. It was like the flick of an eyelash. But it definitely moved.

Dr. O'Leary asked me to do it again. Then again. Then he went through the ceiling.

"It's a miracle!!!" he shouted.

My wife Angela and I were reading a lot from Psalms and Job. Psalms for the comfort and strength it offered, and Job because it spoke so directly to what I was going through. Here was this successful, prosperous man who had worked so hard and earned so much, who was so faithful to the Lord, and whom Satan tried to destroy, testing him by taking away everything he had. I could relate to that story. Job ultimately passed his test. He lost everything but his faith.

And I had not lost mine.

One afternoon, just before Christmas, I felt like I'd made a lot of progress, but I was still so far from doing anything close to walking. I couldn't even lift my leg. I could flex some of the muscles, but I couldn't make it move. And my hands were so limp. I wondered if I was truly strong enough to handle all this. I wondered if I could take it.

And then a voice came to me, a voice as clear as any I'd ever heard. And it said, *"Be strong, my son. You will walk again."*

And Dennis DID walk again. Today, he walks just fine, a true miracle in motion. He's back in his native Oklahoma, where he directs The Dennis Byrd Foundation, which assists kids with spinal cord injuries and other handicaps. When he's not working with the foundation or telling his remarkable story at a speaking engagement, Dennis is continuing his rehabilitation and spending much time with his family. He writes:

I could easily have been destroyed by what happened to me. I could easily have just fallen apart. In every material sense, I was weak and vulnerable. But there is a verse in II Corinthians about that very thing:

And he said to me, "My grace is sufficient for thee, for my strength is made perfect in weakness."

I had become weakness, and I became it in an instant. Only in this weakness was I able to completely lay my entire life at Christ's feet, holding nothing back, putting it all in his hands. He would have to fight the battle for me.

And he did. 🦋

One Left Behind

Very few people have ever heard of Alberta Skinner, because she lived in obscurity. But due to her great perseverance, she's well known in heaven.

In the 1930s, one of the Bible Christian Union's single women missionaries, Alberta Skinner, was serving in the far eastern part of Czechoslovakia. Russian Communists moved in and annexed that section of the country, eventually making it part of the Soviet Union.

The Communists seized the Moody Bible Institute graduate

and told her, "You can leave and never come back, or you can stay and never leave."

She stayed.

For many years, BCU did not hear from her again. All financial support and contact with her family and friends was cut off completely. BCU officials feared the Communists had killed her.

One day, 25 years later, the phone rang in BCU's international headquarters. It was Alberta! She said that she had been allowed to remain behind the Iron Curtain where—though ridiculed and persecuted—she continued to faithfully serve the Lord.

God led her to a godly Russian pastor. They were married and had six sons. Due to their outspoken faith in Christ, they were forced to live in a small wooden structure with a dirt floor. Despite their austere surroundings, they joyfully served the Lord and raised their family. Souls were saved and churches were started and strengthened.

Finally, in 1969, Alberta was allowed to return alone to North America to receive some badly needed dental work. The Communists told her that if she tried to remain in North America, she would risk harm to her husband and boys.

When she called the mission that day, she uttered not a word of complaint or self-pity. Instead, she praised the Lord for His faithfulness and wanted BCU mission officials to know she was fine. She then returned to her family and ministry behind the Iron Curtain. She died several years later.

Alberta Skinner is living proof that there is no such thing as a closed country to a person who is willing to go and never come back. 🐾

Five-finger Exercises
MADELEINE L'ENGLE

An admirer once told Paderewski, the brilliant pianist, that he was a genius. "Before I was a genius, madam," he replied, "I was a bore." In A Circle of Quiet, author Madeleine L'Engle recalls a college course she took on Chaucer. She also speaks of the importance of practice, practice, practice.

In the final exam in the Chaucer course we were asked why he used certain verbal devices, certain adjectives, why he had certain characters behave in certain ways. And I wrote, "I don't think Chaucer had any idea why he did any of these things. That isn't the way people write."

I believe this as strongly now as I did then. Most of what is best in writing isn't done deliberately.

Am I implying that an author should sit around like a pseudomystic in his pad, drinking endless cups of espresso and smoking pot and waiting for enlightenment?

Hardly. That isn't how things happen, either.

Hugh and I heard Rudolf Serkin play Beethoven's *Appassionata* sonata in Symphony Hall in Boston many years ago. It was one of those great, unpredictable moments. When the last notes had been lost in the silence, the crowd not only applauded, cheered, stamped, we stood on our chairs: this doesn't happen often in Boston.

But if Serkin did not practice eight hours a day, every day, the moment of inspiration, when it came, would have been lost; nothing would have happened; there would have been no instrument through which the revelation could be revealed.

I try to remember this when I dump an entire draft of a novel into the wastepaper basket. It *isn't* wasted paper. It's my five-finger exercises. It's necessary practicing before the performance. ❧

God's Giving
ANNIE JOHNSON FLINT

He giveth more grace when the burdens grow greater,
    He sendeth more strength when the labors increase;
To added affliction He addeth His mercies,
    To multiplied trials His multiplied peace.

When we have exhausted our store of endurance,
    When our strength has failed ere the day is half done,
When we reach the end of our hoarded resources
    Our Father's full giving is only begun.

His love has no limit, His grace has no measure,
    His power no boundary known unto men;
For out of His infinite riches in Jesus
    He giveth and giveth and giveth again. &

*Perseverance is more prevailing than violence; and many
things which cannot be overcome when they are together,
yield themselves up when taken little by little.*
PLUTARCH

The Middle Mile

VANCE HAVNER

Vance Havner was a folksy speaker whose commonsense approach to life, bathed in scriptural insight, was an inspiration to thousands in a previous generation. This excerpt is from In Tune with Heaven.

To most of us, the most important parts of a journey are the start and finish. But the part of a trip that really tests the traveler is neither the beginning nor the end but the middle mile.

Anybody can be enthusiastic at the start. The long road invites you, you are fresh and ready to go. It is easy to sing then.

And it is easy to be exuberant at the finish. You may be footsore and weary but you have arrived, the goal is reached, the crown is won. It is not difficult to be happy then.

But on the dreary middle mile when the glory of the start has died away and you are too far from the goal to be inspired by it, on the tedious middle mile when life settles down to its regular routine and monotony—there is the stretch that tires out the traveler. If you can sing along the middle mile, you've learned one of life's most difficult lessons.

This is true of all life's little journeys. A boy hears a great musician and is inspired to undertake a musical career. Years later, he makes his debut and leaps into fame. Both those milestones, his start and his success, are played up in the papers. You hear nothing about the middle mile when he banged a piano until his ears rang, those dull, drab years when he was so often tempted to give it up and be a nobody. But it was the middle mile that made him, that proved the fabric of his soul. . . .

A boy and girl marry. It is easy to be affectionate those first heavenly days when life is a paradise made for two. Fifty years later, they lie in the sunset's glow still in love although time has bent and wrinkled them and silver threads have long since replaced the gold. But it is neither the honeymoon nor the golden wedding that tests the lover. It is the middle stretch, when rent is due and hubby had lost his job and the kids have the whooping cough, that tests the traveler of the matrimonial highway.

A man is converted, "gets religion" we say. It is easy to be spiritual those first great days when the wine of a new affection so intoxicates the soul. A half-century later, he comes to the dark valley and a song is still on his lips and the heavenly vision is still bright within him. But the testing place of his religion was the long middle mile when the enthusiasm of the start had passed and the goal was still far away, when the vision had dimmed a bit and a "sense of things real came doubly strong." . . .

So in life as a whole, it is not for fine beginnings and noble resolutions that we suffer most today. And nobody needs advice on how to be happy at the end of the road, for if you have traveled well, the end of the way will care for itself. It is on the intermediate stretch where the rosy start gives way to long desert marches, where the ordinariness of life bears heaviest on the soul—it is there that we need to know how to keep the inner shrine aglow with the heavenly vision. . . .

This grace of the middle mile the Bible calls "patient continuance." It is a wonderful art that few have mastered. It proves, as nothing else can, that character. And it gets least attention from the world because there is nothing very dramatic about it. There is something theatric in a big start or a glorious finish. There is nothing for a news reporter along the middle mile. It is a lonesome mile, for the crowd is whoopin' 'er up for the fellow who got through. It's a hard mile, for it's too far to go back and a long way to go on. But if you can keep a song within and a smile without on this dreariest stretch of life, if you can learn to transform it into a paradise of its own, you have mastered the greatest secret of victorious living, the problem of the middle mile. &

Drive On!
WINSTON CHURCHILL

Let us go on, then, to battle on every front. Thrust forward every man who can be found. Arm and equip the Forces in bountiful supply. Listen to no parley from the enemy. Vie with our valiant Allies to intensify the conflict. Bear with unflinching fortitude whatever evils and blows we may receive. Drive on through the storm, now that it reaches its fury, with the same singleness of purpose and inflexibility of resolve as we showed to the world when we were all alone. ❧

The difference between perseverance and obstinacy is that one often comes from a strong will and the other from a strong won't.
HENRY WARD BEECHER

And let us not grow weary in well-doing, for in due season we shall reap, if we do not lose heart.
GALATIANS 6:9

The root of all steadfastness is in consecration to God.
ALEXANDER MACLAREN

Resourcefulness

SAMUEL M. ZWEMER was not a man to be easily put off. Perhaps the fact that he was the thirteenth of fifteen children had something to do with it! Whatever the reason, the fact is that he became a tireless worker in the cause of Christ in one of the world's most difficult mission fields, and was known as "the Apostle to Islam." His attitude is illustrated well by his celebrated comment, "If God calls you and no board will send you, bore a hole in the board and go anyway."

I call that resourcefulness. Granted, some might call it pig-headedness—but the point he makes is a good one. There are always ways and means of dealing with life's blockages and hindrances if we refuse to be discouraged and are prepared to take the initiative and use whatever resources are available to us.

Samson is another case in point. Betrayed by his compatriots, bound by ropes, he was suddenly confronted with a thousand men out for his blood. The Spirit of the Lord came upon him, and he snapped the ropes. Grabbing the only weapon available—a donkey's jawbone—he did the job. Then he commented rather poetically,

"With a donkey's jawbone
I have made donkeys of them."

The example is a little bloodthirsty, but the point is clear. If the only resource available is a donkey's jawbone, then the Spirit of God, a marked degree of resourcefulness, and the jawbone might well be all you need.

A very different example is Robinson Crusoe. If ever a man had cause to turn up his toes and die, it was he, cast alone on a desert island. But Crusoe explored his resources and went to work with a will developing what was available to him—with remarkable results. His island became a hive of activity and a center of arts and crafts, none of which he apparently knew he could do before he was put in the position of having to do it.

Or take the example of the little widow lady, destitute and in danger of losing her sons to her creditors. Elisha the prophet came around to help. "What do you have in your house?" he inquired, to which she replied, "Nothing, except a little oil." He calmly told her to collect all the pots and pans she could find and start pouring. She did, and the oil kept coming. Her resources were far greater than she imagined until Elisha helped her discover resourcefulness.

So what does this mean to ordinary folks? Basically it tells us that God has given resources to all of us, and we have the opportunity to discover them and develop them. That's a challenge, and it's also a great cure for boredom and despondency. Look around you—all you may find is a donkey's jawbone. Just grab it and keep swinging! &

The Old Woman and Her Pig

The old woman had difficulty getting home, but she kept trying different things until she succeeded. "If at first you don't succeed, try, try again."

An old woman was sweeping her house, and she found a little crooked sixpence. "What," she said, "shall I do with this little sixpence? I will go to market and buy a little pig."

As she was coming home she came to a stile. The piggy would not go over the stile. She went a little farther, and she met a dog. So she to the dog:

"Dog, dog, bite pig;
Piggy won't get over the stile,
And I shan't get home to-night!"

But the dog would not.

On she went a little farther, and she met a stick. So she said:

"Stick, stick, beat dog;
Dog won't bite pig;
Piggy won't get over the stile,
And I shan't get home to-night!"

But the stick would not.

On she went a little farther, and she met a fire. So she said:

"Fire, fire, burn stick;
Stick won't beat dog;
Dog won't bite pig;
Piggy won't get over the stile,
And I shan't get home to-night!"

But the fire would not.

On she went a little farther, and she met some water. So she said:

"Water, water, quench fire;
Fire won't burn stick;
Stick won't beat dog;
Dog won't bite pig;

Piggy won't get over the stile,
And I shan't get home to-night!"
But the water would not.
On she went a little farther, and she met an ox. So she said:
"Ox, ox, drink water;
Water won't quench fire;
Fire won't burn stick;
Stick won't beat dog;
Dog won't bite pig;
Piggy won't get over the stile,
And I shan't get home to-night!"
But the ox would not.
On she went a little farther, and she met a butcher. So she said:
"Butcher, butcher, kill ox;
Ox won't drink water;
Water won't quench fire;
Fire won't burn stick;
Stick won't beat dog;
Dog won't bite pig;
Piggy won't get over the stile,
And I shan't get home to-night!"
But the butcher would not.
On she went a little farther, and she met a rope. So she said:
"Rope, rope, hang butcher;
Butcher won't kill ox;
Ox won't drink water;
Water won't quench fire;
Fire won't burn stick;
Stick won't beat dog;
Dog won't bite pig;
Piggy won't get over the stile,
And I shan't get home to-night!"
But the rope would not.

On she went a little farther, and she met a rat. So she said:
    "Rat, rat, gnaw rope;
    Rope won't hang butcher;
    Butcher won't kill ox;
    Ox won't drink water;
    Water won't quench fire;
    Fire won't burn stick;
    Stick won't beat dog;
    Dog won't bite pig;
    Piggy won't get over the stile,
    And I shan't get home to-night!"
    But the rat would not.
On she went a little farther, and she met a cat. So she said:
    "Cat, cat, kill rat;
    Rat won't gnaw rope;
    Rope won't hang butcher;
    Butcher won't kill ox;
    Ox won't drink water;
    Water won't quench fire;
    Fire won't burn stick;
    Stick won't beat dog;
    Dog won't bite pig;
    Piggy won't get over the stile,
    And I shan't get home to-night!"
But the cat said to her, "If you will go to yonder cow, and fetch me a saucer of milk, I will kill the rat." So away went the old woman to the cow, and said:
    "Cow, cow, give me a saucer of milk;
    Cat won't kill rat;
    Rat won't gnaw rope;
    Rope won't hang butcher;
    Butcher won't kill ox;
    Ox won't drink water;

Water won't quench fire;
Fire won't burn stick;
Stick won't beat dog;
Dog won't bite pig;
Piggy won't get over the stile,
And I shan't get home to-night!"

But the cow said to her, "If you will go to yonder haymakers, and
fetch me a wisp of hay, I'll give you some milk." So away went the
old woman to the haymakers, and said:

"Haymakers, give me a wisp of hay;
Cow won't give milk;
Cat won't kill rat;
Rat won't gnaw rope;
Rope won't hang butcher;
Butcher won't kill ox;
Ox won't drink water;
Water won't quench fire;
Fire won't burn stick;
Stick won't beat dog;
Dog won't bite pig;
Piggy won't get over the stile,
And I shan't get home to-night!"

But the haymakers said to her, "If you will go to yonder stream,
and fetch us a bucket of water, we'll give you the hay."

So away the old women went. But when she got to the stream,
she found the bucket was full of holes. So she covered the bottom
with pebbles, and then filled the bucket with water, and she went
back with it to the haymakers, and they gave her a wisp of hay.

As soon as the cow had eaten the hay, she gave the old woman
the milk; and away she went with it in a saucer to the cat. As soon
as the cat had lapped up the milk . . . *then*

The cat began to kill the rat;
The rat began to gnaw the rope;

The rope began to hang the butcher;
The butcher began to kill the ox;
The ox began to drink the water;
The water began to quench the fire;
The fire began to burn the stick;
The stick began to beat the dog;
The dog began to bite the pig;
The little pig in a fright jumped over the stile;
And the old woman got home that night! 🐾

Tony the Pony
HELEN NOORDEWIER

A nice story from The Boola Pan, *in which Benjy reminds us that good ideas and hard work help us achieve our objectives.*

Papa's stall in the market place was in the middle, which Papa liked. If you were too far on either end the people did not want to come to you. In the middle everyone walked past and the buying was better. But there was more to the market than fruits and vegetables. There was the popcorn stand and the section for baked goods. At another corner people brought plants to sell, and still another was reserved for homemade articles. There were knitted mittens and pot holders and dolls dressed in many different costumes. There was homemade furniture, and way down at the southern end there were animals for sale–kittens and puppies, rabbits and hamsters, and sometimes little piglets, a few ponies, and a mule or two. Oh, the market was a wonderful place!

The crowds finally finished their buying and there were only a few stragglers left. This was the time of day Benjy liked best. He could leave the cleanup for Papa and he was free to roam for a little while.

Before he knew it, Benjy's feet took him to the part of the

market where the animals were. He stroked the long mane of a dark brown pony, and the pony touched Benjy's ear with his nose. "What do you call him?" he asked the owner.

"Why, that's Tony," the farmer said.

"How much does he cost?" Benjy asked.

"Only fifty dollars," said the farmer. "My barn is getting too small for all I have, and he takes a lot of room."

Fifty dollars! That was more money than Benjy could think of, but oh, how he wanted that pony.

In the meantime, Papa was wondering why Benjy did not come back. He sat in the empty truck and waited. "Humph," he said to himself. "Where is that boy? I'd better go and look for him."

"Benjy! Benjy!" Papa called, but Benjy did not hear. In his mind he was counting dollars—fifty of them.

Suddenly there was Papa standing in front of Benjy and looking a little bit angry.

"This is Tony the Pony, Papa," said Benjy. "He's for sale, and I would like him to be mine."

"And how much does he cost?" Papa asked.

"Fifty dollars," said Benjy.

"Do you have fifty dollars?"

"No, Papa," Benjy said. "Does Papa have fifty dollars?"

"Papa does not!" Papa said. "Not for a pony. What would Mama say if I came home with a horse instead of dollars?"

"Could I earn the dollars, Papa?"

"That will be up to you, my boy. Fifty dollars is a lot of money and you will have to plan how to earn it. But you have three good things: quick hands, fast and willing feet, and a good brain. It will take all three to earn your fifty dollars. But you might figure out how to do it."

All week Benjy thought about how he might earn the money, but he said nothing to Papa about his plans. And Papa said nothing more about the pony. Saturday was market day, and Benjy waited until then.

When Papa brought the truck out beside the mounds of freshly picked vegetables, Benjy stood ready with his goat and his wagon.

"Little One goes to the market today," Benjy said.

"What!" said Papa. "You are going to sell the goat and also the wagon I made you?"

"No! Oh, no, Papa. Little One will work today. He will give rides around the fence that surrounds the market place. Rides for all the children who come with their mothers. Rides for a quarter. You know, Papa, you said that I must figure out how to make the money for Tony."

Papa smiled a little and wrinkled his brow. "What a funny looking load I will have today," he said. "But remember, Benjy, the goat must work only a part of the day or he will be too tired. And the rest of the time I will need you to help me."

Giving the rides was fun for Benjy. He felt very important. With one child in the cart, or two if they were very small, Benjy led Little One by his halter around the long fence. Each quarter he put into the small cloth bag tied to his belt that Mama had made for his marbles. The quarters jingled when he walked and he felt very proud. By noon the bag was full—so full that the quarters did not jingle any more. And Benjy knew it was enough for the little goat. He must not get too tired, and so he tied Little One to the fence on a long rope and took the wagon to Papa beside the truck.

"Look, Papa," he said, as he patted the bag full of quarters. His face was all smiles.

Papa shook his head. "Benjy, Benjy," he said. "You are a little money man! A real little money man!"

The next Saturday was market day again, but it rained.

"There will be no rides today," Papa said.

Benjy was disappointed but he knew there was no way he

could give rides in the rain. He would have to keep busy helping
Papa.

It was slow at the market even though there were coverings
to keep out the rain. People were not in such a hurry today. There
was time to talk.

"Please, mother," a little girl begged as she stood in front of
Papa's stall. "Please, may I have that big pumpkin?"

"No, not today," her mother said. "Your daddy is away from
home and I have never carved a pumpkin."

"I have carved a pumpkin," Benjy said. "I will carve it for
you. For fifty cents I will carve it."

The little girl jumped up and down, clapping her hands.

"Please, mother! Please, mother!" she said.

"All right," the mother said. Turning to Benjy she asked,
"How long will it take?"

"I will do it right away," he said.

But Papa said, "You did not ask me, Benjy. Do you have a
knife?"

"No, Papa," Benjy said. "But the knife you use to cut off carrot
tops and the beet tops is very sharp. And remember, Papa, you said I
had to figure out how to earn the money for Tony all by myself."

"All right," Papa said. "We will try just one."

Benjy went to work. With Papa's felt pen he drew the face on
the pumpkin. He made big, round eyes, a triangle nose and a big
laughing mouth. Cutting the pumpkin was not easy, but Benjy had
done it before so he knew very well how to go about it. Keeping
the eyes round was the hardest part, but he managed. Papa
watched carefully, smiling now and then to see Benjy work so hard
and so carefully. And in a short time the happy little pumpkin face
was finished.

The little girl was delighted, and Benjy collected his pay—*two*
fifty cent pieces, shiny and new. He put them both in his little
cloth bag.

"Wait a minute," Papa said. "Who grew that pumpkin?"

"God sent the sun and the rain, Papa," Benjy said.

"And who planted the seed?" Papa asked.

"You did, Papa," Benjy answered.

"So who gets one of those fifty-cent pieces?"

"You do, Papa," Benjy said, and he gave Papa his fair share.

At the end of the day Benjy was only fifty cents richer than he had been in the morning, but he was not sad. He knew what he was going to do. All next week, every day after school he would carve pumpkins. They would be ready for sale on Saturday.

When the market day ended, all the pumpkins were sold, and Benjy's bag was very full. Papa was pleased and so was Benjy.

Before they left the market Benjy asked Papa, "May I go to the animals and see if Tony came to the market today?"

That was fine with Papa. "But don't stay too long," he said.

Benjy left on flying feet. But Tony was not there. For a minute his heart sank, but the owner, Mr. Mikita, was there.

"Did you sell Tony?" Benjy asked.

"No, I have rabbits to sell today," Mr. Mikita said. "Tony is home in the field today."

"I am going to buy him when I have enough money," Benjy said.

"That's fine," Mr. Mikita said. "I'll keep him for you. By the way, do you have any friends?"

"Oh, yes, lots of friends at school," Benjy said.

"Why don't you buy a rabbit from me? I have one who will have baby rabbits before long, I think, and you could sell them to your friends. That will give you more money and it will help me to sell Tony a little sooner."

"I will take the rabbit," Benjy said, and he took two fifty cent pieces from his bag.

"Oh, oh," Papa said when he saw Benjy walking back. "The money man has another idea. Are you going to sell rabbits next?"

"Baby rabbits, Papa, to my friends, and Mr. Mikita will keep Tony for me. Mr. Mikita lives on the farm next to the schoolhouse."

For the hundredth time, when Benjy came home, the money was shaken out of the sack and counted. He was getting close to his goal now. He had forty-eight dollars and fifty cents. And that was a lot of money.

During the next few days, Papa was doing a lot of thinking and his hands were very busy. Finally he was finished.

When Benjy came home from school the next day, he did not know that the new stall in the barn had an occupant.

"Go upstairs and change your clothes, Benjy," Mama said. "There will be a cookie when you are ready."

Benjy did as he was told. And then, quite suddenly, Mama and Papa heard him crying. He came running down the stairs.

"My money, my money," he cried. "My money is gone!"

"Now, now," Mama said. "Dry your tears. Your money is in the barn.

"In the *barn*!" Benjy said. "Why is it in the barn? It is not safe there."

"Oh, I think it is very safe," Papa said. "Come, I will show you."

The barn was quite dark, but Papa said, "Look, Benjy! Look over there in the corner."

"Tony," Benjy cried, and he ran and threw his arms around the pony, kissing his mane over and over while tears of happiness trickled down his face.

"Oh, thank you, Papa!" he said again and again.

"Look up," Papa said. "See what the sign over the stall says."

Benjy stepped back and read what Papa had painted on a big, beautiful board. It said:

Tony the Pony
Presented to Benjy
by himself 🐾

The Boy Who Always Finished What He Started

Even as a young boy, Thomas Edison demonstrated the truthfulness of the famous comment he made later in life: "Genius is 1% inspiration and 99% perspiration."

One day during the critical period of the Civil War, a newsboy in Detroit went into the office where he daily obtained his supply of papers.

"What is the news?" he questioned.

"Haven't you heard?" asked another newsboy who stood nearby. "There has just been a big battle at Pittsburg Landing."

"Oh!" exclaimed the boy, and he extracted a pencil from his pocket and began to make some calculations.

"What are you trying to figure out, Tom?" the other boy asked.

"How many papers I shall need today," he replied, as he turned and approached the circulation manager's desk.

"I want one thousand newspapers," said young Edison.

The circulation manager of the *Detroit Free Press* looked in amazement at the lad who made this astonishing request.

"Have you the money?" he asked.

"No, sir," replied Edison.

"Then get out."

The boy went directly upstairs to the office of the publisher.

"I want fifteen hundred papers, Mr. Storey," said the boy. Then he explained that the people along the line of the railroad where he had a run as train newsboy would be eager to get the news of the battle of Pittsburg Landing.

"Can you pay for them?" asked Mr. Storey.

"As soon as I sell them," answered the boy. Mr. Storey wrote something on a slip of paper and the boy took it down to the circulation manager.

"*Fifteen* hundred!" growled the man. "I thought you only wanted a thousand!"

"Oh, I thought I might as well be refused fifteen hundred papers as a thousand," grinned the boy. And that is the spirit that helped Thomas Edison, the world's greatest inventor, to success.

Tom knew that the people along the line would be anxious to hear the news. He had no money, but he had courage and, what is better, the habit of thinking things out, that is, of thinking ahead. Usually he sold about sixty papers along this train route. How could he sell fifteen hundred?

He had thought that all out in advance. He went to a telegraph operator who was fond of reading, and said to him, "If you will wire ahead to every stop that there has been a big battle and that I am coming with papers telling the story and giving a list of the dead and wounded, I will send you a daily paper and two magazines a month for six months." Thus bargained young Edison.

"I will do it," agreed the operator.

When young Edison reached his first stop, Utica, there was a large crowd of people waiting at the station.

"At first I thought the crowd was going on an excursion," said Mr. Edison in relating the incident, "but I soon realized they were waiting for the papers. I sold more than half of my papers there, and at Mount Clemens and Port Huron I sold the remainder."

As a young man, and with only a dollar in his pocket, Thomas Edison went to New York City looking for work. Three nights he slept on park benches. One day he went without food. While he was in the office of a gold and stock indicator company the stock ticker stopped and there was great excitement.

He said, "I think I can fix it for you." He opened the ticker lifted a loose contact sprint that had fallen between the wheels, and it started up again.

Just as he did this the man who had a big interest in the

ticker service saw him. "We are having trouble with this service. If you can keep it going for us I will give you three hundred dollars a month," he said.

"I was amazed when I heard this," Mr. Edison said later, "but I remained calm and agreed to do it, demanding an advance in 'good faith.' I really did not want it for 'good faith' but for food, as I had not eaten for nearly thirty hours."

Mr. Edison learned why the ticker would not work well and improved it, securing a patent. When the company asked him for how much he would sell it, he thought of asking five thousand dollars. "I will let the company make the first offer," he said to himself. They gave him forty thousand dollars; so he made exactly thirty-five thousand dollars by using his judgment.

All the world knows of his rapid rise after that. This money enabled him to build a laboratory and carry on experiments. He invented the quadruplex telegraph, the incandescent light, the phonograph, moving pictures, speaking parts of the telephone, appliances for use on electric railways, storage batteries, and scores of other great things. ❧

The Crow and the Pitcher
AESOP

A thirsty Crow, after looking in vain for water to drink, at last saw some in the bottom of a pitcher. Seeing this water made him more thirsty than ever, and he began to plan how he could get it. He finally hit upon a scheme. By dropping pebbles into the pitcher and doing so until he brought the water near enough to the top so that he could reach it, he had all he wanted. Then he said to himself, "Well, I know now, that little by little does the trick." ❧

Through the Roof

When this sick man's friends ran into a problem, they were not easily discouraged. As related in chapter five of the Gospel of Luke, these men found a way to get their sick friend to Jesus. But I wonder who paid for the roof!

"Jesus will help you," some friends told the sick man. "We will take you to Him."

The sick man could not walk. So his friends carried him on his bed. They took him through the streets of town. They took him to the house where Jesus was teaching.

But when they came to the house they could not get in. There were too many people. Everyone wanted to see Jesus.

"What shall we do?" one of the friends asked. "We'll never get through that crowd."

"Then let's go over the crowd," said another friend. "We'll go up on the roof and let our friend down through the roof to see Jesus."

The friends picked up the bed with the sick man on it. They climbed up some outside stairs to the roof of the house. Then, slowly and carefully, they took some parts of the roof off. They tied ropes to the four corners of their friend's bed and let the sick man down through the hole in the roof.

Slowly and gently the bed came right down into the middle of the crowd, right by Jesus. Jesus looked at the man who had come down through the roof. Then He smiled.

"Your sins are forgiven," Jesus said.

Some of the Jewish leaders were upset. "Only God can forgive sins. Who does this Man think He is?"

But Jesus knew what they were thinking, so He said, "You are right. Only God can forgive sins. Therefore, I will show you that I can forgive sins." Then Jesus turned to the sick man and said, "Stand up!"

The man did not know what to do. He couldn't walk. But

Jesus was telling him to stand up. He did so.

Then Jesus said, "Pick up your bed and walk."

So the man did what Jesus said. He picked up his bed, and to everyone's surprise he began to walk.

"Thank You, thank You," the man told Jesus."

He walked out of the house and down the street toward home.

All the people watched the man walk. "Thank God," they said. "Thank God that Jesus can make us well again." ❧

Queequeg Gets on Board
HERMAN MELVILLE

One of the most interesting characters in Melville's classic, Moby Dick, is a former cannibal called Queequeg. His intense desire to know more about Christianity led him through many difficulties and adventures.

Queequeg was a native of Kokovoko, an island far away to the West and South. It is not down in any map; true places never are.

When a new-hatched savage, running wild about his native woodlands in a grass clout, followed by the nibbling goats, as if he were a green sapling; even then, in Queequeg's ambitious soul, lurked a strong desire to see something more of Christendom than a specimen whaler or two. His father was a High Chief, a King; his uncle a High Priest; and on the maternal side he boasted aunts who were the wives of unconquerable warriors. There was excellent blood in his veins—royal stuff; though sadly vitiated, I fear, by the cannibal propensity he nourished in his untutored youth.

A Sag Harbour ship visited his father's bay, and Queequeg sought a passage to Christian lands. But the ship, having her full complement of seamen, spurned his suit; and not all the King his father's influence could prevail. But Queequeg vowed a vow. Alone in his canoe, he paddled off to a distant strait, which he knew the ship must pass through when she quitted the island. On one side was a coral reef; on the other a low tongue of land, covered with mangrove thickets that grew out into the water. Hiding his canoe, still afloat, among these thickets, with its prow seaward, he sat down in the stern, paddle low in hand; and when the ship was gliding by, like a flash he darted out; gained her side; with one backward dash of his foot capsized and sank his canoe; climbed up the chains; and throwing himself at full length upon the deck, grappled a ring-bolt there, and swore not to let it go, though hacked in pieces.

In vain the captain threatened to throw him overboard; suspended a cutlass over his naked wrists; Queequeg was the son of a King, and Queequeg budged not. Struck by his desperate dauntlessness, and his wild desire to visit Christendom, the captain at last relented, and told him he might make himself at home. But this fine young savage—this sea Prince of Wales, never saw the captain's cabin. They put him down among the sailors, and made a whaleman of him. But like the Czar Peter content to toil in the shipyards of foreign cities, Queequeg disdained no seeming ignominy, if thereby he might happily gain the power of enlightening his untutored countrymen. For at bottom—so he told me—he was actuated by a profound desire to learn among the Christians the arts whereby to make his people still happier than they were; and more than that, still better than they were. ❧

Preparing for China
HOWARD AND GERALDINE TAYLOR

Young Hudson Taylor confronted immense difficulties in his desire to take the Gospel to China. In Hudson Taylor in Early Years: The Growth of a Soul, *Taylor's son and daughter-in-law tell how he tackled the problems one by one and achieved his purpose.*

"It seemed to me highly probable," Hudson Taylor said, "that the work to which I was thus called might cost my life. China was not open then as it is now. Few missionary societies had representatives there, and few books on the subject were accessible to me. I learned, however, that a minister in my native town possessed a copy of Medhurst's *China*, and calling upon him ventured to ask a loan of the book.

"This he kindly granted, inquiring why I wished to read it. I told him that God had called me to spend my life in missionary service in that land.

" 'And how do you propose to go there?' he inquired.

"I answered that I did not at all know; that it seemed to me probable that I should need to do as the Twelve and the Seventy had done in Judea, go without purse or scrip, relying on Him who had sent me to supply all my need.

"Kindly placing his hand on my shoulder, the minister replied, 'Ah, my boy, as you grow older you will become wiser than that. Such an idea would do very well in the days when Christ Himself was on earth, but not now.'

"I have grown older since then, but not wiser. I am more and more convinced that if we were to take the directions of our Master and the assurance He gave to His first disciples more fully as our guide, we should find them just as suited to our times as to those in which they were originally given.

"Medhurst's book on China emphasized the value of Medical Missions there, and this directed my attention to medical studies as a mode of preparation.

"My beloved parents neither disapproved nor encouraged my desire to engage in missionary work. They advised me, with such convictions, to use all the means in my power to develop the resources of body, mind and soul, and to wait prayerfully upon God, quite willing, should He show me that I was mistaken, to follow His guidance, or to go forward if in due time He should open the way to missionary service. The importance of this advice I have since had occasion to prove. I began to take more exercise in the open air to strengthen my general health. My feather bed was soon dispensed with, and as many other comforts as possible, in order to prepare for a rougher sort of life. I began also to do what Christian work was in my power, in the way of tract distribution, Sunday-school teaching, and visiting the poor and sick as opportunity afforded."

Another form of preparation entered upon with ardor was the study of Chinese, that formidable task requiring, as Milne put it, "bodies of iron, lungs of brass, heads of oak, hands of spring-steel, eyes of eagles, hearts of apostles, memories of angels and lives of Methuselah." Courageous in his inexperience, Hudson Taylor set to work, despite the fact that he had neither teacher nor books with the exception of that one little volume of the writings of St. Luke. A grammar would have cost no less than four guineas, and a dictionary could hardly have been purchased for fifteen. Needless to say he had neither. But hard work and ingenuity accomplished wonders, as may be judged from the fact that within a few weeks he and the cousin who was with him in the shop had found out the meaning of over five hundred characters.

"The method we pursue is as follows," he wrote to his sister on February 14. "We find a short verse in the English version, and then look out a dozen or more (also in English) that have one word in common with it. We then turn up the first verse in Chinese, and search through all the others for some character in common that seems to stand for the English word. This we write down on a slip of paper as its probable equivalent. Then we look all through the Chinese Gospel for this same character in different connections. It occurs as a rule pretty frequently. And if in every case we find the same word in the English version, we copy the character in ink into our dictionary, adding the meaning in pencil. Afterwards, if further acquaintance shows it to be the true meaning, we ink that over also. At first we made slow progress, but now we can work much faster, as with few exceptions we know all the most common characters. In our dictionary we have four hundred and fifty-three put down as certain, and many others that are not fully proved. About two hundred more we know as certain that we have not copied into the dictionary yet, and many besides that are only probable.

"I have begun to get up at five in the morning," he continued, "and so find it necessary to go to bed early at night. I must study if I mean to go to China. I am fully decided to go, and am making every preparation I can. I intend to rub up my Latin, to learn Greek and the rudiments of Hebrew, and to get as much general information as possible. I need all your prayers."

Opportunity

EDWARD ROWLAND SILL

Attitude is 90% of the battle!

This I beheld, or dreamed it in a dream:—
    There spread a cloud of dust along a plain;
And underneath the cloud, or in it, raged
    A furious battle, and men yelled, and swords
Shocked upon swords and shields. A prince's banner
    Wavered, then staggered backward, hemmed by foes.
A craven hung long the battle's edge
    And thought, "Had I a sword of keener steel—
That blue blade that the king's son bears—but this
    Blunt thing!" he snapped and flung it from his hand,
And lowering crept away and left the field.
    Then came the king's son, wounded, sore bestead,
And weaponless, and saw the broken sword,
    Hilt-buried in the dry and trodden sand,
And ran and snatched it, and with battle-shout
    Lifted afresh he hewed his enemy down,
And saved a great cause that heroic day. ❧

Self-discipline

HAVE YOU EVER made New Year's resolutions and by February forgotten what they were? Have you ever eaten a chocolate fudge sundae and immediately said, "I shouldn't have eaten that?" Or lost your temper and promptly regretted it? Each time this happened, you felt some kind of inner conflict. Different parts of you were going in different directions. This experience has been addressed by philosophers and dramatists, therapists and clergymen from time immemorial. Depending on the discipline involved, the explanations have varied.

Nobody described it better than the apostle Paul when he lamented, "I have the desire to do what is good, but I cannot carry it out. For what I do is not the good I want to do; no, the evil I do not want to do—this I keep on doing." His explanation was that he had a problem with indwelling sin or, as he sometimes called it, "the flesh." The Scriptures also talk about the negative impact of "the world" on our lives. Of course, "the Devil" completes this unholy trinity. Given that we are confronted with these formidable forces within and without, it is clear that steps must be taken to deal with them so that our lives are not dominated by negative, destructive factors. These steps include self-discipline. But what is involved?

First, there must be a recognition of weakness or vulnerability. To deny this is not only to fly in the face of reality, but also to endanger one's own well-being. Mark Twain could joke, "It's easy to

111

stop smoking. I've done it dozens of times," but after the laughter we have to admit that such lack of self-discipline is injurious to one's health!

Second, there has to be a desire for change, a seeking after improvement. A grander goal, a finer focus, like that of the athlete seeking a record or the student competing for a scholarship, must be established and deeply longed for.

Third, practical ways of reaching the desired objective must be explored and spelled out in manageable steps. As we know, the best way to eat an elephant is in bite-sized pieces.

Fourth, the price has to be paid, for the discipline of self is no easy matter. No quick fixes exist. Henry Wadsworth Longfellow had it right when he wrote:

"The heights by great men reached and kept
Were not attained by sudden flight,
But they, while their companions slept
Were toiling upward in the night."

Fifth, the enabling for this endeavor is available through the gift of God's Spirit for, as Paul reminds us, self-control is one aspect of the fruit of the Spirit.

A final word. Before we learn how to discipline ourselves, we all need to learn discipline by being disciplined or discipled by someone else. Usually this discipline has to be imposed and, as any well-brought-up child or well-trained person will testify, the experience may not be pleasant. But that child will also live to thank his parents, and the trainee will become a trainer of fine people in time. ❧

Table Manners

GELETT BURGESS

Oops! Look out for Goops! Gelett Burgess's Goops have been around since 1900, and they're just as funny and useful today. If you can find a copy of Goops and How to Be Them: A Manual of Manners for Polite Infants, *your whole family will profit!*

The Goops they lick their fingers,
    And the Goops they lick their knives;
They spill their broth on the tablecloth—
    Oh, they lead disgusting lives!
The Goops they talk while eating,
    And loud and fast they chew;
And that is why I'm glad that I
    Am not a Goop—are you?

Carrots!

L. M. MONTGOMERY

The young heroine of Anne of Green Gables *had bright red hair and a temper to match. While we sympathize with her in her provocation and admire her spirit, we must admit that her temper needs some work!*

When Mr. Phillips was in the back of the room hearing Prissy Andrews' Latin, Diana whispered to Anne.

"That's Gilbert Blythe sitting right across the aisle from you, Anne. Just look at him and see if you don't think he's handsome."

Anne looked accordingly. She had a good chance to do so, for the said Gilbert Blythe was absorbed in stealthily pinning the long yellow braid of Ruby Gillis, who sat in front of him, to the back of her seat. He was a tall boy, with curly brown hair, roguish hazel eyes and a mouth twisted into a teasing smile. Presently Ruby Gillis started up to take a sum to the master; she fell back into her seat with a little shriek, believing that her hair was pulled out by the roots. Everybody looked at her and Mr. Phillips glared so sternly that Ruby began to cry. Gilbert had whisked the pin out of sight and was studying his history with the soberest face in the world; but when the commotion subsided he looked at Anne and winked with inexpressible drollery.

"I think your Gilbert Blythe *is* handsome," confided Anne to Diana, "but I think he's very bold. It isn't good manners to wink at a strange girl."

But it was not until the afternoon that things really began to happen.

Mr. Phillips was back in the corner explaining a problem in algebra to Prissy Andrews and the rest of the scholars were doing pretty much as they pleased, eating green apples, whispering, drawing pictures on their slates, and driving crickets, harnessed to strings, up and down the aisle. Gilbert Blythe was trying to make Anne Shirley look at him and failing utterly, because Anne was at that moment totally oblivious, not only of the very existence of Gilbert Blythe, but of every other scholar in Avonlea school and of Avonlea school itself. With her chin propped on her hands and her eyes fixed on the blue glimpse of the Lake of Shining Waters that the west window afforded, she was far away in a gorgeous dreamland, hearing and seeing nothing save her own wonderful visions.

Gilbert Blythe wasn't used to putting himself out to make a girl look at him and meeting with failure. She *should* look at him, that redhaired Shirley girl with the little pointed chin and the big eyes that weren't like the eyes of any other girl in Avonlea school.

Gilbert reached across the aisle, picked up the end of Anne's long red braid, held it out at arm's length and said in a piercing whisper, "Carrots! Carrots!"

Then Anne looked at him with a vengeance!

She did more than look. She sprang to her feet, her bright fancies fallen into cureless ruin. She flashed one indignant glance at Gilbert from eyes whose angry sparkle was swiftly quenched in equally angry tears.

"You mean, hateful boy!" she exclaimed passionately. "How dare you!"

And then—Thwack! Anne had brought her slate down on Gilbert's head and cracked it—slate, not head—clear across.

Avonlea school always enjoyed a scene. This was an especially enjoyable one. Everybody said, "Oh" in horrified delight. Diana gasped. Ruby Gillis, who was inclined to be hysterical, began to cry. Tommy Sloane let his team of crickets escape him altogether while he stared openmouthed at the tableau.

Mr. Phillips stalked down the aisle and laid his hand heavily on Anne's shoulder.

"Anne Shirley, what does this mean?" he said angrily.

Anne returned no answer. It was asking too much of flesh and blood to expect her to tell before the whole school that she had been called "Carrots." Gilbert it was who spoke up stoutly.

"It was my fault, Mr. Phillips. I teased her."

Mr. Phillips paid no heed to Gilbert.

"I am sorry to see a pupil of mine displaying such a temper and such a vindictive spirit," he said in a solemn tone, as if the mere fact of being a pupil of his ought to root out all evil passions from the hearts of small imperfect mortals. "Anne, go and stand on the platform in front of the blackboard for the rest of the afternoon."

Anne would have infinitely preferred a whipping to this punishment, under which her sensitive spirit quivered as from a whiplash. With a white, set face she obeyed. Mr. Phillips took a chalk crayon and wrote on the blackboard above her head.

"Ann Shirley has a very bad temper. Ann Shirley must learn to control her temper," and then read it out loud so that even the primer class, who couldn't read writing, should understand it.

Anne stood there the rest of the afternoon with that legend above her. She did not cry or hang her head. Anger was still too

115

hot in her heart for that and it sustained her amid all her agony of humiliation. With resentful eyes and passion-red cheeks she confronted alike Diana's sympathetic gaze and Charlie Sloane's indignant nods and Josie Pye's malicious smiles. As for Gilbert Blythe, she would not even look at him. She would *never* look at him again! She would never speak to him!!

When school was dismissed Anne marched out with her red head held high. Gilbert Blythe tried to intercept her at the porch door.

"I'm awful sorry I made fun of your hair, Anne," he whispered contritely. "Honest I am. Don't be mad for keeps, now."

Anne swept by disdainfully, without look or sign of hearing. "Oh, how could you, Anne?" breathed Diana as they went down the road, half reproachfully, half admiringly. Diana felt that *she* could never have resisted Gilbert's plea.

"I shall never forgive Gilbert Blythe," said Anne firmly. "And Mr. Phillips spelled my name without an *e*, too. The iron has entered into my soul, Diana."

Diana hadn't the least idea what Anne meant but she understood it was something terrible. ❧

Some Determined Young Men
KEN TAYLOR

Daniel and his friends have been captured by the Babylonians and taken away from their homeland. The king wanted them to do something that they knew was wrong. This is the story, from Daniel 1, of how they stood up to him.

King Nebuchadnezzar of Babylon decided that he needed some new advisors, so he started a school to train some of the Israeli boys who had been captured at Jerusalem. He said that all the students at the school must be handsome, quick to learn, and in perfect health. He wanted them to learn everything there was to know.

They would attend his school for three years, and then would work for the king as his advisors and government officials.

Among those chosen to go to school were four Jewish boys whose names were Daniel, Shadrach, Meshach, and Abednego. These young men had a problem: they loved God and wanted to obey Him, but the king didn't want them to. The king said that they should pray to idols before every meal and thank them for the food. But God said no. So what should they do?

Daniel and his three friends decided to ask the king for permission to eat other food, instead of food for which the idols had been thanked.

Daniel talked to one of his teachers about it. This man liked Daniel a lot, but he didn't dare give permission. "I'm afraid it will make the king angry," he said. "If he notices that you look paler and thinner than the young men who eat the food blessed by the idols, he will be angry with me and kill me."

"Please let us try it for just ten days," Daniel begged. "Give us only vegetables and water, and after ten days see if we don't look as well as the fellows who eat the other food. If we don't, then we will go ahead and eat the same as the others do."

The teacher finally agreed, and they were fed vegetables and water for ten days. At the end of that time they looked better and healthier than any of the others! So from then on they could eat whatever they wanted to. God helped them become wise, and He made Daniel able to understand the meaning of dreams.

At the end of their three years' training, the teachers brought them to the palace. There King Nebuchadnezzar talked with them and soon realized that these four Jewish boys were the best students of all! They always knew the right answers when the king was puzzled, and the king discovered that they were ten times smarter than the wisest men in his kingdom. ✿

Grandpa's Great Race
LILI FOLDES

Young people need to learn self-discipline; old people need to remember it. This story of a Swedish "Supergrandpa" should help.

Anyone in Sweden will tell you that Gustaf Håkansson won the longest bicycle race ever held there. But it's not quite as simple as that. It was the strange way he did it that made him the hero of the Swedish people and caused him to be known as "Supergrandpa."

"Go home to your rocking chair," the judges told him when he tried to enter the race. "You're twenty-six years over the age limit." Gustaf was sixty-six years old!

It was to be a tremendously hard and tiring race. The course would run almost the whole length of Sweden—from Haparanda, just south of the Arctic Circle, 1094 miles down to Ystad, at the southern end of Sweden. There was a Grand Prize of 5000 kronor ($1000).

Cyclists were warned not to enter the race unless they were in perfect condition. From the thousand or so men who applied, the judges picked fifty young athletes for the race and took them up to Haparanda by train. There they had a scientifically planned rest and lived on special energy diets for days before starting off.

But nobody offered to pay Gustaf's fare, so he hopped on his bike and pedaled the thousand miles to Haparanda.

Shortly after the fifty young men had started. Gustaf was off on his own private bicycle race, with his snow-white beard waving in the breeze. The judges had given him no racing number so he wore a huge zero on his chest.

They could keep him out of the race but they couldn't keep him off the road.

It wasn't until he had pedaled about a hundred miles that Gustaf was given his nickname. In the quiet little town of Lulea a ten-year-old youngster saw this Santa Claus in shorts and beret whiz past. "Look!" the child exclaimed. "There goes *Stålfarfar!*" That is best translated as Supergrandpa, for *Stålman* is the Swedish name of Superman, and *farfar* means grandfather. A news photographer overheard the child's remark. He took a picture of the old man and sent the astounding story to his newspaper. The nickname stuck.

For seven days the story of this sixty-six-year-old truck driver and his fantastic feat of endurance was front-page news in the Swedish newspapers. As he pedaled south hundreds of people waited for him at every bend of the road. A nation of seven million levelheaded Swedes turned into an eager mass of Supergrandpa fans. Newsreels, newspapers and radio commentators reported everything the old man said and did.

At the end of each day's run, the fifty young cyclists had a good night's rest, but Grandpa pedaled through three days and nights without a wink.

As the race went on, the newspapers gave pages to Supergrandpa's life story. The people of Sweden learned that he had not taken up bicycling until he was past forty. Before that he had been too busy making a living as a farm hand and truck driver. But when his ten children were grown up, he said one day to his wife, "I am going up north to Lapland. I want to see the midnight sun."

His wife pointed out that he had no money. "All you need to see the world is a bicycle and two strong legs," he told her. And, with a loaf of bread, a jug of water and a raincoat, he pedaled off. When he reached the Arctic he spent the summer doing odd jobs on farms to earn his keep. When the days began to shorten he headed his bicycle toward home. For years afterward he spent the dark winter evenings telling his friends about the wonderful summer he had spent in the "land of the midnight sun."

Six days, fourteen hours and twenty minutes after starting,

Supergrandpa crossed the finishing line. He was a good twenty-four hours ahead of the boys. Altogether, he had had ten hours' sleep on the way.

In Ystad thousands cheered him. The fire brigade band played victory marches and the crowd smothered him with flowers, as he hugged his wife happily. Then they carried him on their shoulders to the police station, where he posed for photographers. The people of Sweden showered all sorts of gifts upon him, including mattresses and several dozen armchairs, so that he could rest at last.

The next week, with one of his sons acting as chauffeur, Supergrandpa was driven in a car to a private audience with the King.

Naturally, Supergrandpa did not get the 5000-kronor Grand Prize, for officially he was not in the race. But makers of bicycles and cars paid him a small fortune for the privilege of using his name in their advertisements.

I remember asking Supergrandpa what he would do with the money. He smiled at me with his clear blue eyes. "I'll give it all to my children, so that they can afford to let their children grow up to be themselves. It's got so that if somebody behaves naturally these days, he's considered odd. I know that people in my village thought I was mad to pedal all the way up to the Arctic. But I believe they respect me now."

Fan letters poured in. Many of them were addressed simply to *Stålfarfar* without proper name or address. Supergrandpa's favorite letter came from a man in Uppsala: "I am your age, dear Gustaf Håkansson, and I was an ailing old man before you came along. But your example made me feel young, healthy and happy again. God bless you!" &

Demosthenes' Self-improvement Program
PLUTARCH

Demosthenes ranks highly in everybody's list of all-star orators. But his great abilities did not come naturally or easily. Plutarch, the great Greek biographer, describes the extreme labor and self-discipline that went into the development of Demosthenes' skills.

When Demosthenes first addressed himself to the people, he met with great discouragements, and was derided for his strange and uncouth style, which was cumbered with long sentences and tortured with formal arguments to a most harsh and disagreeable excess. Besides, he had, it seems, a weakness in his voice, a perplexed and indistinct utterance and a shortness of breath, which, by breaking and disjointing his sentences, much obscured the sense and meaning of what he spoke.

. . . Being convinced how much grace and ornament language acquires from action, he began to esteem it a small matter, and as good as nothing for a man to exercise himself in declaiming, if he neglected enunciation and delivery. Hereupon he built himself a place to study in under ground (which was still remaining in our time), and hither he would come constantly every day to form his action and to exercise his voice; and here he would continue, oftentimes without intermission, two or three months together, shaving one half of his head, that so for shame he might not go abroad, though he desired it ever so much.

Nor was this all, but also made his conversation with people abroad, his common speech, and his business, subservient to his studies, taking from hence occasions and arguments as matter to work upon. For as soon as he was parted from his company, down he would go at once into his study, and run over everything in order that had passed, and the reasons that might be alleged for and against it. Any speeches, also, that he was present at, he would go over again with himself, and reduce into periods; and whatever others spoke to him, or he to them, he would correct, transform, and vary several ways. Hence it was that he was looked upon as a person of no great natural genius, but one who owed all the power and ability he had in speaking to labour and industry. Of the truth of which it was thought to be no small sign that he was very rarely heard to speak upon the occasion, but though he were by name frequently called upon by the people, as he sat in the assembly, yet he would not rise unless he had previously considered the subject, and came prepared for it. 🐾

The Gentleman
JOHN HENRY NEWMAN

Newman, a nineteenth-century religious leader and reformer, was an educator, poet, and writer as well. In The Idea of a University Defined, *his brief description of a gentleman contains more sound, challenging information on what his society considered appropriate masculine behavior than we are likely to find in any contemporary treatise of similar length.*

It is almost a definition of a gentleman to say he is one who never inflicts pain. This description is both refined and, as far as it goes, accurate. He is mainly occupied in merely removing the obstacles which hinder the free and unembarrassed action of those about him, and he concurs with their movements rather than takes the initiative himself. His benefits may be considered as parallel to what are called comforts or conveniences in arrangements of a personal nature; like an easy chair or a good fire, which do their part in dispelling cold and fatigue, though nature provides both means of rest and animal heat without them. The true gentleman in like manner carefully avoids whatever may cause a jar or a jolt in the minds of those with whom he is cast—all clashing of opinion, or collision of feeling, all restraint, or suspicion, or gloom, or resentment; his great concern being to make everyone at their ease and at home. He has his eyes on all his company; he is tender toward the bashful, gentle toward the distant, and merciful toward the absurd; he can recollect to whom he is speaking; he guards against unreasonable allusions, or topics which may irritate; he is seldom prominent in conversation, and never wearisome. He makes light of favors while he does them, and seems to be receiving when he is conferring. He never speaks of himself except when compelled, never defends himself by a mere retort, he has no ears for slander or gossip, is scrupulous in imputing motives to those who interfere with him, and interprets everything for the best. He is never mean or little in his disputes, never takes unfair advantage, never mistakes personalities or sharp saying for arguments, or insinuates evil which he dare not say out. From a long-sighted prudence, he observes the maxim of the ancient sage, that we should ever conduct ourselves toward our enemy as if he were one day to be our friend. He has too much good sense to be affronted at insults, he is too well employed to remember injuries, and too indolent to bear malice. He is patient, forbearing, and resigned, on philosophical principles; he submits to pain because it is inevitable, to bereavement because it is irreparable, and to death because it is his destiny. If he engages in controversy of any kind, his disciplined intellect preserves him from the blundering discourtesy of better, perhaps, but less educated minds, who, like blunt weapons, tear and hack, instead of cutting clean, who mistake the point in argument, waste their strength on trifles, misconceive their adversary, and leave the question more involved than they find it. He may be right or wrong in his opinion, but he is too clearheaded to be unjust; he is as simple as he is forcible, and as brief as he is decisive. Nowhere shall we find greater candor, consideration, indulgence; he throws himself into the minds of his opponents; he accounts for their mistakes. He knows the weakness of human reason as well as its strength, its province and its limits. If he be an unbeliever, he will be too profound and large-minded to ridicule religion or to act against it; he is too wise to be a dogmatist or fanatic in his infidelity. He respects piety and devotion; he even supports institutions as venerable, beautiful, or useful, to which he does not assent; he honors the ministers of religion, and it contents him to decline its mysteries without assailing or denouncing them. He is a friend of religious toleration, and that not only because his philosophy has taught him to look on all forms of faith with an impartial eye, but also from the gentleness and effeminacy of feeling which is the attendant on civilization. &

A Father's Advice
WILLIAM SHAKESPEARE

In Hamlet, Act I, Scene III, Polonius gives his son Laertes great advice before sending him to France. In Shakespeare's English the reading is not easy, but the comprehending is most beneficial.

Yet here, Laertes! aboard, aboard, for shame!
    The wind sits in the shoulder of your sail,
And you are stay'd for. There; my blessing with you!
    And these few precepts in thy memory
See thou character. Give thy thoughts no tongue,
    Nor any unproportion'd thought his act.
Be thou familiar, but by no means vulgar.
    Those friends thou hast, and their adoption tried,
Grapple them to thy soul with hoops of steel;
    But do not dull thy palm with entertainment
Of each new-hatch'd, unfledged comrade. Beware
    Of entrance to a quarrel, but being in,
Bear't that the opposed may beware of thee.
    Give every man thy ear, but few thy voice;
Take each man's censure, but reserve thy judgement.
    Costly thy habit as thy purse can buy,
But not express'd in fancy; rich, not gaudy;

For the apparel oft proclaims the man,
And they in France of the best rank and station
      Are of a most select and generous chief in that.
Neither a borrower nor a lender be;
      For loan oft loses both itself and friend,
And borrowing dulls the edge of husbandry.
      This above all: to thine own self be true,
And it must follow, as the night the day,
      Thou canst not then be false to any man.
Farewell: my blessing season this in thee! &

Susanna Wesley's Rules of Order
REBECCA LAMAR HARMON

In Susanna, Mother of the Wesleys, *Rebecca Lamar Harmon recounts Mrs. Wesley's rules for maintaining order in a large household. To our modern ears, this sounds more like boot camp than family, but the overarching rule was "Strength guided by kindness." It's hard to argue with that.*

There were several bye-laws observed among us. I mention them here because I think them useful.

1. It had been observed that cowardice and fear of punishment often lead children into lying till they get a custom of it which they cannot leave. To prevent this, a law was made that whoever was charged with a fault of which they were guilty, if they would ingenuously confess it and promise to amend should not be beaten. This rule prevented a great deal of lying, and would have done more if one in the family would have observed it. But he could not be prevailed upon, and therefore was often imposed on by false colours and equivocations which none would have used but one, had they been kindly dealt with; and some in spite of all would always speak truth plainly.

125

2. That no sinful action, as lying, pilfering at church or on the Lord's day, disobedience, quarreling, etc. should ever pass unpunished. . . .

3. That no child should be ever chid or beat twice for the same fault, and that if they amended they should never be upbraided with it afterwards.

4. That every signal act of obedience, especially when it crossed, upon their own inclinations, should be always commended, and frequently rewarded according to the merits of the case.

5. That if ever any child performed an act of obedience, or did anything with an intention to please, though the performance was not well, yet the obedience and intention should be kindly accepted, and the child with sweetness directed how to do better for the future.

6. That propriety [the rights of property] be invariably preserved, and none suffered to invade the property of another in the smallest matter, though it were but of the value of a farthing or a pin, which they might not take from the owner without, much less against, his consent. This rule can never be too much inculcated on the minds of children; and from the want of parents or governors doing it as they ought, proceeds that shameful neglect of justice which we may observe in the world.

7. That promises be strictly observed; and a gift once bestowed, and so the right passed away from the donor, be not resumed, but left to the disposal of him to whom it was given, unless it were conditional, and the condition of the obligation not performed.

8. That no girl be taught to work till she can read very well; and that she be kept to her work with the same application and for the same time that she was held to in reading. This rule also is much to be observed, for the putting children to learn sewing before they can read perfectly is the very reason why so few women can read fit to be heard, and never to be well understood.

Mrs. Wesley's practice, which she termed "conquering their will" or "subjecting the will" merits a word of comment. At first glance one might think this meant breaking the spirit of her children, but nothing could be further from the truth.

To manage such a large family, attend to the farming, and conduct school daily for all her children Mrs. Wesley was obliged to work out a rigid regimen. She set up her household under as strict a discipline as that of a company of soldiers, each child being amenable to properly constituted authority which was hers. Like the military, Susanna's stringent regime was not simply for more efficient handling of a large group of people, but as better preparation of each member of the company for the battle of life ahead. Her system was always geared to a future when each individual child should have reached a state of maturity and could regulate his own life. The formation of character was ever the end of all her striving. 🐾

Resolutions for Living
JONATHAN EDWARDS

Jonathan Edwards, onetime president of Princeton University, is regarded by many as the greatest theologian-philosopher America has produced. His personal disciplines clearly played a major role in the development of his character and abilities.

During Jonathan Edwards' preparation for the ministry . . . he formed a series of *resolutions*, to the number of seventy, intended obviously for himself alone, to regulate his own heart and life, but fitted also, from their Christian simplicity and spiritual-mindedness, to be eminently useful to others. . . . It should be remembered they were all written before he was twenty years of age. As he was wholly averse to all profession and ostentation; and as these resolutions themselves were plainly intended for no other eye than his own, except the eye that is omniscient; they may be justly considered as the basis of his conduct and character, the plan by which he governed the secret as well as the publick actions of his life. As such they will deeply interest the reader, not only as they unfold the inmost mind of their author, but as they also show, in a manner most striking and convincing to the conscience, what is the true foundation of great and distinguished excellence.

He was too well acquainted with human weakness and frailty, even where the intentions are most sincere, to enter on any resolutions rashly, or from a reliance on his own strength. He therefore in the outset looked to God for aid, who alone can afford success in the use of the best means, and in the intended accomplishment of the best purposes. This he places at the head of all his other important rules, that his whole dependence was on the grace of God, while he still proposes to recur to a frequent and serious perusal of them, in order that they might become the habitual directory of his life.

RESOLUTIONS

"Being sensible that I am unable to do any thing without God's help, I do humbly entreat him, by his grace, to enable me to keep these Resolutions, so far as they are agreeable to his will, for Christ's sake.

Remember to read over these Resolutions once a week.

1. *Resolved,* "That *I will do whatsoever* I think to be most to the glory of God, and my own good, profit, and pleasure, in the whole of my duration; without any consideration of the time, whether now, or never so many myriads of ages hence. *Resolved,* to do whatever I think to be my duty, and most for the good and advantage of mankind in general. *Resolved,* so to do, whatever *difficulties* I meet with, how many soever, and how great soever.

2. *Resolved,* To be continually endeavoring to find out some *new contrivance* and invention to promote the forementioned things.

3. *Resolved,* If ever I shall fall and grow dull, so as to neglect

to keep any part of these Resolutions, to repent of all I can remember, when I come to myself again.

4. *Resolved*, Never *to do* any manner of thing, whether in soul or body, less or more, but what tends to the glory of God, nor *be*, nor *suffer* it, if I can possibly avoid it.

5. *Resolved*, Never to lose one moment of time, but to improve it in the most profitable way I possibly can.

6. *Resolved*, To live with all my might, while I do live.

7. *Resolved*, Never to do any thing, which I should be afraid to do if it were the last hour of my life.

8. *Resolved*, To act, in all respects, both speaking and doing, as if nobody had been so vile as I, and as if I had committed the same sins, or had the same infirmities or failings, as others; and that I will let the knowledge of their failings promote nothing but shame in myself, and prove only on occasion of my confessing my own sins and misery to God. *Vid.* July 30.

9. *Resolved*, To think much, on all occasions, of my dying, and of the common circumstances which attend death.

10. *Resolved*, When I feel pain, to think of the pains of martyrdom, and of hell.

11. *Resolved*, When I think of any theorem in divinity to be solved, immediately to do what I can towards solving it, if circumstances do not hinder.

12. *Resolved*, If I take delight in it as a gratification of pride, or vanity, or on any such account, immediately to throw it by.

13. *Resolved*, To be endeavoring to find out fit objects of liberality and charity.

14. *Resolved*, Never to do any thing out of revenge.

15. *Resolved*, Never to suffer the least motions of anger towards irrational beings.

16. *Resolved*, Never to speak evil of any one, so that it shall tend to his dishonour, more or less, upon no account except for some real good.

17. *Resolved,* That I will live so, as I shall wish I had done when I come to die.

18. *Resolved,* To live so, at all times, as I think is best in my most devout frames, and when I have the clearest notions of the things of the gospel, and another world.

19. *Resolved,* Never to do any thing, which I should be afraid to do, if I expected it would not be above an hour before I should hear the last trump.

20. *Resolved,* To maintain the strictest temperance in eating and drinking.

21. *Resolved,* Never to do any thing, which if I should see in another, I should count a just occasion to despise him for, or to think any way the more meanly of him." ❧

My Kingdom
LOUISA MAY ALCOTT

I do not ask for any crown
    But that which all may win;
Nor try to conquer any world
    Except the one within.
Be THOU my guide until I find
    Led by a tender hand,
The happy kingdom in myself
    And dare to take command. ❧

Wisdom

THOMAS GRAY was of the opinion that all men are "condemn'd alike to groan," so he decided that there was no point in mankind knowing in advance what the future holds. "Since sorrow never comes too late and happiness too swiftly flies," he concluded, "Where ignorance is bliss, 'tis folly to be wise."

We might concede his point when it comes to life's sorrows that lie ahead, but we should not assume that when he said " 'tis folly to be wise" he meant it is smart to be stupid!

The ancients were fascinated with the concept of wisdom, even if moderns show relatively little interest in the subject. Plato talked about four virtues: wisdom, temperance, courage, and justice. He insisted that wisdom was "chief and leader of the divine class of goods." By wisdom he meant much more than the accumulation of knowledge—wisdom was knowledge translated into action.

The Hebrews had a similar insight into wisdom; in fact, their word for wisdom originally meant skill, and was used to describe the skill of a sailor negotiating rough water, a judge dealing with a tough case, or a craftsman at work at his bench. So wisdom became for them the practical knowledge necessary to live skillfully. This of necessity assumed living skillfully by the Lord's standards; hence the great statement of the Old Testament, "the fear of the Lord is the beginning of wisdom."

Jesus made a similar point in His parable of the wise man and the foolish man. One built his house on the rock, the other on the sand. When the storm came, the foolish man's house collapsed, but the wise man's house on the rock stood firm. The wise man was the one who, Jesus said, "hears these words of mine and puts them into practice."

In his ministry to the Greeks and Romans, Paul ran into problems on the issue of wisdom. They were convinced, with some justification, of their own knowledge and expertise in many fields, but rejected the wisdom that Paul preached because it incorporated the message of the cross. This they found offensive, and they "became wise in their own conceits."

A similar situation exists today. With apologies to John Naisbitt of *Megatrends*, you could say "we are drowning in knowledge but starved for wisdom." In spite of the explosion of knowledge, the saturation of information, and the proliferation of educational opportunities in our culture, the practical skills to live wisely and well before the Lord are conspicuously absent.

We should heed the words of Solomon,
"Blessed is the man who finds wisdom,
    the man who gains understanding,
for she is more profitable than silver
    and yields better returns than gold.
She is more precious than rubies;
    nothing you desire can compare with her." ❧

Adam Raccoon and the Flying Machine
GLEN KEANE

High above the oak trees, Sam, the little sparrow, twirled and looped through the air . . . landing on a glider that Adam Raccoon had just finished building. "Ready to try it out?" Sam asked cheerfully.

"Yep, now I'll be able to fly like you, Sam."

Puffing and panting, Adam and Sam pushed and pulled the glider to the top of a very high cliff.

"All set!" Adam said, as Sam gave him a final nudge.

"You did it, Adam! You're flying!" Sam shouted as the glider soared.

As quickly as the glider flew, it dropped, leaving Adam floating in midair.

He fell into the arms of King Aren, who was passing by at that very moment. "You'll never fly that way, Adam. But I may have just the thing you need."

And King Aren led Adam and Sam up a high mountain to his storehouse of wonderful treasures.

As King Aren opened the massive door, a bright light shone from within.

Adam and Sam stood amazed at the many strange and wonderful things they saw.

Soon King Aren returned pushing a large crate.

"What's that?" Adam shouted excitedly.

"You'll see as soon as you put it together."

"All right! No problem!" Adam said as he scrambled onto the crate.

"Hold on, Adam. You'll need this instruction book to show you how to do it. You'll also need someone to help explain it to you.

Meet Ernest Turtle. Be sure to listen to him."

After King Aren left, Adam, Ernest, and Sam went to the business of opening the crate. They tugged and pulled with all of their might, and suddenly . . . the crate burst open, sending the three flying.

"Wow! Look at all this stuff! Where do we begin?" Adam said.

Ernest handed Adam the instruction book. "I think we'd better start here."

Adam started to read. " 'Find Section A and screw in Bolt 32 to Air Turbine D.' Ah, this is gonna take too long," Adam sighed.

"Of course it will!" said the voice of the professor, who suddenly strolled out from behind the bushes. He was a distinguished-looking billy goat. "What do you expect when you do something the old-fashioned way?

"We have the New Way now," he said, tossing the book into the bushes. "There's one simple rule. Do whatever feels right to you."

Much to Ernest's dismay, Adam started sticking whatever part onto whichever piece felt right to him.

Soon King Aren stopped by to see how things were going. "Where's the book, Adam?"

"Oh, that book was old fashioned. The professor showed me the New Way."

"I can't watch," King Aren said, as Adam continued to build.

"King Aren, I'm done!" Adam shouted. "Isn't it great?"

"Well, Adam, what is it?" King Aren asked as he investigated the odd-looking contraption.

"It's a Flying Machine, of course," Adam replied. "See, you just hop in this seat, pull back this lever, and . . ." The machine started to shake.

"Adam, I think you'd better get down. That crazy machine looks dangerous."

"Oh, but the professor said it's safe. Right, professor?"

"That's right. Safer than standing on the ground," the professor answered, hiding behind a tree.

"Want to ride with me?" Adam asked.

"I'd love to, but I . . . er . . . uh . . . just remembered I've got some important reading to do. Good luck!"

"I'll go, I'll go!" Sam volunteered. He hopped in back as Adam started the countdown.

"10 . . . 9 . . . 8 . . . "

With a roar the machine took off, wildly out of control, cutting a path through Master's Wood.

"Help!" Adam screamed as animals dived for cover.

The machine climbed high into the sky like a rocket.

Adam frantically tried to gain control, pulling switches and hitting buttons.

Suddenly the ship turned and plummeted toward earth.

SPLASH! As the water settled, everyone watched for Adam and Sam to surface.

"Look out below!" Up above they saw Sam flapping his wings with all his might, clinging to Adam who was in a faint.

Dropping into King Aren's arms, the groggy raccoon awoke. "Mayday! Mayday! We're going down!"

"Adam, you're back on the ground," the king said gently.

Hopping out of the king's arms, Adam ran to Ernest's side. "Oh, please give me another chance, King Aren. I'll follow the book and listen to Ernest this time, I promise."

King Aren agreed. The next day the flying machine was pulled out of the lake.

They started to build once again.

Adam was surprised at how much he enjoyed the hard work.

Weeks later as King Aren was taking his daily walk he was startled by a voice. "Hello down there. This is the X-25 Jet Hawk calling King Aren."

High above the trees Adam was hovering in his new Flying

Machine. "Adam, you did it!" King Aren shouted.

"Not by myself," he replied, holding up the book with Sam and Ernest sitting beside him. "Now let's see what it can do!"

Then Adam, Sam, and Ernest gave the greatest air show that anyone in Master's Wood had ever seen. 🐿

The Town Mouse and the Country Mouse
AESOP

Sometimes the things that seem most attractive are the most dangerous. Wise people understand this and take steps to avoid life's traps, however appealing they appear to be at first glance.

The Country Mouse was very happy that his city cousin, the Town Mouse, had accepted his invitation to dinner. He gave his city cousin all the best food he had, such as dried beans, peas, and crusts of bread. The Town Mouse tried not to show how he disliked the food and picked a little here and tasted a little there to be polite. After dinner, however, he said, "How can you stand such food all the time? Still I suppose here in the country you don't know about any better. Why don't you go home with me? When you have once tasted the delicious things I eat, you will never want to come back here." The Country Mouse not only kindly forgave the Town Mouse for not liking his dinner, but even consented to go that very evening to the city with his cousin. They arrived late at night; and the City Mouse, as host, took his Country Cousin at once to a room where there had been a big dinner. "You are tired," he said. "Rest here, and I'll bring you some real food." And he brought the Country Mouse such things as nuts, dates, cake, and fruit. The Country Mouse thought it was all so good, he would like to stay there. But before he had a chance to say so, he heard a terrible roar, and looking up, he saw a huge creature dash into the room. Frightened half out of his wits, the Country Mouse ran from the table, and round and round the room, trying to find a hiding place. At last he found a place of safety. While he stood there trembling he made up his mind to go home as soon as he could get safely away; for, to himself, he said, "I'd rather have common food in safety than dates and nuts in the midst of danger." &

Curdie and His Mother
GEORGE MACDONALD

Nineteenth-century author George MacDonald's versatile writings, including his children's fantasies, greatly influenced C.S. Lewis and G.K. Chesterton. In this excerpt from The Princess and the Goblin, *young Curdie learns that it is not wise to disbelieve what we do not understand.*

"But how did you find your way to me?" [Curdie asked.]

"I told you already," answered Irene, "by keeping my finger upon my grandmother's thread, as I am doing now."

"You don't mean you've got the thread here?"

"Of course I do. I have told you so ten times already. I have hardly—except when I was removing the stones—taken my finger off it. There!" she added, guiding Curdie's hand to the thread. "You feel it yourself, don't you?"

"I feel nothing at all," replied Curdie.

"Then what can be the matter with your finger? I feel it perfectly. To be sure it is very thin, and in the sunlight looks just like the thread of a spider, but I can't think why you shouldn't feel it as well as I do."

Curdie was too polite to say he did not believe there was any thread there at all. What he did say was: "Well, I can make nothing of it."

"I can, though, and you must be glad of that, for it will do for

137

both of us," returned Irene confidently. . . .

Up the stair they went, and the next and the next, and
through the long rows of empty rooms, and up the little tower stair,
Irene growing happier and happier as she ascended. There was no
answer when she knocked at the door of the workroom, nor could
she hear any sound of the spinning wheel. Once more her heart
sank within her, but only for one moment, as she turned and
knocked at the other door.

"Come in," answered the sweet voice of her grandmother, and
Irene opened the door and entered, followed by Curdie.

"You darling!" cried the lady, who was seated by a fire of red
roses mingled with white. "I've been waiting for you, and indeed
getting a little anxious about you, and beginning to think whether
I had not better go and fetch you myself."

As she spoke she took the little princess in her arms and
placed her upon her lap. She was dresed in white now, looking if
possible more lovely than ever.

"I've brought Curdie, Grandmother. He wouldn't believe
what I told him and so I've brought him."

"Yes, I see him. He is a good boy, Curdie, and a brave boy.
Aren't you glad you've got him out?"

"Yes, Grandmother. But it wasn't very good of him not to
believe me when I was telling him the truth."

"People must believe what they can, and those who believe
more must not be hard upon those who believe less. I doubt if you
would have believed it all yourself if you hadn't seen some of it."

"Ah! yes, Grandmother, I daresay you are right. But he'll
believe now."

"I don't know that," replied her grandmother.

"Won't you, Curdie?" said Irene, looking round at him as she
asked the question.

He was standing in the middle of the floor, staring, and

looking srangely bewildered. . . .

"Make a bow to my grandmother, Curdie," she said.

"I don't see any grandmother," answered Curdie rather gruffly.

. . . "But don't you hear my grandmother talking to me?" asked Irene, almost crying.

"No. I hear the cooing of a lot of pigeons. If you won't come down, I will go without you. I think that will be better, anyhow, for I'm sure nobody who met us would believe a word we said to them. They would think we made it all up. I don't expect anybody but my own father and mother to believe me. They know I wouldn't tell a story."

"And yet you won't believe me, Curdie?" pleaded the princess, now fairly crying with vexation and sorrow.

"No. I can't, and I can't help it," said Curdie, turning to leave the room.

"What shall I do, Grandmother?" sobbed the princess, turning her face to the lady's bosom and shaking with suppressed sobs.

"You must give him time," said her grandmother. "And you must be content not to be believed for a while. It is very hard to bear; but I have had to bear it, and shall have to bear it many a time yet. I will take care of what Curdie thinks of you in the end. You must let him go now."

. . . Curdie went up the mountain neither whistling nor singing, for he was vexed with Irene for "taking him in," as he called it. And he was vexed with himself for having spoken to her so rudely.

His mother gave a cry of joy when she saw him, and at once set about getting him something to eat, asking him questions all the time, which he did not answer so cheerfully as usual. When his meal was ready, she left him to eat it, and hurried to the mine to let his father know he was safe. When she came back, she found him fast asleep upon her bed. Nor did he wake until his father came home in the evening.

"Now, Curdie," his mother said, as they sat at supper, "tell us the whole story from beginning to end, just as it all happened."

Curdie obeyed, and told everything to the point where they came out upon the lawn in the garden of the king's house.

"And what happened after that?" asked his mother. "You haven't told us all. You ought to be very happy at having got away from those demons, and instead of that I never saw you so gloomy. There must be something more. Besides, you do not speak of that lovely child as I should like to hear you. She saved your life at the risk of her own, and yet somehow you don't seem to think much of it."

"She talked such nonsense!" answered Curdie, "and told me a pack of things that weren't a bit true. I can't get over it."

"What were they?" asked his father. "Your mother may be able to throw some light upon them."

Then Curdie made a clean breast of it, and told them everything. They all sat silent for some time, pondering the strange tale.

At last Curdie's mother spoke. "You confess, my boy," she said, "there is something about the whole affair you do not understand?"

"Yes, of course, Mother," he answered. "I cannot understand how a child knowing nothing about the mountain, or even that I was shut up in it, should come all that way alone, straight to where I was, then, after getting me out of the hole, lead me out of the mountain, too, where I should not have known a step of the way if it had been as light as in the open air."

"Then you have no right to say what she told you was not true. She did take you out, and she must have had something to guide her. Why not a thread as well as a rope, or anything else? There is something you cannot explain, and her explanation may be the right one."

"It's no explanation at all, Mother. I can't believe it."

"That may be only because you do not understand it. If you did, you would probably find it was an explanation, and believe it thoroughly. I don't blame you for not being able to believe it, but I do blame you for fancying such a child would try to deceive you. Why should she? Depend upon it, she told you all she knew. Until you found a better way of accounting for it all, you might at least have been more sparing of your judgment."

"That is what something inside me has been saying all the time," said Curdie, hanging down his head. "But what do you make of the grandmother? That is what I can't get over. To take me up to an old garret, and try to persuade me against the sight of my own eyes that it was a beautiful room, with blue walls and silver stars, and no end of things in it, when there was nothing there but an old tub and a withered apple and a heap of straw and a sunbeam!"

"Didn't she speak as if she saw those other things herself, Curdie?"

"Yes. That's what bothers me. You would have thought she really believed that she saw every one of the things she talked about."

"Perhaps some people can see things other people can't see, Curdie," said his mother gravely. "I think I will tell you something I saw myself once—only perhaps you won't believe me either!"

"Oh, Mother, Mother!" cried Curdie, bursting into tears. "I don't deserve that, surely!"

"But what I am going to tell you is very strange," persisted his mother. "If having heard it you were to say I must have been dreaming, I don't know that I should have any right to be vexed with you, though I know at least that I was not asleep."

"Do tell me, Mother. Perhaps it will help me to think better of the princess."

"That's why I am tempted to tell you," replied his mother. "But first, I may as well mention that, according to old whispers, there is something more than common about the king's family.

141

There were strange stories told concerning them—all good stories—but strange, very strange. What they were I cannot tell, for I only remember the faces of my grandmother and my mother as they talked together about them. There was wonder in their eyes, and they whispered, and never spoke aloud.

"But what I saw myself was this: your father was going to work in the mine one night, and I had been down with his supper. It was soon after we were married, and not very long before you were born. He came with me to the mouth of the mine, and left me to go home alone; for I knew the way almost as well as the floor of our own cottage. It was pretty dark, but I got along perfectly well, never thinking of being afraid, until I reached a spot you know well enough, Curdie, where the path has to make a sharp turn out of the way of a great rock on the left-hand side. When I got there, I was suddenly surrounded by about half a dozen of the cobs, the first I had ever seen, although I had heard tell of them often enough. One of them blocked up the path, and they all began tormenting and teasing me in a way it makes me shudder to think of even now."

"If I had only been with you!" cried father and son in a breath.

The mother gave a funny little smile, and went on.

"They had some of their horrible creatures with them, too, and I must confess I was dreadfully frightened. They had torn my clothes very much, and I was afraid they were going to tear me to pieces, when suddenly a great white soft light shone upon me.

"I looked up. A broad ray, like a shining road, came down from a large globe of silvery light, not very high up, indeed not quite so high as the horizon, so it could not have been a new star or another moon or anything of that sort. The cobs stopped persecuting me, and looked dazed, and I thought they were going to run away, but presently they began again. The same moment, however, down the path from the globe of light came a bird, shining like silver in the sun. It gave a few rapid flaps first, and then, with its wings straight out, shot sliding down the slope of the light. It looked to me just like a white pigeon. But whatever it was, when the cobs caught sight of it coming straight down upon them, they took to their heels and scampered away across the mountain, leaving me safe, only much frightened. As soon as it had sent them off, the bird went gliding again up the light, and the moment it reached the globe the light disappeared, just as if a shutter had been closed over a window, and I saw it no more. But I had no more trouble with the cobs that night or ever after."

"How strange!" exclaimed Curdie.

"Yes, it was strange; but I can't help believing it, whether you do or not," said his mother.

"You don't think I'm doubting my own mother?" cried Curdie.

"There are other people in the world quite as well worth believing as your own mother," said she. "I don't know that I'm so much the fitter to be believed that I happen to be your mother, Mr. Curdie. There are mothers far more likely to tell lies than the little girl I saw talking to the primroses a few weeks ago. She's a good girl, I am certain, and that's more than being a princess. Depend upon it, you will have to be sorry for behaving so to her, Curdie. You ought at least to have held your tongue." &

About Elizabeth Eliza's Piano
LUCRETIA P. HALE

In facing life's problems, large and small, silly solutions should be avoided and wise advice always followed. Elizabeth Eliza learns this lesson from "the lady from Philadelphia" in this story from The Peterkin Papers.

Elizabeth Eliza had a present of a piano, and she was to take lessons of the postmaster's daughter.

They decided to have the piano set across the window in the parlor, and the carters brought it in, and went away.

After they had gone the family all came in to look at the piano; but they found the carters had placed it with its back turned toward the middle of the room, standing close against the window.

How could Elizabeth Eliza open it? How could she reach the keys to play upon it?

Solomon John proposed that they should open the window, which Agamemnon could do with his long arms. Then Elizabeth Eliza should go round upon the piazza, and open the piano. Then she could have her music-stool on the piazza, and play upon the piano there.

So they tried this; and they all thought it was a very pretty sight to see Elizabeth Eliza playing on the piano, while she sat on the piazza, with the honeysuckle vines behind her.

It was very pleasant, too, moonlight evenings. Mr. Peterkin liked to take a doze on his sofa in the room; but the rest of the family liked to sit on the piazza. So did Elizabeth Eliza, only she had to have her back to the moon. All this did very well through the summer; but, when the fall came, Mr. Peterkin thought the air was too cold from the open window, and the family did not want to sit out on the piazza.

Elizabeth Eliza practised in the mornings with her cloak on; but she was obliged to give up her music in the evenings the family shivered so.

One day, when she was talking with the lady from Philadelphia, she spoke of this trouble.

The lady from Philadelphia looked surprised, and then said, "But why don't you turn the piano round?"

One of the little boys pertly said, "It is a square piano."

But Elizabeth Eliza went home directly, and, with the help of Agamemnon and Solomon John, turned the piano round.

"Why did we not think of that before?" said Mrs. Peterkin. "What shall we do when the lady from Philadelphia goes home again?" ❧

A Wise Ruling

King Solomon had a well-deserved reputation as a very wise man. He needed to be; in his capacity as king, he was faced with many problems in need of solution—as this story from I Kings 3 shows.

Now two prostitutes came to the king and stood before him. One of them said, "My lord, this woman and I live in the same house. I had a baby while she was there with me. The third day after my child was born, this woman also had a baby. . . .

"During the night this woman's son died because she lay on him. So she got up in the middle of the night and took my son from my side while I your servant was asleep. She put him by her breast and put her dead son by my breast. The next morning, I got up to nurse my son—and he was dead! But when I looked at him closely in the morning light, I saw it wasn't the son I had borne."

The other woman said, "No! The living one is my son; the dead one is yours." . . . And so they argued before the king.

The king said, "This one says, 'My son is alive and your son is dead,' while that one says, 'No! Your son is dead and mine is alive.' "

Then the king said, "Bring me a sword." So they brought a sword for the king. He then gave an order: "Cut the living child in two and give half to one and half to the other."

The woman whose son was alive was filled with compassion for her son and said to the king, "Please my lord, give her the living baby! Don't kill him!"

But the other said, "Neither I nor you shall have him. Cut him in two!"

Then the king gave his ruling: "Give the living baby to the first woman. Do not kill him; she is his mother."

When all Israel heard the verdict the king had given, they held the king in awe, because they saw that he had wisdom from God to administer justice. 🦗

The Righteous Man
PSALM 1:1-6, NIV

Blessed is the man
    who does not walk in the counsel of the wicked
or stand in the way of sinners
    or sit in the seat of mockers.
But his delight is in the law of the LORD,
    and on his law he meditates day and night.
He is like a tree planted by streams of water
    which yields its fruit in season
and whose leaf does not wither.
    Whatever he does prospers.

Not so the wicked!
    They are like chaff
    that the wind blows away.
Therefore the wicked will not stand in the judgment.
    nor sinners in the assembly of the righteous.

For the LORD watches over the way of the righteous,
    but the way of the wicked will perish. 🍂

Wisdom outweighs any wealth.
SOPHOCLES

Who Are the Wise Men?
B. Y. WILLIAMS

Who were the Wise Men in the long ago?
    Not Herod, fearful lest he lose his throne;
Not Pharisees too proud to claim their own;
    Not priests and scribes whose province was to know;
Not money-changers running to and fro;
    But three who traveled, weary and alone,
With dauntless faith, because before them shone
    The Star that led them to a manger low.

Who are the Wise Men now, when all is told?
    Not men of science; not the great and strong;
Not those who wear a kingly diadem;
    Not those whose eager hands pile high the gold;
But those amid the tumult and the throng
    Who follow still the STAR of Bethlehem. 🐦

The Treasure of Wisdom
HENRY GARIEPY

The ancient Book of Job wrestles with major issues, one of which is mankind's place in the divine scheme of things. Discovering one's place in the universe leads to true wisdom.

But where can wisdom be found? (Job 28:12)
    Our poet-author describes in graphic terms man's mining for treasure buried deep in the earth. Scientist Jastro calls this chapter "one of the most impressive bits of literature in the entire Old Testament." "He searches the farthest recesses" for silver, gold and precious gems. As man tunnels the earth:

Sapphires come from its rocks,
  and its dust contains nuggets of gold.
No bird of prey knows that hidden path,
  no falcon's eye has seen it. . . .
He tunnels through the rock;
  His eyes see all its treasures.
He searches the sources of the rivers
  and brings hidden things to light (28:6-11)

After describing how man's most diligent effort is required to find earth's hidden treasures, he gives us his bottom line: "But where can wisdom be found?" (28:12) It is posed, of course, as a rhetorical question. Wisdom, a greater treasure than all the precious metals and jewels of earth, is inaccessible. No Herculean effort, no technology known to man can find wisdom. Man's ingenuity is marvelous, but it cannot discover wisdom—it is not to be found in the land of the living (28:13), nor in the depth of the sea (28:14), nor can it be bought—it is beyond price (28:15-19).

But Job gave the answer to man's search for wisdom—"God understands the way to it and He alone knows where it dwells" (28:23). This chapter ends with Job's one-sentence summary on wisdom: "The fear of the Lord—that is wisdom, and to shun evil is understanding" (28:28). Centuries later, Milton gave us a paraphrase of this insight: "The end of all learning is to know God and out of the knowledge to love and serve Him."

Wisdom comes from God. Every time we open our Bible, it speaks to us. When we commune with God in prayer, we hear its accents. When we see a godly life, we encounter its eloquence. When we worship, its whispered secrets fall on our ears.

If men will search so arduously for the lesser treasures of earth, how much more should we be willing to expend ourselves to be enriched with the largesse of God's wisdom. It too is a hard-won treasure. It requires a passionate longing for what God has for us.

We must diligently explore and ferret out the riches of prayer, of God's Word, of worship and praise, and then we will discover the priceless treasure of wisdom from God.

A.W. Tozer reminds us of the cost of wisdom: "Let a man become enamored of Eternal Wisdom and set his heart to win her and he takes on himself a full-time, all-engaging pursuit. . . . Thereafter his whole life will be filled with seekings and findings, self-repudiations, tough disciplines and daily dying as he is being crucified unto the world and the world unto him."

Let us also remember that Job gained his greatest wisdom in the school of affliction. Malcom Muggeridge shares this remarkable testimony in *A Twentieth Century Testimony*: "Indeed I can say with complete truthfulness that everything I have learned in my seventy-five years in this world, everything that has truly enhanced and enlightened my existence, has been through affliction and not through happiness." It is in the deepest recesses of life's journeyings that we find God's priceless treasures.

God of wisdom, forgive my foolish ways. Lead me each day to the source of all wisdom, the One "in whom are hidden all the treasures of wisdom and knowledge." 🍂

Two Kinds of Wisdom
JAMES 3:13-18, NIV

Who is wise and understanding among you? Let him show it by his good life, by deeds done in the humility that comes from wisdom. But if you harbor bitter envy and selfish ambition in your hearts, do not boast about it or deny the truth. Such "wisdom" does not come down from heaven but is earthly, unspiritual, of the devil. For where you have envy and selfish ambition, there you find disorder and every evil practice.

But the wisdom that comes from heaven is first of all pure; then peace loving, considerate, submissive, full of mercy and good fruit, impartial and sincere. Peacemakers who sow in peace raise a harvest of righteousness. ❧

The Point of Education
SAMUEL JOHNSON

In the modern debate on education, Johnson's brief statement of objectives still makes a lot of sense.

The supreme end of education is expert discernment in all things—the power to tell the good from the bad, the genuine from the counterfeit, and to prefer the good and the genuine to the bad and the counterfeit. ❧

The Reflections in the River
F. W. BOREHAM

There's the knowledge that comes from books and the experience that comes from life. But true wisdom comes from God and shows us ourselves as we really are by divine reckoning. In this selection from The Golden Milestone, Boreham describes a young girl's sudden experience of looking "into the mystery of her own soul."

The reflections in the river were simply perfect. Every leaf and twig was most exquisitely mirrored in the tranquil waters. The great cliffs were duplicated in the depths, and one could even trace the grain in the strata, and the geological markings, in the inverted representation below. . . . And as the little steamer made her way round the bends and up the reaches of the lovely river, ruining with the wash from her stern the charming water-colours that we had admired from her bows, it seemed to me that the reflections of life hold a wealthy philosophy peculiarly their own. Here is a pretty picture from all Caine's *Scapegoat* that will serve us for a starting-point.

"It was one of those wonderful days that followed the coming of sight and speech to little Naomi. She had been deaf and dumb and blind; her mother died when she was born; and poor Israel, her father, thought that the affliction of his treasure was the curse of God upon him. But at last hearing came to her, and speech; and last of all, she saw. Israel could not make enough of it. He was like a child in his glee. He awoke her in the mornings, and took her for rambles over the hills. And one day they went down to the beach and he took her for a row on the smooth and shining waters.

"It was a morning of God's own making, and, for joy of its loveliness no less than of her own bounding life, Naomi rose in the boat and opened her lips, arms to the breeze while it played with the rippling currents of her hair, as if she could drink and embrace it. At that moment a new and dearer wonder came to her, such as every maiden knows whom God has made beautiful, yet none remembers the hour when she knew it first. For, tracing with her eyes the shadow of the cliff and of the continent of cloud that sailed double in two seas of blue, she leaned over the side of the boat, and then saw the reflection of another and lovelier vision.

" 'Father,' she cried in alarm, 'a face in the water! Look!'

" 'It is your own, my child,' said Israel.

" 'Mine!' she cried.

" 'The reflection of your face,' said Israel; 'the light and water make it.'

"The marvel was hard to understand," Hall Caine goes on. "There was something ghostly in this thing that was herself and yet not herself. She leaned back in the boat and asked Israel if it was still in the water. But when at length she grasped the mystery, the artlessness of her joy was charming. Whenever the boat was at rest she leaned over its bulwark and gazed down into the blue depths. . . .

"She clapped her hands and looked again, and there in the

still water was the wonder of her dancing eyes.

" 'Oh, how very beautiful!' she cried, and when she saw her lips move as she spoke, and her sunny hair fall about her restless head, she laughed and laughed again with her heart of glee."

It was a great and terrible and beautiful day in the life of Naomi when, suddenly, in the depths of the shining waters she came upon herself, was the wonder of her own face, and looked down through her own blue eyes into the mystery of her own soul. And it was a great and terrible and beautiful day in most of our lives when we were overtaken by a similar experience. The prodigal son, for example. The clause on which the whole story swings, as on a pivot, is simply this: "He came to himself." He found himself, as Naomi found herself, and as most of us, at some time or other, have found ourselves, gazing into his own sad face, and reading the secrets of his own empty soul. ❧

The fear of the Lord is the beginning of Wisdom,
And the knowledge of the Holy One is understanding.
PROVERBS 9:10

Work

IT IS NOT UNUSUAL for people to dislike Mondays and to look forward to Fridays. "Thank God it's Friday," they say, even if that it is the only thing they thank Him for. This attitude has a lot to say about modern man's approach to work. The proliferation of bumper stickers chronicling such sentiments as "I'd rather be fishing" or any number of other preferred activities confirms the impression. Work is not a favorite activity for a lot of people.

For many, work is sheer drudgery to be endured until the whistle blows and real life begins. For others work is nothing more than the means to put bread on the table and clothes on the kids' backs, keeping the proverbial wolf from the door.

This is a far cry from the old adage *Orare est laborare, laborare est orare:* "To pray is to work, to work is to pray." This ancient sentiment echoing down the centuries reminds us of days when some people really did think that worship and work were bound up in each other. Whence came this idea?

"In the beginning God created" reminds us that God was not averse to work. He worked for six days and then rested; He gave instructions to mankind, "Six days shalt thou labor." We should be thankful He did, for as Milton explained, man is His "master work, the end of all yet done; a creature who not prone and brute as other creatures, but endued with sanctity of reason, might . . . worship God supreme who made him chief of all His works."

Jesus showed the way when He worked for many years in the

153

carpenter's shop at Nazareth. The early church was taught in no uncertain terms that idleness was not to be countenanced, and that if a man would not work he should not eat. Paul even told slaves to approach their work, menial and demeaning though it often was, with a positive attitude. He said, "Whatever you do, work at it with all your heart, as working for the Lord not men. . . . It is the Lord Christ you are serving."

But having said that, we need to bear in mind that there is a reason that work can become a bore. It's called the Fall. One of the consequences of human rebellion against God is that work can become drudgery, and labor can degenerate into little more than "sweat of the brow" and blisters. But redemption is designed to roll back the consequences of the Fall. So what do we do?

First, we head to work thanking God for a new day.

Second, we acknowledge His great gifts of time and energy and skill and offer them back to Him as an act of worship.

Third, we recognize that work done for Him has significance and work done well bears testimony to our faith.

Fourth, we sense what a privilege it is to earn a wage in order to support our dependents, have something to give to those in need, and to offer gifts to the Lord in worship.

Fifth, we make sure that we teach our children that work is good and that God loves to see us active on the job. ❦

The Camel's Hump
RUDYARD KIPLING

This poem is the finale of "How the Camel Got Its Hump," one of Kipling's Just So Stories. If we don't have enough to do-oo-oo, Kipling warns, we'll get the hump—and there's only one cure—getting something worthwhile to do-oo-oo!

The Camel's hump is an ugly lump
    Which well you may see at the Zoo;
But uglier yet is the hump we get
    From having too little to do.

Kiddies and grown-ups too-oo-oo,
If we haven't enough to do-oo-oo,
    We get the hump—
    Cameelious hump—
The hump that is black and blue!

We climb out of bed with a frouzly head
    And a snarly-yarly voice.
We shiver and scowl and we grunt and we growl
    At our bath and our boots and our toys;

And there ought to be a corner for me
(And I know there is one for you)
    When we get the hump—
    Cameelious hump—
The hump that is black and blue!

The cure for this ill is not to sit still,
    Or frowst with a book by the fire;
But to take a large hoe and a shovel also,
    And dig till you gently perspire;

And then you will find that the sun and the wind,
And the Djinn of the Garden too,
    Have lifted the hump—
    The horrible hump—
The hump that is black and blue!

I get it as well as you-oo-oo—
If I haven't enough to do-oo-oo!
    We all get hump—
    Cameelious hump—
Kiddies and grown-ups too! 🐾

The Little Red Hen
HELEN DEAN FISH

This favorite nursery story reminds us that laziness and selfishness are never attractive.

Once upon a time there was a little red hen who lived in a little house on the edge of a big forest. She could cook and she could sew, and she swept and dusted that little house every day.

She had a garden where she planted corn and potatoes and peas and sunflowers.

With the little red hen lived a cat and a rat and a mouse. The little red hen cooked their meals and took good care of them, but they were very lazy and never did anything to help her.

One morning the sun came up bright and early and woke the little red hen. She popped out of bed and prepared the breakfast: a saucer of cream for the cat, a bowl of corn for the rat, and a plate of wheat for the mouse. And a little blue dish of breadcrumbs for herself.

Then she woke the cat, the rat, and the mouse. The cat washed himself and the rat and mouse brushed their whiskers, and they all sat down to breakfast, and ate up every bit. When she had washed and dried the dishes and the little blue dish, and put them away, and swept the kitchen with her little broom, the little red hen said, "Today I think I will bake a beautiful cake."

The cat said, "Goody!"

The rat said, "Goody! Goody!"

The mouse said, "Goody! Goody! Goody!"

Then the little red hen asked, "Who will go to the woodpile and fetch some wood to heat the oven and bake my beautiful cake?"

The cat said, "I won't."

The rat said, "I won't."

The mouse said, "I won't."

So the little red hen said, "Then I'll have to go and do it, myself." And she did. Then the little red hen said, "Who will go to the meadow and milk the cow and bring fresh milk to put in my beautiful cake?"

The cat said, "I won't."

The rat said, "I won't."

The mouse said, "I won't."

So the little red hen said, "Then I'll have to go and do it myself."

So she did.

Then the little red hen said, "Who will go to the nest and find eggs to beat into my beautiful cake?"

The cat said, "I won't."

The rat said, "I won't."

The mouse said, "I won't."

And the little red hen said, "Then I must go and do it myself."

So she did.

Then the little red hen said, "Who will go to the shop and buy butter and sugar and flour to put in my beautiful cake?"

The cat said, "I won't."

The rat said, "I won't."

The mouse said, "I won't."

And the little red hen said, "Then I must go and do it myself."

So she did.

Then the little red hen took a bowl and a big spoon and mixed butter and sugar and eggs and milk and flour. And she beat the dough and put it in three pans and put them in the oven.

The cat sat by the oven door and waited.

The rat sat by the oven door and sniffed.

The mouse sat by the oven door and looked as if she were getting ready to nibble.

When the cake was baked to a turn, the little red hen took it out of the oven and it smelled so delicious that the cat and the rat and the mouse frisked about the floor. It smelled so delicious that the old fox far away in his den in the forest, and all the little kit-foxes, sniffed the air and said, "What is that beautiful smell?"

The old fox said, "It smells to me as if the little red hen is baking today." And pretty soon he took down the sack that hung by the door of the den, and said to his wife: "I think I'll go see the little red hen. Perhaps I can bring a nice fresh cake home for the kits. And perhaps I will bring the little red hen home, too. She will make us a fine dinner. So put the pot on to boil and wait."

And the old fox came out of the forest and loped along very softly toward the little red hen's house.

In the meantime the little red hen set the layers of cake on the table to cool, and then she took a bowl and made frosting. First she spread the frosting on the first layer. Then she put the second layer on top of that and frosted—all over, very carefully. And then she put the third layer on top of that and frosted all over the whole cake, *very* carefully. And it looked perfectly delicious.

Then the little red hen said, "Now who will help me eat the cake?"

The cat said, "I will!"

The rat said, "I will!"

And the mouse said, "I will!"

But the little red hen said, "No you won't, I'm going to eat it myself!"

Just then the old fox put his head in the window.

When the little red hen saw him, she was so frightened that she flew up to the top of the cabinet and hid behind the clock.

The cat hid under the bed.

The rat went into his big hole behind the stove.

And the mouse went into her little hole behind the door.

The fox came in the kitchen door and looked all around. "Nobody home?" he asked. "But my, what a fine cake! I might as well eat it up."

And he was about to gobble the cake when the little red hen flew down at him in a rage and tried to drive him away by flapping her wings and pecking at him. The old fox laughed, "Ha! Ha!" and grabbed the little red hen and popped her in his sack and tied her up and went out of the house so fast that he forgot the cake.

He loped along toward his den. But the sun was hot and the fox had come a long way and when he saw a shady tree by the roadside he lay down to rest for a bit. And before he knew it, he had fallen asleep.

As soon as the little red hen heard him snore, she took her little pair of scissors out of her apron pocket and snipped a hole in the sack just big enough to creep out of. When she was out she quickly found a rock that weighed about as much as she did, and put it in the hole she had cut. Then she took her needle and thread and sewed up the hole.

Then she ran toward home as fast as she could run.

When the old fox woke from his nap he grabbed the sack and started off home. He was in such a hurry to put the little red hen in the pot to boil that he didn't notice that it was a rock bouncing in the sack on his back instead of the little red hen. When he got to his den the little kits ran out and said, "Oh, Father, have you brought us the good cake?"

Then the fox remembered that he had forgotten to bring the cake but he said, "No, my dears, but I have something much better, a plump little red hen." And he opened the sack and his wife took the lid off the boiling pot and he dropped in the rock with a great splash. So then the old fox knew that the wise little red hen had out-witted him again. He was very cross and the fox's family had no dinner at all that day.

But the little red hen ran home across the fields until she came to the little house, and there was the cake safe and sound on the table looking more delicious than ever.

The cat heard her and came out from under the bed.

The rat came out of his hole behind the stove.

And the mouse came from behind the door.

They were so glad to see their dear little red hen safe at home again that they promised they would never be selfish and lazy any more.

So the little red hen forgave them and they were very happy and ate the cake all up—every crumb of it. 🐾

A dictionary is the only place where you will find success before work.
AUTHOR UNKNOWN

The Glorious Whitewasher
MARK TWAIN

Tom Sawyer, like most boys, preferred playing to working. In one of the best known of The Adventures of Tom Sawyer, *he learns that "work" is not a specific task, but is doing what you're obliged to do. Nothing wrong with that!*

Saturday morning was come, and all the summer world was bright and fresh, and brimming with life. There was a song in every heart; and if the heart was young the music issued at the lips. There was cheer in every face and a spring in every step. The locust trees were in bloom and the fragrance of the blossoms filled the air. . . .

Tom appeared on the sidewalk with a bucket of whitewash and a long-handled brush. He surveyed the fence, and all gladness left him and a deep melancholy settled down upon his spirit. Thirty yards of board fence nine feet high. Life to him seemed hollow, and existence but a burden. Sighing he dipped his brush and passed it along the topmost plank; repeated the operation; did it again; compared the insignificant whitewashed streak with the far-reaching continent of unwhitewashed fence, and sat down on a tree-box discouraged.

. . . He began to think of the fun he had planned for this day, and his sorrows multiplied. Soon the free boys would come tripping along on all sorts of delicious expeditions, and they would make a world of fun of him for having to work—the very thought of it burnt him like fire. He got out his worldly wealth and examined it—bits of toys, marbles, and trash; enough to buy an exchange of *work*, maybe, but not half enough to buy so much as half an hour of pure freedom. So he returned his straitened means to his pocket and gave up the idea of trying to buy the boys. At this dark and hopeless moment an inspiration burst upon him! Nothing less than a great, magnificent inspiration.

He took up his brush and went tranquilly to work. Ben Rogers hove in sight presently—the very boy, of all boys, whose ridicule he had been dreading. Ben's gait was the hop-skip-and-jump—proof enough that his heart was light and his anticipations high. He was eating an apple, and giving a long, melodious whoop, at intervals, followed by a deep-toned ding-dong-dong, ding-dong-dong, for he was personating a steamboat. As he drew near, he slackened speed, took the middle of the street, leaned far over to starboard and rounded to ponderously and with laborious pomp and circumstance—for he was personating the *Big Missouri*, and considered himself to be drawing nine feet of water. He was boat and captain and engine bells combined. . . .

"Stop her, sir! Ting-a-ling-ling!" The headway ran almost out and he drew up slowly toward the sidewalk. . . .

Tom went on whitewashing—paid no attention to the steamboat. Ben stared a moment and then said:

"Hi-*yi*! *You're* up a stump, ain't you!"

No answer. Tom surveyed his last touch with the eye of an artist, then he gave his brush another gentle sweep and surveyed the result, as before. Ben ranged up alongside of him. Tom's mouth watered for the apple, but he stuck to his work. Ben said:

"Hello, old chap, you got to work, hey?"

Tom wheeled suddenly and said:

"Why, it's you, Ben! I warn't noticing."

"Say—*I'm* going in a-swimming, *I* am. Don't you wish you could? But of course you'd ruther *work*—wouldn't you? Course you would!"

Tom contemplated the boy a bit, and said:

"What do you call work?"

"Why, ain't *that* work?"

Tom resumed his whitewashing, and answered carelessly:

"Well, maybe it is, and maybe it ain't. All I know is, it suits Tom Sawyer."

"Oh come, now, you don't mean to let on that you *like* it?"

The brush continued to move.

"Like it? Well, I don't see why I oughtn't to like it. Does a boy get a chance to whitewash a fence every day?"

That put the thing in a new light. Ben stopped nibbling his apple. Tom swept his brush daintily back and forth—stepped back to note the effect—added a touch here and there—criticized the effect again—Ben watching every move and getting more and more interested, more and more absorbed. Presently he said:

"Say, Tom, let *me* whitewash a little."

Tom considered, was about to consent; then altered his mind,

"No—no—I reckon it wouldn't hardly do, Ben. You see, Aunt Polly's awful particular about this fence—right here on the street, you know—but if it was the back fence I wouldn't mind and *she* wouldn't. Yes, she's awful particular about this fence; it's gotta be done very careful; I reckon there ain't one boy in a thousand, maybe two thousand, that can do it the way it's got to be done."

"No—is that so? Oh come, now—lemme just try. Only just a little—I'd let *you*, if it was *me*, Tom."

"Ben, I'd like to, honest Injun; but Aunt Polly—well, Jim wanted to do it, but she wouldn't let him; Sid wanted to do it, and she wouldn't let Sid. Now don't you see how I'm fixed? If you was to tackle this fence and anything was to happen to it—"

"Oh, shucks, I'll be just as careful. Now lemme try. Say—I'll give you the core of my apple."

"Well, here— No, Ben, now don't. I'm afeared—"

"I'll give you *all* of it!"

Tom gave up the brush with reluctance in his face, but alacrity in his heart. And while the late steamer *Big Missouri* worked and sweated in the sun, the retired artist sat on a barrel in the shade close by, dangled his legs, munched his apple, and planned the slaughter of more innocents. There was no lack of material; boys happened along every little while; they came to jeer, but remained to whitewash. By the time Ben was fagged out, Tom had traded the next chance to Billy Fisher for a kite, in good repair;

and when *he* played out, Johnny Miller bought in for a dead rat and a string to swing it with—and so on, and so on, hour after hour. And when the middle of the afternoon came, from being a poor poverty-stricken boy in the morning, Tom was literally rolling in wealth. He had, besides the things before mentioned, twelve marbles, part of a jew's-harp, a piece of blue bottle glass to look through, a spool cannon, a key that wouldn't unlock anything, a fragment of chalk, a glass stopper of a decanter, a tin soldier, a couple of tadpoles, six firecrackers, a kitten with only one eye, a brass doorknob, a dog collar—but no dog—the handle of a knife, four pieces of orange peel, and a dilapidated old window sash.

He had a nice, good, idle time all the while—plenty of company—and the fence had three coats of whitewash on it! If he hadn't run out of whitewash, he would have bankrupted every boy in the village.

Tom said to himself that it was not such a hollow world, after all. He had discovered a great law of human action, without even knowing it—namely, that in order to make a man or a boy covet a thing, it is only necessary to make the thing difficult to attain. If he had been a great and wise philosopher, like the writer of this book, he would now have comprehended that Work consists of whatever a body is *obliged* to do and Play consists of whatever a body is not obliged to do. And this would help him understand why constructing artificial flowers or performing on a treadmill is work, while rolling tenpins or climbing Mont Blanc is only amusement. There are wealthy gentlemen in England who drive four-horse passenger coaches twenty or thirty miles on a daily line, in the summer, because the privilege costs them considerable money; but if they were offered wages for the service, that would turn it into work and then they would resign.

The boy mused awhile over the substantial change which had taken place in his worldly circumstances, and then wended toward headquarters to report. 🐛

That's Not Fair!
MATTHEW 20:1-16, SLB

We were always taught that "an honest day's work deserves an honest day's pay." How does that fit with this story Jesus told?

Here is another story about the Kingdom of Heaven. "The owner of an estate went out early one morning. He needed to hire workers to harvest his field. He agreed to pay them $20 a day and sent them out to work.

"A couple of hours later he saw some men standing around in the marketplace. They had nothing to do. So he sent them also into his fields. He told them he would pay them whatever was right at the end of the day. At noon he did the same thing. And he did it again around three o'clock in the afternoon.

"At five o'clock that evening he was in town again. He saw some more men standing around. He asked them, 'Why haven't you been working today?'

" 'Because no one hired us,' they replied.

" 'Then go on out and join the others in my fields,' he said.

"That evening he told the paymaster to call the men in and pay them. He was to begin by paying the last men first. When the men hired at five o'clock were paid, each was given $20. Then the men hired earlier came to get their pay. They thought that they would get much more. But they, also, were paid $20.

"They were upset! They said, 'Those men worked only one hour. But you've paid them just as much as us. And we worked all day in the scorching heat.'

" 'Friend,' he answered one of them, 'I did you no wrong! Didn't you agree to work all day for $20? Take it and go. It is my desire to pay all the same. Is it against the law to give away my money if I want to? Should you be angry because I am kind?' And so it is that the last shall be first and the first, last." 🐦

The Village Blacksmith

HENRY WADSWORTH LONGFELLOW

We talk about role models. The village blacksmith has always been a favorite of ours.

Under a spreading chestnut-tree
    The village smithy stands;
The smith, a mighty man is he,
    With large and sinewy hands;
And the muscles of his brawny arms
    Are strong as iron bands.

His hair is crisp, and black, and long;
    His face is like the tan;
His brow is wet with honest sweat,
    He earns whate'er he can,
And looks the whole world in the face,
    For his owes not any man.

Week in, week out, from morn till night,
    You can hear his bellows blow;
You can hear him swing his heavy sledge,
    With measured beat and slow,
Like a sexton ringing the village bell,
    When the evening sun is low.

And children coming home from school
    Look in at the open door;
They love to see the flaming forge,
    And hear the bellows roar,
And catch the burning sparks that fly
    Like chaff from a threshing-floor.

He goes on Sunday to the church,
    And sits among his boys;
He hears the parson pray and preach,
    He hears his daughter's voice
Singing in the village choir,
    And it makes his heart rejoice.

It sounds to him like her mother's voice
    Singing in Paradise!
He needs must think of her once more,
    How in the grave she lies;
And with his hard, rough hand he wipes
    A tear out of his eyes.

Toiling, — rejoicing, — sorrowing,
    Onward throughout life he goes;
Each morning sees some task begin,
    Each evening sees it close;
Something attempted, something done,
    Has earned a night's repose.

Thanks, thanks to thee, my worthy friend,
    For the lesson thou has taught!
Thus at the flaming forge of life
    Our fortunes must be wrought;
Thus on its sounding anvil shaped
    Each burning deed and thought.

Lord of All Pots and Pans
AUTHOR UNKNOWN

This poem beautifully illustrates St. Paul's instruction, "Whatever you do, work at it with all your heart, as working for the Lord, not for men" (Colossians 3:23).

Lord of all pots and pans and things
    Since I've no time to be
A saint by doing lovely things
    Or watching late with thee,
Or dreaming in the dawnlight,
    Or storming heaven's gates,
Make me a saint by getting meals
    And washing up the plates.

Thou who didst love to give men food
    In room or by the sea,
Accept this service that I do—
    I do it unto thee. 🦋

The Plowman
GEOFFREY CHAUCER

One of the more attractive pilgrims in The Canterbury Tales *is the plowman, who is ready to "work all the day . . . without expecting pay." A rare breed indeed!*

The brother of the Parson came along:
    A *Plowman* used to work, and very strong.
A kindly, simple laboring man was he,
    Living in peace and perfect charity.
With all his heart he loved God best, and then
    His neighbor as himself. For poorer men
He'd thresh and dig and plow—work all the day

In heavy toil without expecting pay:
It was enough if Christ approve his deed.
He rode a mare, the poor man's humble steed. ❧

To Work with a Will
DANIEL DEFOE

Defoe's The Life and Adventures of Robinson Crusoe *is well worth the read. Our hero on his desert island could have been forgiven if he had complained about being overworked, underpaid, and inadequately affirmed. He didn't. As we read in this selection, Crusoe set to work with a will, and in so doing shows us that there is dignity in work that is often overlooked.*

This want of tools made every work I did go on heavily, and it was near a whole year before I had entirely finished my little pale or surrounded habitation. The piles or stakes, which were as heavy as I could well lift, were a long time in cutting and preparing in the woods, and more by far in bringing home, so that I spent some times two days in cutting and bringing home one of those posts, and a third day in driving it into the ground; for which purpose I got a heavy piece of wood at first, but at last bethought my self of one of the iron crows, which however, tho' I found it, yet it made driving those posts or piles very laborious and tedious work.

But what I need I ha' been concerned at the tediousness of any thing I had to do, seeing I had time enough to do it in? Nor had I any other employment if that had been over, at least that I could foresee, except the ranging the island to seek for food, which I did more or less every day.

Having now brought my mind a little to relish my condition, and given over looking out to sea to see if I could spy a ship; I say, giving over these things, I began to apply my self to accommodate my way of living, and to make things as easy to me as I could.

I have already described my habitation, which was a tent under the side of a rock, surrounded with a strong pale of posts and cables, but I might now rather call it a wall, for I raised a kind of wall up against it of turfs, about two foot thick on the out-side, and after some time, I think it was year and a half, I raised rafters from it leaning to the rock, and thatched or covered it with bows of trees, and such things as I could get to keep out the rain, which I found at some times of the year very violent.

I have already observed how I brought all my good into this pale, and into the cave which I had made behind me. But I must observe too that at first this was a confused heap of goods, which as they lay in no order, so they took up all my place, I had no room to turn my self; so I set my self to enlarge my cave and works farther into the earth, for it was a loose sandy rock, which yielded easily to the labour I bestowed on it: and so when I found I was pretty safe as to beasts of prey, I worked side-ways to the right hand into the rock, and then turning to the right again worked quite out and made me a door to come out, on the out-side of my pale or fortification.

This gave me not only egress and regress, as it were a back way to my tent and to my storehouse, but gave me room to stow my goods.

And now I began to apply my self to make such necessary things as I found I most wanted, as particularly a chair and a table; for without these I was not able to enjoy the few comforts I had in the world; I could not write, or eat, or do several things with so much pleasure without a table.

So I went to work; and here I must needs observe, that as reason is the substance and original of the mathematicks, so by stating and squaring every thing by reason, and by making the most rational judgement of things, every man may be in time master of every mechanick art. I had never handled a tool in my life, and yet in time, by labour, application, and contrivance, I found at last that I wanted nothing but I could have made it, especially if I had had tools; however, I made abundance of things, even without tools, and some with no more tools than an adze and a hatchet, which perhaps were never made that way before, and that with infinite labour. For example, if I wanted a board, I had no other way but to cut down a tree, set it on an edge before me, and hew it flat on either side with my axe, till I had brought it to be thin as a plank, and then dub it smooth with my adze. It is true, by this method I could make but one board out of a whole tree, but this I had no remedy for but patience, any more than I had for the prodigious deal of time and labour which it took me up to make a plank or board. But my time or labour was little worth, and so it was as well employed one way as another. . . .

I felled a cedar tree: I question much whether Solomon ever had such a one for the building of the temple at Jerusalem. It was five foot ten inches diameter at the lower part next the stump, and four foot eleven inches diameter at the end of twenty two foot, after which it lessened for a while, and then parted into branches. It was not without infinite labour that I felled this tree; I was twenty days hacking and hewing at it at the bottom; I was fourteen more getting the branches and limbs and the vast spreading head of it cut off, which I hacked and hewed through with axe and hatchet, and inexpressible labour; after this, it cost me a month to shape it, and dub it to a proportion, and to something like the bottom of a boat, that it might swim upright as it ought to do. It cost me near three months more to clear the in-side, and work it out so as to make an exact boat of it. This I did indeed without fire, by meer malett and chissel, and by the dint of hard labour, till I had brought it to be a very handsome periagua, and big enough to have carry'd six and twenty men, and consequently big enough to have carry'd me and all my cargo.

When I had gone through this work, I was extremely delighted with it. The boat was really much bigger than I ever saw a canoe or periagua, that was made of one tree, in my life. Many a weary stroke it had cost, you may be sure; and there remained nothing but to get it into the water; and had I gotten it into the water, I make no question but I should have began the maddest voyage, and the most unlikely to be performed, that ever was undertaken.

But all my devices to get it into the water failed me; tho' they cost me infinite labour too. It lay about one hundred yards from the water, and not more. But the first inconvenience was, it was up hill towards the creek; well, to take away this discouragement, I resolved to dig into the surface of the earth, and so make a declivity. This I begun, and it cost me a prodigious deal of pains; but who grutches pains, that have their deliverance in view? But when this was worked through, and this difficulty managed, it was still much at one; for I could no more stir the canoe than I could the other boat.

Then I measured the distance of ground, and resolved to cut a dock or canal, to bring the water up to the canoe, seeing I could not bring the canoe down to the water. Well, I began this work, and when I began to enter into it, and calculate how deep it was to be dug, how broad, how the stuff to be thrown out, I found that by the number of hand I had, being none but my own, it must have been ten or twelve years before I should have gone through with it: for the shore lay high, so that at the upper end it must have been at least twenty foot deep; so at length, tho' with great reluctancy, I gave this attempt over also.

This grieved me heartily, and now I saw, tho' too late, the folly of beginning a work before we count the cost, and before we judge rightly of our own strength to go through with it.

In the middle of this work, I finished my fourth year in this place, and kept my anniversary with the same devotion, and with as much comfort as ever before; for by a constant study and serious application of the word of God, and by the assistance of His grace, I gained a different knowledge from what I had before. ❧

An Unforgettable Day's Work
C. Everett Koop

Work well done has its own rewards, as Dr. Koop relates in this dramatic incident recounted in Koop: The Memoirs of America's Family Doctor.

I'll never forget my most spectacular diaphragmatic hernia. A garbled telephone call from a nearby hospital described what could only be a dying newborn with a diaphragmatic hernia. Once again I sprinted down to my car in the cobblestone courtyard, raced eleven blocks to the other hospital, parked my car on the sidewalk, and rushed into the lobby, only to find the elevators were not running. So I ran up to the ninth floor, wrapped the baby in a blanket, ran down the same nine floors and placed the baby on the floor of my car by the heater. Back at the Children's Hospital, I ran up two flights to the operating room and laid the baby on the operating table. By now the little fellow was dark blue and apparently lifeless. Without taking any sterile precautions, I slashed an incision across the left side of his chest, inserted my fingers, and pulled out the abdominal organs that had made their way up into the chest, thereby relieving the pressure on the lungs and the heart. Then I began to massage his tiny heart with one finger. It began to beat, and—a great sign—the edges of the wound began to bleed. We cleaned the wound as much as we could, inserted an endotracheal tube into the baby, and I completed the operation. I made the incision when the infant was only fifty-five minutes old. He remains my youngest patient. ❧

To Labor Passionately
DOROTHY L. SAYERS

In The Mind of the Maker *Dorothy L. Sayers, noted British detective fiction writer, decides that even the manufacture of lavatory cisterns can lead to "a vision splendid."*

Profit, and indeed all remuneration beyond the subsistence that enables a man to go on working, is desired because it offers an escape from work into activities more congenial and more generally admired. If the service of the machines remains hateful, men will not serve them for love; so that if the hope for escape no longer offers an inducement to work, the machines will stop, and the former conditions recur, by the inevitable dialectics of their nature. Nor will a Christian love of humanity be encouraged by the multiplication of products whose effect upon the human mind is to debase and pervert it. We cannot deal with industrialism or unemployment unless we lift work out of the economic, political and social spheres and consider it also in terms of the work's worth and the love of the work, as being in itself a sacrament and manifestation of man's creative energy.

The attitude of the artist to this question is instructive. It is true that he, like everybody else, derives remuneration from his work. The remuneration is frequently beyond the amount necessary to enable him to go on working. What is remarkable about him is the way in which he commonly employs the escape-from-work which the extra remuneration allows him. If he is genuinely an artist, you will find him using his escape-from-work in order to do what he calls "my own work," and nine times out of ten, this means *the same work* (i.e., the excercise of his art) *that he does for money.* The peculiar charm of his escape is that he is relieved, not from the work, but from the money. His holidays are all busman's holidays.

What distinguishes him here from the man who works to live is, I think, his desire to see the fulfillment of the work. Whether it is possible for a machine-worker to feel creatively about his routine job I do not know; but I suspect that it is, provided and so long as the worker eagerly desires that before all things else the work shall be done. What else causes the armaments worker to labor passionately when he knows that the existence of his country is threatened, but that his heart travels along the endless band with the machine parts and that his imagination beholds the fulfillment of the work in terms, not of money, but of the blazing gun itself, charged with his love and fear. As the author of *Ecclesiasticus* says, he "watches to finish the work"; for once, that is, he sees the end-product of his toil exactly as the artist always sees it, in a vision of Idea, Energy, and Power. It is unfortunate that so little effort should be made by Church or State to show him the works of peace in the same terms. Is the man, for example, engaged in the mass-production of lavatory cisterns encouraged to bring to his daily monotonous toil the vision splendid of an increasingly hygienic world? I doubt it; yet there is much merit in sanitary plumbing—more, if you come to think of it, than there is in warfare. ❧

Wise in Work
BEN SIRA

Ben Sira was a teacher of young male aristocrats in Jerusalem. He clearly felt that the leisure class had marked advantages over the working class, but he nevertheless recognized that it is the workers who "maintain the state of the world." This reading is from Ecclesiasticus 38:24-34.

The scribe's profession increases his wisdom;
 whoever is free from toil can become a wise man.
How can he become learned who guides the plow,
 who thrills in wielding the goad like a lance,
Who guides the ox and urges on the bullock,
 and whose every concern is for cattle?
His care is for plowing furrows,

and he keeps a watch on the beasts in the stalls.
So with every engraver and designer
    who, laboring night and day,
Fashions carved seals,
    and whose concern is to vary the pattern.
His care is to produce a vivid impression,
    and he keeps watch till he finishes his design.
So with the smith standing near his anvil,
    forging crude iron.
The heat from the fire sears his flesh,
    yet he toils away in the furnace heat.
The clang of the hammer deafens his ears,
    His eyes are fixed on the tool he is shaping.
His care is to finish his work,
    and he keeps watch till he perfects it in detail.
So with the potter sitting at his labor
    revolving the wheel with his feet.
He is always concerned for his products,
    and turns them out in quantity.
With his hands he molds the clay,
    and with his feet softens it.
His care is for proper coloring,
    and he keeps watch on the fire of his kiln.
All these men are skilled with their hands,
    each one an expert at his own task;
Without them no city could be lived in,
    and wherever they stay, they need not hunger.
They do not occupy the judge's bench,
    nor are they prominent in the assembly;
They set forth no decisions or judgements,
    nor are they found among the rulers;
Yet they maintain God's ancient handiwork,
    and their concern is for exercise of their skill. ❧

⋇ Spiritual Values ⋇

Devotion

DRIVING ALONG THE FREEWAY on the way to church early one Sunday morning, I almost collided with the car in front of me when it braked sharply without warning. The driver should have displayed a bumper sticker announcing, "I brake for geese," for that was what she had done. There in front of her car was a mother goose shepherding her family of gawky goslings across the busy thoroughfare. She appeared to be oblivious to the traffic, so concerned was she about the well-being of her offspring. Despite the very real possibility of rear-end collisions, I paused gratefully to take in the picture of domestic devotion. As I pondered the slightly modified old question, "Why did the goose cross the road?" I observed her wholehearted devotion both to her cause (getting across) and to her little ones.

I recently read a book about the Red Guards who, in their devotion to Chairman Mao, engineered a disastrous reign of terror, and I wondered at their commitment to such a violent cause. Just after I returned from a visit to Japan, I heard about a suicidal Japanese cult. I marveled at the bearded guru's hold over his followers and their extraordinary devotion to him and his incredible schemes.

On the other hand, I have also seen the devotion of a mother to her sick infant as she refused to leave his hospital bed, holding his tiny hand, wiping his fevered brow, never noticing that she had not eaten or slept for endless hours. Ezra, the hard-working scribe,

179

"devoted himself to the study and observance of the law." His friend and colleague Nehemiah said, "I devoted myself to this wall," referring to the wall he was rebuilding around devastated Jerusalem. David prayed, "Guard my life, for I am devoted to you." The new converts in Jerusalem "devoted themselves to the apostles' teaching." The widow in the church was expected to be known for "devoting herself to all kinds of good deeds," while all the believing community were taught to "be devoted to one another in brotherly love."

There was plenty of room for devotion then . . . and there is yet today. The human capacity for devotion to a cause or a relationship is immense, but the sad truth is that devotion to self is becoming increasingly more popular. This kind of devotion knows no bounds. And it can lead only to the fracturing of lives and the fragmenting of cultures. We need models of devotion, and where better to start than in the utter devotion of the Lord to His ancient erring people, Israel? And will there ever be a more graphic example than that of Jesus, who in the extremity of Gethsemane said, in agony, "Not My will, but Yours be done," thereby devoting Himself to the Father and His cause. If these examples of God's devotion to us seem too far out of reach, there is ample proof that the work of God in many lives, both biblical and contemporary, has led to lives of devotion and expressions of dedication for our learning and encouragement. We should read them with relish and emulate them with gratitude, drawing constantly on the resources we need, and which God Himself supplies for the kind of lives to which He unerringly calls us. 🦌

Freddy the Farm Horse
PAUL HAMLYN

Freddy was young, but he learned an important lesson: contentment comes from doing well what you're meant to do, rather than wishing you could do something else.

Freddy was a young farm horse. He lived with his mother Flossie in a field next to the farmyard. In the field opposite, there was a beautiful black racehorse. Flossie admired the racehorse very much and wished she was like him instead of just being a farm horse.

"When *you* grow up," she said to Freddy, "I want *you* to be a racehorse."

But Freddy didn't want to be a racehorse. Anyway, he didn't *feel* like a racehorse. He just felt like a farm horse, heavy and rather slow, and suitable for pulling along the farm carts—which was what he liked doing. He liked the farm animals and he liked the kind farmer. He hoped that one day the farmer would drive him to market, because this was something he'd heard about but never seen and that was all he wanted.

Then one morning the farmer came along and said: "Now, Freddy, it's time to get you into training."

Freddy wondered what he meant as he was led away. But his mother was sure he was off to be a racehorse and neighed proudly: "There goes my racehorse son."

So Freddy was glad when the farmer harnessed him to a small cart, because this meant that he wasn't going to make him race.

Next the farmer put some calves into the cart. Freddy could hardly believe his ears when the farmer said: "Off we go now to market."

Freddy trotted along pulling the cart carefully behind him, so as not to jolt the little calves. He did feel proud when they reached the market and the farmer said: "You did that job very well, Freddy. You shall come to market again."

When they got home Freddy rushed to tell his mother what an exciting place the market was. "And I'm not being trained to be a racehorse at all. I'm being trained to take calves to market, and do the job well," he neighed. "But, oh dear," he added, "I feel tired now."

Freddy lay down on the soft grass and fell fast asleep.

His mother looked at him and neighed softly. "Perhaps you're not meant to be a racehorse after all," she said. "But I'm proud of you just the same. You'll make a fine farm horse."

And she lay down and went to sleep beside him. 🐎

Aristarchus
JOHN KNAPP II

You don't remember Aristarchus? You'll find him named in all these places: Acts 19:29, Acts 20:4, Acts 27:2, Colossians 4:10, and Philemon 24.

If you aren't too fancy,
　　Just an ordinary carcass,
Consider the example
　　Of a man called Aristarchus.

Five times the Bible tells us
　　How his faith refused to bend;
Quietly he served the Lord,
　　Enduring to the end. 🐎

Two Devoted Believers
Virginia Muir

Simeon and Anna were very old. Many things had happened in their lives. But they were always devoted to the Lord and His service. Their story comes from chapter 2 of Luke's gospel.

The Law told new parents to do several special things. First, they were to dedicate their first baby boy to God. When the baby was eight days old, the parents were to name him. Of course, Mary and Joseph named their baby Jesus because that is what the angel had told Mary to do.

Later, they traveled to Jerusalem and took baby Jesus to the Temple. They offered a sacrifice of two young pigeons, as the law required.

At the Temple they saw an old man named Simeon. He spent a lot of time in the Temple, because once God had told him he would not die until he had seen the baby who would become the Messiah—the Savior. Simeon had seen many baby boys brought to the Temple, but so far he had not seen the one who was God's Son.

As soon as Simeon saw the baby Jesus, he knew this was the right baby at last! He took Jesus from Mary and held him lovingly.

Simeon prayed, "O Lord, now I can die in peace. I have seen the baby who will bring your salvation to the world."

Another very old person who lived in the Temple was Anna. She had been a prophet for many years. Anna, too, recognized Jesus as the Messiah. She prayed a prayer of thanks for the Savior, then she hurried to tell everyone she met that the Messiah had been born. ❧

In the Bleak Mid-winter
CHRISTINA ROSSETTI

What can we give to the Lord who has everything? The gift He desires is our loving devotion—our heart.

In the bleak mid-winter
    Frosty wind made moan,
Earth stood hard as iron,
    Water like a stone;
Snow had fallen, snow on snow,
    Snow on snow,
In the bleak mid-winter,
    Long ago.

Our God, heav'n cannot hold him
    Nor earth sustain;
Heav'n and earth shall flee away
    When he comes to reign.
In the bleak mid-winter
    A stable-place sufficed
The Lord God Almighty
    Jesus Christ.

Enough for him, whom cherubim
    Worship night and day,
A breastful of milk,
    And a mangerful of hay;
Enough for him, whom angels
    Fall down before,
The ox and ass and camel
    Which adore.

Angels and archangels
    May have gathered there,
Cherubim and seraphim
    Thronged the air:
But only his mother
    In her maiden bliss
Worshipped the Beloved
    With a kiss.

What can I give him,
    Poor as I am?
If I were a shepherd
    I would bring a lamb;
If I were a wise man
    I would do my part;
Yet what I can I give him—
    Give my heart. ❧

Mary Jones and Her Bible
MIG HOLDER

This is the traditional and well-loved story of a young girl who saved her money for six years and walked twenty-five miles to obtain her own copy of the Bible.

Mary Jones lived about two hundred years ago on the very edge of a little Welsh village. Her family was quite poor, so she and her mother and father had to work very hard to make a living.

    Mary couldn't read or write, and there was no school for her to go to. So every day she had to help her mother clean the house and look after the garden. Every day they baked bread and stirred the stew. Every evening they mended and patched their clothes. Every day Mary fed the hens.

Mostly Mary was happy; but sometimes she got tired of doing the same jobs over and over again. She would stand in the garden and look down the valley, wishing she had a friend to play with. The Jones family rarely saw anyone else; their nearest neighbor was half a mile away.

But Sunday was their rest day. The big loom was silent, the house was spick and span, and Mary and her mother baked enough bread on Saturday to last over till Monday. On Sunday morning, whatever the weather, the family set off over the hill to chapel.

It was two miles to the village, but Mary was used to walking and knew each step brought her nearer to her few friends— children of the other families who lived in the valley. They shouted and waved to each other outside the chapel, exchanging news at the top of their voices, until, all too soon, the grown-ups told them to quiet down and go into the meeting.

The service was always very long. Mary liked singing the hymns, but her heart would sink when the minister stood up to begin his sermon. His voice seemed to drone on for hours, and it was so difficult to understand what he was saying.

Sometimes, when the minister was reading from the huge black Bible, Mary would try to imagine what it would be like to be able to read. Once she had crept to the front of the chapel after service and stood on tiptoe to peer at the strange black squiggles running across the page. She couldn't understand how anyone could make head or tail of them!

Then one Sunday the minister said: "I have a very special announcement." He cleared his throat importantly. "We are to have a school in the village. All children may attend. The new school will open next week."

Mary could hardly believe what she heard!

But it was true. A special teacher was to come and set up a school in the chapel building for three whole months. Not only would Mary have the chance to learn to read and write—she would also see her friends every day! She couldn't wait! The days seemed to pass even more slowly than usual, and the jobs her mother asked her to do seemed even more boring.

When the day came for Mary to start school, she was so excited that she woke up while it was still dark. She lay staring out of her bedroom window at the black sky. Suddenly she was afraid. Suppose it was too hard? Suppose she couldn't do it and the others laughed at her? Along with her excitement, she felt a tight knot of worry in her stomach.

Mary was glad when dawn at last crept slowly over the hills. She jumped out of bed, quickly put on the clean clothes she had laid out the night before, and crept downstairs. She cut some bread and cheese for lunch and wrapped it carefully in a square cloth. Then she woke her parents, said good-bye to them, and set off to walk the two miles to school.

When she arrived, most of the other children were already waiting excitedly outside the chapel. At last Mr. Ellis, the teacher, opened the door. They all filed in and sat down.

Mr. Ellis handed out slates and sticks of chalk, and showed them how to draw letter shapes. The chalk made a horrible squeaky noise on the slate, but Mary scarcely noticed, concentrating hard, poking out the tip of her tongue with the effort. She had never enjoyed herself so much!

Mary learned quickly, and could soon read a whole page at a time. She loved reading the stories of Jesus and the long-ago adventures of people such as Noah and Jonah. One day, on the long walk home from school, Mary found herself wondering what it would be like to have a book of her own.

Suddenly she had an idea! She rushed home and burst in on her parents.

"I've decided. I'm going to save up for a Bible of my own!"

187

There was no answer. She looked at her mother and father. Instead of being pleased, they seemed worried.

"But books are so expensive," said her mother at last. "More than people like us can afford. I wouldn't want you to be disappointed."

"Don't you start getting above yourself now, girl," added her father.

Mary was upset.

"I *will* do it!" she shouted. "If I have to save up for twenty years. Anyway, I *can* read. You wait till next Sunday; you'll see!"

She burst into tears and marched up to her bedroom. Her parents looked miserably at each other.

Later that evening, Mary's father went to his workshop and, by the light of a candle, made a strong wooden box. When it was finished, he hid it under his workbench.

The next day he brought out the box.

"We know how much you want a Bible," he said. "We'll do all we can to help you. Here's a box to keep your savings in."

"You can have two chickens of your own, and sell their eggs," said her mother.

"And one of my hives shall be yours, so that you can sell the honey from the bees," added her father.

"Oh, thank you, thank you." Mary hugged them. "I'll work and work until I get my Bible."

And that is exactly what she did.

When there was any wool left over from mother's knitting, Mary begged it to knit brightly-colored socks that she could sell at the market. When harvest-time came round, Mary went to work for nearby farmers, helping tie and stack the bundles of grain. But it was exhausting work, and she was paid only a few pennies a day.

The pile of coins in Mary's money-box seemed to grow so slowly. Quite often she was tempted to give up and spend the money on a pretty dress or a new pair of shoes. But then she would remind herself that every extra penny in the box brought her nearer to having the Bible she dreamed of.

Six whole years passed. Six long winters and six harvests. Mary was now quite grown-up—fifteen years old! But in all that time, however busy she was, Mary never let go of her resolve.

One winter's evening, she took down the box from the mantelpiece and tipped her pile of coins out onto the table. She counted and then counted again, just to be sure.

"Mother, Father, guess what! Only a few pence more, and I shall have enough money to buy my Bible! I can't wait for Sunday—I'll ask the minister how to get one. Then, as soon as I've saved that last bit, I'll be ready."

But Mary was in for a surprise. After chapel, she waited patiently for a chance to speak to the minister.

"Mr. Hugh," she began. "You know that I've been saving up for a Bible. . . ."

Mr. Hugh held up his hand. " . . . A little bird told me that you have almost enough money now. Some of us in the village have taken a small collection to make up the amount you need."

He pressed a little bag of coins into her hand.

Mary was overwhelmed. She knew that most of the village people could not really afford to give away any of their money.

"Please, please thank them all for me," she said. "Now—tell me where I have to go to get my Bible."

"Mary," Mr. Hugh said. "The nearest place is Bala, and that is twenty-five miles away. Thirteen times as far as you walk to chapel!"

"I'm used to walking," said Mary simply.

"But Mary, suppose when you arrive, there are no Bibles left?"

Mary turned smiling eyes up to his.

"I know there will be," she said.

Mary's parents knew that, after she had been saving for so long, there was no way they would stop her going on her long journey. So, very early one morning, they hugged her and waved her off, praying that God would look after her.

In her hand Mary held a knotted cloth full of bread and cheese to eat on the way. In her pocket was a purse full of the money she had saved. Over her shoulder hung a special leather bag which she had sewn to bring back her precious Bible in. And in her head she carried a name and address that the minister had given her. He had a friend who lived in Bala, and had told Mary that as soon as she arrived, she was to find Mr. Edwards' house, and he would be sure to help her.

At first it was easy. Mary knew all the paths near her own village. It was a bright, sunny day, and she stepped out lightly, humming as she went.

When the sun was high in the sky, she guessed it was about midday. She sat down by a stream to rest, drank some of the clear water, and rinsed her aching feet. She ate most of the bread and cheese, carefully saving some in case she needed it later.

After lunch, Mary set off again, but now the way seemed harder. The hill-paths seemed steeper, the ground stonier, and the sun even hotter than before. Mary had already been walking for seven hours, and there was still a long way to go. Her legs were stiff and tired, and more than once she stumbled on the stony path, tears springing to her eyes from pain and exhaustion.

Finally she came up a winding path to the top of a wooded hill. When she rested on the stile at the top, she looked down and saw, at last, the town of Bala spread out before her.

From somewhere Mary seemed to find new energy. She practically flew down the grassy hillside to the edge of the town, and it seemed no time at all before she found her way to the house where Mr. Edwards lived. As the door swung open, she suddenly felt shy.

Her words came out all in a rush.

"Please sir, the minister at Abergynolwyn said you are a friend of his—my name is Mary Jones—and I have been saving up for six years to buy a Bible—and he said . . ."

"Hold on a minute," said a gentle voice. "Come inside and tell me from the beginning."

Mary looked up into the kind face of Mr. Edwards and then followed him into the house. When he had heard all of Mary's story, he was quite amazed.

"And you walked twenty-five miles just today?" he asked. Mary nodded. She was suddenly so tired she could barely stand up.

"Then first you need a good meal and a good night's sleep. Tomorrow we shall see about getting your Bible."

Mr. Edwards' maid led Mary away to the kitchen for a good dinner, and then tucked her up in a huge soft bed covered with a patchwork quilt. As her head touched the white pillow, Mary fell straight to sleep, dreaming of what tomorrow would bring.

Next morning Mr. Edwards explained that they would need to call on a Mr. Charles, who had received a parcel of Welsh Bibles from London, and would be able to sell one to Mary.

"I just hope he has some left," said Mr. Edwards under his breath, as they hurried through the narrow streets.

"You're very lucky," smiled Mr. Charles when they explained why they had come. "This is the very last one."

He took out a beautifully-bound, brand-new Bible and passed it to Mary. She took it in both hands and stared at it for a long moment. Her own Bible at last! She could hardly believe it. Then she gave Mr. Charles her purse full of money, and tucked the Bible safely into her leather bag.

"Read it carefully and learn from it," said Mr. Charles as he waved good-bye.

"I will—and thank you!" called Mary, hurrying up the street.

The journey home seemed so much shorter than the day before. Mary sped over the hillsides, clasping her leather bag. But she was very tired by the time she saw the lamplights of her own village in the distance. Her mother and father and all her friends were waiting at the edge of the village.

Mary held the Bible high above her head. "I got it! I got it!" she shouted. And to herself she added, "Now at last I can read my own Bible in my own language."

Long after Mary had left for home, Mr. Charles sat in his study thinking about the girl who had saved for so long and walked so far to get a Welsh Bible of her own. Bibles in Welsh were in very short supply, and, even when they could be found, they were much too expensive for ordinary people to afford. Mr. Charles made up his mind to do something about it.

And so a few months later, at a great meeting of important men and women in London, Mr. Charles climbed on the platform and said: "Ladies and gentlemen, I would like to tell you a true story about a little girl called Mary Jones. . . ."

And all the people listened spellbound as he described how Mary had patiently saved her money and walked all the way to Bala to get the Bible she had dreamed of. When he had finished there was silence. Then suddenly people were scrambling to their feet.

"We must print more Welsh Bibles," cried one.

"And make them cheaper," shouted someone else.

And from a loud voice at the back: "Why not Bibles in every language?"

So, there and then, a society was formed to make Bibles in every language for people all over the world.

Mr. Charles would never have imagined that today, two hundred years later, that same organization would still be at work. It is called the British and Foreign Bible Society. Together with Bible

Societies in many other countries, it has translated the Bible into almost two thousand languages. So today almost anyone who wants to can buy a Bible in their own language—without having to save for so long, or walk so far, as Mary Jones. ❧

The Altar
GEORGE HERBERT

This seventeenth-century pastor-poet said his poems were "a picture of the many spiritual conflicts that have passed between God and my soul, before I could subject mine to the will of Jesus my master." In this poem, the conflict has ceased and devotion reigns supreme.

A broken ALTAR, Lord, thy servant rears,
Made of a heart, and cemented with tears:
      Whose parts are as thy hand did frame;
     No workman's tool hath touched the same.
         A HEART alone
         Is such a stone,
         As nothing but
         Thy pow'r doth cut.
         Or my hard heart
         Meets in this frame,
         To praise thy name.
     That, if I chance to hold my peace,
      These stones to praise thee may not cease.
O let thy blessed SACRIFICE be mine,
And sanctify this ALTAR to be thine. ❧

To Gain What He Cannot Lose
ELISABETH ELLIOT

*The brief life of Jim Elliot was one of unusual devotion in one so young. His martyr-
dom, along with that of four equally devoted men, served to challenge thousands to re-
evaluate their priorities. His story, told here by his widow, Elisabeth, in* Shadow of
the Almighty, *still stirs the heart.*

When Jim was a college student in 1949 he wrote these words: "*He
is no fool who gives what he cannot keep to gain what he cannot lose.*"

Seven years later, on a hot Sunday afternoon, far from the
dormitory room where those lines were written, he and four other
young men were finishing a dinner of baked beans and carrot
sticks. They sat together on a strip of white sand on the Curaray
River, deep in Ecuador's rain forest, waiting for the arrival of a
group of men whom they loved, but had never met—savage Stone
Age killers, known to all the world now as Aucas.

Two days before, the hope of years had been partially fulfilled.
Three of these Indians had met them on the beach where they now
sat. The first friendly contact, long anticipated and carefully prepared for, had been completely successful. The young man and his
two women companions stepped off the jungle green on the other
side of the river, and after slight hesitation, accepted the hand of
Jim Elliot, who led them across the river to the other white men.
At first the naked tribespeople were distrustful, and with reason.
They had known of white men who flew in great birds similar to
that which now stood beside them on the sand, who had proved
that they could not be trusted. But somehow they had sensed,
throughout the long weeks when these five men had attempted to
show them their friendship, that there was no "catch" here.

The white men had at first dropped gifts to the Aucas, similar
to those they had received in other years—machetes, cooking pots,
ribbons, cloth. These things were most welcome, and the Indians
began to wait for the sound of that yellow *ayamu* which appeared

with regularity (though whether a people who cannot count beyond three would recognize the seven-day rhythm is questionable). When the sound of the motor was heard, they would run from the manioc patches, from inside the great, oval-shaped, leaf-thatched houses, or from down river where they had been fishing in their dugout canoes. There they were again—those strange, white-faced men, waving and shouting, then lowering a bucket on a rope, from which the Indians could grab all manner of delights. And what was that? Suddenly a voice boomed through the air—in their own language! The man was speaking to them.

"Come! We are your friends. We like you. We are your friends."

Could it be that they did not intend to take away the Indians' land, to destroy their crops, to kill their people, as others had done? There were some who began to believe. An idea came to them. Why not encourage these men? Would it not be worthwhile to find out what their true intentions were? Might there not be greater gains for the Indians if they played along with the strangers?

. . . Back at the beach on the Curaray, the five men waited eagerly the next day for the return of their friends. Pacing the beach as before, they shouted the few phrases they had learned of the Auca language, phrases elicited from an escaped member of the tribe who lived on an hacienda near one of the mission stations. But their calls were answered only by the stillness of the virgin jungle on both sides of the winding river. Once a tree fell, alerting them all to tense expectancy. Nothing happened. Finally Jim Elliot looked at his watch.

"Okay, boys—I give them five minutes. If they don't show up, I'm going over!"

Wisdom prevented his carrying out this threat, but the long afternoon brought no reward for their vigil.

The "neighbors" were apparently in conference—should they

return and invite the white men to their village? Who should go? They could not know with what eagerness and longing they were awaited.

Sunday morning dawned clear. Again God had answered prayer. The river had not risen to obliterate the little landing strip, and the skies were good for flying. Nate, the pilot, took off. After circling the Indian village, he spotted about ten Aucas making their way along the beach in the direction of the four foreigners.

"This is it, guys!" he shouted as the Piper bounced onto the beach. "They're on their way!"

Nate's wife was informed by radio of the expected contact and was asked to stand by again at 4:30 p.m.

Lunch over, the men busied themselves fixing up a miniature "jungle" and model house in the sand, with the intention of demonstrating to the savages how to build an airstrip, should they be interested enough to want the white men to come and live among them. Then the five missionaries sang together, as they had so often done, spontaneously and joyously:

"We rest on Thee, our Shield and our Defender,
We go not forth alone against the foe.
Strong in Thy Strength, safe in Thy keeping tender,
We rest on Thee, and in Thy name we go.

"We rest on Thee, our Shield and our Defender,
Thine is the battle, Thine shall be the praise.
When passing through the gates of pearly splendor,
Victors, we rest with Thee through endless days."

Committing themselves and all their carefully laid plans to Him who had so unmistakably brought them thus far, they waited for the Aucas.

Before four-thirty that afternoon the quiet waters of the Curaray flowed over the bodies of the five comrades, slain by the men they had come to win for Christ, whose banner they had borne. The world called it a nightmare of tragedy. The world did not recognize the truth of the second clause in Jim Elliot's credo: "He is no fool who gives what he cannot keep to gain what he cannot lose." 🐎

Kicking a Habit
STUART BRISCOE

A true story of a young man we knew who found help from the Lord in a problem area of his life. This excerpt is from Transforming the Daily Grind.

I well remember a young man who was a member of a group that my wife and I took to Holland for a conference. He had a problem with smoking. Every evening he used to go alone to a quiet canal for his evening cigarette. The boy was absolutely addicted and had been since he was about twelve years old. In fact, he smoked so heavily that he had to manufacture his own supplies.

One night I talked to the group about the words of the Lord Jesus when he stated, "You will know the truth, and the truth will set you free" (John 8:32). Then I showed that when the Lord said the truth would do the emancipating, He was referring to Himself, for he added, "So if the Son sets you free, you will be free indeed" (John 8:36). Obviously He was using the term *truth* as a description of Himself. I tried to show the young people that whatever was binding them in their Christian experience, the Lord through His indwelling life could and would set them free.

Unknown to me, there was a hungry boy listening. He was hungry to be rid of the habit that was his master. He heard that a Christian is a person who has a power greater than any other power within him. Therefore, he knew that for him to claim to be a Christian but at the same time to be dominated by a lesser power than the Spirit of God was a contradiction. So he evaluated his grave clothes and knew that they had to go.

As usual, he went down to the canal. But for the first time he went there longing to be set free. He did an unusual thing. He took out his cigarettes and threw them into the canal, one at a time. As each cigarette fell into the water, he repeated the words that he believed with all his heart, "So if the Son sets you free, you will be free indeed." He testifies to this day that the Lord had the victory over this thing.

Naturally he still had many battles over this problem. Many times he longed for a calming, soothing smoke. The Lord hadn't taken away his desire, and the Lord hadn't given him a new strength of willpower. Every time he claimed the promise of God, however, and each time he counted on the adequacy of his Lord, he was set free. &

A Sweet Delight in God
JONATHAN EDWARDS

Regarded by many as a classic of spiritual experience, Jonathan Edwards's Personal Narrative *allows us to look into the spiritual life of one of America's greatest sons.*

I had a variety of concerns and exercises about my soul from my childhood; but had two more remarkable seasons of awakening, before I met with that change by which I was brought to those new dispositions, and that new sense of things, that I have since had. The first time was when I was a boy, some years before I went to college, at a time of remarkable awakening in my father's congregation. I was then very much affected for many months, and concerned about the things of religion, and my soul's salvation; and was abundant in duties. I used to pray five times a day in secret, and to spend much time in religious talk with other boys, and used to meet with them to pray together. I experienced I know not what kind of delight in religion. My mind was much engaged in it, and had much self-righteous pleasure; and it was my delight to abound in religious duties. I with some of my school-mates joined together, and built a booth in a swamp, in a very retired spot, for a place of prayer. And besides, I had particular secret places of my own in the woods, where I used to retire by myself; and was from time to time much affected. My affections seemed to be lively and easily moved, and I seemed to be in my element when engaged in religious duties. And I am ready to think, many are deceived with such affections, and such a kind of delight as I then had in religion, and mistake it for grace.

But in process of time, my convictions and affections wore off; and I entirely lost all those affections and delights and left off secret prayer, at least as to any constant performance of it; and returned like a dog to his vomit, and went on in the ways of sin.

. . . The first instance that I remember of that sort of inward, sweet delight in God and divine things that I have lived much in since, was on reading those words, I Tim. 1:17. *Now unto the King eternal, immortal, invisible, the only wise God, be honor and glory forever and ever, Amen.* As I read the words, there came into my soul, and was as it were diffused through it, a sense of the glory of the Divine Being; a new sense, quite different from any thing I ever experienced before. Never any words of scripture seemed to me as these words did. I thought within myself, how excellent a being that was, and how happy I should be, if I might enjoy that God, and be wrapt up in heaven, and be as it were swallowed up in him forever! I kept saying, and as it were singing over these words of scripture to myself; and went to pray to God that I might enjoy him, and prayed in a manner quite different from what I used to do; with a new sort of affection. But it never came into my thought, that there was anything spiritual, or of a saving nature in this.

From about that time, I began to have a new kind of apprehensions and ideas of Christ, and the work of redemption, and the glorious way of salvation by him. And inward, sweet sense of these things, at times, came into my heart; and my soul was led away in pleasant views and contemplations of them. And my mind was greatly engaged to spend my time in reading and meditating on Christ, on the beauty and excellency of his person, and the lovely way of salvation by free grace in him. I found no books so delightful to me, as those that treated of these subjects. 🐛

*The pursuit of God will embrace the labor of bringing our total
personality into conformity to His. . . . I speak of a voluntary exalting of
God to His proper station over us and a willing surrender of our whole
being to the place of worshipful submission which the Creator-creature
circumstance makes proper.*
A.W. TOZER

Faith

I FLY REGULARLY. In airplanes, that is! First I go to the airport, check the schedule, and decide if I believe that what it says is correct. Then I buy a ticket, trusting that in exchange for my money the airline will take me to my destination. Then I check out the airplane and the crew and satisfy myself that the equipment is in good shape and the crew are wide awake. I have already come to the conclusion that airplanes fly, of course. All this effort leads me to believe that if I get on the airplane, I will fly. But I don't move an inch despite my fervent belief. Something else is necessary.

I must walk down the ramp, find my seat, sit down, fasten my seat belt, and relax. Then something wonderful happens. The engines start, the plane roars down the runway, the nose lifts off, and suddenly I'm flying. But I do not jump up from my seat shouting, "I'm flying. I'm flying! I've conquered gravity. I'm free." I *expected* that the properties of the airplane would be transferred to me if I committed myself to it.

So it is with faith. Faith first of all *believes* certain things to be true. Then faith *trusts* itself to that of which it is convinced. Then faith *expects* to receive what was promised and lives in the good of it.

The importance of faith cannot be overemphasized. We are saved by faith (Ephesians 2:8.); we live by faith (Romans 1:17); by faith we stand (II Corinthians 1:24); it is the prayer of faith that is effective (James 5:15); and the victory we enjoy comes through faith (I John 5:4). But faith is only as valid as its object. I could have great faith that an old rust bucket will fly, but I might crash by faith. Or I could sincerely believe that the New York flight is going to Los Angeles and be sincerely wrong. Atheists believe! They believe that there is no God. And they trust that this belief is true and live their lives accordingly. They have lots of faith; they believe sincerely; but what they believe is not true.

Some people believe that what the Bible says about Jesus is true, but they never trust themselves to Him for salvation, or they do not commit their lives to Him as their Lord and Master. What they believe is true, but their belief does not include trust, and so they miss out on the benefits of His grace.

The longer I sit on an airplane, the more I trust it. In fact, I trust it so much that I even forget that I'm flying way up in the air. It's as if my faith grows stronger, the longer I trust. I am so convinced that I will fly that I am not surprised when I do—but I would be very shocked if I suddenly stopped! In the same way, the longer I believe God's word and trust myself to His care, the more my faith grows. And it shows! Real, genuine faith in the Lord changes our lives, and people see the difference. What can people expect to see in the lives of those who live by faith? Paul said, "The only thing that counts is faith expressing itself through love" (Galatians 5:6). 🐾

Anthea in Rome

G. G. MARTIN

The story of Anthea, a beautiful young Christian slave who was put into a Roman dungeon to await the time she would be thrown to the lions, is one of extraordinary faith in action. It comes from a book called Under the Roman Eagle.

Anthea sat in a corner of the dark prison in the straw, thinking of her home in Britain, her village under the oak trees, where the long, long sunlight played through the pleasant afternoons. Suddenly she was awakened from her thoughts by a disturbance at the end of the long dungeon. Hurrying toward her, accompanied by an armed guard, was her mistress, Flavia!

"Anthea!" Flavia stretched forth her hands, and was unable to say more. For a moment her eyes filled with tears as she glanced around at the dripping walls, the filthy straw, and the stone floor. Recovering herself, she exclaimed quickly, "My dear Anthea, I have come to have you released, if I can. My father does not know of this visit, nor would he allow it, but I have many friends in the palace of Nero; they will help you to flee from here."

Anthea pressed her hand and murmured, "I thank you!"

"I have authority that will grant you full pardon," continued Flavia, "if you will come with me at once to the temple of Jupiter and merely burn a little incense at the altar. You only need show yourself before certain witnesses. Come with me at once, Anthea."

Anthea half-turned away from her. Freedom! What a temptation! She saw the discreet but curious stares of the other prisoners all around. Unable to answer at once she asked, "What would become of me, noble Flavia? I am a slave, and you say your father—"

"Have no fear, for I have arranged to sell you to Lucan, Antonia's brother. It seems he once saw you when I was visiting at his palace, and it is his influence that has obtained my pass into the dungeons. Through him I am able to offer you freedom."

"Sell me to Lucan!"

"Why do you hesitate?" continued Flavia in surprise. "You know the Antoninus family is one of the first in Rome. You would have nothing to fear in their possession."

"It is not that—" Anthea straightened her shoulders unconsciously. "I am a Christian, Flavia, and I cannot deny my Lord. Making an offering to an idol is against my faith. I wish I could thank you and noble Lucan as I ought, but I cannot accept freedom at the price of my belief."

"I would almost become a Christian myself," were Flavia's parting words. "Your strength is so amazing. Would that I knew what upholds you so calmly!"

Anthea was disturbed, but she did not regret her refusal. She had made her choice, and if need be, she was willing to die for her Christ. 🙙

The Captain's Faith
LUKE 7:1-10, SLB

The story of the centurion reminds us that faith means we not only believe that God can, but also expect that He will.

Jesus finished his sermon and then went back to the city of Capernaum.

At that time, a Roman army captain's slave was sick and near death. When the captain heard about Jesus, he sent some Jewish elders to speak to him. He told them to ask Jesus to come and heal his slave. So they begged Jesus to come with them and help the man. They told him what a good person the captain was.

"If anyone deserves your help, it is he," they said. "For he loves the Jews. He even built a synagogue for us!"

Jesus went with them. But just before they got to the house, the captain sent some friends with a message. They said, "Sir, don't trouble yourself by coming to my home. For I am not worthy of any such honor. I am not even worthy to come and meet you. Just speak a word from where you are. If you do, I know that my servant boy will be healed! I know, because I am under the authority of my superior officers. And I have authority over my men. I only need to say, 'Go!' and they go. Or I might say, 'Come!' and they come. And to my slave, 'Do this or that,' and he does it. So just say, 'Be healed!' If you do, my servant will be well again!"

When he heard this, Jesus was amazed. And he turned to the crowd following him. "I have never met a man with faith like this," he said. "None of all the Jews in Israel have such faith!"

Then the captain's friends went back to his house. And they found the slave completely healed. &

No Is an Answer
Amy Carmichael

At a very early age, Amy Carmichael prayed for blue eyes, but her brown eyes stayed brown! A good thing, too, because Amy became a daring missionary in India, where blue eyes would have marked her as a foreigner. Sometimes we need to have faith that "No" is an answer to prayer!

Just a tiny little child
    Three years old,
And a mother with a heart
    All of gold.
Often did that mother say,
    Jesus hears us when we pray,
For He's never far away
    And He always answers.

Now, that tiny little child
    Had brown eyes,

And she wanted blue instead
    Like blue skies.
For her mother's eyes were blue
    Like forget-me-nots. She knew
All her mother said was true,
    Jesus always answered.

So she prayed for two blue eyes,
    Said "Good night,"
Went to sleep in deep content
    And delight.
Woke up early, climbed a chair
    By a mirror. Where, O where
Could the blue eyes be? Not there;
    Jesus hadn't answered.

Hadn't answered her at all;
    Never more
Could she pray; her eyes were brown
    As before.
Did a little soft wind blow?
    Came a whisper soft and low,
"Jesus answered. He said, No;
    Isn't No an answer?"

*Faith is the means by which the infirmity of man
lays hold on the infinity of God.*
JOHN BLANCHARD

Jesus and the Children
MARK 10:13-16, NIV

What does faith look like? Like a young child trusting a loving parent.

People were bringing little children to Jesus to have him touch them, but the disciples rebuked them. When Jesus saw this, he was indignant. He said to them, "Let the little children come to me, and do not hinder them, for the kingdom of God belongs to such as these. I tell you the truth, anyone who will not receive the kingdom of God like a little child will never enter it."

And he took the children in his arms, put his hands on them and blessed them. 🍂

Thoughts before Surgery
JOSEPH BAYLY

Lying on a cart waiting for surgery, Joe Bayly muses on life and death. Like the apostle Paul, he concludes, "For to me to live is Christ and to die is gain." That's the way to approach surgery . . . and everything else! This selection is taken from Bayly's
Heaven.

It's six-thirty on a Tuesday morning. Here I am waiting. Waiting to be wheeled into an operating room at Mayo Clinic's Methodist Hospital.

For some reason I am at the beginning of the long line of carts, soon to number thirty, each holding another human being who also waits. Next to me is a man in his eighties, beyond him a man younger than I. The older man is asleep, the younger is himself a medical doctor. I learn this when another stops to talk briefly with him.

"Does being a doctor help at a time like this?" I ask.

"Not really," he answers with a wry smile. "It's a mixed bag."

A nurse stops at the head of my cart, reads the piece of adhesive tape on my forehead, then asks, "What's your name?"

"Bayly," I answer. "Joseph Bayly."

She moves to the sleeping older man next to me, reads his name, but doesn't disturb him. Then on to the doctor, and so down the line.

As people are wheeled past me to take their places farther down, I nod or smile at the ones who are still awake. Otherwise I wait.

For what?

I wait for the merciful anesthesia, then the surgeon, and then . . . to come back to consciousness in the room where dear Mary Lou, my wife of thirty-two winters—and summers—also waits.

Or to come back to consciousness in the presence of my Lord Christ.

The surgery will not be very serious, there is little risk, but I am equally at peace, as far as I can plumb the depths of my heart, with either prospect.

I wonder how many others in the long white line have this hope. How would I feel, approaching the radical surgical procedures some of them face, without it? Would I have their courage?

My courage is Christ. My hope is Christ and the door to heaven He flung open by His own death for my sins, my hope His resurrection.

What will heaven be like, whether I go there as result of this operation (a remote possibility), or go there later (a certainty)?

Heaven will be my eternal home with Christ. I'll just move into the part of His Father's house He prepared for me. No fixing up that home, no parts unfinished, no disappointments on moving day. No, He's prepared it. He's made it completely ready, completely perfect, completely mine.

What's a home like, one that He prepares?

A place of peace and beauty, of joy and glory, of celestial music, of fresh, unchanging, purest love.

I'll say: "Hello, Lord. I'm tired." And He'll say, "Rest, because I have work for you to do."

"Rest?"

"Yes, remember that I myself rested on the seventh day of creation. So, rest is not incompatible with heaven's perfection."

"And work?"

"Of course. Did you think heaven would be an eternal Sunday afternoon nap? My people serve Me in heaven. I have work for you to do." 🙠

My Heart Was Strangely Warmed
JOHN WESLEY

On the evening of May 24, 1738, John Wesley came to faith—an event that changed the course of his life and the history of Britain. Here the event is described in his own words, from The Journal of John Wesley.

In the evening I went very unwillingly to a society in Aldersgate Street, where one was reading Luther's preface to the Epistle to the Romans. About a quarter before nine, while he was describing the change which God works in the heart through faith in Christ, I felt my heart strangely warmed. I felt I did trust in Christ, Christ alone, for salvation; and an assurance was given me that He had taken away my sins; even mine, and saved me from the law of sin and death.

I began to pray with all my might for those who had in a more especial manner despitefully used me and persecuted me. I then testified openly to all there what I now first felt in my heart. But it was not long before the enemy suggested, "This cannot be faith; for where is thy joy?" Then was I taught that peace and victory over sin are essential to faith in the Captain of our salvation; but that, as to the transports of joy that usually attend the beginning of it, especially in those who have mourned deeply, God sometimes giveth, sometimes withholdeth, them according to the counsels of His own will.

After my return home, I was much buffeted with temptations, but I cried out, and they fled away. They returned again and again. I as often lifted up my eyes, and He "sent me help from his holy place." And herein I found the difference between this and my former state chiefly consisted. I was striving, yea, fighting with all my might under the law, as well as under grace. But then I was sometimes, if not often, conquered; now, I was always conqueror.

Thursday, 25.—The moment I awakened, "Jesus, Master," was in my heart and in my mouth; and I found all my strength lay in keeping my eye fixed upon Him and my soul waiting on Him continually. Being again at St. Paul's in the afternoon, I could taste the good word of God in the anthem which began, "My song shall be always of the loving-kindness of the Lord: with my mouth will I ever be showing forth thy truth from one generation to another." Yet the enemy injected a fear, "If thou dost believe, why is there not a more sensible change?" I answered (yet not I), "That I know not. But this I know, I have 'now peace with God.' " 🐾

The First Swallow
F. W. BOREHAM

F. W. Boreham was a British pastor who ministered in Australia and New Zealand. His many books hold countless treasures of observation and spiritual insight. Watch as he follows the swallow with the keen eye of faith in this excerpt from The Golden Milestone.

Yesterday afternoon I saw the first swallow of another summer! It was one of those fragrant and delicious spring days that seem to have all the ecstasy and song of summertime dancing through their tranquil hours. The grass was a sheen of emerald—greener than any tint that a painter would dare to place upon his canvas. Just beyond, the river shimmered in the sunshine. And suddenly, skimming gracefully along the grass, and circling over the water, touching first the one and then the other with a camel-hair delicacy, my swallow darted. I could see that it was very, very happy to be back again, and I was no less delighted to welcome it. . . .

Now since watching my swallow by the riverside yesterday I have been trying to analyze these poignant emotions that are aroused in autumn and in springtime by the going and the coming of the swallows. I am convinced that, when I see the swallows leaving the russet autumn, and preparing for their northward flight, there is something deeper in my sadness than a mere shrinking from a winter that is too mild to have any terrors. And I am equally certain that the keen delight that is mine when my heart leaps up to greet the first swallow in August is far greater than a smug relief at the passing of the cold.

Why does the swallow migrate? How does the swallow know when to turn its face to the ocean? How does it know in which direction to go? I do not know. And, what is more, the swallow does not know! Yes, that is the beauty of it—the swallow does not know. You tell me that the swallow knows *instinctively*. But what is instinct? You do not explain a thing, or lessen its mystery, by giving it a name.

> A fire mist and a planet,
>> A crystal and a cell,
> A jelly-fish and a saurian,
>> And a cave where the cave-men dwell;
> Then a sense of law and beauty,
>> A face turned from the clod—
> Some call it Evolution,
>> And others call it God.

It is better—far better to call it God and be done with it.
And, in exactly the same way, there is this wondrous force that
guides the swallow:

Some people call it instinct,
And others call it God.

It is better, I repeat, to call it God. Far better. Now at this
point the study of the swallow becomes of vast importance to me.
For in many respects I am very like the swallow. I move through
life guided by a force that I cannot explain. By what strange
impulse was I impelled to follow this profession—this and no
other? By what freak of fate did I marry this wife—this and no
other? By what stroke of fortune did I settle in this land—this and
no other? Looking back on life, it seems almost like a drift; we
seem to have reached this position by the veriest chance. And yet
it has all turned out too well to be the result of chance. The fact is
that like the swallow we acted instinctively. And that instinct was
God! We say with Browning's Paracelsus:

I see my way as birds their trackless way.
I shall arrive! What time, what circuit first,
I ask not: but unless God send His hail,
Or blinding fireballs, sleet or stifling snow,
In some time, His good time, I shall arrive:
He guides me and the bird. In His good time! ♣

Seek First the Kingdom
MATTHEW 6:25-33, KJV

Therefore I say unto you, Take no thought for your life, what ye
shall eat, or what ye shall drink; nor yet for your body, what ye
shall put on. Is not the life more than meat, and the body than raiment? Behold the fowls of the air: for they sow not, neither do they
reap, nor gather into barns; yet your heavenly Father feedeth them.

Are ye not much better than they? Which of you by taking thought can add one cubit unto his stature? And why take ye thought for raiment? Consider the lilies of the field, how they grow; they toil not, neither do they spin: And yet I say unto you, That even Solomon in all his glory was not arrayed like one of these. Wherefore, if God so clothe the grass of the field, which today is, and tomorrow is cast into the oven, shall he not much more clothe you, O ye of little faith? Therefore take no thought, saying, What shall we eat? or, What shall we drink? or, Wherewithal shall we be clothed? For your heavenly Father knoweth that ye have need of all these things. But seek ye first the kingdom of God, and his right-eousness; and all these things shall be added unto you. ❧

On Christian Doctrine
ST. AUGUSTINE

Augustine, in his own earnest way, looks at his faith and gets himself into a kind of chicken-and-egg discussion. This is the beginning of Book One of The Confessions.

Great art Thou, O Lord, and greatly to be praised; great is Thy power, and Thy wisdom infinite. And Thee would man praise; man, but a particle of Thy creation, man, that bears about him his mortality, the witness of his sin, the witness, that "Thou resistest the proud": yet would man praise Thee; he, but a particle of Thy creation. Thou awakest us to delight in Thy praise; for Thou madest us for Thyself, and our heart is restless until it repose in Thee. Grant me, Lord, to know and understand which is first, to call on Thee or to praise Thee? and, again, to know Thee or to call on Thee? For who can call on Thee, not knowing Thee? For he that knoweth Thee not may call on Thee as other than Thou art. Or is it rather that we call on Thee that we may know Thee? "But how shall they call on Him in Whom they have not believed? or how shall they believe without a preacher?" And they that seek the Lord shall praise Him. For they that seek shall find Him, and they that find shall praise Him. I will seek Thee, Lord, by calling on Thee; and will call on Thee, believing in Thee; for to us hast Thou been preached. My faith, Lord, shall call on Thee, which Thou hast given me, wherewith Thou hast inspired me, through the Incarnation of Thy Son, through the ministry of the Preacher. 🙢

Lead, Kindly Light
JOHN HENRY NEWMAN

As Newman was returning to England from Sicily, he thought of his faith life as a journey, which he describes in this well-known poem.

Lead, kindly Light, amid the encircling gloom,
    Lead thou me on;
The night is dark, and I am far from home,
    Lead thou me on.
Keep thou my feet; I do not ask to see
The distant scene; one step enough for me.

I was not ever thus, nor prayed that thou
    Should'st lead me on;
I loved to choose and see my path, but now
    Lead thou me on.
I loved the garish day; and spite of fears,
Pride ruled my will; remember not past years.

So long thy power has blessed me, sure it still
    Will lead me on,
O'er moor and fen, o'er crag and torrent, till
    The night is gone,

And with the morn those angel faces smile,
Which I have loved long since, and lost awhile. 🦋

The Sunnier Side of Doubt
ALFRED, LORD TENNYSON

*In which Tennyson, nineteenth-century British poet laureate, reminds even the most
skeptical among us that faith is not only reasonable but necessary.*

Thou canst not prove the Nameless, O my son,
    Nor canst thou prove the world thou movest in,
Thou canst not prove that thou art body alone,
    Nor canst thou prove that thou art spirit alone,
Nor canst thou prove that thou art both in one.
    Thou canst not prove thou art immortal, no,
Nor yet that thou art mortal—nay, my son,
    Thou canst not prove that I, who speak with thee,
Am not thyself in converse with thyself,
    For nothing worthy proving can be proven,
Nor yet disproven. Wherefore thou be wise,
    Cleave ever to the sunnier side of doubt,
And cling to Faith beyond the forms of Faith!
    She reels not in the storm of warring words,
She brightens at the clash of "yes" and "no,"
    She sees the best that glimmers thro' the worst,
She feels the sun is hid but for a night,
    She spies the summer thro' the winter bud,
She tastes the fruit before the blossom falls,
    She hears the lark within the songless egg,
She finds the fountain where they wail'd "Mirage!" 🦋

Faith and Love
JOHN MILTON

Paul told the Galatians, "The only thing that counts is faith expressing itself through love." Milton illustrates this in the following poem.

When Faith and Love which parted from thee never,
  Had ripen'd thy just soul to dwell with God,
  Meekly thou didst resign this earthly load
  Of Death, call'd Life; which us from Life doth sever.
Thy Works and Alms and all thy good Endeavour
  Staid not behind, nor in the grave were trod;
  But as Faith pointed with her golden rod,
  Follow'd thee up to joy and bliss for ever.
Love led them on, and Faith who knew them best
  Thy hand-maids, clad them o'er with purple beams
  And azure wings, that up they flew so drest,
And speak the truth of thee on glorious Theams
  Before the Judge, who thenceforth bid thee rest
  And drink thy fill of pure immortal streams. 🐦

An English Prayer
FIFTEENTH CENTURY

The life of faith is one where faith touches every part of life.

God be in my head, and in my understanding;
 God be in my eyes, and in my looking;
God be in my mouth, and in my speaking;
 God be in my heart, and in my thinking;
God be at my end, and in my departing. 🐦

Holiness

ONE DAY MOSES was way out in the desert looking after his father-in-law's sheep when he saw a strange sight. A bush was burning—nothing unusual about that—but it was not burning up. That was very unusual. So he went to have a closer look. He got a terrible shock when God spoke to him from the bush. "Don't come any closer, Moses. Take off your sandals. You are standing on holy ground."

Now the ground where Moses was standing didn't look any different from the ground all around it. It was sandy and rocky and full of weeds and thorn bushes. Bugs buzzed and worms wriggled. It was, to all appearances, just ordinary desert dirt. What then did God mean? Surely He was not suggesting that this was extra-special dirt! No. He meant that it was ordinary ground that was different because He had set it apart for His special purposes. And that is what "holy" means. Set apart.

God is holy. He is set apart, totally different from us. We are sinful; He is without sin. We are limited by time and space; He inhabits eternity. All His characteristics and attributes are set apart from ours. His love, His mercy, His anger are all totally different from ours. Now when God calls people to Himself and saves them because of Christ's sacrifice, He sets apart those people for Himself. So they too are holy. Another word for "holy" is "sanctified," which is related to the word "saint." Believers are called saints not because they are perfect, but because they have been set apart by

God for His special purposes.

This presents a great challenge to the believers, or "holy ones." They now have to learn to behave in a manner that is appropriate to their new station in life. So God, who says that believers are holy, now tells us, "Be holy, because I am holy." We now have to *be* what we have *become*. If that sounds complicated, let me remind you what happens when a man marries a woman. The moment the minister pronounces the couple "man and wife," the man is a husband. He has been set apart to husbandry! But he doesn't know much about it, so he has to start learning to be what he has become. He has the rest of his married life to learn and grow in this regard. The same is true of the Christian life!

This all sounds very intimidating, but remember that in order for us to live this way, God gives us "His Spirit, the Holy One." He imparts new desires, teaches us new things, and empowers us to live differently. And the word for that is holiness. ❧

Mrs. Rosey-Posey and the Chocolate Cherry Treat

ROBIN JONES GUNN

It's not easy to be different, especially when we are young. But sometimes different is best because different is right.

Right in the middle of Poppyville, at the end of Marigold Lane, stands a big yellow house.

All the children in Poppyville love this house.

They love to play in the attic. They love to roller-skate on the porch. And they love to feed the ducks in the pond.

But what the children love most about this house is Mrs. Rosey-Posey. She has a thousand secrets. When she gets a twinkle-sparkle-zing look in her eyes, she is about to give away one of those secrets.

One sunny Saturday, Mrs. Rosey-Posey saw Natalie sitting on her porch swing.

"Mercy me!" cried Mrs. Rosey-Posey. "Such a frown! Whatever is the matter, Natalie Olivia?"

Mrs. Rosey-Posey always calls the children by their first two names. Not the way your mother does when she's upset with you. But it's like she's calling you "Prince" or "Princess."

"It's not fair!" Natalie told Mrs. Rosey-Posey. "All my friends went to the movies without me."

"Why?" asked Mrs. Rosey-Posey.

"My mom and dad said I could not go. They said it was not the kind of movie I should see."

"And your friends went anyway?" Mrs. Rosey-Posey asked.

"Yes," said Natalie. "My parents were the only parents who said no."

"Mercy me!" said Mrs. Rosey-Posey, shaking her head. "You are right. That is not fair to your friends at all!"

"What?" Natalie cried. "What do you mean it is not fair to my friends? I think it is not fair to me!"

Natalie looked at Mrs. Rosey-Posey. She had that twinkle-sparkle-zing look in her eyes.

"Natalie Olivia," she said. "Did you know that you have been set apart? Your parents are helping you make the right choice."

"Set apart?" Natalie said. "What does that mean?"

"Come with me," said Mrs. Rosey-Posey. She took Natalie by the hand.

"Natalie Olivia," she said. "You are about to learn the secret of the fine china plate."

And off they marched to the kitchen.

"This morning I picked cherries," said Mrs. Rosey-Posey. "Then I dipped them in chocolate. Would you like some?"

"Oh, yes!" said Natalie.

Mrs. Rosey-Posey pulled a dirty paper plate out of the trash. "Would you like me to put your cherries on this plate?" Mrs. Rosey-Posey asked with a smile.

"Well," said Natalie, "if that is all you have. . . ."

"Goodness, no!" said Mrs. Rosey-Posey. "I have other plates. Clean plates. Special plates. Plates which I have kept set apart."

They went into the dining room. Natalie sat down. Mrs. Rosey-Posey put three plates in front of her.

First, the dirty paper plate.

Then a plain brown dinner plate.

Then a beautiful, fine china plate with gold trim.

"Which plate would you like to use for your cherries?" Mrs. Rosey-Posey asked.

"This one," Natalie said. She pointed to the fine china plate.

Mrs. Rosey-Posey scooped the cherries onto it. "Why did you pick this one?" she asked.

"Well, the paper plate was dirty," Natalie explained. "The dinner plate was boring. But this one is beautiful."

"Indeed!" said Mrs. Rosey-Posey. She sat down next to Natalie. "Now I shall tell you the story of the fine china plate."

Natalie popped a cherry into her mouth. She nodded and listened with her heart.

"Once there was a dinner plate. She was young and free. With all her heart she wanted to be special. She wanted to serve the King.

"Her friends called to her one day, 'Come with us! We're going to get smeared with beans and hot dogs!'

"The dinner plate wanted to go. But she thought, *If I were a fine china plate, I would never get smeared with beans and hot dogs.*

" 'I cannot go,' she told her friends. 'I want to keep clean. The King might want to use me someday.'

"Her friends laughed. 'Little Miss Set-Apart thinks she is too good for us.' And they went on without her.

"The dinner plate felt sad. Being set apart is sometimes very lonely.

"Then one day, the King came! He was looking for a clean plate that He could use.

"All the plates lined up.

" 'Pick me! Pick me!' they cried.

"The dinner plate looked at her friends. They were no longer dinner plates! They had turned into paper plates! Dark bean stains covered their sagging edges.

"Suddenly the King reached for the lonely dinner plate. He smiled. 'I am glad you stayed clean. You made the right choice. I will now turn you into a fine china plate and use you to serve others.' "

Mrs. Rosey-Posey leaned forward. "Do you know what all the paper plates said?"

"No, what?" Natalie asked.

"They shouted, 'It's not fair! Pick us! Turn us into china plates too!' "

Natalie laughed. "They had a choice. They did not have to get covered with beans and hot dogs. They could have said no. The dinner plate did."

"Mercy me!" said Mrs. Rosey-Posey. "Perhaps they needed someone to help them make the right choice."

"You mean the way my parents helped me today? They wanted me to stay clean. So they said no to the movie."

"Indeed!" said Mrs. Rosey-Posey.

It was quiet for a moment. Then Mrs. Rosey-Posey whispered, "Natalie Olivia, what kind of plate would you like to be?"

Natalie looked into Mrs. Rosey-Posey's dancing eyes. She saw a silver tear.

Natalie sat up. She spoke in a clear voice. "I would like to be a fine china plate. The kind of plate the King can use."

Then Mrs. Rosey-Posey took a pen out of her pocket. She picked up Natalie's plate and wrote on the back of it.

"This is for you," Mrs. Rosey-Posey said. "Treasure it always." She handed the china plate to Natalie.

Natalie looked on the back of the plate. It said:
For Natalie Olivia
Love always, Mrs. Rosey-Posey
II Timothy 2:21

"What does II Timothy 2:21 say?" asked Natalie.

"It says, 'If you stay away from sin you will be like one of these dishes made of purest gold—the very best in the house—so that Christ himself can use you for his highest purposes.' "

"Wow!" Natalie hugged Mrs. Rosey-Posey. "You make me feel so special. How can I ever thank you?"

"Natalie Olivia," said Mrs. Rosey-Posey. "You are special. You are set apart, just like a fine china plate. Stay clean, my dear one. And I promise you, one day the King will use you."

Thunder on the Mountain
E. B. R. HIRSH

We are always ready to think about God's love, mercy, and kindness, but we must never forget that He is first and foremost a holy God. This means that He is quite different from us, and we should approach Him with awe and reverence, as the children of Israel learn in Exodus 19-24.

The children of Israel had been traveling three months when they came to the desert of Sinai. At the foot of the mountain of Sinai they pitched their tents.

Moses went up the mountain, and God spoke to him, saying: "The children of Israel have seen what I did to the Egyptians and how I led them to this place.

"Tell them that if they listen to My voice and keep My covenant, they will become a kingdom of priests and a holy people."

Moses came down and spoke the words of the Lord to the people.

And they said: "All that the Lord has said, we will do."

Then God said to Moses: "I will come to you in a thick cloud so the people will know when I speak to you.

"Go and bless them, and let them wash their clothes and prepare themselves for two days. On the third day I will appear to them."

On the morning of the third day there was lightning and thunder, and a thick cloud surrounded the mountain. A loud sound like a trumpet-blast was heard, and all the people trembled.

Mount Sinai was covered with smoke, and the smoke rose up as if from a great furnace. The whole mountain shook violently.

The trumpet sound grew louder. Moses spoke, and God answered with another great sound of thunder. Then the Lord called Moses to the top of the mountain, and Moses went up.

God spoke all these words to Moses, the words of the Ten

Commandments. . . .

When the people saw the lightning and heard the thunder and the sound of the trumpet, they were afraid and stood a long way off while Moses went near the thick darkness.

There the Lord spoke to Moses at great length, setting out many other laws which the people of Israel must understand and obey. And Moses told them to the people to be their guide in treating each other justly.

The people said: "Everything the Lord has said, we will do."

Then Moses built an altar to the Lord with twelve pillars, one for each of the twelve tribes of Israel. The people made sacrifices to the Lord and worshiped Him. ❧

Ceiling Zero
JOSEPH BAYLY

Joe Bayly's imaginary friend Herb Gooley had many adventures, all of which had a point—usually sharp! This story comes from a collection called The Gospel Blimp *and Other Modern Parables.*

My roommate is a guy named Gooley. Herb Gooley.

He transferred to this crummy little school in the boondocks about six months ago. When he first arrived, we were all asking why he left a big, well-known college at the beginning of his senior year. Everybody's heard of it; nobody's heard of us.

Only thing we have that they don't have is a flight school. What they have, and we don't have, would fill a book.

One night I ask Herb straight out, "Why did you come here?"

"One reason," he says. "Last Christmas vacation I learned to fly. So I decided to switch to a flight school, a place where everyone could fly. That's why I'm here."

I should explain that I don't mean flying planes or gliders or balloons or anything. I mean we can fly, period.

We can step out of a window and be airborne. I remember my first flight—it was while I was still in high school—off a barn in the Blue Ridge Mountains. Some of the guys and girls here have been flying ever since they were little kids.

So the reason Herb Gooley gave for coming here made sense. Except for one thing, which he couldn't have known before he came. It's the sort of thing you don't learn from a catalog.

Gooley is a sensitive guy—withdrawn. Doesn't talk to many people. But there's some reason for being as he is: for one thing, he got off to a bad start.

I've never seen a happier freshman than Gooley, when he first showed up. I don't mean that he was actually a freshman—like I said, he was a transfer senior. But he had that same stupid innocence.

One of those hot afternoons in September—like so many days when school has just begun—I was stripped to the waist, arranging my clothes on hangers, when this new student comes through the window. He flew in—our room is on the third floor of Derwin Hall.

"I'm Herb Gooley," he says. "Boy, have I ever been looking forward to coming here."

"To this crummy school? Why?" I ask.

He looks sort of surprised. "Why, because it's a flight school. You can fly, can't you? The other guys in this dorm can fly, can't they? And the girls—just think of having a flying date. Wow!"

Should I tell him straight off, or should I let him find out for himself?

I guess I'm sort of chicken, because I decide not to say anything. Let someone else tell him.

"Yeah, this is a flight school, all right. We can all fly, including the profs—and the administration. You can have that bed over there by the door, Gooley. And that dresser, and either closet, except that I've got my things in this one. The public relations department can fly, too. They prepare the catalog."

He doesn't say anything, but begins to unpack. First thing out of his suitcase is a copy of *Aerodynamic Theory*. It goes on his desk.

Around five-thirty I head for the dining hall. "Coming along?" I ask.

"Not yet," Gooley says. "Don't wait for me. I want to finish here first. I'll be along before it closes."

So I walk on over and go through the cafeteria line. I find my crowd and sit down to eat with them.

We're on dessert, when there's a little stir over by the door.

"What do we have here?" someone asks.

"An exhibitionist."

"A new student, you can tell that. Nobody else would fly on campus."

Sure enough—it's Herb Gooley, my new roommate. He comes through the door and touches down gently, by the stack of trays and the silver holder. He's got a smooth technique.

Everybody gets sort of quiet. I don't know about the others, but suddenly I'm thinking about some of my flights in high school days.

"You're too late," this battle-ax who runs the cafeteria says. "We close at six-thirty."

The clock on the wall says six-thirty. She's absolutely right, which is what she always is.

"Serves him right," a girl going back for seconds on iced tea says, loud enough for Herb to hear. "He's just a show-off."

Gooley looks sort of hurt, but he doesn't say anything, either to battle-ax or to battle-ax, junior grade. He just heads out the door. Walking.

"He'll learn," someone at my table says. "We all learned."

And he did, during the next few weeks.

First thing he finds out is that here nobody flies. In spite of this being a flight school, and everyone can fly—theoretically—we're all grounded.

There's a lot of talk about flight, of course, a daily flight hour. But nobody flies.

Some of us came here planning to be flight instructors. I myself wanted to teach Africans how to fly, but that didn't last long.

Actually, the deadest things are the flight courses. They use *Aerodynamic Theory* as the text, but you'd never recognize it. One flight out of a hayloft has more excitement to it than a year of that course.

One night we get into a discussion on our floor of the dorm.

"Look, Gooley," one of the guys says. "Tell us about the college you were in before you came here. Is it true that they have more exciting courses than we do here?"

"A lot of them, yes," Gooley says. "But they don't know anything about how to fly."

"Are the girls there real swingers?"

"I guess so. But they can't fly."

The way Herb answers sort of frustrates the guys who are asking the questions, because they would jump at a chance to transfer to the school he came from.

"I think this flying isn't all it's cracked up to be," one of them says.

"I feel the same way," another chimes in. "And besides, it seems sort of selfish to me to fly when the rest of the world is walking."

"Not only selfish. To them you look like some kind of a nut, up there above the ground. From here on in, any flights I take are going to be when there's nobody around to see me."

"Besides, the world needs to be taught how to walk. And pavements and roads need to be improved."

"Did any of you read John Robin's book? It's a pretty strong critique of *Aerodynamic Theory*, and he does an effective job of questioning the usual foundations of flight. The significant thing is that Robin is a flyer, not a walker."

That was the only time I ever heard Herb Gooley swear. Then he dived out the window. (It was a cold night, but fortunately we had opened the window because the room was getting stuffy. If we hadn't, I think Herb would have gone right through the glass.)

He didn't return until early next morning. I heard him at the window and got up to open it. It had begun to snow, and he was covered. He looked nearly exhausted, but happier than I'd seen him since the day he first arrived.

That night marked a change in Herb Gooley, a change that came to affect the whole school. Only, I didn't know it at the time.

He began to fly again. On campus.

Now when you're with flyers, flying isn't remarkable—actually it's the basic minimum, it's taken for granted. What worries us is perfection, and it's sort of embarrassing—around other flyers—to try an extra little maneuver, or to stay aloft longer than usual. There can be such a letdown. And the competition is so keen. There's always someone who can fly better than you.

That's the reason nobody flies here. At least they didn't, not until Gooley took it up again.

Like the flight prof says, "This is a school for flying, not an airport. You've come here to learn more about flying, not to fly. We want to teach you how to fly with real conviction." Then he draws diagrams on the blackboard. And he walks across the campus.

Meanwhile, Herb is getting better and better. I mean his flying is improving. You can see him on a moonlit night, trying all sorts of flight gymnastics.

Moonlit nights. That brings me to another side of the change in Gooley.

He began to have flying dates. Not many—none of the girls, except one or two, would be caught dead on a flight date, especially with Herb.

What can you talk about on a flying date? What can you do? I ask you.

We discuss it while Gooley's out of the dorm. He's out a lot those last months of school. Not just flying or on flight dates, but teaching a bunch of kids to fly at the community center in town, studying *Aerodynamic Theory* with a little group of students. The guys can't understand why Herb keeps at it.

"Sure we can fly—at least as well as that guy Gooley. But after all, real life is down here on the earth. It's not as if we were birds."

"Besides, we've got to learn to relate to the walkers. And that's a lot harder to do than flying."

"I've found—I don't know about the rest of you guys—but I've found that they're not much interested in my flying ability. I mean, the walkers aren't. So it's important to show them that I can walk."

"Don't get me wrong. It's not that I'm against flying. I'm not. But you don't have to fly to be for flying."

So the year ends.

We graduate.

I ask Gooley, while we're packing, what he plans to do next year.

"Grad school," he says. "In a walking university. You see, I was reading *Aerodynamic Theory* the other day, where it says that you can take off best against the wind." ❧

What we need is not new truth, but that the truth which we already know become active and effective in our lives.
WILLIAM BARCLAY

Holy, Holy, Holy
ISAIAH 6:1-7, KJV

Because the Lord is holy, He calls us to be holy. So holiness starts with an understanding of God such as Isaiah received in his famous vision.

In the year that King Uzziah died I saw also the Lord sitting upon a throne, high and lifted up, and his train filled the temple. Above it stood the seraphim: each one had six wings; with twain he covered his face, and with twain he covered his feet, and with twain he did fly. And one cried unto another, and said, Holy, holy, holy, is the LORD of hosts: the whole earth is full of his glory. And the posts of the door moved at the voice of him that cried, and the house was filled with smoke. Then said I, Woe is me! for I am undone; because I am a man of unclean lips, and I dwell in the midst of a people of unclean lips: for mine eyes have seen the King, the LORD of hosts. Then flew one of the seraphim unto me, having a live coal in his hand, which he had taken with the tongs from off the altar: And he laid it upon my mouth, and said, Lo, this hath touched thy lips; and thine iniquity is taken away, and thy sin purged. 🐾

Restored
LARRY BURKETT

Restoring classic automobiles has become a favorite hobby of mine. It gives me great satisfaction to see an old car restored to its original design and beauty.

One of my projects was a '57 Ford Thunderbird convertible. When I first saw it, the car had a reasonably good appearance with a shiny, powder blue finish. I purchased the car and intended to do some light touch-up work and then paint it red. Was I in for a surprise! When I began to remove the layers of paint, the real condition of the car's body became evident. Through years of neglect, rust had corroded much of the front end and the passenger side door. Although the outside looked fine, beneath the surface corruption was just waiting to break through.

Restoring the car turned into a monumental task that required completely dismantling the car and replacing the defective parts. The work was tedious, but I couldn't take any shortcuts. Any corrosion left untouched would show through later, and my work would be for nothing.

Just as I work systematically to restore cars to mint condition, God works to restore me to the condition that He intended for all of us before the Fall. I need to allow God to strip away my veneer of self-righteousness, to dismantle my old self, and then to refinish me with the glossy coat of righteousness, to restore me to "showroom" condition in the likeness of His Son.

The Apostle Paul wrote, "If any man is in Christ, he is a new creature; the old things passed away; behold, new things have come" (II Corinthians 5:17, NASB).

No life is beyond God's ability to save and to repair. God patiently peels away all my attempts to "fix" myself; instead, He renews me from within. That process may be painful, but the result is a life that reflects God's handiwork and brings glory to Him! ❧

A People above Reproach
EDWARD GIBBON

Gibbon's Decline and Fall of the Roman Empire is still highly regarded. He was often skeptical of Christianity, but he acknowledged the real thing when he saw it, as in this description of early believers.

When the new converts had been enrolled in the number of the faithful, and were admitted to the sacraments of the church, they found themselves restrained from relapsing into their past disorders by another consideration of a less spiritual but of a very innocent and respectable nature. Any particular society that has departed from the great body of the nation, or the religion to which it belonged, immediately becomes the object of universal as well as invidious observation. In proportion to the smallness of its numbers, the character of the society may be affected by the virtue and vices of the persons who compose it; and every member is engaged to watch with the most vigilant attention over his own behaviour, and over that of his brethren, since, as he must expect to incur a part of the common disgrace, he may hope to enjoy a share of the common reputation.

When the Christians of Bithynia were brought before the tribunal of the younger Pliny, they assured the proconsul that, far from being engaged in any unlawful conspiracy, they were found by a solemn obligation to abstain from the commission of those crimes which disturb the private or public peace of society, from theft, robbery, adultery, perjury, and fraud. Near a century afterwards, Tertullian with an honest pride could boast that very few Christians had suffered by the hand of the executioner, except on account of their religion. Their serious and sequestered life, averse to the gay luxury of the age, inured them to chastity, temperance, economy, and all the sober and domestic virtues. As the greater number were of some trade or profession, it was incumbent on them, by the strictest integrity and the fairest dealing, to remove the suspicions which the profane are too apt to conceive against the appearances of sanctity. The contempt of the world exercised them in the habits of humility, meekness, and patience. The more they were persecuted, the more closely they adhered to each other. Their mutual charity and unsuspecting confidence has been remarked by infidels, and was too often abused by perfidious friends. 🐛

Be Holy
I PETER 1:13-21, NIV

Peter knew that the Christians were going to have a difficult time, but he encouraged them to live holy lives in the midst of their problems.

Therefore, prepare your minds for action; be self-controlled; set your hope fully on the grace to be given you when Jesus Christ is revealed. As obedient children, do not conform to the evil desires you had when you lived in ignorance. But just as he who called you is holy, so be holy in all you do; for it is written: "Be holy, because I am holy."

Since you call on a Father who judges each man's work impartially, live your lives as strangers here in reverent fear. For you know that it was not with perishable things such as silver or gold that you were redeemed from the empty way of life handed down to you from your forefathers, but with the precious blood of Christ, a lamb without blemish or defect. He was chosen before the creation of the world, but was revealed in these last times for your sake. Through him you believe in God, who raised him from the dead and glorified him, and so your faith and hope are in God. 🦂

London, 1802
WILLIAM WORDSWORTH

Wordsworth lamented England's moral decline and longed for Milton's "cheerful godliness"—an example greatly needed then and now.

Milton! thou should'st be living at this hour;
    England hath need of thee; she is a fen
Of stagnant waters: altar, sword, and pen,
    Fireside, the heroic wealth of hall and bower,
Have forfeited their ancient English dower

In inward happiness. We are selfish men;
Oh! raise us up, return to us again;
    And give us manners, virtue, freedom, power.
Thy soul was like a Star, and dwelt apart:
    Thou hadst a voice whose sound was like the sea:
Pure as the naked heavens, majestic, free,
    So didst thou travel on life's common way,
In cheerful godliness; and yet thy heart
    The lowliest duties on herself did lay. ❧

The Pursuit of Holiness
JONATHAN EDWARDS

To the modern mind, thoughts of holiness are all too often coupled with visions of rigidity, otherworldliness, and austerity, and accordingly tend to be most unappealing. Jonathan Edwards's Personal Narrative *reveals something much more attractive.*

My sense of divine things seemed gradually to increase, until I went to preach at New York, which was about a year and a half after they began; and while I was there, I felt them, very sensibly, in a higher degree than I had done before. My longings after God and holiness, were much increased. Pure and humble, holy and heavenly Christianity, appeared exceedingly amiable to me. I felt a burning desire to be in every thing a complete Christian; and conform to the blessed image of Christ; and that I might live, in all things, according to the pure and blessed rules of the gospel. I had an eager thirsting after progress in these things; which put me upon pursuing and pressing after them. It was my continual strife day and night, and constant inquiry, how I should *be* more holy, and *live* more holily, and more becoming a child of God, and a disciple of Christ. I now sought an increase of grace and holiness, and a holy life, with much more earnestness, than ever I sought grace before I had it. I used to be continually examining myself, and studying and contriving for likely ways and means, how I should live holily, with far greater diligence and earnestness, than ever I pursued any thing in life; but yet with too great a dependence on my own strength; which afterwards proved a great damage to me. My experience had not then taught me, as it has done since my extreme feebleness and impotence, every manner of way; and the bottomless depths of secret corruption and deceit there was in my heart. However, I went on with my eager pursuit. . . .

The heaven I desired was a heaven of holiness; to be with God, and to spend my eternity in divine love, and holy communion with Christ. My mind was very much taken up with contemplations on heaven, and the enjoyments there; and living there in perfect holiness, humility and love. And it used at that time to appear a great part of the happiness of heaven, that there the saints could express their love to Christ. It appeared to me a great clog and burden, that what I felt within, I could not express as I desired. The inward ardor of my soul, seemed to be hindered and pent up, and could not freely flame out as it would. I used often to think, how in heaven this principle should freely and fully vent and express itself. Heaven appeared exceedingly delightful, as a world of love; and that all happiness consisted in living in pure, humble, heavenly, divine love.

I remember the thoughts I used then to have of holiness; and said sometimes to myself, "I do certainly know that I love holiness, such as the gospel prescribes." It appeared to me, that there was nothing in it but what was ravishingly lovely; the highest beauty and amiableness—a *divine* beauty; far purer than any thing here upon earth; and that every thing else was like mire and defilement, in comparison of it.

Holiness, as I then wrote down some of my contemplations on it, appeared to me to be of a sweet, pleasant, charming, serene, calm nature; which brought an inexpressible purity, brightness, peacefulness and ravishment to the soul. In other words, that it

made the soul like a field or garden of God, with all manner of
pleasant flowers; all pleasant, delightful, and undisturbed; enjoying
a sweet calm, and the gently vivifying beams of the sun. The soul
of a true Christian, as I then wrote my meditations, appeared like
such a little white flower as we see in the spring of the year; low
and humble on the ground, opening its bosom to receive the pleasant beams of the sun's glory; rejoicing as it were in calm rapture;
diffusing around a sweet fragrancy; standing peacefully and lovingly, in the midst of other flowers round about; all in like manner
opening their bosoms, to drink in the light of the sun. There was
no part of creature holiness, that I had so great a sense of its loveliness, as humility, brokenness of heart and poverty of spirit; and
there was nothing that I so earnestly longed for. My heart panted
after this, to lie low before God, as in the dust; that I might be
nothing, and that God might be ALL, that I might become as a
little child. &

Character and Conduct
E. M. BOUNDS

Conduct is what we do;
    character is what we are.
Conduct is the outward life;
    character is the life unseen, hidden within,
    yet evidenced by that which is seen.
Conduct is external, seen from without;
    character is internal—operating within. . . .
Character is the state of the heart,
    conduct is its outward expression.
Character is the root of the tree,
    conduct, the fruit it bears. &

Joyfulness

IT'S AN ODD THING, but if you really experience something that gives you deep joy, you always want more. That which satisfies still leaves one dissatisfied. So if you see an exciting ball game, you can't wait to see a replay of the most exciting parts. Or if you attend a wonderful concert, you clap till your hands are sore to persuade the artist to give one more encore—and then you buy a CD to play on the way home!

C. S. Lewis developed this insight throughout his life, and was eventually convinced that this insatiable inner desire for joy was an argument for the existence of God and heaven. As he reasoned, every innate desire within us suggests a means of satisfying that desire. But the desire for joy cannot be totally and perfectly satisfied by earthly, temporal things; therefore the answer to joy must be found beyond earth, time, and creation—that is, in an eternal One. Ultimate joy will be found in heaven with the Lord.

Does this mean that we cannot expect joy on earth? Not at all! It means that every experience of joy "in the now" is merely a foretaste of real joy "in the then," but we can and should enjoy it nevertheless. God has filled the world with reasons for joy. Wordsworth's heart "leaped up" when he beheld a rainbow in the sky and "danced with the daffodils" as he recollected a scene by the lake.

Jesus told His disciples that as they lived obediently in fellowship with Him, they could count on His continuing love. They would experience His joy, and as a result their joy would be complete. This was clearly the case after Christ had returned to the Father, and these disciples embarked on their ministries. They met together and found great joy in worship. They found intense delight in seeing lives changed through the Gospel. In fact, they shared the joy of heaven, where we are told the angels rejoice over sinners coming to repentance. Not that everything was easy for them—far from it—but they exhibited a remarkable resilience. Paul summarized their prevailing attitude when he said, "We also rejoice in our sufferings, because we know that suffering produces perseverance; perseverance, character; and character, hope."

But we must ask, "How is it possible to know joy even in the midst of trying circumstances?" The answer lies in the fact that joy is the "fruit of the Spirit" and comes from knowing what the Lord's will is and doing it. There truly is "joy in serving Jesus."

Nest Building

FRANCES HODGSON BURNETT

Mary Lennox, heroine of The Secret Garden, *was not a very happy or pleasant child at the start of the tale. But in her secret garden she discovered the joys of God's wonderful creation.*

On that very first morning when the sky was blue again Mary wakened very early. The sun was pouring in slanting rays through the blinds and there was something so joyous in the sight of it that she jumped out of bed and ran to the window. She drew up the blinds and opened the window itself and a great waft of fresh, scented air blew in upon her. The moor was blue and the whole world looked as if something Magic had happened to it. There were tender little fluting sounds here and there and everywhere, as if scores of birds were beginning to tune up for a concert. Mary put her hand out of the window and held it in the sun.

"It's warm—warm!" she said. "It will make the green points push up and up and up, and it will make the bulbs and roots work and struggle with all their might under the earth."

She knelt down and leaned out of the window as far as she could, breathing big breaths and sniffing the air until she laughed because she remembered what Dickon's mother had said about the end of his nose quivering like a rabbit's.

"It must be very early," she said. "The little clouds are all pink and I've never seen the sky look like this. No one is up. I don't even hear the stable boys."

A sudden thought made her scramble to her feet.

"I can't wait! I am going to see the garden!"

. . . She put on her clothes in five minutes. She knew a small side door which she could unbolt herself and she flew downstairs in her stocking feet and put on her shoes in the hall. She unchained and unbolted and unlocked and when the door was open she sprang across the step with one bound, and there she was standing on the grass, which seemed to have turned green, and with the sun pouring down on her and warm sweet wafts about her and the fluting and twittering and singing coming from every bush and tree. She clasped her hands for pure joy and looked up in the sky and it was so blue and pink and pearly and white and flooded with springtime light that she felt as if she must flute and sing aloud herself and knew that thrushes and robins and skylarks could not possibly help it. She ran around the shrubs and paths toward the secret garden.

"It is all different already," she said. "The grass is greener and things are sticking up everywhere and things are uncurling and green buds of leaves are showing. This afternoon I am sure Dickon will come."

The long warm rain had done strange things to the herbaceous beds which bordered the walk by the lower wall. There were things sprouting and pushing out from the roots of clumps of plants and there were actually here and there glimpses of royal purple and yellow unfurling among the stems of crocuses. Six months before, Mistress Mary would not have seen how the world was waking up, but now she missed nothing.

When she had reached the place where the door hid itself under the ivy, she was startled by a curious loud sound. It was the caw-caw of a crow and it came from the top of the wall, and when she looked up, there sat a big glossy-plumaged blue-black bird, looking down at her very wisely indeed. She had never seen a crow so close before and he made her a little nervous, but the next moment he spread his wings and flapped away across the garden. She hoped he was not going to stay inside and she pushed the door open wondering if he would. When she got fairly into the garden she saw that he probably did intend to stay because he had alighted on a dwarf apple-tree and under the apple-tree was lying a little reddish animal with a busy tail, and both of them were watching the stooping body and rust-red head of Dickon, who was kneeling on the grass working hard.

Mary flew across the grass to him.

"Oh, Dickon! Dickon!" she cried out. "How could you get here so early! How could you! The sun has only just got up!"

He got up himself, laughing and glowing, and tousled; his eyes like a bit of the sky.

"Eh!" he said. "I was up long before him. How could I have stayed abed! Th' world's all fair begun again this mornin', it has. An' it's workin' an' hummin' an' scratchin' an' pipin' an' nest-buildin' an' breathin' out scents, till you've got to be out on it 'stead o' lyin' on your back. When th' sun did jump up, th' moor went mad for joy, an' I was in the midst of th' heather, an' I run like mad myself, shoutin' an' singin'. An' I come straight here. I couldn't have stayed away. Why, th' garden was lyin' here waitin'!"

Mary put her hands on her chest, panting, as if she had been running herself.

"Oh, Dickon! Dickon!" she said. "I'm so happy I can scarcely breathe!"

Seeing him talking to a stranger, the little bush-tailed animal rose from its place under the tree and came to him, and the rook, cawing once, flew down from its branch and settled quietly on his shoulder.

"This is th' little fox cub," he said, rubbing the little reddish animal's head. "It's named Captain. An' this here's Soot. Soot he flew across th' moor with me an' Captain he run same as if th' hounds had been after him. They both felt same as I did."

Neither of the creatures looked as if he were the least afraid of Mary. When Dickon began to walk about, Soot stayed on his shoulder and Captain trotted quietly close to his side.

"See here!" said Dickon. "See how these has pushed up, an' these an' these! An' eh! Look at these here!"

He threw himself upon his knees and Mary went down beside

241

him. They had come upon a whole clump of crocuses burst into purple and orange and gold. Mary bent her face down and kissed and kissed them.

"You never kiss a person in that way," she said when she lifted her head. "Flowers are so different."

He looked puzzled but smiled.

"Eh!" he said, "I've kissed mother many a time that way when I come in from th' moor after a day's roamin' an' she stood there at th' door in th' sun, lookin' so glad an' comfortable."

They ran from one part of the garden to another and found so many wonders that they were obliged to remind themselves that they must whisper or speak low. He showed her swelling leaf buds on rose branches which had seemed dead. He showed her ten thousand new green points pushing through the mould. They put their eager young noses close to the earth and sniffed its warmed springtime breathing; they dug and pulled and laughed low with rapture until Mistress Mary's hair was as tumbled as Dickon's and her cheeks were almost as poppy red as his.

There was every joy on earth in the secret garden that morning. . . . ❧

Jabberwocky
Lewis Carroll

From Through the Looking-Glass, *just a little bit of fun! After all, what good is joy if you can't have fun?*

'Twas brillig, and the slithy toves
    Did gyre and gimble in the wabe:
All mimsy were the borogoves,
    And the mome raths outgrabe.

"Beware the Jabberwock, my son!
   The jaws that bite, the claws that catch!
Beware the Jubjub bird, and shun
   The frumious Bandersnatch!"

He took his vorpal sword in hand:
   Long time the manxome foe he sought—
So rested he by the Tumtum tree,
   And stood awhile in thought.

And, as in uffish thought he stood,
   The Jabberwock, with eyes of flame,
Came whiffling through the tulgey wood,
   And burbled as it came!

One, two! One, two! And through and through
   The vorpal blade went snicker-snack!
He left it dead, and with its head
   He went galumphing back.

"And hast thou slain the Jabberwock?
   Come to my arms, my beamish boy!
O frabjous day! Callooh! Callay!"
   He chortled in his joy.

'Twas brillig, and the slithy toves
   Did gyre and gimble in the wabe:
All mimsy were the borogoves,
   And the mome raths outgrabe.

   "You seem very clever at explaining words, Sir," said Alice.
"Would you kindly tell me the meaning of the poem *Jabberwocky?*"
   "Let's hear it," said Humpty Dumpty. "I can explain all the

243

poems that ever were invented—and a good many that haven't been invented just yet."

This sounded very hopeful, so Alice repeated the first verse:

" 'Twas brillig, and the slithy toves
Did gyre and gimble in the wabe;
All mimsy were the borogoves,
And the mome raths outgrabe."

"That's enough to begin with," Humpty Dumpty interrupted: "there are plenty of hard words there. 'Brillig' means four o'clock in the afternoon—that time when you begin *broiling* things for dinner."

"That'll do very well," said Alice: "and slithy?"

"Well, 'slithy' means 'lithe and slimy.' 'Lithe' is the same as 'active.' You see it's like a portmanteau—there are two meanings packed into one word."

"I see it now," Alice remarked thoughtfully: "and what are 'toves'?"

"Well, 'toves' are something like badgers—they're something like lizards—and they're something like corkscrews."

"They must be very curious creatures."

"They are that," said Humpty Dumpty: "also they make their nests under sundials—also they live on cheese."

"And what's to 'gyre' and to 'gimble'?"

"To 'gyre' is to go round and round like a gyroscope. To 'gimble' is to make holes like a gimlet."

"And the 'wabe' is the grassy plot round a sundial, I suppose?" said Alice, surprised at her own ingenuity.

"Of course it is. It's called a 'wabe,' you know, because it goes a long way before it, and a long way behind it—"

"And a long way beyond it on each side," Alice added.

"Exactly so. Well then, 'mimsy' is 'flimsy and miserable' (there's another portmanteau for you). And a 'borogove' is a thin shabby-looking bird with its feathers sticking out all round—something like a live mop."

"And then 'mome raths'?" said Alice. "If I'm not giving you too much trouble."

"Well, a 'rath' is sort of a green pig: but 'mome' I'm not certain about. I think it's short for 'from home'—meaning that they'd lost their way, you know."

"And what does 'outgrabe' mean?"

"Well, 'outgribing' is something between bellowing and whistling, with a kind of sneeze in the middle: however, you'll hear it done, maybe—down in the wood yonder—and when you've once heard it you'll be quite content. Who's been repeating all that hard stuff to you?"

"I read it in a book," said Alice. ♞

A Joyous Transformation
CHARLES DICKENS

Old Ebeneezer Scrooge of A Christmas Carol *was miserable and made everyone around him miserable—until he saw himself as he really was. His life was suddenly changed and his joy contagious.*

Yes! And the bedpost was his own. The bed was his own, the room was his own. Best and happiest of all, the Time before him was his own, to make amends in!

"I will live in the Past, the Present, and the Future!" Scrooge repeated, as he scrambled out of bed. "The Spirits of all Three shall strive within me. O Jacob Marley! Heaven and the Christmastime be praised for this! I say it on my knees, old Jacob, on my knees!"

He was so fluttered and so glowing with his good intentions, that his broken voice would scarcely answer to his call. He had been sobbing violently in his conflict with the Spirit, and his face was wet with tears.

"They are not torn down," cried Scrooge, folding one of his

bed-curtains in his arms—"they are not torn down, rings and all. They are here—I am here—the shadows of the things that would have been may be dispelled. They will be. I know they will!"

His hands were busy with his garments all this time; turning them inside out, putting them on upside down, tearing them, mislaying them, making them parties to every kind of extravagance.

"I don't know what to do!" cried Scrooge, laughing and crying in the same breath, and making a perfect Laocoön of himself with his stockings. "I am as light as a feather, I am as happy as an angel, I am as merry as a schoolboy. I am as giddy as a drunken man. A merry Christmas to everybody! A happy New Year to all the world! Hallo here! Whoop! Hallo!"

He had frisked into the sitting-room, and was now standing there, perfectly winded.

"There's the saucepan that the gruel was in!" cried Scrooge, starting off again, and going round the fireplace. "There's the door by which the Ghost of Jacob Marley entered! There's the corner where the Ghost of Christmas Present sat! There's the window where I saw the wandering Spirits! It's all right, it's all true, it all happened. Ha, ha, ha!"

Really, for a man who had been out of practice for so many years, it was a splendid laugh, a most illustrious laugh. The father of a long, long line of brilliant laughs!

"I don't know what day of the month it is," said Scrooge. "I don't know how long I have been among the Spirits. I don't know anything. I'm quite a baby. Never mind. I don't care. I'd rather be a baby. Hallo! Whoop! Hallo here!"

He was checked in his transports by the churches ringing out the lustiest peals he had ever heard. Clash, clash, hammer; ding, dong, bell! Bell, dong, ding; hammer, clang, clash! Oh, glorious, glorious!

Running to the window, he opened it, and put out his head. No fog, no mist; clear, bright, jovial, stirring, cold; cold, piping for the blood to dance to; golden sunlight; heavenly sky; sweet fresh air; merry bells. Oh, glorious! Glorious!

"What's today?" cried Scrooge, calling downward to a boy in Sunday clothes, who perhaps had loitered in to look about him.

"Eh?" returned the boy, with all his might of wonder.

"What's today, my fine fellow?" said Scrooge.

"Today!" replied the boy. "Why, *Christmas Day.*"

"It's Christmas Day!" said Scrooge to himself. "I haven't missed it. The Spirits have done it all in one night. They can do anything they like. Of course they can. Of course they can. Hallo, my fine fellow!"

"Hallo!" returned the boy.

"Do you know the poulterer's, in the next street but one, at the corner?" Scrooge inquired.

"I should hope I did," replied the lad.

"An intelligent boy!" said Scrooge. "A remarkable boy! Do you know whether they've sold the prize Turkey that was hanging up there?—Not the little prize Turkey, the big one?"

"What, the one as big as me?" returned the boy.

"What a delightful boy!" said Scrooge. "It's a pleasure to talk to him. Yes, my buck!"

"It's hanging there now," replied the boy.

"Is it?" said Scrooge. "Go and buy it."

"Walk-ER" exclaimed the boy.

"No, no," said Scrooge. "I am in earnest. Go and buy it, and tell 'em to bring it here, that I may give them the directions where to take it. Come back with the man, and I'll give you a shilling. Come back with him in less than five minutes, and I'll give you half a crown!"

The boy was off like a shot. He must have had a steady hand at a trigger who could have got a shot off half so fast.

"I'll send it to Bob Cratchit's," whispered Scrooge, rubbing his hands, and splitting with a laugh. "He sha'n't know who sends it.

It's twice the size of Tiny Tim. Joe Miller never made such a joke as sending it to Bob's will be!"

The hand in which he wrote the address was not a steady one, but write it he did, somehow, and went downstairs to open the street door, ready for the coming of the poulterer's man. As he stood there, waiting his arrival, the knocker caught his eyes.

"I shall love it as long as I live!" cried Scrooge, patting it with his hand. "I scarcely ever looked at it before. What an honest expression it has in its face! It's a wonderful knocker!—Here's the Turkey. Hallo! Whoop! How are you? Merry Christmas!"

It *was* a Turkey! He never could have stood upon his legs, that bird. He would have snapped 'em short off in a minute, like sticks of sealing-wax.

"Why, it's impossible to carry that to Camden Town," said Scrooge. "You must have a cab."

The chuckle with which he said this, and the chuckle with which he paid for the Turkey, and the chuckle with which he paid for the cab, and the chuckle with which he recompensed the boy, were only to be exceeded by the chuckle with which he sat down breathless in his chair again, and chuckled till he cried.

Shaving was not an easy task, for his hand continued to shake very much and shaving requires attention, even when you don't dance while you are at it. But if he had cut the end of his nose off, he would have put a piece of sticking-plaster over it, and been quite satisfied.

He dressed himself "all in his best," and at last got out into the streets. The people were by this time pouring forth, as he had seen them with the Ghost of Christmas Present; and walking with his hands behind him, Scrooge regarded every one with a delighted smile. He looked so irresistibly pleasant, in a word, that three or four good-humored fellows said, "Good morning, sir! A merry Christmas to you!" And Scrooge said often afterward, that of all the blithe sounds he had ever heard, those were the blithest in his ears.

He had not gone far, when, coming on toward him he beheld the portly gentleman who had walked into his counting-house the day before, and said, "Scrooge and Marley's, I believe?" It sent a pang across his heart to think how this old gentleman would look upon him when they met, but he knew what path lay straight before him, and he took it.

"My dear sir," said Scrooge, quickening his pace, and taking the old gentleman by both his hands, "How do you do? I hope you succeeded yesterday. It was very kind of you. A merry Christmas to you, sir!"

"Mr. Scrooge?"

"Yes," said Scrooge. "That is my name, and I fear it may not be pleasant to you. Allow me to ask your pardon. And will you have the goodness—" Here Scrooge whispered in his ear.

"Lord bless me!" cried the gentleman, as if his breath were taken away. "My dear Mr. Scrooge, are you serious?"

"If you please," said Scrooge. "Not a farthing less. A great many back payments are included in it, I assure you. Will you do me that favor?"

"My dear sir," said the other, shaking hands with him, "I don't know what to say to such munifi—"

"Don't say anything, please," retorted Scrooge. "Come and see me. Will you come and see me?"

"I will!" cried the old gentleman. And it was clear he meant to do it.

"Thankee," said Scrooge. "I am much obliged to you. I thank you fifty times. Bless you!"

He went to church, and walked about the streets, and watched the people hurrying to and fro, and patted the children on the head, and questioned beggars, and looked down into the kitchens of houses, and up to the windows, and found that everything could yield him pleasure. He had never dreamed that any walk—that anything—could give him so much happiness. 🍂

Joyful, Joyful, We Adore Thee
HENRY VAN DYKE

Discovering the Lord as the "wellspring of the joy of living" is one of life's greatest gifts.

Joyful, joyful, we adore thee,
    God of glory, Lord of love;
Hearts unfold like flowers before thee,
    Opening to the sun above.
Melt the clouds of sin and sadness,
    Drive the dark of doubt away;
Giver of immortal gladness,
    Fill us with the light of day.

All thy works with joy surround thee,
    Earth and heaven reflect thy rays,
Stars and angels sing around thee,
    Center of unbroken praise.
Field and forest, vale and mountain,
    Flowery meadow, flashing sea,
Chanting bird and flowing fountain,
    Call us to rejoice in thee.

Thou art giving and forgiving,
    Ever blessing, ever blest,
Wellspring of the joy of living,
    Ocean depth of happy rest!
Thou our Father, Christ our Brother,
    All who live in love are thine;
Teach us how to love each other,
    Lift us to the Joy divine. ❧

Psalm of Thanks
I CHRONICLES 16:23-34, NIV

King David's joy knew no limits when he organized the return of the Ark of the Covenant to Jerusalem. He wrote this psalm and encouraged the people to sing it joyfully!

Sing to the Lord, all the earth;
>   proclaim his salvation day after day.
Declare his glory among the nations,
>   his marvelous deeds among all peoples.
For great is the Lord and most worthy of praise;
>   he is to be feared above all gods.
For all the gods of the nations are idols,
>   but the Lord made the heavens.
Splendor and majesty are before him;
>   strength and joy in his dwelling place.
Ascribe to the Lord, O families of nations,
>   ascribe to the Lord glory and strength,
>   ascribe to the Lord the glory due his name.
Bring an offering and come before him;
>   worship the Lord in the splendor of his holiness.
Tremble before him, all the earth!
>   The world is firmly established; it cannot be moved.
Let the heavens rejoice, let the earth be glad;
>   let them say among the nations, "The Lord reigns!"
Let the sea resound, and all that is in it;
>   let the fields be jubilant, and everything in them!
Then the trees of the forest will sing,
>   they will sing for joy before the Lord,
>   for he comes to judge the earth.
Give thanks to the Lord, for he is good;
>   his love endures forever.

Living by God's Surprises
HAROLD L. MYRA

The apostle Paul said, surprisingly, "In all our troubles my joy knows no bounds."
Helmut Thielicke, the great German pastor and theologian, testified to the same quality
of joy in the horrors of World War II.

When Thielicke said "We live by God's surprises," he had personally suffered under the Nazis. As a pastor he wrote to young soldiers about to die; he comforted mothers and fathers and children after the bombs killed their loved ones. He preached magnificent sermons week after week as bombs blew apart his church and the lives and dreams of his parishioners. He spoke of God not only looking in love at His suffering people, weeping with them as they were surrounded by flames, but of God's hand reaching into the flames to help them, His own hand scorched by the fires.

From the depths of suffering and the wanton destruction during the Nazi regime, Thielicke held out a powerful Christian hope. To Germans disillusioned by the easily manipulated faith of their fathers, he quoted Peter Wust: "The great things happen to those who pray. But we learn to pray best in suffering."

Prayer, suffering, joy, and the surprises of God . . . . they are all tightly enmeshed. But most shrink from the above statement, seeing suffering as the surest killer of both joy and "great things."

When we are rightly related to God, life is full of joyful uncertainty and expectancy . . . we do not know what God is going to do next; He packs our lives with surprises all the time.

What a strange idea: "joyful uncertainty." Most of us view uncertainty as cause for anxiety, not joy. Yet this call to expectancy rings true. The idea of standing on tiptoe to see what God is going to do next, can transform our way of seeing. Prayers go maddeningly unanswered, as well as marvelously fulfilled. Prayer becomes the lens through which we begin to see from God's perspective. 🍂

252

I Wandered Lonely as a Cloud

WILLIAM WORDSWORTH

Poet William Wordsworth (1770-1850) found that dancing daffodils can work joyful wonders for the most pensive mood.

I wandered lonely as a cloud
    That floats on high o'er vales and hills,
When all at once I saw a crowd,
    A host, of golden daffodils;
Beside the lake, beneath the trees,
    Fluttering and dancing in the breeze.

Continuous as the stars that shine
    And twinkle on the milky way,
They stretched in never-ending line
    Along the margin of a bay:
Ten thousand saw I at a glance,
    Tossing their heads in sprightly dance.

The waves beside them danced; but they
    Outdid the sparkling waves in glee;
A poet could not but be gay,
    In such a jocund company;
I gazed—and gazed—but little thought
    What wealth the show to me had brought:

For oft, when on my couch I lie
    In vacant or in pensive mood,
They flash upon that inward eye
    Which is the bliss of solitude;
And then my heart with pleasure fills,
    And dances with the daffodils. ❧

The Secret of Joy
BILLY GRAHAM

The Bible says, "A cheerful heart is good medicine, but a crushed spirit dries up the bones" (Proverbs 17:22).

If the heart has been attuned to God through faith in Christ, then its overflow will be joyous optimism and good cheer.

Out West an old sheepherder had a violin, but it was out of tune. He had no way of tuning it, so in desperation he wrote to one of the radio stations and asked them at a certain hour on a certain day to strike the tone "A." The officials of the station decided they would accommodate the old fellow, and on that particular day the true tone of the "A" was broadcast. His fiddle was thus tuned, and once more his cabin echoed with joyful music.

We have to be tuned to God. We will never be free from discouragement and despondency until we know and walk with the very fountainhead of joy.

Christ Himself is the Christian's secret of joy: "Though you have not seen Him, you love Him; and even though you do not see Him now, you believe in Him and are filled with an inexpressible and glorious joy" (I Peter 1:8). 🎵

Do not grieve, for the joy of the Lord is your strength.
NEHEMIAH 8:10

Obedience

ONE DAY JESUS MET a Roman centurion whose very special servant was seriously ill. Though he was an important man, the centurion thought he was not worthy to meet Jesus personally—but he did want His help. He sent some of the Jewish elders with a message: if Jesus would just say the word, he had no doubt that his servant would recover. He said, "For I myself am a man under authority with soldiers under me. I tell this one, 'Go' and he goes; and that one 'Come' and he comes. I say to my servant 'Do this' and he does it."

The centurion understood authority both as one who administered it and as one who responded to it. He had no difficulty understanding the authority of Jesus; he believed that if Jesus told the illness to "Go," it would go! Jesus was greatly impressed. He said He had not seen such great faith in all of Israel—and this man was a Roman!

Obedience starts with the recognition of legitimate authority. God is the ultimate authority, but He has delegated some authority to humans. Parents, for example, have authority over children, and governments are ordained by God to have authority in the affairs of state. Unfortunately, children don't always want to do what their parents say, and adults don't always obey the laws that their governments enact. Granted, this disobedience may be warranted, if the parents or the government direct people to do what God has forbidden or deny them the freedom to do what He has instructed them to do. But much of the time disobedience is related to an attitude of resistance or rebellion.

There is nothing new about this. The sad story of resistance to God's authority started with the angel who rebelled against God and brought his rebellious attitude down to Eden, persuading our forebears to disobey.

Fortunately Jesus was obedient to the Father's will, came down to earth, and died and rose again that the consequences of disobedience—sin—might be forgiven. But those who are forgiven their rebellion are expected to become obedient. Peter said, "As obedient children, do not conform to the evil desires you had when you lived in ignorance." And Jesus made it clear, after He had given His disciples an example of appropriate behavior, that knowing what to do is not enough. He said, "Now that you know these things, you will be blessed if you do them."

Being obedient is not always easy, but if children are taught correctly and given the proper models of obedience, they can learn respect for authority and responsiveness to instructions from an early age. This will save everyone a lot of pain in later life. 🐾

Silly to Fuss
PAUL HAMLYN

Sometimes a "should do" becomes a "must do."

Why must I wash behind my ears?
    That's what I want to know.
Why can't I just wash hands and knees?
    Places that really show.

Who's going to *look* behind my ears?
    It seems so odd to fuss.
Besides, I think it's waste of soap,
    Oh well, all right! If I *must!*

The Tale of Peter Rabbit
BEATRIX POTTER

Beatrix Potter's little friend Peter Rabbit didn't like doing what he was told. As the old Dutchman said, "He got too late, smart."

Once upon a time there were four little Rabbits, and their names were Flopsy, Mopsy, Cotton-tail, and Peter. They lived with their Mother in a sandbank, underneath the root of a very big fir-tree.

"Now, my dears," said old Mrs. Rabbit one morning, "you may go into the fields or down the lane, but don't go into Mr. McGregor's garden: your Father had an accident there; he was put in a pie by Mrs. McGregor. Now run along, and don't get into mischief; I am going out."

Then old Mrs. Rabbit took a basket and her umbrella, and went through the wood to the baker's. She bought a loaf of brown bread and five currant buns.

Flopsy, Mopsy, and Cotton-tail, who were good little bunnies, went down the lane to gather blackberries; but Peter who was very naughty, ran straight away to Mr. McGregor's garden, and squeezed under the gate!

First he ate some lettuces and some French beans; and then he ate some radishes; and then, feeling rather sick he went to look for some parsley.

But round the end of a cucumber frame, whom should he meet but Mr. McGregor!

Mr. McGregor was on his hands and knees planting out young cabbages, but he jumped up and ran after Peter, waving a rake and calling out, "Stop thief!"

Peter was most dreadfully frightened; he rushed all over the garden, for he had forgotten the way back to the gate.

He lost one of his shoes among the cabbages, and the other shoe amongst the potatoes.

After losing them, he ran on four legs and went faster, so that I think he might have got away altogether if he had not unfortunately run into a gooseberry net, and got caught by the large buttons on his jacket. . . .

Peter gave himself up for lost, and shed big tears; but his sobs were overhead by some friendly sparrows, who flew to him in great excitement, and implored him to exert himself.

Mr. McGregor came up with a sieve, which he intended to pop upon the top of Peter; but Peter wriggled out just in time, leaving his jacket behind him. And rushed into the toolshed, and jumped into a can. It would have been a beautiful thing to hide in, if it had not had so much water in it.

Mr. McGregor was quite sure that Peter was somewhere in the toolshed, perhaps hidden underneath a flower-pot. He began to turn them over carefully, looking under each.

Presently Peter sneezed—"Kertyschoo!" Mr. McGregor was after him in no time, and tried to put his foot upon Peter, who jumped out of the window, upsetting three plants. The window was too small for Mr. McGregor and he was tired of running after Peter. He went back to his work.

Peter sat down to rest; he was out of breath and trembling with fright, and he had not the least idea which way to go. Also he was very damp with sitting in that can.

After a time he began to wander about, going lippity—lippity—not very fast, and looking all around.

He found a door in a wall; but it was locked, and there was no room for a fat little rabbit to squeeze underneath.

An old mouse was running in and out over the stone door-step, carrying peas and beans to her family in the wood. Peter asked her the way to the gate, but she had such a large pea in her mouth that she could not answer. She only shook her head at him. Peter began to cry.

Then he tried to find his way straight across the garden, but he became more and more puzzled. Presently, he came to a pond where Mr. McGregor filled his water-cans. A white cat was staring at some goldfish; she sat very, very still, but now and then the tip of her tail twitched as if it were alive. Peter thought it best to go away without speaking to her; he had heard about cats from his cousin, little Benjamin Bunny.

He went back towards the toolshed, but suddenly, quite close to him, he heard the noise of a hoe—scr-r-ritch, scratch, scratch, scritch. Peter scuttered underneath the bushes. But presently, as nothing happened, he came out, and climbed upon a wheel-barrow, and peeped over. The first thing he saw was Mr. McGregor hoeing onions. His back was turned toward Peter, and beyond him was the gate!

Peter got down very quietly off the wheel-barrow, and started running as fast as he could go, along a straight walk behind some black-currant bushes.

Mr. McGregor caught sight of him at the corner, but Peter did not care. He slipped underneath the gate, and was safe at last in the wood outside the garden.

Mr. McGregor hung up the little jacket and the shoes for a scare-crow to frighten the blackbirds.

Peter never stopped running or looked behind him till he got home to the big fir-tree.

He was so tired that he flopped down upon the nice soft sand on the floor of the rabbit hole, and shut his eyes. His mother was busy cooking; she wondered what he had done with his clothes. It was the second little jacket and pair of shoes that Peter had lost in a fortnight!

I am sorry to say that Peter was not very well during the evening. His mother put him to bed, and made some camomile tea; and she gave a dose of it to Peter!

"One tablespoonful to be taken at bedtime."

But Flopsy, Mopsy, and Cotton-tail had bread and milk and blackberries for supper. ❧

A Pillar of Pepper
JOHN KNAPP II

There are two good reasons for being obedient. One, it's smart. Two, it's right! See Genesis 19:15-26 and Numbers 12.

Since Mrs. Lot sinned
    And was clearly at fault,
God let her change into
    A pillar of salt.

But when Miriam sinned
    She became a poor leper
Instead of something like
    A pillar of pepper.

Since sinning may change us
    In ways you can see,
I plan to be good
    So you'll recognize me.

But recognize also,
    I plan to obey
Because Jesus, my Savior,
    Wants it that way. 🍃

Adam and Eve Disobey God

Try to imagine how different the world would have been if Adam and Eve had been obedient. Here's a retelling of their story from chapters 2 and 3 of Genesis.

The man God created was called Adam. And God brought all the animals and birds to the man and let him name them.

The woman God created was Eve. God knew that it was not good for people to be alone. So it was His plan from this time on for a man and a woman to leave the homes of their parents and get married, love each other, and have children.

Adam and Eve lived in Eden, the most beautiful garden in all the world. God made it for them. He gave them only one rule. They were not to eat the fruit from one certain tree in the garden.

One day as Eve was walking alone in the garden, she came to this special tree. In it was a snake. "Has God told you that you may not eat the fruit from this tree?" the snake asked.

"We may eat from every tree but this one," Eve said. "If we eat from this one, God said we would die."

"You won't die," the snake said. "If you eat the fruit, you will be wise."

Eve looked at the fruit. It looked so good. She tasted it. "I must give some to Adam," she said. She did, and Adam ate it, too.

Suddenly Adam and Eve were afraid. They ran and hid.

But God called them. "Have you eaten this fruit? I told you not to eat it," God said.

"Eve gave it to me," Adam said, trying to blame her.

"The snake told me to eat it," Eve said, trying to blame someone else.

Then God had to do something He did not want to do. He had to punish them for disobeying Him.

"You must leave the garden I made for you," God said. "You must go out and work hard for your food."

So Adam and Eve left the garden called Eden. They looked back. In the path was a sword of fire! Guards stood by it. Adam and Eve could never go back!

God was sorry for them. "I love you," God said. "If you love and obey Me, I will help you." But God would not make them obey. Adam and Eve had to choose for themselves whether they would obey or disobey God. 🐾

Raising Responsible Children
SUSANNA WESLEY

Obedience, respect for authority, doing what we are told—none of these things comes easily. Happy the person who learns them in early years. Susanna Wesley's accomplished children were unstinting in their appreciation for their remarkable mother, whose wisdom is shared in this excerpt.

As self-will is the root of all sin and misery, so whatever cherishes this in children ensures their after wretchedness and irreligion: whatever checks and mortifies it, promotes their future happiness and piety. This is still more evident if we farther consider that religion is nothing else than doing the will of God and not our own; that the one grand impediment to our temporal and eternal happiness being this self-will, no indulgence of it can be trivial, no denial unprofitable. Heaven or hell depends on this alone, so that the parent who studies to subdue it in his child works together with God in the renewing and saving a soul. The parent who indulges it does the Devil's work; makes religion impracticable, salvation unattainable, and does all that in him lies to damn his child body and soul for ever.

Our children were taught as soon as they could speak the Lord's prayer, which they were made to say at rising and bedtime constantly, to which, as they grew bigger, were added a short prayer for their parents, and some collects, a short catechism, and some portion of Scripture as their memories could bear. They were very early made to distinguish the Sabbath from other days, before they could well speak or go. They were as soon taught to be still at family prayers, and to ask a blessing immediately after, which they used to do by signs, before they could kneel or speak.

They were quickly made to understand they might have nothing they cried for, and instructed to speak handsomely for what they wanted. They were not suffered to ask even the lowest servant for aught without saying "Pray give me such a thing"; and the servant was chid if she ever let them omit that word.

Taking God's name in vain, cursing and swearing, profanity, obscenity, rude ill-bred names, were never heard among them; nor were they ever permitted to call each other by their proper names without the addition of brother or sister.

There was no such thing as loud playing or talking allowed of, but everyone was kept close to business for the six hours of school. And it is almost incredible what may be taught a child in a quarter of a year by a vigorous application, if it have but a tolerable capacity and good health. Kezzy excepted, all could read better in that time than the most of women can do as long as they live. Rising out of their places, or going out of the room, was not permitted except for good cause; and running into the yard, garden, or street, without leave, was always esteemed a capital offence. ❧

Philip and the Ethiopian
FULTON OURSLER

Sometimes God tells us to do things that we don't understand at the time. But later we learn why, just as Philip did. This retelling of Acts 8 is from The Greatest Faith Ever Known.

Fond farewells echoed from the crowds of Samaritan converts as the two apostles and Philip the evangelist descended into the Vale of Shechem and started their long walk back to Jerusalem.

At the end of that journey Philip, for the first time in his career as a Christian, had a supernatural experience. An angel spoke to him and told him what to do.

Now Philip was well schooled in the history of visitations of the past: the celestial visitors who came without wings and broke bread, or wrestled, or beckoned, and who gave divine instructions from the days of Abraham, Isaac, and Jacob down to the Annunciation when Mary learned that she was to become the mother of Christ. He knew, too, of the recent delivery of the twelve apostles from prison.

But Philip the evangelist had never expected that any such thing would happen to him, or that the voice of an angel would be a prelude to a special miracle.

Dusk had spread a veil of deepening lavender and gold over the tawny walls and gates and the fortified towers of Jerusalem when Philip heard a voice that could belong only to an angel:

"Philip, arise!"

The young missionary had been lying on his folded blanket ready for a night's sleep. He sprang to his feet, obedient and alert.

"Arise and go toward the south, into the way that goes down from Jerusalem unto Gaza, which is desert."

With the same unquestioning agreeableness of the patriarch Abraham, Philip instantly did as he was told. He was weary from the journey to Samaria and the excitements of the visit there. He had hoped to remain in Jerusalem. But in the gathering darkness, with no sleep and with very little preparation, he explained about the vision to Peter, picked up his blanket, and started off briskly, walking southward.

Why should he go to Gaza? That town, ancient even before the long-ago days of Joshua, was the southernmost of the five principal cities of the Philistines. In Gaza Samson had met Delilah and had his head shaved, and there too had brought the Temple crashing down upon his Philistine captors and himself. But now the region of that caravan city was desert.

Why should Philip go there? He walked for nearly two days, southwest on the road to Gaza, before he understood.

At a resting place near a wayside inn he saw a chariot drawn up in the shade. Two horses released from the shafts were tethered to a palm tree, and there, lurched forward in the gilded and ornamented vehicle, sat a dark-skinned man arrayed in costly garments of colored brocade. In his hand he held an open scroll, on which Philip could make out the shape of Hebrew characters.

Another traveler, leaving the inn refreshed, noticed Philip's interest in the dusky wayfarer.

"He's quite a figure," the newcomer explained. "The landlord was just telling me all about him. He is an Ethiopian!"

Philip nodded agreeably; obviously the studious man in the golden chariot hailed from the land we call Nubia, whose extreme northern boundary was then near the first cataract of the Nile. But the merchant who had just dined, and well, was eager to tell Philip more about him.

"This one is a eunuch who says he is not a eunuch."

Philip stared blankly, as the chatterer continued:

"But yes! He has the title of being eunuch, and is a personage of great authority in Ethiopia. He has charge of all the treasure of the queen mother, Candace. And, while he has the title of eunuch, as well as the title of treasurer, he says that having the title of

265

eunuch in his country does not necessarily mean that he is actually a eunuch. Oh, no! For centuries, real eunuchs were employed in such positions of responsibility. But he says that the word eunuch in the official title has long since lost its meaning."

Philip did not pay close attention to the man's prattle. Some inner compulsion trained his interest solely on the Ethiopian.

With a polite nod of his head and a lift of the hand, the deacon sped his loquacious companion on his way. Then as he stood alone, once again Philip the evangelist heard the angelic voice:

"Go near and join yourself to this chariot."

Philip approached the dark stranger. He could hear him toilsomely, haltingly reading from his scroll. And he saw that the scroll was the Book of Isaiah.

Philip's shadow fell on the hands of the queen's treasurer.

"Do you understand what you are reading there?" asked Philip gently.

The eunuch held his place with a forefinger as he looked up, puzzled and humbled. With a great sigh he asked:

"How can I? How can I unless somebody explains it to me?"

And moving over, with a smile that showed great, clean pearly teeth, he made room for Philip to sit beside him.

"What part of Isaiah are you reading?" asked Philip, and the Ethiopian, voice soft and reverent, repeated these verses:

"He was led as a sheep to the slaughter; and like a lamb without voice before his shearer, so opened He not His mouth:

"In His humility His judgment was taken away. His generation who shall declare, for His life shall be taken from the earth?"

Was that beyond the Ethiopian's understanding? Yes, unless someone should guide him. Who is the Bible talking about in those two verses? Could Philip explain?

Most certainly he could and would. He had seen these prophecies, made by Isaiah nearly a thousand years before, come true so recently that Jerusalem was still talking about it. Jesus

Christ had most certainly been led as a lamb to the slaughter. Often He had referred to Himself as the Lamb of God that takes away the sin of the world. And Jesus had not opened His mouth to defend Himself before the razor-edged attack of Annas and Caiphas. He had been humiliated and judged, and His life was taken from the earth.

The Ethiopian listened attentively. Tired of sitting in the chariot, he rolled up the scroll and slid it up his sleeve, as he walked with Philip through a patch of woods. Not far off they could hear the ripple and splash of flowing water.

The Ethiopian financier asked penetrating questions. A most unusual fellow, Philip realized; a black man from the wild-tribe regions of Cush, who, putting aside all the idolatry which surrounded him, had learned Hebrew and was reading the Law and the Prophets.

Soon they returned, hitched the horses again to the chariot, and resumed the journey with Philip riding beside the eager stranger.

"Then," St. Luke reported, "Philip, opening his mouth and beginning at this Scripture, preached unto him Jesus."

They came to the tumbling, noisy little stream that rambled through the patch of woods on its way to the sea and the inquisitive eunuch asked another question:

"Philip, see—here is water. What hinders me to be baptized?"

"What hinders you, Ethiopian? Nothing. You want to be baptized. If you believe with all your heart, you may."

And the Ethiopian answered, as he looked into Philip's eyes: "I believe that Jesus Christ is the Son of God."

The horses were reined to a halt, and the great tether stones with holes in them were thrown to the ground, their chains fastened to the necks of the steeds. Now the two men forced their way through the brambles and down to the stream edged with green and bending tamarisks. There the money master of the Queen of Ethiopia was baptized and became a Christian. ❦

Dr. Johnson's Letter to Mr. Drummond

JAMES BOSWELL

Samuel Johnson (1709–1784) wrote the first dictionary of the English language, in which he defined more than 40,000 words. But he knew that the most important book was the Bible. His friend Boswell recorded the following incident in his Life Of Johnson.

He wrote this year a letter, not intended for publication, which has, perhaps, as strong marks of his sentiment and style, as any of his compositions. The original is in my possession. It is addressed to the late Mr. William Drummond, bookseller in Edinburgh, a gentleman of good family, but small estate, who took arms for the house of Stuart in 1745; and during his concealment in London till the act of general pardon came out obtained the acquaintance of Dr. Johnson, who justly esteemed him as a very worthy man. It seems, some of the members of the society in Scotland for propagating Christian knowledge, had opposed the scheme of translating the holy scriptures into the Erse or Gaelick language, from political considerations of the disadvantage of keeping up the distinction between the Highlanders and the other inhabitants of North-Britain. Dr. Johnson being informed of this, I suppose by Mr. Drummond, wrote with a generous indignation as follows:

TO MR. WILLIAM DRUMMOND

   Sir, I did not expect to hear that it could be, in an assembly convened for the propagation of Christian knowledge, a question whether any nation uninstructed in religion should receive instruction; or whether that instruction should be imparted to them by a translation of the holy books into their own language. If obedience to the will of God be necessary to happiness, and knowledge of his will be necessary to obedience, I know not how he that withholds this knowledge, or delays it, can be said to love his neigh-

bour as himself. He that voluntarily continues ignorance, is
guilty of all the crimes which ignorance produces; as to him
that should extinguish the tapers of a lighthouse, might
justly be imputed the calamities of shipwrecks. Christianity
is the highest perfection of humanity; and as no man is
good but as he wishes the good of others, no man can be
good in the highest degree who wishes not to others the
largest measures of the greatest good. To omit for a year, or
for a day, the most efficacious method of advancing
Christianity, in compliance with any purposes that termi-
nate on this side of the grave, is crime of which I know not
that the world has yet   had an example, except in the
practice of the planters of America, a race of mortals whom,
I suppose, no other man wishes to resemble. 🐚

The Sermon
HERMAN MELVILLE

In this scene from Moby Dick, *Father Mapple's congregation of seafaring folk listened
with rapt attention to his imaginative sermon retelling the story of Jonah's disobedience.*

Father Mapple rose, and in a mild voice of unassuming authority
ordered the scattered people to condense. "Star board gangway,
there! Side away to larboard—larboard gangway to starboard!
Midships! Midships!"

There was a low rumbling of heavy sea-boots among the
benches, and a still slighter shuffling of women's shoes, and all was
quiet again, and every eye on the preacher.

He paused a little; then kneeling in the pulpit's bows, folded
his large brown hands across his chest, uplifted his closed eyes, and
offered a prayer so deeply devout that he seemed kneeling and
praying at the bottom of the sea.

This ended, in prolonged solemn tones, like the continual

tolling of a bell in a ship that is foundering at sea in a fog—in such tones he commenced reading [a] hymn.

Nearly all joined in singing this hymn, which swelled high above the howling of the storm. A brief pause ensued; the preacher slowly turned over the leaves of the Bible, and at last, folding his hand down upon the proper page, said: "Beloved shipmates, clinch the last verse of the first chapter of Jonah—'And God had prepared a great fish to swallow up Jonah.'

"Shipmates, this book, containing only four chapters—four yarns—is one of the smallest strands in the mighty cable of the Scriptures. Yet what depths of the soul does Jonah's deep sea-line sound! What a pregnant lesson to us is this prophet! What a noble thing is that canticle in the fish's belly! How billow-like and boisterously grand! We feel the floods surging over us; we sound with him to the kelpy bottom of the waters; seaweed and all the slime of the sea is about us! But *what* is this lesson that the book of Jonah teaches? Shipmates, it is a two-stranded lesson; a lesson to us all as sinful men, and a lesson to me as a pilot of the living God. As sinful men, it is a lesson to us all, because it is a story of the sin, hardheartedness, suddenly awakened fears, the swift punishment, repentance, prayers, and finally the deliverance and joy of Jonah. As with all sinners among men, the sin of this son of Amittai was in his willful disobedience of the command of God—never mind now what that command was, or how conveyed—which he found a hard command. But all the things that God would have us do are hard for us to do—remember that—and hence, He oftener commands us than endeavours to persuade. And if we obey God, we must disobey ourselves; and it is in this disobeying ourselves, wherein the hardness of obeying God consists.

"With this sin of disobedience in him, Jonah still further flouts at God, by seeking to flee from Him. He thinks that a ship made by men will carry him into countries where God does not reign, but only the Captains of this earth. He skulks about the wharves of Joppa, seeks a ship that's bound for Tarshish. There lurks, perhaps, a hitherto unheeded meaning here. By all accounts Tarshish could have been no other city than the modern Cadiz. That's the opinion of learned men. And where is Cadiz, shipmates? Cadiz is in Spain; as far by water, from Joppa, as Jonah could possibly have sailed in those ancient days, when the Atlantic was an almost unknown sea. Because Joppa, the modern Jaffa, shipmates, is on the most easterly coast of the Mediterranean, the Syrian; and Tarshish or Cadiz more than two thousand miles to the westward from that, just outside the Straits of Gibraltar. See ye not then, shipmates, that Jonah sought to flee world-wide from God? Miserable man! Oh! Most contemptible and worthy of all scorn; with slouched hat and guilty eye, skulking from his God; prowling among the shipping like a vile burglar hastening to cross the seas. So disordered, self-condemning is his look, that had there been policemen in those days, Jonah, on the mere suspicion of something wrong, had been arrested ere he touched a deck. How plainly he's a fugitive! No baggage, not a hat-box, valise, or carpet-bag— no friends accompany him to the wharf with their adieux. At last, after much dodging search, he finds the Tarshish ship receiving the last items of her cargo; and as he steps on board to see its Captain in the cabin, all the sailors for the moment desist from hoisting in the goods, to mark the stranger's evil eye. Jonah sees this; but in vain he tries to look all ease and confidence; in vain essays his wretched smile. Strong intuitions of the man assure the mariners he can be no innocent. In their gamesome but still serious way, one whispers to the other—'Jack, he's robbed a widow;' or, 'Joe, do you mark him; he's a bigamist;' or, 'Harry lad, I guess he's the adulterer that broke jail in old Gomorrah, or belike, one of the missing murderers from Sodom.' Another runs to read the bill that's stuck against the spile upon the wharf to which the ship is moored, offering five hundred gold coins for the apprehension of a parricide, and containing a description of his person. He reads, and looks from

Jonah to the bill; while all his sympathetic shipmates now crowd round Jonah, prepared to lay their hands upon him. Frighted Jonah trembles, and summoning all his boldness to his face, only looks so much the more a coward. He will not confess himself suspected; but that itself is strong suspicion. So he makes the best of it; and when the sailors find him not to be the man that is advertised, they let him pass, and he descends into the cabin.

" 'Who's there?' cries the Captain at his busy desk, hurriedly making out his papers for the Customs—'Who's there?' Oh! How that harmless question mangles Jonah! For the instant he almost turns to flee again. But he rallies. 'I seek a passage in the ship to Tarshish; how soon sail ye, sir?' Thus far the busy Captain had not looked up to Jonah, though the man now stands before him; but no sooner does he hear that hollow voice, than he darts a scrutinizing glance, 'We sail with the next coming tide,' at last he slowly answered, still intently eyeing him. 'No sooner, sir?'—'Soon enough for any honest man that goes a passenger.' Ha! Jonah! That's another stab. But he swiftly calls away the Captain from that scent. 'I'll sail with ye,'—he says,—'the passage money, how much is that?—I'll pay now.' For it is particularly written, ship-mates, as if it were a thing not to be overlooked in this history, 'that he paid the fare thereof' ere the craft did sail. And taken with the context, this is full of meaning.

"Now Jonah's Captain, shipmates, was one whose discern-ment detects crime in any, but whose cupidity exposes it only in the penniless. In this world, shipmates, sin that pays its way can travel freely, and without a passport; whereas Virtue, if a pauper, is stopped at all frontiers. So Jonah's Captain prepares to test the length of Jonah's purse, ere he judge him openly. He charges him thrice the usual sum; and it's assented to. Then the Captain knows that Jonah is a fugitive; but at the same time resolves to help a flight that paves its rear with gold. Yet when Jonah fairly takes out his purse, prudent suspicions still molest the Captain. He rings every coin to find a counterfeit. Not a forger, any way, he mutters; and Jonah is put down for his passage. 'Point out my state-room, sir,' says Jonah now, 'I'm travel-weary; I need sleep.' 'Thou look'st like it,' says the Captain, 'there's thy room.' Jonah enters, and would lock the door, but the lock contains no key. Hearing him foolishly fumbling there, the Captain laughs lowly to himself, and mutters something about the doors of convicts' cells being never allowed to be locked within. All dressed and dusty as he is, Jonah throws himself into his berth, and finds the little state-room ceiling almost resting on his forehead. The air is close, and Jonah gasps. Then, in that contracted hole, sunk, too, beneath the ship's water-line, Jonah feels the heralding presentiment of that stifling hour, when the whale shall hold him in the smallest of his bowel's wards.

"Screwed at its axis against the side, a swinging lamp slightly oscillates in Jonah's room; and the ship, heeling over towards the wharf with the weight of the last bales received, the lamp, flame and all, though in slight motion, still maintains a permanent obliquity with reference to the room; though, in truth, infallibly straight itself, it but made obvious the false, lying levels among which it hung. The lamp alarms and frightens Jonah; as lying in his berth his tormented eyes roll around the place, and this thus far successful fugitive finds no refuge for his restless glance. But that contradiction in the lamp more and more appalls him. The floor, the ceiling, and the side, are all awry. 'Oh! So my conscience hangs in me!' he groans, 'Straight upward, so it burns; but the chambers of my soul are all in crookedness!'

"Like one who after a night of drunken revelry hies to his bed, still reeling, but with conscience yet pricking him, as the plungings of the Roman race-horse but so much the more strike his steel tags into him; as one who in that miserable plight still turns and turns in giddy anguish, praying God for annihilation until the fit be passed; and at last amid the whirl of woe he feels, a deep stupor steals over him, as over the man who bleeds to death, for conscience is the wound, and there's naught to staunch it; so, after sore wrestlings in his berth, Jonah's prodigy of ponderous misery drags him drowning down to sleep.

"And now the time of tide has come; the ship casts off her cables; and from the deserted wharf the uncheered ship for Tarshish, all careening, glides to sea. That ship, my friends, was the first of recorded smugglers! The contraband was Jonah. But the sea rebels; he will not bear the wicked burden. A dreadful storm comes on, the ship is like to break. But now when the boatswain calls all hands to lighten her; when boxes, bales, and jars are tumbling overboard; when the wind is shrieking, and the men are yelling, and every plank thunders with trampling feet right over Jonah's head; in all this raging tumult, Jonah sleeps his hideous sleep. He sees no black sky and raging sea, feels not the reeling timbers, and little hears he or heeds he the far rush of the mighty whale, which even now with open mouth is cleaving the seas after him. Aye, shipmates, Jonah was gone down into the sides of the ship—a berth in the cabin as I have taken it, and was fast asleep. But the frightened master comes to him, and shrieks in his dead ear, 'What meanest thou, O sleeper! Arise!' Startled from his lethargy by that direful cry, Jonah staggers to his feet, and stumbling to the deck, grasps a shroud, to look out upon the sea. But at that moment he is sprung upon by a panther billow leaping over the bulwarks. Wave after wave thus leaps into the ship, and finding no speedy vent runs roaring fore and aft, till the mariners come nigh to drowning while yet afloat. And ever, as the white moon shows her affrighted face from the steep gullies in the blackness overhead, aghast Jonah sees the rearing bowsprit pointing high upward, but soon beat downward again towards the tormented deep.

"Terrors upon terrors run shouting through his soul. In all his cringing attitudes, the God-fugitive is now too plainly known. The sailors mark him; more and more certain grow their suspicions of him, and at last, fully to test the truth, by referring the whole matter to high Heaven, they fall to casting lots, to see for whose cause this great tempest was upon them. The lot is Jonah's; that discovered, then how furiously they mob him with their questions. 'What is thine occupation? Whence comest thou? Thy country? What people?' But mark now, my shipmates, the behavior of poor Jonah. The eager mariners but ask him who he is, and where from; whereas, they not only receive an answer to those questions, but likewise another answer to a question not put by them, but the unsolicited answer is forced from Jonah by the hard hand of God that is upon him.

" 'I am a Hebrew,' he cries—and then—'I fear the Lord the God of Heaven who hath made the sea and the dry land!' Fear him, O Jonah? Aye, well mightest thou fear the Lord God *then!* Straightway, he now goes on to make a full confession; whereupon the mariners became more and more appalled, but still are pitiful. For when Jonah, not yet supplicating God for mercy, since he but too well knew the darkness of his deserts,—when wretched Jonah cries out to them to take him and cast him forth into the sea, for he knew that for *his* sake this great tempest was upon them; they mercifully turn from him, and seek by other means to save the ship. But all in vain; the indignant gale howls louder; then, with one hand raised invokingly to God, with the other they not unreluctantly lay hold of Jonah.

"And now behold Jonah taken up as an anchor and dropped into the sea; when instantly an oily calmness floats out from the east, and the sea is still, as Jonah carries down the gale with him, leaving smooth water behind. He goes down in the whirling heart of such a masterless commotion that he scarce heeds the moment when he drops seething into the yawning jaws awaiting him; and the whale shoots-to all his ivory teeth, like so many white bolts, upon his prison. Then Jonah prayed unto the Lord out of the fish's belly. But observe his prayer, and learn a weighty lesson. For sinful as he is, Jonah does not weep and wail for direct deliverance. He feels that his dreadful punishment is just. He leaves all his deliverance to God, contenting himself with this, that spite of all his pains and pangs, he will still look towards His holy temple. And here, shipmates, is true and faithful repentance; not clamorous for pardon, but grateful for punishment. And how pleasing to God was this conduct in Jonah, is shown in the eventual deliverance of him from the sea and the whale. Shipmates, I do not place Jonah before you to be copied for his sin, but I do place him before you as a model for repentance. Sin not; but if you do, take heed to repent of it like Jonah." ❧

When he returns for His own, He is not going to ask us how much we memorized or how often we met for study. No, He will want to know "What did you do about my instructions?"

CHARLES R. SWINDOLL

Prayerfulness

WHEN JESUS WAS TALKING to His disciples He said, *"When you pray,"* not *"If you pray."* There's a big difference. He expected them to be men of prayer. Alfred, Lord Tennyson wrote,

> "More things are wrought by prayer
> Than this world dreams of. Wherefore, let thy voice
> Rise like a fountain for me night and day.
> For what are men better than sheep or goats
> That nourish a blind life within the brain,
> If, knowing God, they lift not hands of prayer
> Both for themselves and those who call them friend?
> For so the whole round earth is every way
> Bound by gold chains about the feet of God."

What better, indeed, are men than sheep or goats, if they claim to believe in the God of the Universe but treat Him with benign neglect and do not take the trouble to develop a relationship of intimacy with Him? The uniqueness of our humanity is found in our God-given capacity to function in the physical, social, and spiritual realms simultaneously—a privilege granted to none but humans in the divine scheme of things. But unless devotion to revealed truth is fostered, and the response of prayer and praise is nurtured, the spiritual dimension withers and dies, and the gold chains rust.

Prayer is first and foremost a declaration of dependence. It is the language of a submissive heart recognizing its place in the divinely ordained structure of the universe. It is the only appropriate language of creatures who are so painfully dependent that they cannot even keep themselves alive, cannot forgive their own sin or make themselves eligible for heaven. We refer, of course, not to the infamous prayer of the man who "prayed" to God by thanking Him that he was so far superior to the rest of mankind, but rather to the prayer of his neighbor who cried out, "Be merciful to me, a sinner." The language of the Lord's Prayer puts it in perspective:

Our Father, who art in heaven,
   hallowed be Thy name.
   thy kingdom come,
   thy will be done
      on earth as it is in heaven.
Give us this day our daily bread.
And forgive us our trespasses,
   as we forgive those
      who trespass against us.
And lead us not into temptation,
   but deliver us from evil.
For Thine is the Kingdom,
   and the power, and the glory,
   for ever and ever. Amen.

But note that prayer is also a declaration of desire. What we pray for readily identifies the inner priorities of our lives. So in order that we might learn correct dependence and proper desires early in life, let's make sure that we teach our children to pray by praying with them and for them. 🦌

Grandma's Prayer
ARLETA RICHARDSON

Jesus' disciples asked him, "Teach us to pray." We still need to learn today. This story from In Grandma's Attic *teaches some basic things about prayer.*

The day was very hot, and I flopped down on the steps where Grandma was shelling peas for supper.

"Oh, dear," I complained. "Why does it have to be so hot? Couldn't we pray that the Lord would send us some cold weather?"

Grandma laughed and threw me a pod to chew on.

"It will be cooler when the sun goes down," she said. "I don't think the Lord wants us to pray for something like that. In fact, I learned that lesson the hard way."

The heat suddenly seemed a littler easier to bear if there was to be a story, so I settled back on the step and waited expectantly. Grandma smiled to herself and began.

"It happened the summer I was nine years old," she said. "It was a day in August, much like this one. Pa had been up to the house several times for a cool drink, and finally said to Ma, 'I guess I'll have to give up on the fences until later. It's just too hot to work out there. But if this heat doesn't let up so I can finish, we won't be able to get in to town on Saturday. I'll have to work early in the morning and after the sun goes down.'

"Pa returned to the barn, and I sat beside the cellar door thinking about what I had heard. Not go to town on Saturday! That just couldn't be! Sarah Jane and I had planned the whole day, and I just couldn't miss it.

"I turned the problem over in my mind for some time," Grandma continued. "What could I do about the heat? Nothing, of course. And if Pa said no trip, then it was no trip.

"After supper, Pa took down the big Bible for prayers. The Scripture he chose perked me up considerably. He read, 'If you ask anything in My name, I will do it.'

"That was the answer! I'd pray for cool weather tomorrow so that Pa could finish his fences. While Pa thanked the Lord for His goodness to us and asked His blessing on our home, I had just one request: 'Please make it cool tomorrow.' "

Grandma rocked a moment as she thought.

"I awoke early the next morning," she said, "and ran to the window to look for clouds. I knew at once that my prayer was not answered. The sun was coming up, and the sky was clear. It promised to be as hot as yesterday or perhaps even hotter.

"I ate breakfast in glum silence. Maybe I hadn't prayed hard enough. Or maybe I didn't promise enough in return. As soon as I had finished helping Ma in the kitchen, I hurried to my room to ask the Lord again for cool weather. This time I promised to be obedient, kind to my brothers, and more help to Ma.

"I was so sure I had been heard that it was no surprise to hear Ma say, shortly after noon, 'Would you look at those black clouds coming over! Mabel, run and shut the windows in the boys' room. I believe it's going to rain!'

"The sky grew black and a chill breeze came around the porch as I watched the results of my prayers. To tell the truth, I was becoming a bit worried. This didn't look like an ordinary rain storm to me. And it wasn't. In a few minutes, the clouds broke and it began to hail. Pep ran yipping under the porch, and I hurried inside to be nearer to Ma.

"The storm was over in a short time. Pa and the boys came in from the barn, and Pa dropped heavily into a chair.

" 'Well, Maryanne,' he said, 'that did a lot of damage to the wheat. We may be able to save some of it, but it was pretty badly beaten.'

"I didn't listen further. I ran to my room and threw myself on my bed. The wheat was ruined, and it was all my fault. What would Pa do to me when he found out? I had just prayed for cool weather, not total destruction. Probably I had promised too much this time. What would the family think of me if they knew I had brought on this terrible hailstorm? I was determined that they should not find out.

"But when Pa prayed that evening, and thanked the Lord for His blessing and care, I couldn't stand it any longer. I began to sob and cry, and Ma looked around in concern. Pa picked me up and put me on his lap, and finally the story came out.

" 'Why, Mabel,' said Pa, 'don't you worry about that. Just remember that the Lord doesn't expect us to ask favors for our convenience or pleasure. A hailstorm often follows a hot spell like this, and your prayers didn't bring it on.' "

Grandma picked up the pans to carry them to the kitchen.

"I was comforted by Pa's assurance," she said. "But I didn't forget that day. It taught me to pray for the Lord's will instead of demanding what I wanted." ❧

Elijah and the Prophets of Baal
ELSIE E. EGERMEIER

In this story from 1 Kings 18:17-40, Elijah was on his own, challenging 450 prophets who did not believe in his God. He knew the Lord would answer his prayer, so Elijah dared to ask Him to do a mighty act.

Because Elijah knew God had sent him to speak to the king, he was not afraid. At once King Ahab asked, "Are you the man who has been causing all this trouble?"

Elijah answered, "No, I am not the man who has troubled your country. You and your family are the guilty ones. You have forsaken the Lord God and disobeyed His commandments. You have worshiped the idol Baal. That's what has caused all this trouble. Now have the people of Israel and Jezebel's prophets of Baal meet me at Mount Carmel."

This was one time the king did not give the orders. Instead he did just as Elijah commanded.

When the crowd of curious people gathered at Mount Carmel, they saw Elijah for the first time in three years. They listened quietly while he spoke to them.

"How long are you going to serve first one god and then another?" he asked. "If the Lord is God, follow Him; but if Baal is the true God, then choose him."

Elijah did not ask the people to choose right then. Instead he wanted to prove to them who was the true God. He said, "I and the prophets of Baal have met with you here. I am only one man, but there are four hundred and fifty prophets of Baal. Bring two bullocks for sacrifices. We will build two altars and lay a bullock on each altar. The heathen can call on their gods, and I will call on the Lord God. Let the one who answers by fire be your God."

The people liked this plan. Quickly they brought the offerings for the sacrifices. "What will happen next?" they wondered.

Elijah told the prophets of Baal to choose the bullock they wanted, and he took the one that was left. He said, "Since there are so many of you, you offer your sacrifice first and call on your god. Ask him to send fire."

In a short time the heathen prophets had their sacrifice ready. From morning till noon they prayed. "O Baal, hear us," but there was no answer. They jumped up and down around the altar. Still nothing happened.

Elijah knew their god could not send fire from heaven. At noon he made fun of them, saying, "Cry louder! Maybe he is talking, or gone on a trip. Perhaps he is sleeping and cannot hear you."

The prophets cried louder than ever. They cut themselves with knives so Baal would feel sorry for them and answer their prayer. Still Baal did not answer, and no fire fell from the sky.

When it was time for the evening sacrifice at the temple in Jerusalem, Elijah told all the people to gather around him. As they watched he rebuilt the altar of the Lord that had once stood on this spot. He chose twelve rough stones and piled them together for the altar. Then he dug a ditch around it. On top of the altar he placed the wood.

Elijah wanted to make sure the people would realize God's great power. He commanded, "Bring four barrels of water and pour them on the sacrifice and wood." When this was done, he said, "Do it a second time." A third time he said, "Do it again."

Twelve barrels of water had been poured on the altar. The wood and meat were drenched. The water filled the trench up to the brim.

When everything was ready, Elijah said, "Lord God of Abraham, Isaac, and Israel, let it be known this day that You are God, that I am Your servant, that I have done this to obey You. Hear me, O Lord, hear me that these people may know You are the Lord God and return to worship You."

At once fire fell from the sky and burned up the sacrifice and the wood. Even all the water in the ditch was licked up by the fire.

How amazed the people were! They had never seen anything like this before. Now they were sure Elijah's God was the true God. They fell on their faces and cried, "The Lord, He is God! The Lord, He is God!"

Making sure they would not be tempted to worship Baal again, the people killed all the sinful, heathen prophets. ❧

Prayer for Children
AMY CARMICHAEL

Amy Carmichael, a missionary to India who had no children of her own, gave her life to providing a secure home environment for hundreds of Indian children who had been rescued from temple prostitution. Her love for children was boundless, and that love is illustrated in a prayer that she wrote in poetic form.

Father, hear us, we are praying,
Hear the words our hearts are saying,
We are praying for our children.

Keep them from the powers of evil,
From the secret, hidden peril,
From the whirlpool that would suck them,
From the treacherous quicksand pluck them.

From the worldling's hollow gladness,
From the sting of faithless sadness,
Holy Father, save our children.

Through life's troubled waters steer them,
Through life's bitter battle cheer them,
Father, Father, be Thou near them.
Read the language of our longing,
Read the wordless pleadings thronging,
Holy Father, for our children.
    And wherever they may bide,
        Lead them Home at eventide. 🐾

Peter and the Angel
FULTON OURSLER

The Christians in Jerusalem prayed for Peter, who was in prison, and were surprised when God answered the way He did. The answers to prayer are often filled with surprises. This retelling of Acts 12 is from The Greatest Faith Ever Known.

Close upon midnight of Easter Sunday, Peter was most uncomfortably resting between two soldiers, bound to them with two sets of chains. His cell in the dungeon had bolts, bars, locks, and chains, and guards outside as well.

"Now," the chief guard had said, "you who have such Christian power, let's see you get free of all that!"

Peter did get free, but the chief guard was not allowed to see how.

The soldiers beside him were wide awake and the keepers before the door of the prison tramped back and forth, up and down, on duty and alert.

Peter had been praying unceasingly. Suddenly a most shining and mysterious light, without source or center, arrived luminous and full-blown in that pit of misery, warming and illuminating its darkest corners.

In the midst of that all-suffusing light stood an angel of the Lord. With one touch of ineffable power he smote Peter on the side. He raised Peter from the floor and the apostle heard the heavenly voice:

"Arise up quickly."

The chains fell from Peter's hands and feet as the angel counseled him with great urgency:

"Gird yourself, Peter. Bind on your sandals."

Without a word, Peter obeyed. The two guards lay, transfixed, offering no resistance to this strange scene.

"And now," the angel commanded, "cast your garment about you and follow me."

Peter's mind was in an extraordinary state as he followed instructions. It seemed that he was asleep and dreaming and yet knew that he was not asleep and not dreaming. . . .

The iron gate swung open to them, with no porter to release its hinges, no guard to lift its mighty latch.

"And they went out, and passed on through one street; and immediately the angel departed from him."

. . . In all decisions on the path of life, the follower of Jesus prays for guidance. He looks for it with the eye of the soul, and with the sound ear he listens hopefully. So Peter, alone and freed miraculously in the empty street, "considered the thing" and presently knew exactly what he was to do. He went straight to the house of Mary, Mark's mother, one of the most ardent Christians in the whole Jerusalem band.

. . . Elsewhere in Jerusalem people might still be sleeping, but not in this house. Through the window the apostle could hear voices, low and intense and full of entreaty. Head turned aside, bright eyes half-closed, the greatest of fishermen could make out their words.

They were praying—and for him, as Christians were doing all over the city. All night they had been on their knees. Unwearied, they continued to lift their voices, storming heaven that Peter be spared the wrath of Herod Agrippa and be loosed from prison.

Peter could not help smiling to himself as he knocked gently on the door.

Among the hired servants of the house was a damsel called Rhoda, who answered Peter's knuckles on the shutter.

"Who is it?" she whispered, the never-absent Christian fear of the authorities in her tone.

"It is I. Peter!"

Peter, for whom they had been praying all night long; Peter on their doorstep!

Rhoda was so overcome with gladness that she witlessly left

Peter outside the door still bolted against him, while she rushed down the long corridor and pulled aside the hall curtains, crying above the eager drone of the prayers:

"Listen! Listen! Peter stands before the gate."

Several voices broke the brief and sudden spell of silence, three or four shocked and incredulous Christians, who had been praying all night for this very thing, yet could not believe their answer when it came, all exclaiming together:

"Rhoda! You are mad!"

"No, he's really at the front door."

"You are beside yourself, girl."

"Come and see for yourselves!"

The whole company rose up, some going to the windows over the dewy garden, others following the maid to the door.

Surely, there was Peter! Or was it his angel?

Peter lifted his hand and beckoned them with a cajoling gesture to believe that it was really he, the Peter they all knew, in his own proper person and clad in his right mind. &

The Christian's Tools
HENRY MARTYN

Martyn's life was brief but his influence was far-reaching in India and Persia. His secret was simple.

A workman in time of need would part with everything but his tools; for to lose them would be to lose all. Reading the Word of God and prayer are the tools of the Christian's craft; without them he is helpless. How is it, then, that when time presses, he so often foregoes these, or shortens them? What is this but to sell his tools?

If there be anything I do, if there be anything I leave undone, let me be perfect in prayer. &

After the Stroke
JOHN LEAX

In the summer of 1970, the poet's wife contracted sub-acute bacterial endocarditis. While recovering from it, an embolism from a damaged heart valve broke loose, resulting in a stroke that totally paralyzed her right side and blocked her speech.

The embolism loose
from the heart
lodged in the brain
a sudden confusion of language
paralysis
and the end of speech

As for man, his days are as grass.
Psalm 103:15
Beside your bed, I cannot speak the prayer
that begs for your recovery.
The Groaning Spirit
who gives us leave to pray
withholds that comfort.
He has given me, instead,
sleeplessness,
open eyes to watch
the sweet liquid, fortified,
drip three days
into your needled arm.
My mouth stays shut.

Bless the Lord, O my soul.
Psalm 103:1
It is no easy thing
to bless the Lord in Buffalo
where you lie
stroke still and dumb.

My watch is pointless,
kept only for myself.
The nurses, crisp professionals,
need neither me
nor my questions.
The heart of your room drives
me out into the street.
The 5 AM winter wind
is cold. Its voice,
a quick thin blade, slips
through the layered wool I wear
and speaks deep into my side
the word that alters all.

He hath not dealt with us after our sins, nor rewarded us according to our iniquities.
Psalm 103:10
In the therapy room
they held you by a belt
stood you up
and told you,
Walk.

You thought hard,
clutched the rails
and throwing your foot
like a loose shoe
stepped into the pain
and did not stop
until you'd walked it through.

But there were others there,
almost as young as you,
whose only grace

was the white webbed belt
around their waists.

Who satisfieth thy mouth with good things.
Psalm 103:5a

When your words returned,
they came at random,
jumped from your lips
out of context
and refused to lie down in sentences;

but they did return,
And slowly felt your lips
and tongue divide the syllables
until, one day, dominated,
they spoke as ordered
and blessed the name of God. &

Lessons in Prayer
HOWARD AND GERALDINE TAYLOR

"To learn before leaving England to move man through God by prayer alone"; this and nothing less was Hudson Taylor's objective. The following tale of how he practiced this lesson is from Hudson Taylor in Early Years: The Growth of a Soul.

"At Hull my kind employer, always busy, wished me to remind him whenever my salary became due. This I determined not to do directly, but to ask that God would bring the fact to his recollection, and thus encourage me by answering prayer.

"At one time as the day drew near for the payment of a quarter's salary I was as usual much in prayer about it. The time arrived, but Dr. Hardey made no allusion to the matter. I continued praying. Days passed on and he did not remember, until at length on settling up my weekly accounts one Saturday night, I found myself possessed of only one remaining coin, a half-crown piece. Still, I had hitherto known no lack, and I continued praying.

"That Sunday was a very happy one. As usual my heart was full and brimming over with blessing. After attending Divine Service in the morning, my afternoons and evenings were taken up with Gospel work in the various lodging-houses I was accustomed to visit in the lowest part of the town. . . .

"After concluding my last service about ten o'clock that night, a poor man asked me to go and pray with his wife, saying that she was dying. I readily agreed, and on the way to his house asked him why he had not sent for the priest, as his accent told me he was an Irishman. He had done so, he said, but the priest refused to come without a payment of eighteen pence which the man did not possess, as the family was starving.

"I began to reprove the poor man, telling him that it was very wrong to have allowed matters to get into such a state as he described, and that he ought to have applied to the relieving officer. His answer was that he had done so, and was told to come at eleven o'clock the next morning, but that he feared his wife might not live through the night.

"Ah, thought I, *if only I had two shillings and a sixpence instead of this half-crown, how gladly would I give these poor people a shilling!* But to part with the half-crown was far from my thoughts. I little dreamed that the truth of the matter simply was that I could trust God *plus* one-and-sixpence, but was not prepared to trust Him only, without any money at all in my pocket.

"My conductor led me into a court . . . and up a miserable flight of stairs into a wretched room; and oh, what a sight there presented itself! Four or five children stood about, their sunken cheeks and temples all unmistakably the story of slow starvation, and lying on a wretched pallet was a poor, exhausted mother, with a tiny infant thirty-six hours old moaning rather than crying at her

side, for it too seemed spent and failing. . . . Still a wretched unbe-
lief prevented me from obeying the impulse to relieve their distress
at the cost of all I possessed.

"It will scarcely seem strange that I was unable to say much to
comfort these poor people. I needed comfort myself. I began to tell
them, however, that they must not be cast down; that though their
circumstances were very distressing there was a kind and loving
Father in heaven. But something within me cried, 'You hypocrite!
Telling these unconverted people about a kind and loving Father
in heaven, and not prepared yourself to trust Him without a half-a-
crown.'

"I was nearly choked. How gladly would I have compromised
with conscience, if I had a florin and a sixpence! I would have
given the florin thankfully and kept the rest. But I was not yet prepared to trust in God alone, without the sixpence.

" 'You asked me to come and pray with your wife,' I said to
the man, 'let us pray.' And I knelt down.

"But no sooner had I opened my lips with 'Our Father who
art in heaven,' than conscience said within, 'Dare you mock God?
Dare you kneel down and call Him Father with that half-crown in
your pocket?'

"Such a time of conflict then came upon me as I have never
experienced before or since. How I got through that form of prayer
I know not, and whether the words uttered were connected or disconnected I cannot tell. But I arose from my knees in great distress
of mind.

"The poor father turned to me and said, 'You see what a terrible state we are in, sir. If you can help us, for God's sake do!'

"At that moment the word flashed into my mind, 'Give to
him that asketh of thee.' And in the word of a King there is power.

"I put my hand into my pocket and slowly drawing out the
half-crown, gave it to the man. . . . The joy all came back in full
floodtide to my heart. I could say anything and feel it then, and

the hindrance to blessing was gone—gone, I trust, forever.

"Not only was the poor woman's life saved; but my life, as I fully realised, had been saved too. It might have been a wreck—would have been, probably, as a Christian life—had not grace at that time conquered, and the striving of God's Spirit been obeyed.

". . . Next morning for breakfast my plate of porridge remained, and before it was finished the postman's knock was heard at the door. I was not in the habit of receiving letters on Monday, as my parents and most of my friends refrained from posting on Saturday, so that I was somewhat surprised when the landlady came in holding a letter or packet in her wet hand covered by her apron. I looked at the letter, but could not make out the handwriting. It was either a strange hand or a feigned one, and the postmark was blurred. Where it came from I could not tell. On opening the envelope I found nothing written within; but inside a sheet of blank paper was folded a pair of kid gloves, from which, as I opened them in astonishment, half-a-sovereign fell to the ground.

" 'Praise the Lord,' I exclaimed. 'Four hundred per cent for twelve hours' investment—that is good interest!'

". . . I cannot tell you how often my mind has recurred to this incident, or all the help it has been to me in circumstances of difficulty in afterlife. If we are faithful to God in little things, we shall gain experience and strength that will be helpful to us in the more serious trials of life."

But this was not the end of the story, nor was it the only answer to prayer that was to confirm his faith at this time. For the chief difficulty still remained. Dr. Hardey had not remembered; and though prayer was unremitting, other matters appeared entirely to engross his attention. It would have been so easy to remind him. But what then of the lesson upon the acquirement of which Hudson Taylor felt his future usefulness depended—"to move man through God, by prayer alone"?

"This remarkable and gracious deliverance," he continued, "was a great joy to me as well as a strong confirmation of faith. But of course ten shillings however economically used will not go very far, and it was none the less necessary to continue in prayer, asking that the larger supply which was still due might be remembered and paid. All my petitions, however, appeared to remain unanswered, and before a fortnight elapsed I found myself pretty much in the same position that I had occupied on the Sunday night already made so memorable. Meanwhile I continued pleading with God more and more earnestly that He would Himself remind Dr. Hardey that my salary was due.

"Of course it was not the want of money that distressed me. That could have been had at any time for the asking. But the question uppermost in my mind was this: 'Can I go to China? or will my want of faith and power with God prove so serious an obstacle as to preclude my entering upon this much-prized service?'

... "Above five o'clock that Saturday afternoon, when Dr. Hardey had finished writing his prescriptions . . . he threw himself back in his arm-chair . . . and began to speak of the things of God. All at once he said: 'By the by, Taylor, is not your salary due again?'

"My emotion may be imagined. I had to swallow two or three times before I could answer. . . . How thankful I felt at that moment! God surely had heard my prayer and caused him in this time of my great need to remember the salary without any word or suggestion from me.

"He replied, 'Oh, I am so sorry you did not remind me! You know how busy I am. I wish I had thought of it a little sooner, for only this afternoon I sent all the money I had to the bank. Otherwise I would pay you at once.'

"It is impossible to describe the revulsion of feeling caused by this unexpected statement. I knew not what to do.

"As soon as Dr. Hardey was gone I had to seek my little sanctum and pour out my heart before the Lord for some time before calmness, and more than calmness, thankfulness and joy were restored. I felt that God had His own way, and was not going to fail me. . . .

"That evening was spent . . . in reading the Word and preparing the subject on which I expected to speak in the various lodging-houses on the morrow. I waited perhaps a little longer than usual. At last about ten o'clock, there being no interruption of any kind, I put on my overcoat and was preparing to leave for home, rather thankful to know that by that time I should have to let myself in with the latchkey, as my landlady retired early. There was certainly no help for that night. . . .

"Just as I was about to turn down the gas, I heard the doctor's step in the garden that lay between the dwelling-house and Surgery. He was laughing to himself very heartily, as though greatly amused. Entering the Surgery he asked for the ledger, and told me that, strange to say, one of his richest patients had just come to pay his doctor's bill. Was it not an odd thing to do? It never struck me that it might have any bearing on my own case, or I might have felt embarrassed. But looking at it simply from the position of an uninterested spectator, I also was highly amused that a man rolling in wealth should come after ten o'clock at night to pay a bill which he could any day have met by a cheque with the greatest ease. It appeared that somehow or other he could not rest with this on his mind, and had been constrained to come at that unusual hour to discharge his liability.

"The account was duly receipted in the ledger, and Dr. Hardey was about to leave, when suddenly he turned and handing me some of the banknotes just received, said to my surprise and thankfulness:

" 'By the way, Taylor, you might as well take these notes. I have no change, but can give you the balance next week.'

"Again I was left, my feelings undiscovered, to go back to my little closet and praise the Lord with a joyful heart that after all I *might go to China.* To me this incident was not a trivial one; and to recall it sometimes, in circumstances of great difficulty, in China or elsewhere, has proved no small comfort and strength." ❧

The Power of Prayer
HAROLD L. MYRA

Midnight! I hear sounds on the roof. Perhaps the red squirrels my dad thought he had gotten rid of? Something swishes and falls heavily. I turn on the outside lights. The snow is melting, coming down in sheets off the roof. The thaw has come.

Yesterday, the trees were helplessly bowed down by snow. Cedars, spruce, aspen, all caught and bent . . . even the birch I had shaken loose hung disconsolately a foot off the ground. But the thaw will change everything.

Tomorrow the sun will shine again. And like God's work through prayer, it will release the captives, break the impasses, and bring warmth to the world's creatures. ❧

The School of Prayer
E. M. BOUNDS

As God's house is, pre-eminently, a house of prayer, prayer should enter into and underlie everything that is undertaken there. . . . As God's house is a house where the business of praying is carried on, so is it a place where the business of making praying people out of prayerless people is done. The house of God is a divine workshop, and there the work of prayer goes on. The house of God is a divine schoolhouse, in which the lesson of prayer is taught; where men and women learn to pray, and where they are graduated in the school of prayer. ❧

Repentance

MARK TWAIN said, "Man is the only animal that blushes; or needs to." Not being experts in animal psychology and physiology, we are not qualified to say whether Twain was right about animals blushing or not. We once had a golden retriever called Prince whose behavior was regularly less than princely, and he did have the grace to look mildly embarrassed when he was caught eating a freshly baked pie. But there can be no doubt about mankind's unique need to blush. We humans have the capability to feel shame when confronted with acts for which we are guilty. Granted, it is possible to experience false shame—feelings of remorse for something when there is in actuality no guilt. But by the same token there is such a thing as false innocence—the refusal or inability to feel shame for actions where real guilt exists.

God has given us the gift of conscience. When properly informed, conscience will lead a person to recognize right from wrong and stimulate appropriate feelings of shame when necessary. Constant abuse of the conscience can lead to its being chloroformed, but exposure to the truth and the prompting of the Spirit can lead a person to recognition of wrong and a desire for forgiveness. This is where repentance comes into the picture.

Repentance comes in different shapes and sizes. Some people repent to get out of a fix, such as the soldier in the foxhole who is sorry for his past sins and promises that if God gets him out of his predicament, he'll never bother Him again. God does, and the soldier doesn't! Or there's the repentance that is sorry for being caught and embarrassed by exposure. But real repentance is born of deep sorrow for sin. It blossoms into a desire for forgiveness, and out of gratitude leads to a rejecting of the sin and a redirection of life.

It is said that men find it hard to say "I'm afraid," "I was wrong," "I'm lost," or "I'm sorry." That being the case, it may be more difficult for men to repent than for women. Regardless of the degree of difficulty, for men as well as women repentance is the way to reconciliation, both spiritually and socially.

When our children were small, we used to teach them to pray by incorporating "please prayers," "thank you prayers" and "sorry prayers" into their youthful devotions. The "please prayers" came easily, and the "thank you prayers" when the children were reminded, but the "sorry prayers" were much harder. Even children don't like to admit that they have done wrong and ask for forgiveness with a commitment to a change in behavior. But we mustn't forget that it is "the kindness of God that leads to repentance." And it is the kindness of God that offers the sweet relief of forgiveness. 🦋

Trouble in the School Yard

CHARLES COLSON AND WILLIAM COLEMAN

Two of the hardest things to say are, "Yes, I did it" and "I'm very sorry." But once we say them, we enjoy great peace.

Remember the last time you knew you did something wrong? Did you feel bad or sad or mad?

I've felt like that, too, when I've done something wrong.

Let me tell you about Mark, who's a lot like you and me. He knows what it's like to disobey.

The ball game had ended, and Mark was the only one left in the school yard. He was unhappy because his team lost. "Oh, well," Mark said as he stuck his hand in his old baseball glove and wiggled his thumb through a hole.

Mark started to walk away, but then he looked up at the school windows. *It sure would be easy to throw a stone through a window*, he thought. He grinned a little grin.

First he looked this way; then he looked that way. Nobody was watching. Mark reached down and picked up a stone.

"Yuck," he said and made an ugly face. "This stone has gum on it." He looked at the gooey mess stuck to his fingers. He rubbed his fingers on his jeans. "What a mess," Mark said to no one as he scraped the gum from his fingers.

Again Mark looked this way; then he looked that way. Nobody was watching. Mark picked up a rock the size of his fist and threw it at a window.

CRASH!

As soon as Mark heard the glass break, he ran across the playground, jumped over a bush, and hurried home.

At supper that night, Mark's chin hung low and almost touched the mashed potatoes. His left eyelid drooped almost closed.

His father said, "You look bad."

His mother said, "You look sad."

His sister said, "You look mad."

Mark wasn't hungry. He said, "May I be excused?"

His father looked at his mother. They said, "Yes."

Mark went outside and sat on the steps. He thought about what he had done. He never could be happy knowing he had thrown a rock through the school window. Soon his father came out and sat with him. "What is wrong, Mark?" he asked.

It was hard, but Mark told his father what he had done. As Mark talked, he began to feel better. They talked about why throwing the rock was wrong and what he must do to make things right. When Mark's father saw that Mark was truly sorry, he said, "I forgive you, son, and God will forgive you, too, if you ask Him."

Mark bowed his head and said, "God, I'm sorry I broke the window. I know it was wrong. Please forgive me." When he lifted his head, Mark knew God had forgiven him just as his father had.

In the morning Mark's father took him to school. Mark was scared, but he told the principal, "I broke the window. I know it was wrong, and I am sorry. What can I do to help fix it?"

Mark felt better when the principal said, "You're a brave boy to come to me. I admire your honesty. Now let's talk about how you can earn money to help buy a new window." Together they made a plan.

I know what it's like to disobey, just as you do. We've all done things that are wrong. And just like Mark, we have to confess our wrongs and try to fix what is wrong. We need to ask God to help us keep from doing wrong again. God has promised always to forgive us when we ask and when we are truly sorry.

"If we confess our sins, he is faithful and just and will forgive us our sins." I John 1:9, NIV 🦋

Pinocchio Becomes a Boy

Carlo Collodi

Geppetto's naughty wooden puppet, through his disobedience and laziness, suffers one scrape after another. In this excerpt from The Adventures of Pinocchio, *we cheer the happy ending that Pinocchio's repentance finally makes possible.*

When [Pinocchio and Geppetto] had gone another hundred yards they saw, at the end of a path in the middle of the fields, a nice little straw hut with a roof of tiles and bricks.

"That hut must be inhabited by someone," said Pinocchio. "Let us go and knock at the door."

They went and knocked.

"Who is there?" said a little voice from within.

"We are a poor father and son without bread and without a roof," answered the puppet.

"Turn the key and the door will open," said the same little voice.

Pinocchio turned the key and the door opened. They went in and looked here, there, and everywhere, but could see no one.

"Oh, where is the master of the house?" said Pinocchio, much surprised.

"Here I am up here!"

The father and son looked immediately up to the ceiling, and there on a beam they saw the Talking Cricket.

"Oh, my dear little Cricket!" said Pinocchio, bowing politely to him.

"Ah! Now you call me your 'dear little Cricket.' But do you remember the time when you threw the handle of a hammer at me, to drive me from your house?"

"You are right, Cricket! Drive me away also . . . throw the handle of a hammer at me; but have pity on my poor papa . . ."

"I will have pity on both father and son, but I wished to

301

remind you of the ill treatment I received from you, to teach you that in this world, when it is possible, we should show courtesy to everybody, if we wish it to be extended to us in our hour of need."

"You are right, Cricket, you are right, and I will bear in mind the lesson you have given me. . . . Tell me, little Cricket, where can I find a tumbler of milk for my poor papa?"

"Three fields off from here there lives a gardener called Giangio who keeps cows. Go to him and you will get the milk you are in want of."

Pinocchio ran all the way to Giangio's house; and the gardener asked him:

"How much milk do you want?"

"I want a tumblerful."

"A tumbler of milk costs a halfpenny. Begin by giving me the halfpenny."

"I have not even a farthing," replied Pinocchio, grieved and mortified.

"That is bad, puppet," answered the gardener. "If you have not even a farthing, I have not even a drop of milk."

"I must have patience!" said Pinocchio, and he turned to go.

"Wait a little," said Giangio. "We can come to an arrangement together. Will you undertake to turn the pumping machine?"

"What is the pumping machine?"

"It is a wooden pole which serves to draw up the water from the cistern to water the vegetables."

"You can try me . . ."

"Well, then, if you will draw a hundred buckets of water, I will give you in compensation a tumbler of milk."

"It is a bargain."

Giangio then led Pinocchio to the kitchen garden and taught him how to turn the pumping machine. Pinocchio immediately began to work; but before he had drawn up the hundred buckets of water the perspiration was pouring from his head to his feet.

Never before had he undergone such fatigue. . . .

And from that day for more than five months he continued to get up at daybreak every morning to go and turn the pumping machine, to earn the tumbler of milk that was of such benefit to his father in his bad state of health. Nor was he satisfied with this; for, during the time that he had over, he learned to make hampers and baskets of rushes, and with the money he obtained by selling them he was able with great economy to provide for all the daily expenses. Among other things he constructed an elegant little wheel chair, in which he could take his father out on fine days to breathe a mouthful of fresh air.

By his industry, ingenuity, and his anxiety to work and to overcome difficulties, he not only succeeded in maintaining his father, who continued infirm, in comfort, but he also contrived to put aside forty pence to buy himself a new coat.

One morning he said to his father:

"I am going to the neighboring market to buy myself a jacket, a cap, and a pair of shoes. When I return," he added, laughing, "I shall be so well dressed that you will take me for a fine gentleman."

And leaving the house he began to run merrily and happily along. All at once he heard himself called by name, and turning around he saw a big Snail crawling out from the hedge.

"Do you not know me?" asked the Snail.

"It seems to me . . . and yet I am not sure . . ."

"Do you not remember the Snail who was lady's maid to the Fairy with blue hair? Do you not remember the time when I came downstairs to let you in, and you were caught by your foot which you had stuck through the house door?"

"I remember it all!" shouted Pinocchio. "Tell me quickly, my beautiful little Snail, where have you left my good Fairy? What is she doing? Has she forgiven me? Does she still remember me? Does she still wish me well? Is she far from here? Can I go and see her?"

To all these rapid, breathless questions the Snail replied in her usual phlegmatic manner:

"My dear Pinocchio, the poor Fairy is lying in bed at the hospital!"

"At the hospital?"

"It is only too true. Overtaken by a thousand misfortunes, she has fallen seriously ill, and she has not even enough to buy herself a mouthful of bread."

"Is it really so? Oh, what sorrow you have given me! Oh, poor Fairy, poor Fairy, poor Fairy! . . . If I had a million I would run and carry it to her . . . but I have only forty pence . . . Here they are: I was going to buy a new coat. Take them, Snail, and carry them at once to my good Fairy."

"And your new coat?"

"What matters my new coat? I would sell even these rags that I have got on to be able to help her. Go, Snail, and be quick; and in two days return to this place, for I hope I shall then be able to give you some more money. Up to this time I have worked to maintain my papa; from today I will work five hours more that I may also maintain my good mamma. Good-by, Snail, I shall expect you in two days."

The Snail, contrary to her usual habits, began to run like a lizard in a hot August sun.

That evening, Pinocchio, instead of going to bed at ten o'clock, sat up till midnight had struck; and instead of making eight baskets of rushes he made sixteen.

Then he went to bed and fell asleep. And while he slept he thought that he saw the Fairy smiling and beautiful, who, after having kissed him, said to him:

"Well done, Pinocchio! To reward you for your good heart I will forgive you for all that is past. Boys who minister tenderly to their parents, and assist them in their misery and infirmities, are deserving of great praise and affection, even if they cannot be cited as examples of obedience and good behavior. Try and do better in the future and you will be happy."

At this moment his dream ended, and Pincocchio opened his eyes and awoke.

But imagine his astonishment when upon awakening he discovered that he was no longer a wooden puppet, but that he had become instead a boy, like all other boys. He gave a glance round and saw that the straw walls of the hut had disappeared, and that he was in a pretty little room furnished and arranged with a simplicity that was almost elegance. Jumping out of bed he found a new suit of clothes ready for him, a new cap, and a pair of new leather boots that fitted him beautifully.

He was hardly dressed when he naturally put his hands in his pockets, and pulled out a little ivory purse on which these words were written: "The Fairy with blue hair returns the forty pence to her dear Pinocchio, and thanks him for his good heart." He opened the purse, and instead of forty copper pennies he saw forty shining gold pieces fresh from the mint.

He then went and looked at himself in the glass, and he thought he was someone else. For he no longer saw the usual reflection of a wooden puppet; he was greeted instead by the image of a bright, intelligent boy with chestnut hair, blue eyes, and looking as happy and joyful as if it were the Easter holidays.

In the midst of all these wonders succeeding each other Pinocchio felt quite bewildered, and he could not tell if he was really awake of if he was dreaming with his eyes open.

"Where can my papa be?" he exclaimed suddenly, and going into the next room he found old Geppetto quite well, lively, and in good humor, just as he had been formerly. He had already resumed his trade of wood carving, and he was designing a rich and beautiful frame of leaves, flowers, and the heads of animals.

"Satisfy my curiosity, dear papa," said Pinocchio, throwing his arms around his neck and covering him with kisses. "How can this sudden change be accounted for?"

"This sudden change in our home is all your doing," answered Geppetto.

"How my doing?"

"Because when boys who have behaved badly turn over a new leaf and become good, they have the power of bringing contentment and happiness to their families."

"And where has the old wooden Pinocchio hidden himself?"

"There he is," answered Geppetto, and he pointed to a big puppet, leaning against a chair, with its head on one side, its arms dangling, and its legs so crossed and bent that it was really a miracle that it remained standing.

Pinocchio turned and looked at it; and after he had looked at it for a short time, he said to himself with great complacency:

"How ridiculous I was when I was a puppet! And how glad I am that I have become a well-behaved boy!" 🪶

John the Baptizer

John's job, retold here from Matthew 3 and John 1:32-34, was to prepare people for the blessings Messiah would bring. The preparation included repentance.

When Jesus was a grown man, his cousin, John, began preaching in the desert of Judea. John dressed in rough clothes made of camels' hair with a leather belt around his waist. He ate what wild food he could find—grasshoppers and wild honey.

He preached from the Old Testament Book of Isaiah and told people to repent from their sins because the Lord's Messiah was coming soon. People came from the city of Jerusalem and all the surrounding towns to hear him preach. Many people repented, and to express their sorrow for having disobeyed God and to show that they wanted to change, they asked John to baptize them in the Jordan River.

But when the religious leaders came out to hear John, he

spoke harshly to them because they were evil. Instead of repenting as they should have, they continued to sin, and worse, they boasted that God had to accept them anyway because they were part of God's people, the Jews.

John warned them that soon God's special Servant was coming who would judge everyone who hadn't repented of their sin.

One day Jesus came down from Galilee to visit John in the desert. He asked John to baptize Him. John, being Jesus' cousin, knew that Jesus lived a holy life, so he said, "Jesus, You are the One who ought to baptize me rather than me baptizing You."

But Jesus said, "No. You must baptize Me."

As soon as Jesus came up out of the water, the Spirit of God came down from heaven and landed on Jesus like a dove. And a voice from heaven said, "This is My Son, whom I love. With You I am well pleased."

John knew something very special had happened, and he started to understand that Jesus was the Messiah, the very Savior-King he had been telling people that God would soon send. ❧

A Message for the Miners
JOHN POLLOCK

The actor David Garrick said that George Whitefield's voice was so beautiful that he could make people cry by pronouncing "Mesopotamia." But the tough coal miners in this story weren't crying because of a voice; they were brought to repentance through the Gospel. This is an excerpt from George Whitefield and the Great Awakening.

Seward and George had been invited to dine that afternoon with an aged Dissenter at Kingswood, a mile or two outside the walls and close to the forest coal mines, where George's thoughts had often strayed since the day in 1737 when a former Mayor of Bristol had called the Kingswood colliers "Indians."

Respectable citizens were afraid of them; they caused violent affrays, had shocked even hard-bitten sailors by digging up the corpse of a murderer whose suicide had cheated them of a public execution to hold high festival round it. They were totally illiterate. Their shacks, like the mines, lay on the far boundaries of four different parishes so they were ignored by the clergy of all. Gin-devils, wife beaters, sodomites—the Bristol world had not a good word for the colliers of Kingswood, and considered that they illustrated perfectly the dictum of Thomas Hobbes: "No arts; no letters; no society; and which is worst of all, continual fear and danger of violent death; and the life of man, solitary, poor, nasty, brutish and short."

Their bodies might be foul but their souls were immortal. And they could only be reached in the open air. Yet to preach in the open air, John Wesley had said, was "a *mad* notion." When George, Seward, and another friend dismounted at the old Dissenter's home on the edge of Kingswood common, George still pondered whether to take this decisive step.

He could see the forest just beyond and the trails leading to the mines. Over dinner he told their host, an "old disciple of the Lord," how "My bowels have long yearned toward the poor colliers, who are very numerous and are as sheep having no shepherd."

The four of them went out at the hour when many coal miners left the pits, and walked towards a rise of ground. Whitefield felt a little afraid of what he was about to do, but if the churches were to be closed against him he should all the more follow his Master's words and go into the highways and hedges. He remarked with a nervous laugh that the Lord Jesus had a mount for his pulpit and the heavens for his sounding board.

He stood on the little hill, on this Saturday, February 17, 1739. He pitched his voice about a hundred yards, to a group of colliers moving towards him. He called out: "Blessed are the poor in spirit, for they shall see the kingdom of heaven!"

The miners stopped and stared. A parson in cassock, gown,

and bands, holding a book and audible at a hundred yards! That young, astonishingly clear voice came again. "Matthew, Chapter 5, verses 1 to 3." They had no idea who Matthew was or what "Chapter" meant but they drew nearer, and heard: "Seeing the multitudes Jesus went up into a mountain: and when he was set, his disciples came unto him: And he opened his mouth, and taught them, saying, Blessed are the poor in spirit: for theirs is the kingdom of heaven."

By now quite a crowd had collected. Almost all were coal miners, the grime of the pits making them look like Indians indeed. George told a story which made them laugh. They had never heard a parson who cracked a joke in a sermon—but they had never heard a parson at all! Seward, who had been exceedingly nervous lest they both be prosecuted under the Conventicle Act, or at least be shunned by clergy and gentry for disorderly conduct, now stood praying and praising silently beside the young clergyman whose words poured out in a torrent. The crowd grew until perhaps two hundred were clustered round Hannam Mount. George Whitefield spoke of hell, black as a pit, of the certainty of judgment for evil done. He turned to talk about "Jesus, who was a friend of publicans and sinners and came not to call the righteous, but sinners to repentance." He spoke of the cross, and the love of God, and brushed tears from his eyes. On and on he went, in dead silence except for his own voice and the slight stirring of wind through the bare trees behind him.

Suddenly he noticed pale streaks forming on grimy faces, on that of a young man on his right, and an old bent miner on his left, and two scarred, depraved faces in front; more and more of them. Whitefield, still preaching, saw the "white gutters made by their tears down their black cheeks." ❦

May One Be Pardoned and Retain th' Offense?

WILLIAM SHAKESPEARE

Claudius, King of Denmark, has murdered his brother, Old Hamlet, by pouring poison in his ear, thus gaining a crown, an ambition, and a queen—his brother's widow. But his conscience gives him no rest. He longs to pray but cannot, to be forgiven but wonders if repentance is real when the gains of sin are still enjoyed. Shakespeare's words from Hamlet, Act III, Scene 3 raise profound questions concerning prayer, repentance, mercy, justice, and forgiveness—both God's and ours.

O, my offense is rank; it smells to heaven;
    It hath the primal eldest curse upon't,
A brother's murder. Pray can I not,
    Though inclination be as sharp as will.
My stronger guilt defeats my strong intent,
    And, like a man to double business bound,
I stand in pause where I shall first begin,
    And both neglect. What if this cursèd hand
Were thicker than itself with brother's blood,
    Is there not rain enough in the sweet heavens
To wash it white as snow? Whereto serves mercy
    But to confront the visage of offense?
And what's in prayer but this twofold force:
    To be forestalled ere we come to fall,
Or pardoned being down? Then I'll look up;
    My fault is past. But O, what form of prayer
Can serve my turn? "Forgive me my foul murder"?
    That cannot be; since I am still possessed
Of those effects for which I did the murder—
    My crown, mine own ambition, and my Queen.
May one be pardoned and retain th' offense?
    In the corrupted currents of this world,
Offense's gilded hand may shove by justice,

And oft 'tis seen the wicked prize itself
Buys out the law. But 'tis not so above;
   There is no shuffling; there the action lies
In his true nature, and we ourselves compelled
   Even to the teeth and forehead of our faults
To give in evidence. What then? What rests?
   Try what repentance can—what can it not?
Yet what can it, when one cannot repent?
   O wretched state, O bosom black as death,
O limèd soul, that struggling to be free,
   Art more engaged! Help, angels, make assay.
Bow, stubborn knees; and heart with strings of steel,
   Be soft as sinews of the new-born babe.
All may be well. ❧

I tell you that in the same way there is more rejoicing
in heaven over one sinner who repents
than over ninety-nine righteous persons
who do not need to repent.
LUKE 15:7

A Psalm of Repentance
PSALM 51, NIV

*This was the prayer of King David when the prophet Nathan came to him after David
had committed adultery with Bathsheba.*

Have mercy on me, O God,
    according to your unfailing love;
according to your great compassion
    blot out my transgressions.
Wash away all my iniquity
    and cleanse me from my sin.
For I know my transgressions,
    and my sin is always before me.
Against you, you only, have I sinned
    and done what is evil in your sight,
so that you are proved right when you speak
    and justified when you judge.
Surely I have been a sinner from birth,
    sinful from the time my mother conceived me.
Surely you desire truth in the inner parts;
    you teach me wisdom in the inmost place.
Cleanse me with hyssop, and I will be clean;
    wash me, and I will be whiter than snow.
Let me hear joy and gladness;
    let the bones you have crushed rejoice.
Hide your face from my sins
    and blot out all my iniquity.
Create in me a pure heart, O God,
    and renew a steadfast spirit within me.
Do not cast me from your presence
    or take your Holy Spirit from me.
Restore to me the joy of your salvation

and grant me a willing spirit, to sustain me.
Then I will teach transgressors your ways,
>and sinners will turn back to you.
Save me from bloodguilt, O God,
>the God who saves me,
>and my tongue will sing of your righteousness.
O Lord, open my lips,
>and my mouth will declare your praise.
You do not delight in sacrifice, or I would bring it;
>you do not take pleasure in burnt offerings.
The sacrifices of God are a broken spirit;
>a broken and contrite heart,
>O God, you will not despise.
In your good pleasure make Zion prosper;
>build up the walls of Jerusalem.
Then there will be righteous sacrifices,
>whole burnt offerings to delight you;
>then bulls will be offered on your altar. ❧

A Blissful Transformation

FYODOR DOSTOEVSKY

The dying priest, Zossima, recounts the kind of life he lived before committing himself to the Lord's service forty years earlier. This story of genuine repentance from The Brothers Karamozov *knows few equals.*

By the time we left the school as officers, we were ready to lay down our lives for the honor of the regiment, but no one of us had any knowledge of the real meaning of honor, and if anyone had known it, he would have been the first to ridicule it. Drunkenness, debauchery and devilry were what we almost prided ourselves on. I don't say that we were bad by nature. All these young men were good fellows, but they behaved badly, and I worst of all. What made it worse for me was that I had come into my own money, and so I flung myself into a life of pleasure, and plunged headlong into all the recklessness of youth.

. . . After four years of this life, I chanced to be in the town of K. where our regiment was stationed at the time. We found the people of the town hospitable, rich, and fond of entertainments. I met with a cordial reception everywhere, as I was of a lively temperament and was known to be well off, which always goes a long way in the world. And then a circumstance happened which was the beginning of it all.

I formed an attachment to a beautiful and intelligent young girl of noble and lofty character, the daughter of people much respected. They were well-to-do people of influence and position. They always gave me a cordial and friendly reception. I fancied that the young lady looked on me with favor and my heart was aflame at such an idea. . . . Then, all of a sudden, we were ordered off for two months to another district.

On my return two months later, I found the young lady already married to a rich neighboring landowner, a very amiable man, still young though older than I was, connected with the best Petersburg society, which I was not, and of excellent education, which I also was not. I was so overwhelmed at this unexpected circumstance that my mind was positively clouded. The worst of it all was that, as I learned then, the young landowner had been a long while betrothed to her, and I had met him indeed many times in her house, but blinded by my conceit I had noticed nothing. And this particularly mortified me; almost everybody had known all about it, while I knew nothing. I was filled with sudden irrepressible fury. With flushed face I began recalling how often I had been on the point of declaring my love to her, and as she had not attempted to stop me or to warn me, she must, I concluded, have been laughing at me all the time. Later on, of course, I reflected and remembered that she had been very far from laughing at me;

on the contrary, she used to turn off any love-making on my part with a jest and begin talking of other subjects; but at that moment I was incapable of reflection and was all eagerness for revenge. . . .

I waited for an opportunity and succeeded in insulting my "rival" in the presence of a large company. I insulted him on a perfectly extraneous pretext, jeering at his opinion upon an important public event—it was in the year 1826—and my jeer was, so people said, clever and effective. Then I forced him to ask for an explanation, and behaved so rudely that he accepted my challenge in spite of the vast inequality between us, as I was younger, a person of no consequence, and of inferior rank. . . . I soon found a second in a comrade, an ensign of our regiment. In those days though duels were severely punished, yet dueling was a kind of fashion among the officers—so strong and deeply rooted will a brutal prejudice sometimes be.

It was the end of June, and our meeting was to take place at seven o'clock the next day on the outskirts of the town—and then something happened that in very truth was the turning point of my life. In the evening, returning home in a savage and brutal humor, I flew into a rage with my orderly Afanasy, and gave him two blows in the face with all my might, so that it was covered with blood. He had not long been in my service and I had struck him before, but never with such ferocious cruelty. And, believe me, though it's forty years ago, I recall it now with shame and pain. I went to bed and slept for about three hours; when I waked up the day was breaking. I got up—I did not want to sleep any more—I went to the window—opened it, it looked out upon the garden; I saw the sun rising; it was warm and beautiful, the birds were singing.

"What's the meaning of it?" I thought. "I feel in my heart as it were something vile and shameful. Is it because I am going to shed blood? No," I thought, "I feel it's not that. Can it be that I am afraid of death, afraid of being killed? No, that's not it, that's not it at all." . . . And all at once I knew what it was: it was because I had

315

beaten Afanasy the evening before! It all rose before my mind, it all was, as it were, repeated over again; he stood before me and I was beating him straight on the face and he was holding his arms stiffly down, his head erect, his eyes fixed upon me as though on parade. He staggered at every blow and did not even dare to raise his hands to protect himself. That is what a man has been brought to, and that was a man beating a fellow creature! What a crime! It was as though a sharp dagger had pierced me right through. I stood as if I were struck dumb, while the sun was shining, the leaves were rejoicing and the birds were trilling the praise of God. . . . I hid my face in my hands, fell on my bed and broke into a storm of tears.

. . . And all at once the whole truth in its full light appeared to me: what was I going to do? I was going to kill a good, clever, noble man, who had done me no wrong, and by depriving his wife of happiness for the rest of her life, I should be torturing and killing her too. I lay thus in my bed with my face in the pillow, heedless how the time was passing. Suddenly my second, the ensign, came in with the pistol to fetch me.

"Ah," said he, "it's a good thing you're up already. It's time we were off, come along!"

I did not know what to do and hurried to and fro undecided; we went out to the carriage, however.

"Wait here a minute," I said to him. "I'll be back directly, I have forgotten my purse."

And I ran back alone, to Afanasy's little room.

"Afanasy," I said, "I gave you two blows on the face yesterday, forgive me," I said.

He started as though he were frightened, and looked at me; and I saw that it was not enough, and on the spot, in my full officer's uniform, I dropped at his feet and bowed my head to the ground.

"Forgive me," I said.

Then he was completely aghast.

"Your honor . . . sir, what are you doing? Am I worth it?"

And he burst out crying as I had done before, hid his face in his hands, turned to the window and shook all over with his sobs. I flew out to my comrade and jumped into the carriage.

"Ready," I cried. "Have you ever seen a conqueror?" I asked him. "Here is one before you."

I was in ecstasy, laughing and talking all the way, I don't remember what about.

He looked at me. "Well, brother, you are a plucky fellow, you'll keep up the honor of the uniform, I can see."

So we reached the place and found them there, waiting for us. We were placed twelve paces apart; he had the first shot. I stood gaily, looking him full in the face; I did not twitch an eyelash, I looked lovingly at him, for I knew what I would do. His shot just grazed my cheek and ear.

"Thank God," I cried, "no man has been killed," and I seized my pistol, turned back and flung it far away into the wood. "That's the place for you," I cried.

I turned to my adversary.

"Forgive me, young fool that I am, sir," I said, "for my unprovoked insult to you and for forcing you to fire at me. I am ten times worse than you and more, maybe. Tell that to the person whom you hold dearest in the world."

I had no sooner said this than they all three shouted at me.

"Upon my word," cried my adversary, annoyed, "if you did not want to fight, why did not you let me alone?"

"Yesterday I was a fool, today I know better," I answered him gaily.

"As to yesterday, I believe you, but as for today, it is difficult to agree with your opinion," said he.

"Bravo," I cried, clapping my hands. "I agree with you there too, I have deserved it!"

"Will you shoot, sir, or not?"

"No, I won't," I said; "if you like, fire at me again, but it would be better for you not to fire."

The seconds, especially mine, were shouting too: "Can you disgrace the regiment like this, facing your antagonist and begging his forgiveness! If I'd only known this!"

I stood facing them all, not laughing now.

"Gentlemen," I said, "is it really so wonderful in these days to find a man who can repent of his stupidity and publicly confess his wrongdoing?"

"But not in a duel," cried my second again.

"That's what's so strange," I said. "For I ought to have owned my fault as soon as I got here, before he had fired a shot, before leading him into a great and deadly sin; but we have made our life so grotesque, that to act in that way would have been almost impossible, for only after I had faced his shot at the distance of twelve paces could my words have any significance for him, and if I had spoken before, he could have said, 'He is a coward, the sight of the pistols has frightened him, no use to listen to him.'

"Gentlemen," I cried suddenly, speaking straight from my heart, "look around you at the gifts of God, the clear sky, the pure air, the tender grass, the birds; nature is beautiful and sinless, and we, only we, are sinful and foolish, and we don't understand that life is heaven, for we have only to understand that life is heaven, for we have only to understand that and it will at once be fulfilled in all its beauty, we shall embrace each other and weep."

I would have said more but I could not; my voice broke with the sweetness and youthful gladness of it, and there was such bliss in my heart as I had never known before in my life. &

The Results of Repentance
EDWARD GIBBON

In this excerpt from The Decline and Fall of the Roman Empire, *Gibbon describes how, in the early Church, "many of the most eminent saints" had previously been among "the most abandoned sinners." Repentance, or penitence as he called it, leads to faith and newness of life.*

But the primitive Christian demonstrated his faith by his virtues; and it was very justly supposed that the Divine persuasion, which enlightened or subdued the understanding, must at the same time purify the heart and direct the actions of the believer. The first apologists of Christianity who justify the innocence of their brethren, and the writers of a later period who celebrate the sanctity of their ancestors, display, in the most lively colours, the reformation of manners which was introduced into the world by the preaching of the Gospel. As it is my intention to remark only such human causes as were permitted to second the influence of revelation, I shall slightly mention two motives which might naturally render the lives of the primitive Christians much purer and more austere than those of their Pagan contemporaries or their degenerate successors—repentance for their past sins, and the laudable desire of supporting the reputation of the society in which they were engaged.

It is a very ancient reproach, suggested by the ignorance or the malice of infidelity, that the Christians allured into their party the most atrocious criminals, who, as soon as they were touched by a sense of remorse, were easily persuaded to wash away, in the water of baptism, the guilt of their past conduct, for which the temples of the gods refused to grant them any expiation. But this reproach, when it is cleared from misrepresentation, contributes as much to the honour as it did to the increase of the church. The friends of Christianity may acknowledge without a blush that many of the most eminent saints had been before their baptism the most abandoned sinners. Those persons who in the world had followed, though in an imperfect manner, the dictates of benevolence and propriety, derived such a calm satisfaction from the opinion of their own rectitude as rendered them much less susceptible of the sudden emotions of shame, of grief, and of terror, which have given birth to so many wonderful conversions. After the example of their Divine Master, the missionaries of the Gospel disdained not the society of men, and especially of women, oppressed by the consciousness, and very often by the effects, of their vices. As they emerged from sin and superstition to the glorious hope of immortality, they resolved to devote themselves to a life, not only of virtue, but of penitence. The desire of perfection became the ruling passion of their soul; and it is well known that, while reason embraces a cold mediocrity, our passions hurry us with rapid violence over the space which lies between the most opposite extremes. ❧

We acknowledge and bewail our manifold sins and wickedness, Which we, from time to time, most grievously have committed, By thought, word, and deed, Against thy Divine Majesty, Provoking most justly thy wrath and indignation against us. We do earnestly repent, And are heartily sorry for these our misdoings; The remembrance of them is grievous unto us; The burden of them is intolerable. Have mercy upon us.
THE BOOK OF COMMON PRAYER

Thankfulness

SOME TIME AGO WE MET with a group of missionary-linguists in Brasilia, the capital city of Brazil. They were working among primitive Indian tribes in South America, first of all learning the language of the tribal groups and then translating the Scriptures into their languages. During a discussion concerning the difficulties encountered in their work, a young missionary said, "In our tribal group there is no word for 'thank you.' Does anyone have any ideas?" To our amazement, every missionary in the discussion group said the same thing. The Indians had no word for 'thank you,' presumably because they had a limited understanding of thankfulness. Now that is hard to imagine!

Human beings thrive on encouragement. Even the thickest-skinned person responds to appreciation. A thank you in the right place can travel a great distance. A mother who, having spent hours preparing a meal, watches it disappear in minutes down hungry teenage throats, is greatly blessed by a simple "Thanks, Mom." A harrassed secretary, pushed to the limits by a demanding boss, finds new desire to please and new energy to serve once the "thanks word" is voiced.

But it is in the spiritual realm that thankfulness needs to be fully appreciated. One of God's chief complaints against humanity is that, despite His self-revelation, "they neither glorified Him as God, nor gave thanks to Him." This does not mean that God was upset because He wasn't adequately appreciated, but rather, that mankind was functioning in a manner that denied human uniqueness. That uniqueness is seen in the capacity to receive revelation of eternal things, to appreciate them, and to articulate that appreciation in thanksgiving. To fail to be thankful is to fail to be fully human.

A good place to start being thankful is at the meal table. Offering thanks does not make the food into something it isn't, but it does make the eaters into something they weren't . . . thankful! Private devotions for young and old train people to read in the Word great truths and to articulate in appropriate language a response of gratitude. Regular worship leads even the most depressed person to thankfulness and lifts even the most discouraged soul to the heights of praise.

The ancient words of the General Thanksgiving say it all:

Almighty God, Father of all mercies, we, thine unworthy servants, do give thee most humble and hearty thanks for all thy goodness and lovingkindness to us, and to all men. We bless thee for our creation, preservation, and all the blessings of this life; but above all for thine inestimable love in the redemption of the world by our Lord Jesus Christ; for the means of grace, and the hope of glory. And we beseech thee, give us that due sense of all thy mercies, that our hearts may be unfeignedly thankful; and that we show forth thy praise, not only with our lips, but in our lives, by giving up ourselves to thy service, and by walking before thee in holiness and righteousness all our days; through Jesus Christ our Lord, to whom, with thee and the Holy Ghost, be all honor and glory, world without end. Amen.

The Creation
CECIL FRANCES ALEXANDER

Eyes full of wonder and lips filled with thanksgiving make for hearts full of joy and lives filled with glory.

All things bright and beautiful,
    All creatures, great and small,
All things wise and wonderful,
    The Lord God made them all.

Each little flower that opens,
    Each little bird that sings,
He made their glowing colors,
    He made their tiny wings.

The rich man in his castle,
    The poor man at his gate,
God made them, high or lowly,
    And ordered their estate.

The purple-headed mountain,
    The river running by,
The sunset and the morning,
    That brightens up the sky;

The cold wind in the winter,
    The pleasant summer sun,
The ripe fruits in the garden—
    He made them every one.

The tall trees in the greenwood,
    The meadows where we play,

323

The rushes by the water
    We gather every day,—

He gave us eyes to see them,
    And lips that we might tell
How great is God Almighty,
    Who has made all things well! 🐎

Casey the Greedy Young Cowboy
MICHAEL P. WAITE

Casey the Cowboy learned that instead of wanting more, he would do better to be thankful for what he had.

    Cowboy Casey had a horse,
A purebred pedal-horse of course.
He raced it 'round the kitchen chairs
And galloped up the hallway stairs.
    He trotted to the living room
To watch his favorite noon cartoon.
His favorite show was *Cowboy Days*,
He watched it while his horsey grazed.
    And as he watched his cowboy show
With bucking broncs and rodeos,
Cowboy Casey had a thought—
"Hey! They've got stuff I haven't GOT!
All those cowboys on TV
Have more cowboy stuff than me!"
    So, Cowboy Casey wrote a list,
He wrote so long he strained his wrist!
'Stuff I Need' he wrote on top,

And then he ran to Mom and Pop.
    "Here," said Casey, "here's a list.
I need this stuff, I must insist!
Every cowboy on TV
Has this stuff . . . but not poor me!"
    His mom and dad were pretty shocked,
A long time passed before they talked.
"This list is rather long," said Dad.
"You're sure you need these things real bad?"
Cowboy Casey nodded, "Yes."
And said, "Make sure you get the best!"
    "Now, Casey," Mom said with a frown.
"I think that you should look around.
We've bought you cowboy hats and boots,
Silver stars and two six-shoots.
But more than that, you shouldn't groan—
You have a family, friends, a home!"
    That made Casey very mad—
Very mad at Mom and Dad!
He jumped upon his horse's back
And stormed outside—the door went SMACK!
    He rolled his pedal-horse along,
Humming angry cowboy songs.
But as he muttered at the sky,
Something near him caught his eye—
    A poster for a rodeo!
A rodeo! What do you know!
With cowboys, hot dogs, bulls, and clowns—
Coming soon to Casey's town!
    Cowboy Casey snatched the sign
And pedaled home in little time.
Forgetting that he'd been so mad,
He showed the sign to Mom and Dad.

"Sure," they said, "we'd love to go—
We'll take you to the rodeo!"
  The rodeo was big and loud.
What a show! And what a crowd!
They rode on bulls and broncos, too,
It was like a dream come true!
  And then there came a big surprise . . .
A cowboy who was Casey's size!
  Casey watched the boy and thought,
"What a swell life that kid's got!
His parents must be really great. . . .
I'll bet that he's not even eight!"
  The boy, whose name was Bronco Bill,
Had a trailer on a hill.
Casey watched Bill go inside,
And then he took a little ride.
  He went and knocked on Bill's front door. . . .
No answer . . . so he knocked once more.
He opened it, and looked around.
Then he heard a sobbing sound—
And there, in tears, was Bronco Bill
Leaning on the windowsill.
  "Oh, my!" said Casey. "Are you hurt?
Did you get shot by Black-eyed Bert?"
"No," sobbed Bill, "I just feel sad.
I wish I had a mom and dad.
I live here all alone, you see,
'Cause I don't have a family!"
  "You mean that's *all*?" said Casey doubting.
"That's no reason to be pouting!
You've got everything you need—
Bulls and guns and broncs with speed!"
"Sure," said Bill, "but I'm alone.

Would you want this for a home?
All the others in the show
Have a home, a place to go.
Look around. What do you see?
Is this a place you'd want to be?"
    The place was small and dark and sad—
No pets, no friends, no Mom and Dad.
"How awfully lonely," Casey thought.
"I'd rather have the life I've got!"
    It all came clear to Casey then—
How awfully thankless he had been. . . .
Thankless for the things he had,
Thankless for his mom and dad.
All this time he'd whined and moaned
While living in a happy home!
    And as he hung his head in shame,
He heard a voice call out his name.
"Casey! Casey! Where are you?
It's time to go, the show is through."
    Quickly Casey got a plan.
"Come on!" he cried, and took Bill's hand.
    "Hey, Mom! Hey, Dad!" Casey screamed.
They turned and both their faces beamed!
"Casey, Son, where did you go?
You had us worried sick, you know!"
    "Meet my new pal, Bronco Bill,
He lives alone up on the hill.
He's even in the rodeo. . . .
He's the best one in the show!
"And he's got tons of cowboy stuff,
But I found out that's not enough.
You see, he has no Mom or Dad. . . .
And that's why Bronco Bill's so sad.

"He really shouldn't be alone. . . .
Don't you think he needs a home?
I could sort of be his brother—
You could be his dad and mother!
'Cause you're the greatest, Mom and Dad—
And having you sure makes me glad!"
    Cowboy Casey's parents smiled
And hugged their little cowboy child.
They hugged his new friend Billy, too—
This thankfulness was something new! ❧

Ten Poor Lepers
JOHN KNAPP II

In which we learn that on one occasion, only ten percent of the people Jesus blessed were thankful (see Luke 17:11-19).

Ten poor lepers,
    sick as they could be,
Lived by themselves
    in the land of Galilee.

Then the Son of Man
    came walking down the road.
"Oh, heal us!" they cried,
    "We bear a heavy load!"

The Lord Jesus Christ
    was touched in his soul;
He spoke unto the ten men
    and all were made whole.

- Leper Number 1 left to find his brother,
- Leper Number 2 ran home to his mother,
- Leper Number 3 set out to get a wife,
- Leper Number 4 simply ran for his life.
- Leper Number 5 paused to count his money,
- Leper Number 6 bought some jam and honey,
- Leper Number 7 wondered what to do,
- Leper Number 8 was glad he was a Jew,
- Leper Number 9 said, "What else is new?"

But Leper Number 10,
    on his knees he fell,
Crying, "Thank you, Lord Jesus,
    for making me well!"

This poor leper
    had his body made new,
But when he thanked Jesus,
    his heart was healed, too. 🐾

Rest and be thankful.
INSCRIPTION ON A STONE SEAT IN THE SCOTTISH HIGHLANDS.

We Thank Thee
AUTHOR UNKNOWN

People say they don't know God's will. Well, what about this: "In everything give thanks, for this is the will of God in Christ Jesus concerning you"? This poem shows us where to start.

For mother-love and father-care,
For brothers strong and sisters fair,
For love at home and here each day,
For guidance lest we go astray,
     Father in Heaven, we thank Thee.

For this new morning with its light,
For rest and shelter of the night,
For health and food, for love and friends,
For ev'rything His goodness sends,
     Father in Heaven, we thank Thee.

For flowers that bloom about our feet,
For tender grass, so fresh, so sweet,
For song of bird and hum of bee,
For all things fair we hear or see,
     Father in Heaven, we thank Thee.

For blue of stream and blue of sky,
For pleasant shade of branches high,
For fragrant air and cooling breeze,
For beauty of the blooming trees,
     Father in Heaven, we thank Thee. ❧

What God Gives
ROBERT HERRICK, SEVENTEENTH CENTURY

What God gives, and what we take,
'Tis a gift for Christ, His sake:

Be the meal of beans and pease,
God be thanked for those and these.
Have we flesh or have we fish,
All are fragments from His dish. 🏵

With Thanksgiving
PHILIPPIANS 4:4-13, NIV

It's worth remembering that these words were written from prison.

Rejoice in the Lord always. I will say it again: Rejoice! Let your gentleness be evident to all. The Lord is near. Do not be anxious about anything, but in everything, by prayer and petition, with thanksgiving, present your requests to God. And the peace of God, which transcends all understanding, will guard your hearts and your minds in Christ Jesus.

Finally, brothers, whatever is true, whatever is noble, whatever is right, whatever is pure, whatever is lovely, whatever is admirable—if anything is excellent or praiseworthy—think about such things. Whatever you have learned or received or heard from me, or seen in me—put it into practice. And the God of peace will be with you.

I rejoice greatly in the Lord that at last you have renewed your concern for me. Indeed, you have been concerned, but you had no opportunity to show it. I am not saying this because I am in need, for I have learned to be content whatever the circumstances.

I know what it is to be in need, and I know what it is to have plenty. I have learned the secret of being content in any and every situation, whether well fed or hungry, whether living in plenty or in want. I can do everything through him who gives me strength.

Robinson Crusoe Counts His Blessings
DANIEL DEFOE

Robinson Crusoe, shipwrecked and castaway on a deserted island, had every reason to be discouraged and depressed. But he did the smart thing—he sat down, looked his problems squarely in the eye, counted his blessings, and gave thanks to God for His goodness.

I now began to consider seriously my condition, and the circumstance I was reduced to, and I drew up the state of my affairs in writing, not so much to leave them to any that were to come after me, for I was like to have but few heirs, as to deliver my thoughts from daily poring upon them, and afflicting my mind; and as my reason began now to master my despondency, I began to comfort my self as well as I could, and to set the good against the evil, that I might have something to distinguish my case from worse, and I stated it very impartially, like debtor and creditor, the comforts I enjoyed against the miseries I suffered, thus:

Evil	Good
I am cast upon a horrible, desolate island, void of all hope of recovery.	But I am alive, and not drowned as all my ship's company was.
I am singled out and separated, as it were, from all the world to be miserable.	But I am singled out too from all the ship's crew to be spared from death; and He that miraculously saved me from

I am divided from mankind, a solitaire, one banished from humane society.

I have not clothes to cover me.

I am without any defence or means to resist any violence of man or beast.

I have no soul to speak to, or relieve me.

death, can deliver me from this condition.

But I am not starved and perishing on a barren place, affording no sustenance.

But I am in a hot climate, where if I had clothes I could hardly wear them.

But I am cast on an island, where I see no wild beasts to hurt me, as I saw on the coast of Africa; and what if I had been shipwrecked there?

But God wonderfully sent the ship in near enough to the shore, that I have gotten out so many necessary things as will either supply my wants, or enable me to supply myself even as long as I live.

Upon the whole, here was an undoubted testimony, that there was scarce any condition in the world so miserable, but there was something negative or something positive to be thankful for in it; and let this stand as a direction from the experience of the most miserable of all conditions in this world, that we may always find in it something to comfort ourselves from, and to set in the description of good and evil, on the credit side of the account.

The rainy season of the autumnal equinox was now come, and I kept the 30th of September in the same solemn manner as before, being the anniversary of my landing on the island, having now been there two years, and no more prospect of being delivered than the first day I came there. I spent the whole day in humble and thankful acknowledgments of the many wonderful mercies which my solitary condition was attended with, and without which it might have been infinitely more miserable. I gave humble and hearty thanks that God had been pleased to discover to me, even that it was possible I might be more happy in this solitary condition, than I should have been in a liberty of society, and in all the pleasures of the world; that He could fully make up to me the deficiencies of my solitary state, and the want of humane society, by His presence and the communications of His grace to my soul, supporting, comforting, and encouraging me to depend upon His providence here, and hope for His eternal presence hereafter.

It was now that I began sensibly to feel how much more happy this life I now led was, with all its miserable circumstances, than the wicked, cursed, abominable life I led all the past part of my days; and now I changed both my sorrows and my joys; my very desires altered, my affections changed their gusts, and my delights were perfectly new from what they were at my first coming, or indeed for the two years past. ❧

It is the duty of all nations to acknowledge the providence of Almighty God, to obey His will, to be grateful for His benefits, and humbly implore His protection and favor.
GEORGE WASHINGTON

A Psalm of Minor Miracles
JOSEPH BAYLY

Thank you
for what Deborah
calls minor miracles
Lord
like finding
a paper bag
a clean one
there on the sidewalk
ten steps after
you prayed for it
or going down
that awful
dirt road
on the side of the mountain
and only passing
four cars
in eight miles. 🐚

Sermon to the Birds
ST. FRANCIS

St. Francis is probably better known for his love of animals and birds than his work as an artist and preacher. No doubt some of the stories of his relations with the animal kingdom owe more to imagination than reality, but this brief "Sermon to the Birds" is delightful and wonderfully illustrates the psalmist's command, "Let everything that has breath, praise the Lord."

My little sisters, the birds, much bounden are ye unto God, your Creator, and always in every place ought ye to praise Him, for that He hath given you liberty to fly about everywhere, and hath also given you double and triple raiment; moreover He preserved your seed in the ark of Noah, that your race might not perish out of the world; still more are ye beholden to Him for the element of the air which He hath appointed for you; beyond all this, ye sow not, neither do you reap; and God feedeth you, and giveth you the streams and fountains for your drink; the mountains and the valleys for your refuge and the high trees whereon to make your nests; and because ye know not how to spin or sew, God clotheth you, you and your children; wherefore your Creator loveth you much, seeing that He hath bestowed on you so many benefits; and therefore, my little sisters, beware of the sin of ingratitude, and study always to give praises unto God. ❧

Murder in the Cathedral
T. S. ELIOT

This tragic story of the murder of Thomas Becket, Archbishop of Canterbury, ends with a chorus of the common people of the cathedral town lifting their voices in thanksgiving, even at the time of an event that outraged the whole of Europe.

THIRD PRIEST
    Let our thanks ascend
    To God, who has given us another Saint in Canterbury.

CHORUS [*While a* Te Deum *is sung in Latin by a choir in the distance.*]
We praise Thee, O God, for Thy glory displayed in all the creatures
    of the earth,
In the snow, in the rain, in the wind, in the storm; in all of Thy
    creatures, both the hunters and the hunted.
For all things exist only as seen by Thee, only as known by Thee,
    all things exist
Only in Thy light, and Thy glory is declared even in that which
    denies Thee; the darkness declares the glory of light.

Those who deny Thee could not deny, if Thou didst not exist; and
their denial is never complete, for if it were so, they would
not exist.

They affirm Thee in living; all things affirm Thee in living; the
bird in the air, both the hawk and the finch; the beast on the
earth, both the wolf and the lamb; the worm in the soil and
the worm in the belly.

Therefore man, whom Thou hast made to be conscious of Thee,
must consciously praise Thee, in thought and in word and in
deed.

Even with the hand to the broom, the back bent in laying the fire,
the knee bent in cleaning the hearth, we, the scrubbers and
sweepers of Canterbury,

The back bent under toil, the knee bent under sin, the hands to
the face under fear, the head bent under grief,

Even in us the voices of seasons, the snuffle of winter, the song of
spring, the drone of summer, the voices of beasts and of birds,
praise Thee.

We thank Thee for Thy mercies of blood, for Thy redemption by
blood. For the blood of Thy martyrs and saints

Shall enrich the earth, shall create the holy places.

For wherever a saint has dwelt, wherever a martyr has given his
blood for the blood of Christ,

There is holy ground, and the sanctity shall not depart from it

Though armies trample over it, though sightseers come with guide-
books looking over it;

From where the western seas gnaw at the coast of Iona,

To the death in the desert, the prayer in forgotten places by the
broken imperial column,

From such ground springs that which forever renews the earth

Though it is forever denied. Therefore, O God, we thank Thee

Who hast given such blessing to Canterbury.

Forgive us, O Lord, we acknowledge ourselves as type of the
    common man,
Of the men and women who shut the door and sit by the fire;
Who fear the blessing of God, the loneliness of the night of God,
    the surrender required, the deprivation inflicted;
Who fear the injustice of men less than the justice of God;
Who fear the hand at the window, the fire in the thatch, the fist in
    the tavern, the push into the canal,
Less than we fear the love of God.
We acknowledge our trespass, our weakness, our fault; we
    acknowledge
That the sin of the world is upon our heads; that the blood of the
    martyrs and the agony of the saints
Is upon our heads.
Lord, have mercy upon us.
Christ, have mercy upon us.
Lord, have mercy upon us.
Blessed Thomas, pray for us. ❧

Prevailing Prayer
DWIGHT L. MOODY

Dwight L. Moody was a tireless, innovative, irrepressible servant of the Lord. The secret comes through in his emphasis on thankfulness.

It is said that in a time of great despondency among the first set-
tlers in New England, it was proposed in one of their public assem-
blies to proclaim a fast. An old farmer arose; spoke of their provoking heaven with their complaints, reviewed their measures, showed
that they had much to be thankful for, and moved that instead of
appointing a day of fasting, they should appoint a day of thanksgiving. This was done; and the custom has been continued ever since.

However great our difficulties, or deep even our sorrows, there is room for thankfulness. Thomas Adams has said: "Lay up in the ark of thy memory not only the pot of manna, the bread of life; but even Aaron's rod, the very scourge of correction, wherewith thou hast been bettered. Blessed be the Lord, not only giving, but taking away, saith Job. God who sees there is no walking upon roses to heaven, puts His children into the way of discipline; and by the fire of correction eats out the rust of corruption. God sends trouble, then bids us call upon Him; promiseth our deliverance; and lastly, all He requires of us is to glorify Him. 'Call upon Me in the day of trouble; I will deliver thee, and thou shalt glorify Me.' " Like the nightingale, we can sing in the night, and say with John Newton,

> Since all that I meet shall work for my good,
> The bitter is sweet, the medicine food;
> Though painful at present, 'twill cease before long,
> And then—oh, how pleasant!—the conqueror's song.

Among all the apostles none suffered so much as Paul; but none of them do we find so often giving thanks as he. Take his letter to the Philippians. Remember what he suffered at Philippi; how they laid many stripes upon him, and cast him into prison. Yet every chapter in that Epistle speaks of rejoicing and giving thanks. There is that well-known passage: "Be careful for nothing, but in everything, by prayer and supplication, with thanksgiving, let your requests be made known unto God." As someone has said, there are here three precious ideas: "Careful for nothing; prayerful for everything; and thankful for anything." We always get more by being thankful for what God has done for us. Paul says again: "We give thanks to God, the Father of our Lord Jesus Christ, praying always for you." So he was constantly giving thanks. Take up any one of his Epistles, and you will find them full of praise to God.

Even if nothing else called for thankfulness, it would always be an ample cause for it that Jesus Christ loved us, and gave Himself for us. A farmer was once found kneeling at a soldier's grave near Nashville. Someone came to him and said: "Why do you pay so much attention to this grave? Was your son buried here?" "No," he said. "During the war my family were all sick, I knew not how to leave them. I was drafted. One of my neighbors came over and said: 'I will go for you; I have no family.' He went off. He was wounded at Chickamauga. He was carried to the hospital, and there died. And, sir, I have come a great many miles, that I might write over his grave these words, 'He died for me.' "

This the believer can always say of his blessed Savior, and in the fact may well rejoice. "By Him therefore, let us offer the sacrifice of praise continually, that is, the fruit of our lips, giving thanks to His name." 🐞

Every true work of art praises God apart from the composer's intentions, because it could not have been written without the gifts which God gave His creation.
A. W. TOZER

RELATIONAL VALUES

Compassion

THE ENGLISH WORD *compassion* comes from two Latin words that together mean "to suffer with." Compassion, although it may start with sympathy, means more than "to feel sorry for." We get some idea of how compassion "suffers with" a person from the example of Jesus. One day He met a leper. This man's life was very difficult, not only because of his physical condition, but also because local convention required that he live separately from his friends and family. People were deeply afraid that if they had contact with him, they would contract his dreadful disease. But when Jesus saw the leper, He had compassion on him and did a remarkable thing—He actually reached out and touched the man. Unthinkable, in that society. The Greek word used to describe the compassion of Jesus suggests that His stomach was tied in knots, so deeply did He feel the man's pain.

The same word is used to describe the feelings of the father of the prodigal son. From the time his unruly and unthankful boy left, the father anxiously looked for his return. When finally he saw his boy making his weary way back home, he could have been angry. He could have said, "He got exactly what he deserved. He made his bed, now he can lie in it." Instead, on seeing the boy's deep anguish and need, he was filled with compassion. He did what senior citizens in his culture did *not* do—he rushed down the middle of the village street to meet him. Most undignified! Sweeping his son into his arms, he offered him forgiveness and reconciliation.

It was compassion for the suffering soldiers in the Crimea that motivated Florence Nightingale to travel to the battlefront to help alleviate their pain. It was compassion for the poorest of the poor that drove Mother Teresa of Calcutta to spend her life ministering to people for whom nobody else cared. Countless other men and women, less known and unheralded, have taken seriously the powerful words of John the Apostle, translated quaintly but searchingly in the King James Version: "But whoso hath this world's good, and seeth his brother have need, and shutteth up his bowels of compassion from him, how dwelleth the love of God in him?" (I John 3:17).

Perhaps the problem for many of us is that we see so much need and feel so inadequate to meet it that we look the other direction and hope it will go away. Like Andrew with his handful of loaves and fishes, told by the Lord to feed the masses, we look at what we have to offer and say, "But what are they among so many?" Surely the answer to that is, "In the hands of the Master, more than enough." If we dare to care and are ready to share, His blessing is there. 🦋

The Real Treasure
Nancy Simpson Levene

Compassion can be costly, as Alex discovered in Apple Turnover Treasure *when she gave away her well-earned reward. But compassion pays dividends, not only in heaven, but in a deep sense of joy and satisfaction for a kind action done well.*

Alex was a hero at school the next day. Everyone had seen her on television. That seemed to be all anyone could talk about. Even children she did not know spoke to her in the hallways and in the lunchroom. At recess, Alex was bombarded with questions from eager schoolmates wanting to know more about her adventures. Even the teachers crowded around her.

Alex enjoyed being the center of attention, but when she got home, she had an even bigger thrill. Officer Fawcett was waiting.

"Hello, Alex," the officer smiled when Alex walked in the door. "I have a surprise for you."

"Really?" Alex's eyes it up.

"The people in our department want to give you something for your help in catching the bicycle thieves. Can you tell me what you would like for a reward?"

"You mean anything I want?" Alex asked.

"Well, I don't think we can give you Royals Stadium," answered Officer Fawcett with a wink. "Perhaps we could manage something smaller though."

Alex thought for a moment. For some reason she could not explain, a picture of Bridget's grandfather popped into her mind.

"I know what I want!" she suddenly exclaimed. "I want a wheelchair!"

"A what?" questioned Officer Fawcett, completely surprised.

"It's for Bridget's grandpa," Alex explained. "He can't walk, and it's too hard for Bridget or her mother to lift him out of bed. Oh, a wheelchair would be perfect!" she clapped her hands. "But would that be too expensive?" she asked a moment later.

345

"I'll see what we can do," Officer Fawcett replied. She shook her head in disbelief. "You are truly an amazing girl."

Even after the bicycle episode was over, Alex continued to walk over to Bridget's house after school. Bridget had become a very good friend.

The girls kept busy. They put the finishing touches on the sun room. They dusted and polished the furniture and arranged dried flowers and leaves in vases around the room. It was such a warm, happy room. They loved to just sit in it and talk.

Then one evening, Officer Fawcett called Alex. She asked if Alex and her family could meet her at Bridget's house the next evening.

"Bridget and her family know I am coming," Officer Fawcett told Alex, "but I did not tell them that you were going to come, and I did not tell them about the wheelchair. I wanted to surprise them."

"You mean you got a wheelchair?" Alex asked hopefully.

"Yes, we did," Officer Fawcett replied.

"Brussels sprouts!" Alex cried joyfully.

After her talk with Officer Fawcett, Alex danced around the kitchen. "Whoopee!" she cried and tossed Mother's dish towel in the air. She did a little dance with T-Bone until he barked so loud she had to stop.

"I'm so glad Officer Fawcett got a wheelchair for Grandpa!" Alex said to her parents as she collapsed in a kitchen chair beside them.

"We think that what you have done, honey, is wonderful," said Mother giving Alex a hug.

"Yes, Firecracker, giving your reward to Grandpa is a true act of love," said Father.

"Well," Alex shrugged her shoulders, "I guess I will store up some more heavenly treasure."

"Indeed you will," Father replied with a smile. He put his arm around Alex and squeezed her tight. "That's the best kind of treasure you'll ever have."

The next day at school, Alex could hardly keep from telling Bridget about the wheelchair. She could not wait for the day to be over.

Finally, it was time to go to Bridget's house. Janie, Julie, and Lorraine were going too. So was Jason. Alex wanted everyone to share in the joy that night.

When they got to Bridget's house, Officer Fawcett opened the door. She smiled broadly at Alex and her family and friends.

"Come in," she held open the door for them.

"Where is everybody?" Alex asked. The usual chatter was missing. The big house was unusually quiet.

"They are all waiting in Grandpa's room," Officer Fawcett told her. "I asked them to stay there. I told them that I had a surprise for them. I think you ought to push the wheelchair into the room."

"Really?" Alex clapped her hands together excitedly. She couldn't wait to see the look of surprise on the family's faces. "Where is the wheelchair?" she asked.

"Right behind you," laughed Officer Fawcett.

Alex turned to see several police officers gathered on the front porch of the house. Two of them were carrying a brand-new, shiny wheelchair.

"Oh, this is great!" Alex and her family and friends exclaimed. When the wheelchair was set down, Alex sat in it to test it out.

Officer Fawcett disappeared into the back of the house. Soon she reappeared and motioned everyone to follow her. Alex slowly pushed the wheelchair across the wooden floors to Grandpa's room.

There was stunned silence when Alex and the wheelchair appeared at the entrance to Grandpa's bedroom. Bridget and her mother stared at Alex with wide-open mouths.

Alex pushed the wheelchair over to Grandpa's bed. "This wheelchair is for you," she told the elderly man. "I got a reward for helping catch the boys who stole our bicycles, and I decided the best thing to do would be to give it to you."

The old man's eyes filled with tears as he listened to Alex. Trembling, he grasped her hands and held them tight. Staring into Grandpa's grateful eyes, Alex knew that she had made the right decision. This was the treasure. This was the treasure that the Lord was storing in heaven for her that very moment. On earth, the treasure could only be known as LOVE.

Cautiously, Grandpa slid out of his bed and onto the seat of the wheelchair. Bridget put slippers on his feet while her mother arranged a small blanket on his lap.

Alex got the honor of being the first one to push Grandpa. They visited the sun room they had fixed up just for him. They then proceeded to the kitchen where everyone ate Bridget's apple turnovers and cookies provided by the police department. It was a wonderful celebration, and Alex could not remember ever being so happy. She and her family and friends laughed and talked for a long time. Finally, when it was quite late, everyone said good-bye.

"You know, this might sound funny," Alex told her parents as they drove home from Bridget's house, "but when you do something good for someone, God gives you two treasures."

"Two treasures?" Father asked.

"Yeah," Alex replied. "He not only stores treasure for you in heaven, but He also makes you feel really good while you're still here on earth."

Father laughed. "I bet God has a big treasure chest in heaven just waiting for you, Firecracker. And remember, where your treasure is, there your heart is also."

"Yeah," Alex sighed happily. "I guess my heart is pretty close to heaven right now."

"And that's just where it belongs," said Father. 🐾

The Good Samaritan

JENNY ROBERTSON

When a man who was arguing with Jesus asked, "Who is my neighbor?" Jesus told the famous story of the Good Samaritan (see Luke 10) by way of an answer. It's the man in the ditch who needs compassion!

As well as teaching people about God and how to please him, Jesus wanted to show people how they should treat one another. Once one of the religious leaders asked Jesus a question. "What must I do to go to heaven when I die?"

Jesus knew that the questioner was a clever man who was really trying to catch him out, so he asked another question in return.

"God gave us a law to tell us how to please him. What does it say?"

"We must love God with all our heart and love our neighbors just as much as we love ourselves," answered the man.

"Then that is what you must do," answered Jesus simply.

"Well, but who is my neighbor?" the clever man asked. And Jesus told a story to answer him.

The road from Jerusalem to Jericho goes through lonely country where there are plenty of rocks for robbers to hid behind. Nobody liked using the road, especially when they were on their own. One day a traveler set out from Jerusalem, and sure enough, before he had gone very far, a gang of thieves leapt out and attacked him. They snatched his bags, stripped off his cloak and beat him up. Then they ran off, leaving him badly hurt. He would certainly die if no one came by to help him.

As he lay there, he heard footsteps coming along the road. He was too weak to shout or move, but he felt sure that whoever it was would see him.

The passerby was a priest. He was going to Jerusalem to pray in the temple. He noticed the man, but he was too scared to stop in case the robbers attacked him, too. Hastily he crossed over the road and walked by on the other side.

A little later another man came down the road. He was on his way to the temple, too. He looked at the wounded man for a moment, but then he crossed the road as well, and went on his way, leaving the man lying in the hot sun.

At last a Samaritan came by, riding on a donkey. Jews and Samaritans hated one another, but this man felt sorry for the wounded Jew. He got off his donkey and searched in his bags for some cool oil and wine which he had with him. He used them to clean the man's cuts. Then he tore up his own clothes for bandages. He lifted the man on to his donkey and took him to an inn where he looked after him all night.

Next morning the Samaritan had to go on with his journey. He gave the innkeeper two silver coins.

"Look after him well," he said. "If you have to spend more money, I will repay you when I come back."

"Who do you think really cared for the man who was robbed?" Jesus asked the clever man at the end of his story.

"The one who looked after him!" came the reply.

The clever man didn't like admitting it was the Samaritan, one of the Jews' enemies!

But Jesus replied, "Then you must go and behave in the same way." ❧

Biblical orthodoxy without compassion is surely the ugliest thing in the world.
FRANCIS SCHAEFFER

Ninepence for a Baby
VERA COWIE

Gladys Aylward was a humble parlormaid who longed to be a missionary, but no missions agency would accept her. So she saved her money and bought a ticket to China via Siberia. On arrival she met a "bundle of rags" who became the first of hundreds of young children to be cared for by the parlormaid nobody wanted. This excerpt is from Girl Friday to Gladys Aylward.

On one of Gladys's many treks into the mountains, she had come upon a woman sitting by the roadside with what looked like a bundle of rags in her lap. On closer inspection Gladys, whose insatiable curiosity had more than once landed her in difficult situations, discovered that the bundle contained a baby girl. The child was filthy and hardly recognizable as a human being. Angry questions tumbled over themselves as Gladys sought to control her emotions, while the woman just smiled in a slow, aggravating way.

At last, she said, "Do you want to buy the child? I don't want it. I can't be bothered with it," noting with cruel amusement the devastating effect the child's pathetic condition was having on Gladys's feelings. "If you don't take it, it will die," she continued, with the knowing satisfaction that this soft-hearted Western woman would eventually give in. "How much will you give me for it?"

"I have only ninepence," said Gladys angrily.

"Ninepence will do," replied the woman with glee and offered the smelly, filthy bundle to Gladys.

Without a word she gave the woman all the money she had and with warmth and satisfaction she clasped the child to her heart.

Little did Gladys know that Ninepence, as she called her, was to be only the first of a very large family. ❧

Hearts and Hands
O. HENRY

Read carefully. This story of compassion for an unfortunate man takes a surprising twist at the end!

At Denver, there was an influx of passengers into the coaches on the eastbound B. & M. express. In one coach there sat a very pretty young woman dressed in elegant taste and surrounded by all the luxurious comforts of an experienced traveler. Among the newcomers were two young men, one of handsome presence with a bold, frank countenance and manner; the other a ruffled, glum-faced person, heavily built and roughly dressed. The two were handcuffed together.

As they passed down the aisle of the coach the only vacant seat offered was a reversed one facing the attractive young woman. Here the linked couple seated themselves. The young woman's glance fell upon them with a distant, swift disinterest; then with a lovely smile brightening her countenance and a tender pink tingeing her rounded cheeks, she held out a little gray-gloved hand. When she spoke her voice, full, sweet, and deliberate, proclaimed that its owner was accustomed to speak and be heard.

"Well, Mr. Easton, if you *will* make me speak first, I suppose I must. Don't you ever recognize old friends when you meet them in the West?"

The younger man roused himself sharply at the sound of her voice, seemed to struggle with a slight embarrassment which he threw off instantly, and then clasped her fingers with his left hand.

"It's Miss Fairchild," he said, with a smile. "I'll ask you to excuse the other hand; it's otherwise engaged just at present."

He slightly raised his right hand, bound at the wrist by the shining "bracelet" to the left one of his companion. The glad look in the girl's eyes slowly changed to a bewildered horror. The glow faded from her cheeks. Her lips parted in a vague, relaxing distress. Easton, with a little laugh, as if amused, was about to speak again when the other forestalled him. The glum-faced man had been watching the girl's countenance with veiled glances from his keen, shrewd eyes.

"You'll excuse me for speaking, miss, but, I see you're acquainted with the marshal here. If you'll ask him to speak a word for me when we get to the pen he'll do it, and it'll make things easier for me there. He's taking me to Leavenworth prison. It's seven years for counterfeiting."

"Oh!" said the girl, with a deep breath and returning color. "So that is what you are doing out here? A marshal!"

"My dear Miss Fairchild," said Easton, calmly, "I had to do something. Money has a way of taking wings unto itself, and you know it takes money to keep step with our crowd in Washington. I saw this opening in the West, and—well, a marshalship isn't quite as high a position as that of ambassador, but—"

"The ambassador," said the girl, warmly, "doesn't call any more. He needn't ever have done so. You ought to know that. And so now you are one of these dashing western heroes, and you ride and shoot and go into all kinds of dangers. That's different from the Washington life. You have been missed from the old crowd."

The girl's eyes, fascinated, went back, widening a little, to rest upon the glittering handcuffs.

"Don't you worry about them, miss," said the other man. "All marshals handcuff themselves to their prisoners to keep them from getting away. Mr. Easton knows his business."

"Will we see you again soon in Washington?" asked the girl.

"Not soon, I think," said Easton. "My butterfly days are over, I fear."

"I love the West," said the girl, irrelevantly. Her eyes were shining softly. She looked away out the car window. She began to speak truly and simply, without the gloss of style and manner:

"Mamma and I spent the summer in Denver. She went home a week ago because Father was slightly ill. I could live and be happy in the West. I think the air here agrees with me. Money isn't everything. But people always misunderstand things and remain stupid—"

"Say, Mr. Marshal," growled the glum-faced man. "This isn't quite fair. I'm needin' a drink, and haven't had a smoke all day. Haven't you talked long enough? Take me to the smoker now, won't you? I'm half dead for a pipe."

The bound travelers rose to their feet, Easton with the same slow smile on his face.

"I can't deny a petition for tobacco," he said, lightly. "It's the one friend of the unfortunate. Good-bye, Miss Fairchild. Duty calls, you know." He held out his hand for a farewell.

"It's too bad you are not going East," she said, reclothing herself with manner and style. "But you must go on to Leavenworth, I suppose?"

"Yes," said Easton, "I must go on to Leavenworth."

The two men sidled down the aisle into the smoker.

The two passengers in a seat near by had heard most of the conversation. Said one of them: "That marshal's a good sort of chap. Some of these Western fellows are all right."

"Pretty young to hold an office like that, isn't he?" asked the other.

"Young!" exclaimed the first speaker, "why—Oh! didn't you catch on? Say—did you ever know an officer to handcuff a prisoner to his *right* hand?" ❧

Alexander's Leadership
PLUTARCH

In Plutarch's The Lives of the Noble Grecians and Romans, *we can read about Alexander the Great. Alexander was one of the most powerful men who ever lived, but he was still capable of being generous and considerate. Can you think of a similar story about King David?*

He now, as we said, set forth to seek Darius, expecting he should be put to the hazard of another battle, but heard he was taken and secured by Bessus, upon which news he sent home the Thessalians, and gave them a largess of two thousand talents over and above the pay that was due to them. This long and painful pursuit of Darius— for in eleven days he marched thirty-three hundred furlongs— harassed his soldiers so that most of them were ready to give it up, chiefly for want of water.

While they were in this distress, it happened that some Macedonians who had fetched water in skins upon their mules from a river they had found out came about noon to the place where Alexander was, and seeing him almost choked with thirst, presently filled an helmet and offered it him.

He asked them to whom they were carrying the water; they told him to their children, adding, that if his life were but saved, it was no matter for them, they should be able well enough to repair that loss, though they all perished.

Then he took the helmet into his hands, and looking round about, when he saw all those who were near him stretching their heads out and looking earnestly after the drink, he returned it again with thanks without tasting a drop of it. "For," said he, "if I alone should drink, the rest will be out of heart."

The soldiers no sooner took notice of this temperance and magnanimity upon this occasion, but they one and all cried out to him to lead them forward boldly, and began whipping on their horses. For whilst they had such a king they said they defied both weariness and thirst, and looked upon themselves to be little less than immortal. 🐎

The Doctor and the Street Children
NORMAN WYMER

Thomas John Barnardo was studying medicine in preparation for missionary work in China in the 1800s, when the destitute children of London captured his attention. He never made it to China, but it is estimated he assisted at least 330,000 children who were in desperate need. Norman Wymer tells his story in the biography Dr. Barnardo.

Of the many horrors to which the cholera epidemic drew Barnardo's attention, none disgusted him more than the way in which children were left to wander about the streets at all hours in their rags and tatters, and generally barefooted, with nobody appearing to care what happened to them.

Though still only twenty-one himself, Barnardo had developed already a deep affection and sympathy for youth. His devotion was sincere; his behavior tender, fatherly and, considering his own youthfulness, remarkably mature. Many years later, General Booth of the Salvation Army was heard to say to him: "You look after the children and I'll look after the adults; then together we'll convert the world." Barnardo had no need to wait for this advice. Already, by 1866, the lowliest child seemed more important to him than London's wealthiest citizen, and the more pathetic the child's condition, the more deeply he felt for him.

Barnardo had not lived in London sufficiently long to appreciate fully the tragic position of the children, but in only a few weeks he was convinced that it was far too serious to ignore. Aimless-looking boys and girls, from children who could only just toddle to hefty youths, like the one who pelted him during the hymn singing, comprised more than half his audience at his Sunday prayer meetings in the streets; and the mere sight of them, and of the hundreds of others who lurked in the gutters and alleyways or who frequented the "penny gaffs" and gin palaces, was enough to stir him to action.

As in Dublin, he began by teaching in a Ragged School, volunteering his services at a little school in Ernest Street, just off the Mile End Road, of which he soon became the Superintendent. Though his behavior after the beerhouse scene had gained him many followers by then, he was not appreciated by the pupils at Ernest Street. The children proved rather worse than Dublin's. Not content to pelt him with rotten eggs and oranges, they prepared a more ingenious reception for their new master by wrapping cayenne pepper in paper, to which they then set light, unseen, at various corners of the room. The result was that irritating fumes attacked their noses and throats; and everybody began at once to sneeze and cough, until in the end they had to leave the building. A day or two later they crowned their "victory" by dropping Barnardo bodily out of the window. Since the building, happily, was only of a single storey, Barnardo came to no harm. Though inwardly furious, he picked himself up, flicked the dust off his clothes, and made a dignified return by the door—to the astonishment and disappointment of his attackers. The most subtle of tricks are apt to lose their magic when the victim appears unruffled. In vain the Ragged School children tried out many more during the next fortnight or so; and in the end they ceased their baiting.

After a few weeks Barnardo had won not only their attention but their respect: so much so that the worst offenders became his declared champions. He discovered this unexpectedly one night when walking home from the school to his lodgings. Conscious that six of the roughest boys in his class were shadowing him, he became suspicious and turned swiftly on his heel to challenge them. The youths, however, assured him that they had no mischievous intent. They were following because they had heard that a Stepney tough, well known for his ruthlessness, was planning to waylay their master and punch his head, and they wished to protect him.

Barnardo became so popular with his pupils at Ernest Street that soon many more boys came to his school.

How did Barnardo so quickly win the respect and affection of the once unruly children? Several factors were responsible: his sympathy and understanding, his personal enthusiasm, his faith, and his keen sense of humor which grew more lively year by year. He treated them in a responsible, fatherly manner; but his own youthfulness also helped him to appreciate their feelings better than most fathers. Thus he possessed the ability to combine the outlooks of two generations, with the result that he could be intensely serious or intensely jovial as the occasion required. Though the medical students at the London Hospital seldom saw him laugh, his jovial moods, when in the presence of children, were frequent and infectious. He giggled, he tweaked ears, he bounced. Yet he was not a buffoon. He could turn from gay to serious in an instant, and was able to rivet their attentions equally well in his serious moments by the force of his personality and his ability to make his lessons interesting. Whereas the Bible had been but a name to the children hitherto, Barnardo revealed it to them as a book of wonderful and fascinating stories, deeply relevant to their own lives.

The numbers who flocked to listen to him reading and explaining those stories each Sunday soon became so great that the long, narrow, badly ventilated schoolroom was no longer adequate to accommodate them all, and as many as one hundred or two hundred children had to be refused admittance, week after week.

Delighted by the response but distressed at the thought of turning children away, with the inevitable result that they would make straight for the public houses and gin palaces, or else get into mischief in the streets, Barnardo decided to open a larger and more ambitious school of his own: a school that would be open on one or two evenings, as well as on Sundays, and where the boys and girls could learn their alphabet, how to spell, and perhaps a little simple grammar, rather more intelligently than was normally the case. As grown men and women were often unable to spell or write their own names, and, as ignorance often leads to wickedness, Barnardo felt strongly that such instruction was badly needed. ❧

The Dream
FYODOR DOSTOEVSKY

It is sadly possible for us to live our lives without seeing the needs of others around us. Like Mitya in this famous dream from The Brothers Karamazov, *we need to feel and respond to a "passion of pity."*

He had a strange dream, utterly out of keeping with the place and the time.

He was driving somewhere in the steppes, where he had been stationed long ago, and a peasant was driving him in a cart with a pair of horses, through snow and sleet. He was cold, it was early in November, and the snow was falling in big wet flakes, melting as soon as it touched the earth. And the peasant drove him smartly, he had a fair, long beard. He was not an old man, somewhere about fifty, and he had on a grey peasant's smock. Not far off was a village, he could see the black huts, and half the huts were burnt down, there were only the charred beams sticking up. And as they drove in, there were peasant women drawn up along the road, a lot of women, a whole row, all thin and wan, with their faces a sort of brownish color, especially one at the edge, a tall, bony woman, who looked forty, but might have been only twenty, with a long thin face. And in her arms was a little baby crying. And her breasts seemed so dried up that there was not a drop of milk in them. And the child cried and cried, and held out its little bare arms, with its little fists blue from cold.

"Why are they crying? Why are they crying?" Mitya asked, as they dashed gaily by.

"It's the babe," answered the driver, "the babe weeping."

And Mitya was struck by his saying, in his peasant way, "the babe," and he liked the peasant's calling it a "babe." There seemed more pity in it.

"But why is it weeping?" Mitya persisted stupidly, "why are its little arms bare? Why don't they wrap it up?"

"The babe's cold, its little clothes are frozen and don't warm it."

"But why is it? Why?" foolish Mitya still persisted.

"Why, they're poor people, burnt out. They've no bread. They're begging because they've been burnt out."

"No, no," Mitya, as it were, still did not understand. "Tell me why it is those poor mothers stand there? Why are people poor? Why is the babe poor? Why is the steppe barren? Why don't they hug each other and kiss? Why don't they sing songs of joy? Why are they so dark from black misery? Why don't they feed the babe?"

And he felt that, though his questions were unreasonable and senseless, yet he wanted to ask just that, and he had to ask it just in that way. And he felt that a passion of pity, such as he had never known before, was rising in his heart, that he wanted to cry, that he wanted to do something for them all, so that the babe should weep no more, so that the dark-faced, dried-up mother should not weep, that no one should shed tears again from that moment, and he wanted to do it at once, at once, regardless of all obstacles, with all the recklessness of the Karamazovs. ❧

The Quality of Mercy
WILLIAM SHAKESPEARE

The merchant in The Merchant of Venice *was in a predicament. His deadly enemy, Shylock, was in court claiming the right to a pound of his flesh. The merchant's friend, Portia, makes this moving appeal for compassion in Act IV, Scene I.*

The quality of mercy is not strain'd,
   It droppeth as the gentle rain from heaven
Upon the place beneath: it is twice blest;
   It blesseth him that gives and him that takes:
'Tis mightiest in the mightiest; it becomes
   The throned monarch better than his crown;
His sceptre shows the force of temporal power,
   The attribute to awe and majesty,
Wherein doth sit the dread and fear of kings;
   But mercy is above this sceptred sway;
It is enthroned in the hearts of kings,
   It is an attribute to God himself;
And earthly power doth then show likest God's
   When mercy seasons justice. Therefore, Jew,
Though justice be thy plea, consider this,
   That, in the course of justice, none of us
Should see salvation: we do pray for mercy;
   And that same prayer doth teach us all to render
The deeds of mercy. I have spoke thus much
   To mitigate the justice of thy plea;
Which if thou follow, this strict court of Venice
   Must needs give sentence 'gainst the merchant there. 🐾

Who Is So Low
S. RALPH HARLOW

"Am I my brother's keeper?" asked Cain. "Yes, you are," this sixteenth-century poem replies loudly and clearly.

Who is so low that I am not his brother?
    Who is so high that I've no path to him?
Who is so poor I may not feel his hunger?
    Who is so rich I may not pity him?

Who is so hurt I may not know his heartache?
    Who sings for joy my heart may never share?
Who in God's heaven has passed beyond my vision?
    Who to hell's depths where I may never fare?

May none, then, call on me for understanding,
    May none, then, turn to me for help in pain,
And drain alone his bitter cup of sorrow,
    Or find he knocks upon my heart in vain.

*There is no exercise better for the heart than reaching
down and lifting people up.*
JOHN ANDREW HOLMER

People will not care what you know until they know that you care.
AUTHOR UNKNOWN

Forgiveness

LITTLE JOHNNY WAS VERY UPSET with his brother, Willy. Before he said his prayers, Johnny's mother said to him, "Now I want you to forgive your brother." But Johnny was not in a very forgiving frame of mind. "No, I won't forgive him," he replied. Mother tried persuasion of every motherly variety, to no avail. In desperation she said, "What if your brother were to die tonight? How would you feel if you knew you hadn't forgiven him?" This was too much for Johnny, who reluctantly conceded, "All right, I forgive him . . . but if he's alive in the morning, I'll get him for what he did to me!" Poor little Johnny was expressing in childlike terms what is so often mistaken today for forgiveness.

The English word *forgive* means literally to "give away." When a debt is forgiven, the rights to recoup the funds are "given away." If someone injures me and I forgive him, I give away the freedom to continue being angry and resentful towards the one who wronged me. This, of course can be costly. If I forgive a monetary indebtedness, I release my creditor from responsibility, but I have to absorb the loss myself. If I give away my angry feelings, I must bear the pain without experiencing the satisfaction my angry, resentful reactions provide. That means I relinquish the only means at my disposal to make the offending party pay, and I suffer loss by that transaction.

The forgiveness of sins is, of course, a fundamental aspect of Christian experience. God devised a way whereby He would assume responsibility for man's sin in the person of the God-man, Jesus—and it cost Him His life. Surely there are no more reassuring words than Paul's exultant statement, "There is now therefore no condemnation to those who are in Christ Jesus." Forgiven, no longer responsible, because He has given away His holy anger against our sin by accepting its consequences in Himself.

But there is an essentially practical application to all this. As we so often pray, "Forgive us our debts as we forgive those who are indebted to us." We need to recognize that our experience of forgiveness is directly related to our ability to forgive. This does not mean that we earn forgiveness by generating a forgiving spirit. Rather, it means that unless we have a forgiving spirit, we are in no condition to appropriate and appreciate forgiveness. The clenched fist cannot receive the gift of a sweet-smelling rose.

We are often encouraged to "forgive and forget." This may be a little unrealistic, because the eradication of the memory bank is not something we are equipped to accomplish. Our minds play tricks, and our memories keep coming back like a song. We may not be able to forget, but we can, through God's grace, reaffirm our forgiveness. &

Sir Humphrey's Honeystands

CHRISTOPHER A. LANE

Freddie was forgiven, but he would not forgive. Can you think of a parable Jesus told that is like the story of Sir Humphrey and Freddie the Fox?

There was once a bear who lived in a beautiful house deep in the forest. He lived a kingly life, and the woodland creatures actually considered him a royal bear, of sorts, and called him Sir Humphrey.

He had gotten rich after he had found an enormous beehive. He had sold the honey from it, and the woodland creatures couldn't seem to get enough of it.

Humphrey soon found himself swamped with so many orders for honey that he couldn't keep up. He looked for other animals to help him with his honey business.

Freddie the Fox was one of the first animals to come forward. Freddie was a clever sort and seemed very willing to help. Before long, Freddie became Humphrey's chief fox and number-one servant.

Now it came about one day, just before naptime, that Edward, the bookkeeping beaver, was in Sir Humphrey's study checking the honey records.

"Are my honeystands doing well?" Sir Humphrey asked.

"Oh, yes, quite well," Edward assured him, adjusting his round spectacles. "In fact, you could say . . . hmmm."

"What is it?" Sir Humphrey asked, sitting forward in his tall padded chair.

"Probably nothing," Edward said. "Just a slight . . . discrepancy. The numbers here don't seem to add up correctly. It seems that one of your servants has—um—'borrowed' several jars of your honey and failed to return them or to pay you."

Sir Humphrey was silent for a moment, his nose wrinkled up as he wondered what this meant. "One of my trusted servants?" he asked finally.

"Yes, sir. According to these figures, he owes you 100 jars."

"100 jars!!?" Sir Humphrey nearly fell from his seat. "What on earth could anyone do with 100 jars of honey?"

Edward shook his head. "I have no idea, sir. But I certainly advise you to find out."

"Oh, I assure you, Ed, I will find out at once! Reginald!!!" he roared.

A regal-looking hound appeared in a clean, sharp butler's uniform. "You rang, Sir Humphrey?" he asked.

"Yes, Reginald, please summon—" Sir Humphrey paused. "Ed, what was the name of that servant?"

Edward flipped quickly through his papers. "It is Mr. Freddie the Fox."

Humphrey started. "Freddie? Surely you are mistaken."

Edward looked down at his documents and then shrugged his shoulders. "It's no mistake, sir," he said. "Freddie the Fox owes you honey."

"Unthinkable. Reginald, bring Mr. Fox to me at once!"

. . . [Eventually] he heard a knock at the door of his study. "Come in," he said in a deep voice.

Reginald the butler held the door open. "Mr. Fox to see you, sir."

"Send him in. And have Ed my bookkeeper come in as well."

"Good day, Sir Humphrey," Freddie said brightly as he entered the study. "You're lookin' good, sir. Must be the muffins and honey, eh? Oh, it's awful nice of you to have me over like this. What did you want to talk about? You gonna open another honey-stand? I tell ya, I have some ideas about that. I was thinkin' 'bout a place over by the elk lodge. And I—"

"That's not why I've asked you here, Freddie," Sir Humphrey interrupted. "Sit down and listen. Ed, tell Mr. Fox what you found in the records."

"According to these figures, Mr. Fox, you owe Sir Humphrey 100 jars of honey."

Sir Humphrey leaned forward toward the seated fox. "How do you explain this debt?"

"I . . . ah . . ." Freddie stuttered.

"Well," Sir Humphrey asked, "did you take 100 jars?"

"I guess so," Freddie said quietly.

"You guess so!?" Sir Humphrey roared. "Freddie, whatever did you do with 100 jars of honey?"

"I took some home for my family. You remember my family—Lucy, the wife—" He pulled out a wallet filled with photographs. "And there's Dora, our little—"

Sir Humphrey stared intently at Freddie. "Your family couldn't possibly eat that much honey!"

"Um . . . well . . . No, we didn't eat it all. I kind of took some"—his voice sank to a whisper—"outside the forest. And I sold it."

"Where is the money, Freddie?"

"I sort of lost it."

Sir Humphrey gave a long sigh. "What do you mean, you lost it?" he asked, trying not to lose his temper.

"Well, I have this weakness for the ponies, you know, race-horses. I bet it at the racetrack. I thought maybe I could make a little easy money."

Sir Humphrey sank into his tall padded chair. "Let me get this straight, Freddie. You stole my honey, sold it without my permission, and gambled away the profits?"

"That about says it," the fox agreed. "I'll pay you back, though. Don't worry. Just give me a little time."

Sir Humphrey rose. "You will pay me back immediately! If you must, sell everything you own."

"But sir," Freddie pleaded, "you can't mean that. What about my family? How will we live?"

"You should have thought about that before you took my honey."

"Oh, please, sir," Freddie whined, falling to his knees before the wealthy bear. "Please, Sir Humphrey, give me one more chance. You are such a kind, forgiving bear. I really am sorry, sir. What I did was wrong, I know that. Please forgive me. I've learned my lesson. If you'll only be patient with me, I'll pay you back, every single jar. Please, sir . . . "

"Oh, get up," Sir Humphrey said, taking his seat again. "I should have you thrown into jail, but I can see that you are sorry for what you did. I forgive you."

"Oh, thank you, sir!" Freddie cried. "I'll start paying you back as soon as—"

"You could never repay it all," the wealthy bear said, shaking his head. "Ed, strike out his debt."

"Sir?" the bookkeeper questioned.

"Cancel it. Give him a fresh start." Rising again, Sir Humphrey offered the fox his paw.

"Oh, Sir Humphrey, thank you, thank you," the overjoyed fox said. "I'll never forget your generosity and kindness. Thank you!"

"Now back to work with you," Sir Humphrey motioned, "you crazy fox."

Later that same day, an elderly mole dressed in worn, tattered clothing approached one of Sir Humphrey's honeystands. His name was Barnabas, and he was a poor mole who could only afford to buy very small amounts of honey at a time.

"Good day, Mrs. Rabbit," the elderly mole said timidly.

"Why, hello there, Barnabas," the rabbit clerk answered cheerily. "I haven't seen you around lately. What can I do for you?"

"I—I was wondering," he said hesitantly, "if I might have a bit of honey, a small cup perhaps?"

"Of course," she said. Lowering her voice, she said, "Would you like me to put it on your bill?"

"Oh, yes, please, if it's not too much trouble."

Mrs. Rabbit hopped over to the honey bin, dipped out a generous cupful of the sticky golden nectar, and handed it over the counter to the hungry, waiting mole. She wrote down "one cup" on a bill as Barnabas slowly started home.

Just then Freddie the Fox arrived. He visited each honeystand every day to check up on the employees and to make sure that the business was running smoothly.

He walked right into Barnabas, who had stopped to sample the delicious syrup.

"Oh, excuse me, sir," Barnabas apologized as his honey spilled over onto the ground.

"You old fool!" Freddie hissed, wiping droplets of honey from his smooth, shiny coat. Suddenly Freddie recognized the mole. "Hey, aren't you Barnabas? Let's see your money, fella."

"I haven't any at the moment, but—"

"I put it on his bill, Mr. Fox," Mrs. Rabbit explained.

"Oh, no, you don't!" Freddie ordered. "No more, no honey. In fact," he said, shuffling through his notes, "let me see. Barnabas, Barnabas . . . Aha! According to my records, you already owe me for one cup of honey."

"Yes, I know sir, but—"

"No buts about it." Freddie grabbed the elderly mole by the coat. "Pay up!"

"Mr. Fox!" Mrs. Rabbit protested. "Please don't shake him."

"Where'd you hide your money, mole? You've gotta pay up right now, Barny ol' buddy. Gimme this coat, and that cane, and let me have your hat."

"Mr. Fox!" Mrs. Rabbit pleaded.

"Another word," Freddie the Fox said, baring his sharp white fangs, "and you're fired, Mrs. Rabbit!"

"Please, Mr. Fox. Be patient," Barnabas begged, falling to his knees. "I promise to pay you back."

"I've heard that before," Freddie said. He started yelling, "Police! Police! This man won't pay his bill!"

It took only moments for Freddie's shouts to reach the nearby police station, and soon two badgers arrived in dark blue uniforms.

"What seems to be the problem here?" the first officer questioned.

"This bum won't pay his bill. He owes me for honey and claims he has no money."

"Well, sir, what do you have to say for yourself?" the second badger asked.

"I have no money," Barnabas answered, hanging his head.

"Sorry, fella," the first badger said, "we're gonna have to take you in."

Mrs. Rabbit [was angry]. "I must help old Barnabas. And I know just what to do!"

She quickly closed down the honeystand and made her way to Sir Humphrey's luxurious home.

"Sir Humphrey! Sir Humphrey!" she shouted, hopping up and down. "Oh, it was terrible!"

"Mrs. Rabbit, calm yourself. What is the problem?"

"Oh, sir, it was terrible! He's so cruel! He has no heart, no heart at all, I tell you!" And Mrs. Rabbit told Sir Humphrey all about what had happened.

When she was done, there was a long silence. Then Sir Humphrey bared his huge white teeth and let out a long, deep growl. "Why, that ungrateful little fox! Reginald!! Reginald!!" he roared.

"Yes, sir," the butler replied, coming into the parlor.

"Have Freddie the Fox summoned at once!"

Later, when Freddie the Fox arrived, he strutted into the parlor after Reginald had announced him. "Say there, Sir H. What's up? Got a problem I can help you iron out? Say, thanks again for overlooking that honey jar mix-up."

"Be quiet. You," Sir Humphrey pointed with his big paw, "are a worthless servant!"

"Huh?"

"First you steal from me. That's bad enough. But then you go and have a respectable mole thrown into prison."

"Oh, I got you. You mean that Barnabas. Listen, Sir H, he's a bum, always trying to get something for nothin'. I turned him over to the police. That's the last time he'll bother us."

"You should have forgiven him."

"Hey, he owed me!" Freddie objected.

"If that is your attitude, Freddie, I have no choice but to take action. If you cannot forgive this small debt, then neither will your debt be forgiven you."

"What?"

"Reginald!" Sir Humphrey roared.

"Sir?" the butler responded.

"Call the police!" he ordered.

"Very good, sir," Reginald replied before reaching over to ring a bell hanging near the doorway.

"The police!?" Freddie screeched. "What are you doing?"

"Freddie," Sir Humphrey explained, "you will be residing in the local jail until you pay back all the honey you owe me."

"But—but—" the fox stuttered, "you can't do that."

Soon Reginald opened the door. "Sir Humphrey, the law enforcement officers have arrived."

"This is he, officers," Sir Humphrey pointed. "Freddie the Fox."

"Come along, Mr. Fox," one officer said. He and the other officer grabbed Freddie by the scruff of his neck and carried him down the hallway and out the door toward the jail, where he became known as "the fox who wouldn't forgive." He remains in jail to this day, still paying back his debt to Sir Humphrey. He now has only 95 $1/2$ jars of honey to go. ❧

The Forgiving Father
LUKE 15:11-24, NIV

Jesus told this story to illustrate God's concern for sinners and His willingness to forgive them.

Jesus continued: "There was a man who had two sons. The younger one said to his father, 'Father, give me my share of the estate.' So he divided his property between them.

"Not long after that, the younger son got together all he had, set off for a distant country and there squandered his wealth in wild living. After he had spent everything, there was a severe famine in that whole country, and he began to be in need. So he went and hired himself out to a citizen of that country, who sent him to his fields to feed pigs. He longed to fill his stomach with the pods that the pigs were eating, but no one gave him anything.

"When he came to his senses, he said, 'How many of my father's hired men have food to spare, and here I am starving to death! I will set out and go back to my father and say to him: Father, I have sinned against heaven and against you. I am no longer worthy to be called your son; make me like one of your hired men.' So he got up and went to his father.

"But while he was still a long way off, his father saw him and was filled with compassion for him; he ran to his son, threw his arms around him and kissed him.

"The son said to him, 'Father, I have sinned against heaven and against you. I am no longer worthy to be called your son.'

"But the father said to his servants, 'Quick! Bring the best robe and put it on him. Put a ring on his finger and sandals on his feet. Bring the fattened calf and kill it. Let's have a feast and cele-brate. For this son of mine was dead and is alive again; he was lost and is found.' So they began to celebrate."

A Quarrel Between Sisters

Louisa May Alcott

In which two of Alcott's Little Women, Jo and Amy, learn through a near tragedy the blessings and joys of forgiving and being forgiven.

On going up to put away her best hat, Jo's first look was toward the bureau; for, in their last quarrel, Amy had soothed her feelings by turning Jo's top drawer upside down on the floor. Everything was in its place, however; and after a hasty glance into her various closets, bags, and boxes, Jo decided that Amy had forgiven and forgotten her wrongs.

There Jo was mistaken, for next day she made a discovery which produced a tempest. Meg, Beth, and Amy were sitting together, late in the afternoon, when Jo burst into the room, looking excited, and demanding breathlessly, "Has any one taken my book?"

Meg and Beth said "No," at once, and looked surprised; Amy poked the fire, and said nothing. Jo saw her color rise, and was down upon her in a minute.

"Amy, you've got it!"

"No, I haven't."

"You know where it is, then!"

"No, I don't."

"That's a fib!" cried Jo, taking her by the shoulders, and looking fierce enough to frighten a much braver child than Amy.

"It isn't. I haven't got it, don't know where it is now, and don't care."

"You know something about it, and you'd better tell at once, or I'll make you," and Jo gave her a slight shake.

"Scold as much as you like, you'll never see your silly old book again," cried Amy, getting excited in her turn.

"Why not?"

"I burnt it up."

"What! my little book I was so fond of, and worked over, and meant to finish before Father got home! Have you really burnt it?" said Jo, turning very pale, while her eyes kindled and her hands clutched Amy nervously.

"Yes, I did! I told you I'd make you pay for being so cross yesterday, and I have, so—"

Amy got no farther, for Jo's hot temper mastered her, and she shook Amy till her teeth chattered in her head; crying, in a passion of grief and anger, —

"You wicked, wicked girl! I never can write it again, and I'll never forgive you as long as I live."

Meg flew to rescue Amy, and Beth to pacify Jo, but Jo was quite beside herself; and, with a parting box on her sister's ear, she rushed out of the room up to the old sofa in the garret, and finished her fight alone.

The storm cleared up below, for Mrs. March came home, and, having heard the story, soon brought Amy to a sense of the wrong she had done her sister. . . . Amy's bonfire had consumed the loving work of several years. It seemed a small loss to others, but to Jo it was a dreadful calamity, and she felt that it never could be made up to her. Beth mourned as for a departed kitten, and Meg refused to defend her pet; Mrs. March looked grave and grieved, and Amy felt that no one would love her till she had asked pardon for the act which she now regretted more than any of them.

When the tea-bell rang, Jo appeared, looking so grim and unapproachable that it took all Amy's courage to say meekly, —

"Please forgive me, Jo; I'm very, very sorry."

"I never shall forgive you," was Jo's stern answer; and, from that moment, she ignored Amy entirely. . . .

As Jo received her good-night kiss, Mrs. March whispered gently, —

"My dear, don't let the sun go down upon your anger; forgive each other, help each other, and begin again to-morrow."

Jo wanted to lay her head down on the motherly bosom, and cry her grief and anger all away; but tears were an unmanly weakness, and she felt so deeply injured that she really *couldn't* quite forgive yet. So she winked hard, shook her head, and said, gruffly because Amy was listening, —

"It was an abominable thing, and she don't deserve to be forgiven."

With that she marched off to bed, and there was no merry or confidential gossip that night.

Amy was much offended that her overtures of peace had been repulsed, and began to wish she had not humbled herself, to feel more injured than ever, and to plume herself on her superior virtue in a way which was particularly exasperating. Jo still looked like a thunder-cloud, and nothing went well all day. . . .

"Everybody is so hateful, I'll ask Laurie to go skating. He is always kind and jolly, and will put me to rights, I know," said Jo to herself, and off she went.

Amy heard the clash of skates, and looked out with an impatient exclamation, —

"There! She promised I should go next time, for this is the last ice we shall have. But it's no use to ask such a cross-patch to take me."

"Don't say that; you *were* very naughty, and it *is* hard to forgive the loss of her precious little book; but I think she might do it now, and I guess she will, if you try her at the right minute," said Meg. "Go after them; don't say anything till Jo has got good-natured with Laurie, then take a quiet minute, and just kiss her, or do some kind thing, and I'm sure she'll be friends again, with all her heart."

"I'll try," said Amy, for the advice suited her; and, after a flurry to get ready, she ran after the friends, who were just disappearing over the hill. . . .

Jo heard Amy panting after her run, stamping her feet and blowing her fingers, as she tried to put her skates on; but Jo never turned, and went slowly zigzagging down the river, taking a bitter, unhappy sort of satisfaction in her sister's troubles. She had cherished her anger till it grew strong, and took possession of her, as evil thoughts and feelings always do, unless cast out at once. As Laurie turned the bend, he shouted back, —

"Keep near the shore; it isn't safe in the middle."

Jo heard, but Amy was just struggling to her feet, and did not catch a word. Jo glanced over her shoulder, and the little demon she was harboring said in her ear, —

"No matter whether she heard or not, let her take care of herself."

Laurie had vanished round the bend; Jo was just at the turn, and Amy, far behind, striking out toward the smoother ice in the middle of the river. For a minute Jo stood still, with a strange feeling at her heart; then she resolved to go on, but something held and turned her round, just in time to see Amy throw up her hands and go down, with the sudden crash of rotten ice, the splash of water, and a cry that made Jo's heart stand still with fear. . . .

She tried to call Laurie, but her voice was gone; she tried to rush forward, but her feet seemed to have no strength in them; and, for a second, she could only stand motionless, staring, with a terror-stricken face, at the little blue hood above the black water. Something rushed swiftly by her, and Laurie's voice cried out,—

"Bring a rail; quick, quick!"

How she did it, she never knew; but for the next few minutes she worked as if possessed, blindly obeying Laurie, who was quite self-possessed, and, lying flat, held Amy up by his arm and hockey till Jo dragged a rail from the fence, and together they got the child out, more frightened than hurt.

"Now then, we must walk her home as fast as we can; pile our things on her, while I get off these confounded skates," cried Laurie, wrapping his coat round Amy , and tugging away at the straps, which never seemed so intricate before.

Shivering, dripping, and crying, they got Amy home; and, after an exciting time of it, she fell asleep, rolled in blankets, before a hot fire. During the bustle Jo had scarcely spoken, but flown about, looking pale and wild, with her things half off, her dress torn, and her hands cut and bruised by ice and rails and refractory buckles. When Amy was comfortably asleep, the house quiet, and Mrs. March sitting by the bed, she called Jo to her, and began to bind up the hurt hands.

"Are you sure she is safe?" whispered Jo, looking remorsefully at the golden head, which might have been swept away from her sight forever under the treacherous ice.

"Quite safe, dear; she is not hurt, and won't even take cold, I think, you were so sensible in covering and getting her home quickly," replied her mother cheerfully.

"Laurie did it all; I only let her go. Mother, if she *should* die, it would be my fault"; and Jo dropped down beside the bed, in a passion of penitent tears, telling all that had happened, bitterly condemning her hardness of heart, and sobbing out her gratitude for being spared the heavy punishment which might have come upon her.

"It's my dreadful temper! I try to cure it; I think I have, and then it breaks out worse than ever. O Mother, what shall I do? what shall I do?" cried poor Jo, in despair.

"Watch and pray, dear; never get tired of trying; and never think it is impossible to conquer your fault," said Mrs. March, drawing the blowzy head to her shoulder, and kissing the wet cheek so tenderly that Jo cried harder than ever.

"You don't know, you can't guess how bad it is! It seems as if I could do anything when I'm in a passion; I get so savage, I could hurt anyone, and enjoy it. I'm afraid I *shall* do something dreadful some day, and spoil my life, and make everybody hate me. O Mother, help me, do help me!"

"I will, my child, I will. Don't cry so bitterly, but remember this day, and resolve, with all your soul, that you will never know another like it. Jo, dear, we all have our temptations, some far greater than yours, and it often takes us all our lives to conquer them. . . . My child, the troubles and temptations of your life are beginning, and may be many; but you can overcome and outlive them all if you learn to feel the strength and tenderness of your Heavenly Father as you do that of your earthly one. The more you love and trust Him, the nearer you will feel to Him, and the less you will depend on human power and wisdom. His love and care never tire or change, can never be taken from you, but may become the source of lifelong peace, happiness, and strength. Believe this heartily, and go to God with all your little cares, and hopes, and sins, and sorrows, as freely and confidingly as you come to your mother."

Jo's only answer was to hold her mother close, and, in the silence which followed, the sincerest prayer she had ever prayed left her heart without words; for in that sad, yet happy hour, she had learned not only the bitterness of remorse and despair, but the sweetness of self-denial and self-control; and, led by her mother's hand, she had drawn nearer to the Friend who welcomes every child with a love stronger than that of any father, tenderer than that of any mother.

Amy stirred, and sighed in her sleep; and, as if eager to begin at once to mend her fault, Jo looked up with an expression on her face which it had never worn before.

"I let the sun go down on my anger; I wouldn't forgive her, and to-day, if it hadn't been for Laurie, it might have been too late! How could I be so wicked?" said Jo, half aloud, as she leaned over her sister, softly stroking the wet hair scattered on the pillow.

As if she heard, Amy opened her eyes, and held out her arms, with a smile that went straight to Jo's heart. Neither said a word, but they hugged one another close, in spite of the blankets, and everything was forgiven and forgotten in one hearty kiss. 🍂

Jacob Seeks Peace

VIRGINIA MUIR

Esau had good reason to be angry with his brother Jacob. And Jacob had good reason to be afraid. But when they finally met after many years, as recounted in Genesis 32 and 33, Esau forgave his brother.

The closer Jacob got to his homeland, the more he wondered how Esau would feel about him coming back. It had been twenty years since Jacob had tricked Esau and stolen Esau's blessing. Was Esau still angry with him? Did he perhaps even want to kill him? He decided to send messengers to Esau to tell him he was coming and that he wanted to be friends. He also told them to tell Esau all about the things that had happened to him during the twenty years they had been apart.

The messengers came back and said, "Esau is coming out to meet you, and he has four hundred men with him." That really scared Jacob! He divided his family, servants, and flocks into two groups. If Esau should attack, at least one group might be able to escape. Next, Jacob prayed that God would protect him from Esau's anger. He thanked God for all the good things that had happened to him in Haran, and for the riches he now had, even though he knew he didn't deserve them.

Then Jacob gathered many of his sheep, goats, camels, cattle, and donkeys—several hundred animals in all—as a gift for Esau. He sent servants ahead with groups of these animals to meet his brother. He thought a big present like that might make Esau less angry with him. Maybe they would be able to be friends after all.

. . . Finally the moment came for Jacob and Esau to meet. Jacob went on ahead of his family and servants and flocks. As he came close to Esau he bowed down seven times to show his respect for his brother. Esau ran to meet him and put his arms around him, hugging and kissing him. They were so glad to see each other that they both cried for joy.

When Esau saw Jacob's large family, he asked, "Who are all these women and children with you?"

Jacob replied, "These are the children God has given me." And he introduced his wives and children to Esau.

Esau asked, "And why did you send all those sheep and goats and other animals to me?"

Jacob said, "I sent them as a gift—to make you feel friendly toward me."

"Oh, no," Esau said, "I have all the flocks and herds I need. You keep them." But Jacob insisted, and finally Esau accepted them.

Esau offered to travel with Jacob the rest of the way, but Jacob was still a little bit afraid of him. He thought he'd be safer if Esau was out in front where he could keep his eye on him! He told Esau to go on ahead and he and his family would follow more slowly. And that's what they did.

So God answered Jacob's prayer and reunited him with Esau, and the brothers could be friends after twenty long years apart. ❧

An Act of the Will
CORRIE TEN BOOM

Corrie ten Boom was imprisoned in a Nazi concentration camp with her father and sister. Only Corrie survived the ordeal, and after her release she traveled all over the world preaching the love of Christ and the joy of forgiveness. But one day her message of forgiveness was put to the ultimate test, as she tells in her book Tramp for the Lord.

It was in a church in Munich that I saw him—a balding, heavyset man in a gray overcoat, a brown felt hat clutched between his hands. People were filing out of the basement room where I had just spoken, moving along the rows of wooden chairs to the door at the rear. It was 1947 and I had come from Holland to defeated

Germany with the message that God forgives.

It was the truth they needed most to hear in that bitter, bombed-out land, and I gave them my favorite mental picture. Maybe because the sea is never far from a Hollander's mind, I liked to think that that's where forgiven sins were thrown. "When we confess our sins," I said, "God casts them into the deepest ocean, gone forever. And even though I cannot find a Scripture for it, I believe God then places a sign out there that says, NO FISHING ALLOWED."

The solemn faces stared back at me, not quite daring to believe. There were never questions after a talk in Germany in 1947. People stood up in silence, in silence collected their wraps, in silence left the room.

And that's when I saw him, working his way forward against the others. One moment I saw the overcoat and the brown hat; the next, a blue uniform and a visored cap with its skull and cross-bones. It came back with a rush: the huge room with its harsh over-head lights; the pathetic pile of dresses and shoes in the center of the floor; the shame of walking naked past this man. I could see my sister's frail form ahead of me, ribs sharp beneath the parchment skin. *Betsie, how thin you were!*

The place was Ravensbruck and the man who was making his way forward had been a guard—one of the most cruel guards.

Now he was in front of me, hand thrust out: "A fine message, Fraulein! How good it is to know that, as you say, all our sins are at the bottom of the sea!"

And I, who had spoken so glibly of forgiveness, fumbled in my pocketbook rather than take that hand. He would not remember me, of course—how could he remember one prisoner among those thousands of women?

But I remembered him and the leather crop swinging from his belt. I was face-to-face with one of my captors and my blood seemed to freeze.

"You mentioned Ravensbruck in your talk," he was saying. "I was a guard there." No, he did not remember me.

"But since that time," he went on, "I have become a Christian. I know that God has forgiven me for the cruel things I did there, but I would like to hear it from your lips as well. Fraulein,"—again the hand came out—"will you forgive me?"

And I stood there—I whose sins had again and again to be forgiven—and could not forgive. Betsie had died in that place—could he erase her slow terrible death simply for the asking?

It could not have been many seconds that he stood there—hand held out—but to me it seemed hours as I wrestled with the most difficult thing I had ever had to do.

For I had to do it—I knew that. The message that God forgives has a prior condition: that we forgive those who have injured us. "If you do not forgive men their trespasses," Jesus says, "neither will your Father in heaven forgive your trespasses."

I knew it not only as a commandment of God, but as a daily experience. Since the end of the war I had had a home in Holland for victims of Nazi brutality. Those who were able to forgive their former enemies were able also to return to the outside world and rebuild their lives, no matter what the physical scars. Those who nursed their bitterness remained invalids. It was as simple and as horrible as that.

And still I stood there with the coldness clutching my heart. But forgiveness is not an emotion—I knew that too. Forgiveness is an act of the will, and the will can function regardless of the temperature of the heart. "Jesus, help me!" I prayed silently. "I can lift my hand. I can do that much. You supply the feeling."

And so woodenly, mechanically, I thrust my hand into the one stretched out to me. And as I did, an incredible thing took place. The current started in my shoulder, raced down my arm, sprang into our joined hands. And then this healing warmth seemed to flood my whole being, bringing tears to my eyes.

"I forgive you, brother!" I cried. "With all my heart."

For a long moment we grasped each other's hands, the former guard and the former prisoner. I had never known God's love so intensely as I did then. But even so, I realized it was not my love. I had tried, and did not have the power. It was the power of the Holy Spirit as recorded in Romans 5:5, " . . . because the love of God is shed abroad in our hearts by the Holy Ghost which is given unto us." &

The Squint-Eyed Preacher
JOHN POLLOCK

George Whitefield did much more than just preach forgiveness—he practiced it! Excerpted from George Whitefield and the Great Awakening.

[The following incident neatly sums] up George Whitefield's profound influence during his second Boston visit.

A man had been making a hit in the taverns by mimicking him for money. He went to a lecture in order to gather more scraps of sermons for use in his act, and having got enough tried to leave in the middle, only to find all movement impossible since every inch of aisle was occupied. Whether he wished or not, he had to stay, and no man could stay where Whitefield preached and shut his ears (as a boy in Philadelphia discovered who went to the field-preaching to throw stones and found his arms literally pinned to his sides by the crush; he stayed and was converted). The man therefore set himself to pick up more gems for ridicule until, as he listened and watched, he found himself gripped by an appalling sense of sacrilege and guilt. He felt turned inside out.

He left in a daze, at the end, sure he could only find peace of mind by apologizing to the squint-eyed preacher who was so easy to mimic and hard to resist. He dared not approach him: he had heard those thundering tones conveying the awful judgment of God until the people winced.

He approached old Dr. Prince instead, whose name he knew from the famous periodical *The Christian History* in which Prince chronicled the Awakening in terms which even Whitefield thought sometimes extravagant. Prince assured him George Whitefield could be gentle as a dove, and promised to intercede.

He told Whitefield: "You will shortly be favored with the company of a very pensive and uncommon person. He is a man of good parts, ready wit, lively imagination who has been preaching you over a bottle!"

Next day at mid-morning George sat in John Smith's parlor where he received Gospel visitants. He heard a tentative tap on the door. He opened it and identified the caller at once "by the paleness, pensiveness and horror of his countenance."

The man hung his head and said in a low voice: "Sir, can you forgive me?"

George smiled. "Yes, sir. Very readily. Please sit down." And without allowing another word of contrition or apology, "I preached to him the Gospel." ❧

Self-Righteousness
JOHN BYROM

"He is a sinner," you are pleased to say.
　　Then love him for the sake of Christ, I pray.
If on His gracious words you place your trust,
　　"I came to call the sinners, not the just,"
Second His call; which if you will not do,
　　You'll be the greater sinner of the two. ❧

Friendliness

OLIVER WENDELL HOLMES wrote in "An After-dinner Poem,"
> Sweet is the scene where genial friendship plays,
> The pleasing game of interchanging praise.

Who among us does not prefer praise to criticism? And who does not enjoy the sweet scene where praise begets praise and friendships bloom? A little affirmation here, a dash of adulation there, a spoonful of appreciation mixed in, and over all a pervasive sense of adoration. Sounds good, doesn't it? But sadly there is all too often a lack of genuine affirmation in our world, and rare is the unfeigned acknowledgment of achievement. Competition has beaten out commendation, and while weeping with those who weep may not be too difficult, rejoicing with those who rejoice is not always what we want to do, particularly if they rejoice over receiving what we had sought for ourselves. But real friends are genuinely glad when their friends succeed, and deep friendship thrills to the other's delight. Friendship of this kind in the present scene is a precious gift, a rare gem.

Jesus told the humorous story of a man whose friend arrived at his house at midnight looking for something to eat. Unfortunately the man was out of bread, so his friend was out of luck, but together they got a third friend out of bed . . . a little out of sorts, I might add. But because they were friends, the bread was delivered, the hungry friend was fed, the first man went back to bed, and friendship won the day—or the night, to be more precise.

Friendship not only offers praise, it gets out of bed at midnight to share. It may grumble, but not for long.

Friendship levels with friends—in love, of course. I call it "loveling." Any brave or insensitive soul may tell you an unpleasant truth and in so doing exacerbate the problem. But only a friend has the right and the nerve to say what needs to be said, unpleasant though it may be, with a loving concern for your well-being and deep interest in your welfare. As Proverbs reminds us,

"The kisses of an enemy may be profuse,
but faithful are the wounds of a friend."

Where do we find such friends? An old proverb insists that "he that would have friends must show himself friendly." Good point! It is as we take the trouble to work at a relationship where supporting and affirming, caring and sharing (even at midnight) are normative, that friendship buds and blossoms.

As for our children, let us remember that the day comes all too soon when peers matter more than parents. Wise parents work at developing positive peer pressure while they are still in a position to call the shots! You can't pick your child's friends any more than you can choose your relatives, but you can steer your impressionable child to the right kind of friends, and this must be done for the child's greater good. &

A Lion and a Mouse
AESOP

Always make friends. One day you may need them. And if not, they may need you!

A Mouse one day happened to run across the paws of a sleeping Lion and wakened him. The Lion, angry at being disturbed, grabbed the Mouse, and was about to swallow him, when the Mouse cried out, "Please, kind Sir, I didn't mean it; if you will let me go, I shall always be grateful; and, perhaps, I can help you some day." The idea that such a little thing as a Mouse could help him so amused the Lion that he let the Mouse go. A week later the Mouse heard a Lion roaring loudly. He went closer to see what the trouble was and found his Lion caught in a hunter's net. Remembering his promise, the Mouse began to gnaw the ropes of the net and kept it up until the Lion could get free. The Lion then acknowledged that little friends might prove great friends. ❧

Along the Yellow Brick Road
L. FRANK BAUM

When Dorothy and her dog Toto were blown away in a Kansas twister, they landed in a strange country. There they met strange creatures who became good friends. You can read all about them in The Wonderful Wizard of Oz.

When Dorothy awoke, the sun was shining through the trees, and Toto had long been out chasing birds around her. There was the Scarecrow, still standing patiently in his corner, waiting for her.

"We must go and search for water," she said to him.

"Why do you want water?" he asked.

"To wash my face clean after the dust of the road, and to drink, so the dry bread will not stick in my throat."

"It must be inconvenient to be made of flesh," said the

Scarecrow, thoughtfully, "for you must sleep, and eat, and drink. However, you have brains, and it is worth a lot of bother to be able to think properly."

They left the cottage and walked through the trees until they found a little spring of clear water, where Dorothy drank and bathed and ate her breakfast. She saw there was not much bread left in the basket, and the girl was thankful the Scarecrow did not have to eat anything, for there was scarcely enough for herself and Toto for the day.

When she had finished her meal and was about to go back to the road of yellow brick, she was startled to hear a deep groan nearby.

"What was that?" she asked, timidly.

"I cannot imagine," replied the Scarecrow; "but we can go and see."

Just then, another groan reached their ears, and the sound seemed to come from behind them. They turned and walked through the forest a few steps, when Dorothy discovered something shining in a ray of sunshine that fell between the trees. She ran to the place and then stopped short, with a cry of surprise.

One of the big trees had been partly chopped through, and standing beside it, with an uplifted ax in his hands, was a man made entirely of tin. His head and arms and legs were jointed upon his body, but he stood perfectly motionless as if he could not stir at all.

Dorothy looked at him in amazement, and so did the Scarecrow, while Toto barked sharply and made a snap at the tin legs, which hurt his teeth.

"Did you groan?" asked Dorothy.

"Yes," answered the tin man, "I did. I've been groaning for more than a year, and no one has ever heard me before or come to help me."

"What can I do for you?" she inquired softly, for she was

moved by the sad voice in which the man spoke.

"Get an oil-can and oil my joints," he answered. "They are rusted so badly that I cannot move them at all; if I am well oiled, I shall soon be all right again. You will find an oil-can on a shelf in my cottage."

Dorothy at once ran back to the cottage and found the oil-can, and then she returned and asked, anxiously, "Where are your joints?"

"Oil my neck, first," replied the Tin Woodman. So she oiled it, and as it was quite badly rusted, the Scarecrow took hold of the tin head and moved it gently from side to side until it worked freely, and then the man could turn it himself.

"Now oil the joints in my arms," he said. And Dorothy oiled them, and the Scarecrow bent them carefully until they were quite free from rust and as good as new.

The Tin Woodman gave a sigh of satisfaction and lowered his ax, which he leaned against the tree.

"This is a great comfort," he said. "I have been holding that ax in the air ever since I rusted, and I'm glad to be able to put it down at last. Now, if you will oil the joints of my legs, I shall be all right once more."

So they oiled his legs until he could move them freely; and he thanked them again and again for his release, for he seemed a very polite creature, and very grateful.

"I might have stood there always if you had not come along," he said; "so you have certainly saved my life. How did you happen to be here?"

"We are on our way to the Emerald City, to see the great Oz," she answered, "and we stopped at your cottage to pass the night."

"Why do you wish to see Oz?" he asked.

"I want him to send me back to Kansas; and the Scarecrow wants him to put a few brains into his head," she replied.

The Tin Woodman appeared to think deeply for a moment.

Then he said:

"Do you suppose Oz could give me a heart?"

"Why, I guess so," Dorothy answered. "It would be as easy as to give the Scarecrow brains."

"True," the Tin Woodman returned. "So, if you will allow me to join your party, I will also go to the Emerald City and ask Oz to help me."

"Come along," said the Scarecrow heartily; and Dorothy added that she would be pleased to have his company. So the Tin Woodman shouldered his ax, and they all passed through the forest until they came to the road that was paved with yellow brick.

The Tin Woodman had asked Dorothy to put the oil-can in her basket. "For," he said, "if I should get caught in the rain, and rust again, I would need the oil-can badly."

It was a bit of good luck to have their new comrade join the party, for soon after they had begun their journey again, they came to a place where the trees and branches grew so thick over the road that the travelers could not pass. But the Tin Woodman set to work with his ax and chopped so well that soon he cleared a passage for the entire party.

Dorothy was thinking so earnestly as they walked along that she did not notice when the Scarecrow stumbled into a hole and rolled over to the side of the road. Indeed, he was obliged to call to her to help him up again.

"Why didn't you walk around the hole?" asked the Tin Woodman.

"I don't know enough," replied the Scarecrow cheerfully. "My head is stuffed with straw, you know, and that is why I am going to Oz to ask him for some brains."

"Oh, I see," said the Tin Woodman. "But, after all, brains are not the best things in the world."

"Have you any?" inquired the Scarecrow.

"No, my head is quite empty," answered the Woodman; "but

once I had brains, and a heart also; so, having tried them both, I should much rather have a heart."

. . . "All the same," said the Scarecrow, "I shall ask for brains instead of a heart; for a fool would not know what to do with a heart if he had one."

"I shall take the heart," returned the Tin Woodman, "for brains do not make one happy, and happiness is the best thing in the world."

Dorothy did not say anything, for she was puzzled to know which of her two friends was right, and she decided if she could only get back to Kansas and Aunt Em, it did not matter so much whether the Woodman had no brains and the Scarecrow had no heart, or each got what he wanted.

. . . There were few birds in this part of the forest, for birds love the open country where there is plenty of sunshine; but now and then, there came a deep growl from some wild animal hidden among the trees. These sounds made the little girl's heart beat fast, for she did not know what made them; but Toto knew, and he walked close to Dorothy's side and did not even bark in return.

"How long will it be," the child asked of the Tin Woodman, "before we are out of the forest?"

"I cannot tell," was the answer, "for I have never been to the Emerald City. But my father went there once, when I was a boy, and he said it was a long journey through a dangerous country, although nearer to the city where Oz dwells, the country is beautiful. But I am not afraid so long as I have my oil-can, and nothing can hurt the Scarecrow, while you bear upon your forehead the mark of the good Witch's kiss, and that will protect you from harm."

"But Toto!" said the girl anxiously. "What will protect him?"

"We must protect him ourselves, if he is in danger," replied the Tin Woodman.

Just as he spoke, there came from the forest a terrible roar, and the next moment a great Lion bounded into the road. With one blow of his paw, he sent the Scarecrow spinning over and over to the edge of the road, and then he struck the Tin Woodman with his sharp claws. But, to the Lion's surprise, he could make no impression on the tin, although the Woodman fell over in the road and lay still.

Little Toto, now that he had an enemy to face, ran barking toward the Lion, and the great beast had opened his mouth to bite the dog, when Dorothy, fearing Toto would be killed, and heedless of the danger, rushed forward and slapped the Lion upon his nose as hard as she could, while she cried out:

"Don't you dare to bite Toto! You ought to be ashamed of yourself, a big beast like you, to bite a poor little dog!"

"I didn't bite him," said the Lion, as he rubbed his nose with his paw where Dorothy had hit it.

"No, but you tried to," she retorted. "You are nothing but a big coward."

"I know it," said the Lion, hanging his head in shame. "I've always known it. But how can I help it?"

"I don't know, I'm sure. To think of your striking a stuffed man, like the poor Scarecrow!"

"Is he stuffed?" asked the Lion in surprise, as he watched her pick up the Scarecrow and set him upon his feet, while she patted him into shape again.

"Of course he's stuffed," replied Dorothy, who was still angry.

"That's why he went over so easily," remarked the Lion. "It astonished me to see him whirl around so. Is the other one stuffed also?"

"No," said Dorothy, "he's made of tin." And she helped the Woodman up again.

"That's why he nearly blunted my claws," said the Lion. "When they scratched against the tin, it made a cold shiver run down my back. What is that little animal you are so tender of?"

"He is my dog, Toto," answered Dorothy.

"Is he made of tin, or stuffed?" asked the Lion.

"Neither. He's a—a—a meat dog," said the girl.

"Oh! He's a curious animal and seems remarkably small, now that I look at him. No one would think of biting such a little thing, except a coward like me," continued the Lion sadly.

"What makes you a coward?" asked Dorothy, looking at the great beast in wonder, for he was as big as a small horse.

"It's a mystery," replied the Lion. "I suppose I was born that way. All the other animals in the forest naturally expect me to be brave, for the Lion is everywhere thought to be the King of Beasts. I learned that if I roared very loudly every living thing was frightened and got out of my way. Whenever I've met a man, I've been awfully scared; but I just roared at him, and he has always run away as fast as he could go. If the elephants and the tigers and the bears had ever tried to fight me, I should have run myself—I'm such a coward; but just as soon as they hear me roar, they all try to get away from me, and of course I let them go."

"But that isn't right. The King of Beasts shouldn't be a coward," said the Scarecrow.

"I know it," returned the Lion, wiping a tear from his eye with the tip of his tail. "It is my great sorrow and makes my life very unhappy. But whenever there is a danger, my heart begins to beat fast."

"Perhaps you have heart disease," said the Tin Woodman.

"It may be," said the Lion.

"If you have," continued the Tin Woodman, "you ought to be glad, for it proves you have a heart. For my part, I have no heart; so I cannot have heart disease."

"Perhaps," said the Lion thoughtfully, "if I had no heart, I should not be a coward."

"Have you brains?" asked the Scarecrow.

"I suppose so. I've never looked to see," replied the Lion.

"I am going to the great Oz to ask him to give me some," remarked the Scarecrow, "for my head is stuffed with straw."

"And I am going to ask him to give me a heart," said the Woodman.

"And I am going to ask him to send Toto and me back to Kansas," added Dorothy.

"Do you think Oz could give me courage?" asked the Cowardly Lion.

"Just as easily as he could give me brains," said the Scarecrow.

"Or give me a heart," said the Tin Woodman.

"Or send me back to Kansas," said Dorothy.

"Then, if you don't mind, I'll go with you," said the Lion, "for my life is simply unbearable without a bit of courage."

"You will be very welcome," answered Dorothy, "for you will help to keep away the other wild beasts. It seems to me they must be more cowardly than you are if they allow you to scare them so easily."

"They really are," said the Lion, "but that doesn't make me any braver; and as long as I know myself to be a coward, I shall be unhappy."

So once more, the little company set off upon the journey, the Lion walking with stately strides at Dorothy's side. Toto did not approve this new comrade at first, for he could not forget how nearly he had been crushed between the Lion's great jaws; but after a time, he became more at ease, and presently Toto and the Cowardly Lion had grown to be good friends. 🙢

To My Daughter
JILL BRISCOE

Thank you for being a girl. You were a shock to your dad. He didn't believe he could produce one of our kind! I could see the bewilderment in his face as you lay snugly in his arms. "Whatever shall I do with one of these?" he asked me silently. You knew, didn't you. You knew that, man that he was from a man's world, he needed to learn what a woman was all about! Thank you for teaching him—*he's loved it!*

Thank you for being a tomboy. For falling off the donkey and joining in the football, and keeping up with every brother-step along the way! I tried to get you interested in dolls, but you just thumped your friends with them.

Thank you for coming to Christ. I can still see your sticky candy hands clutching at my baking board, your big blue eyes in a still point of their own, wondering if Jesus would want you to put your toys away if you let Him into your heart! I remember! Thank you for coming anyway even when I told you "yes" about the toys! Thank you for loving the Lord I love!

Than you for loving Nanna like you do! I think you love her as much as I! How can that be? It's a miracle . . . I really don't understand—but thank you for loving my mum!

Thank you for choosing the right friends. I just now see why you didn't choose the ones *I* chose for you. You were there on the right level. Thank you for choosing right. That was *very* important.

Thank you for wanting to please us, so hard and always. That was one thing we could depend on.

Thank you for telling me it was time for you to choose your own clothes. It wasn't worth a war—you taught me to keep the wars for bigger things . . . moral issues, questions of discipline—not for bits of cloth!

Thank you for yelling back at me when I got mad. You taught

me that shouting did no good. Nothing got said that way. Screaming didn't settle things. We had to stop and *listen* to each other. Thank you for making me change.

Thank you for bringing me up right. No one else could teach me how to be a parent but you kids. And when I was afraid—thank you for taking me into my bedroom and sitting me on the bed and asking me what was the matter. You asked me if I trusted you and I said yes, but I didn't trust your judgment. Then you asked me how I expected you to develop judgment without experience! I told you my job was to know when you were ready for the experience— "Don't be afraid, Mum," you said—*"I'm not."* "THAT'S WHY I AM," I said! Thank you for that and for teaching me I needn't have worried!

Thank you for challenging me with your discipline. For your running and your study habits, your bright mind you have determined to sharpen, train, and use for Him. Your fresh sweet unspoiled beauty catches my breath and turns it into thankfulness.

Thank you most of all FOR BEING MY FRIEND. For making me forget I'm over forty! For walking on the beach or in the mall with me. For slipping your arm through mine, even when your friends are there without their mothers. For giggling, and sharing and saying—"I'm glad we're super close, Mum!" Can you possibly know what that's worth? How could you tell until you have a child of your own!

And thank you for coming to sing for me, for the way you have worked and played and traveled so many places. Thank you for all those fun times at the airport when you insisted on going to the ladies room five minutes before it was time to board the plane!

And thank you for telling me you won't put me in a home when I'm old and alone—that I can come and live with you! (Although Dad wants to know what makes me think he's going first.) Incidentally, I won't ask that of you, Judy—but thank you anyway!

Thank you last of all for the privilege it's been to be your anchor, and for the confidence you've given us to "set your sail."

Yes, thank you for being a girl! 🐾

A Rift in a Friendship
FULTON OURSLER

Even great people like Paul and Barnabas find difficulties in relationships, as seen in this story from The Greatest Faith Ever Known *(see Acts 15 and 16). Friendships have to be guarded and cared for like tender plants.*

In the very planning of new travels Paul was faced with fresh troubles.

"Let us go again," Paul proposed to Barnabas, "and visit our brethren in every city where we have preached the word of the Lord and see how they do."

Good! Barnabas thought it was an excellent plan. And, he added, why not take his cousin, young Mark, along with them again?

"No!" said Paul. And the argument was on. Paul could not forget his previous disappointment with young Mark. Had Mark not deserted Paul and Barnabas on the first journey, leaving them to carry on their arduous task alone? Why trust him again?

Paul's logic was sound. He intended not only to revisit his first mission outposts but to go on into unknown lands, facing incalculable perils. (Though Paul did not then know it, this second journey was to last more than three years.) For such an enterprise, they would need a helper who could be relied upon. Could Barnabas contradict that fact?

Barnabas' reply put an end to one of the most remarkable of friendships. The contention between them had become so sharp that only action could conclude it. The two men parted in silence and heartache. Barnabas and Mark boarded a ship at the Orontes dock, sailed down the river and out into the Mediterranean, their prow pointed homeward to Cyprus.

Was their parting entirely over Mark? Had Barnabas' defection in quitting the Gentiles when Peter did caused the first deep abyss between these two men?

Let Barnabas and his nephew call on the churches the two missioners had founded on the island of Cyprus. As for Paul, he would go another way. For companion he chose a man he had learned to trust completely, Silas, called Sylvanus, who had originally come down from Jerusalem as one of the agents of the grand council.

But Paul could never shut Barnabas out of his heart. The tent-making Pharisee from Tarsus could never forget that it was Barnabas who found him in the streets of Jerusalem and led him to the Cenacle. Barnabas had stood up for Paul against all those who feared his presence because of the stoning of Stephen. It was Barnabas who had started the evangelizing tour and had invited Paul to join, taking him into partnership. And when Paul's eloquence plainly exceeded his own, even on his home grounds the Cypriote had taken second place with quiet humility. He seemed never to know smallness or meanness.

Together the two missioners had converted thousands. They had run desperate dangers, had been persecuted together, and escaped together. They had known chills and fevers, all kinds of hardship. Yet because of one young and unreliable relative, Mark, whom Peter was to call his adopted son, they were partners in spreading Christ's Gospel no longer.

Perhaps Paul still had a lot to learn, and this second missionary journey would help to school him, not in the concentrated wisdom of books, but in warm flesh and blood human relations. Many of his companions would have said that Paul was hard to get along with. Surrounded by so many and varied antagonists, he may well have been too suspicious.

Whatever Paul's motives, over the question of Mark he stood out against Barnabas and lost him.

It is a severe grief to lose a friend. &

The Best Treasure
JOHN J. MOMENT

There are veins in the hills where jewels hide,
    And gold lies buried deep;
    There are harbor-towns where the great ships ride,
    And fame and fortune sleep;
But land and sea though we tireless rove,
And follow each trail to the end,
    Whatever the wealth of our treasure-trove,
The best we shall find is a friend. &

Spring Cleaning
F. W. BOREHAM

In which the thought of cleaning out a desk leads to memories of love and friendship (excerpt from The Golden Milestone*).*

I have discovered that the pigeon-hole [in the author's desk] is not only a useful but a sacred place. These little squares in front of me are like little chapels, and an atmosphere of reverence and tenderness broods over them. I have here, for example, a bundle of old letters that are very dear to me, and that grow dearer as the days go by. They are all of them from those whom I have loved long since and lost awhile. Whenever I have received a characteristic letter from a friend, a letter that seems saturated in his spirit and echoing with the merriment of his laughter, I have found it impossible to destroy it. Some day, I know, others will scan it, burn it as rubbish, and blame me for not having saved them the trouble. But then, to me, the personality of my friend is woven into the letter, and my friend is mortal. And one day my friend will join the immortals, and I shall go through these piles of letters, and carefully, reverently gather out his letters and transfer them to this sacred little bundle in the corner. The other day I heard of the death, away in East Africa, of my old friend, the Rev. J. J. Doke. He married me, and helped me in more ways than I can tell. His intimate friendship in our old New Zealand days is one of my most cherished memories. And now, in the course of a journey of exploration through Rhodesia, he has fallen, and added his name to the long, long list of Africa's illustrious dead. This morning I went through my hoard of letters, and was delighted to find some of his graphic and chatty epistles. And with chastened emotions, and with tender touch, I have transferred them to that priceless bundle. . . . But I am discovering every year that I cherish with growing affection the precious documents in this rapidly increasing bundle. To re-read these letters is part of life's loftiest worship. It is only when I have shaken the dust of the world from off my spirit that I allow myself to break this seal, and enjoy unbroken fellowship with these pure and earthless ones. Those who sort out my paltry effects at the last may blame me for having accumulated such heaps of rubbish; but I entreat them to reflect, before they condemn me too harshly, on the hallowed hours that I have spent with these spiritual radiations from out the everlasting.

Then, too, every minister treasures some letters whose rereading is very sweet to him. They are from folk who have been helped by him. He will never burn them. In times of discouragement or public censure, he will read them and be comforted. Lord Milner, in his volume of speeches, says that he likes to store up the praise he receives for less cheerful days. "Bank the praise when you get it," he says, "and live upon it when you do not get it, and do not make too much fuss either way." That is a good word for the pigeon-hole.

Nor are these all. It is getting on for twenty years since I exchanged the Old World in the north for this New World beneath the Southern Cross. And never a single mail has reached Australia through all those years that did not bear a letter from my mother. Not one! And am I to be blamed that I have not found it in my heart to commit any one of those welcome messages to the paper basket or the flames? I know that I may never read again all these piles and piles of letters in that dear handwriting. I know, too, that a day must come when some other hands will consign these stacks of letters to the devouring flames. Let other hands do it, say I! It will cost them little enough, and it would almost break my heart. ❧

Keeping Friends
LAURA INGALLS WILDER

In which the author of "The Little House" series writes for adults about friendship, which cannot be demanded but can be wooed.

Sometimes we are a great trial to our friends and put an entirely uncalled-for strain upon our friendships by asking foolish questions.

The Man of the Place and I discovered the other day that we had for some time been saying to our friends, "Why don't you come over?" Can you think of a more awkward question than that? Just imagine the result if that question should always be answered truthfully. Some would reply, "Because I do not care to visit you." Others might say, "Because it is too much trouble," while still others who might care to come would be swamped in trying to enumerate the many little reasons why they had not done so. We decided that we would break ourselves of such a bad habit.

I once had a neighbor who, whenever we met, invariably

asked me why I had not been to visit her. Even when I did go she met me with the query, "Why haven't you been over before?" It was not a very pleasant greeting, and naturally one shuns unpleasantness when one may.

I have another neighbor who will call me on the phone and say: "It has been a long time since we have seen you, and we do want a good visit. Can't you come over tomorrow?" And immediately I wish to go. It does make such a difference how things are said.

Friendship is like love. It cannot be demanded or driven or insisted upon. It must be wooed to be won. The habit of saying disagreeable things or of being careless about how what we say affects others grows on us so easily and so surely if we indulge it.

"Mrs. Brown gave me an unhappy half hour a few days ago," said Mrs. Gray to me. "She said a great many unpleasant things and was generally disagreeable, but it is all right. The poor thing is getting childish, and we must overlook her oddities."

Mrs. Gray is a comparative newcomer in the neighborhood, but I have known Mrs. Brown for years; and ever since I have known her, she has prided herself on her plain speaking, showing very little regard for others' feelings. Her unkindness appears to me not a reversion to the mentality of childhood but simply an advance in the way she was going years ago. Her tongue has only become sharper with use, and her dexterity in hurting the feelings of others has grown with practice.

I know another woman of the same age whom no one speaks of as being childish. It is not necessary to make such an excuse for her because she is still, as she has been for twenty years, helpful and sweet and kind. And this helpfulness and sweetness and kindness of hers has grown with the passing years. I think no one will ever say of her, "Poor old thing, she is childish," as an excuse for her being disagreeable. I know she would hope to die before that time should come.

People do grow childish in extreme old age, of course, and should be treated with tenderness because of it; but I believe that even then the character which they have built during the years before will manifest itself. There is a great difference in children, you know, and I have come to the conclusion that if we live to reach a second childhood, we shall not be bad-tempered, disagreeable children unless we have indulged those traits. 🐾

Friday's Devotion
DANIEL DEFOE

In The Life and Adventures of Robinson Crusoe, *our hero wants to help his friend, Man Friday, to return home. But Friday misunderstands, thinking that Crusoe is angry with him. He asks Crusoe to kill him rather than send him away. What loyal friendship!*

[I said,] "Friday, do not you wish your self in your own country, your own nation?" "Yes," he said, "he be much O glad to be at his own nation." "What would you do there?" said I, "would you turn wild again, eat men's flesh again, and be a savage as you were before?" He lookt full of concern, and shaking his head said, "No, no, Friday tell them to live good, tell them to pray God, tell them to eat corn-bread, cattle-flesh, milk, no eat man again." "Why then," said I to him, "they will kill you." He looked grave at that, and then said, "No, they no kill me, they willing love learn." He meant by this, they would be willing to learn. He added, they learned much of the bearded-mans that come in the boat. Then I asked him if he would go back to them. He smiled at that, and told me he could not swim so far. I told him I would make a canoe for him. He told me he would go, if I would go with him. "I go!" says I, "why, they will eat me if I come there." "No, no," says he, "me make they no eat you; me make they much love you." He meant he would tell them how I had killed his enemies, and saved his life, and so he would make them love me; then he told me as well as he could, how kind they were to seventeen white-men, or bearded-men, as he called them, who came on shore there in distress.

From this time I confess I had a mind to venture over, and see if I could possibly joyn with these bearded-men, who I made no doubt were Spaniards or Portuguese; not doubting but if I could we might find some method to escape from thence; being upon the continent, and a good company together; better than I could from an island 40 miles off the shore, and alone without help. So after some days I took Friday to work again, by way of discourse, and told him I would give him a boat to go back to his nation; and accordingly I carry'd him to my frigate which lay on the other side of the island, and having cleared it of water, for I always kept it sunk in the water, I brought it out, shewed it him, and we both went into it.

I found he was a most dexterous fellow at managing it, would make it go almost as swift and fast again as I could; so when he was in, I said to him, "Well, now, Friday, shall we go to your nation?" He looked very dull at my saying so, which it seems was because he thought the boat too small to go so far. I told him then I had a bigger; so the next day I went to the place where the first boat lay which I had made, but which I could not get into water. He said that was big enough; but then as I had taken no care of it, and it had lain two or three and twenty years there, the sun had split and dry'd it, that it was in a manner rotten. Friday told me such a boat would do very well, and would carry "much enough vittle, drink, bread," that was his way of talking.

Upon the whole, I was by this time so fixed upon my design of going over with him to the continent, that I told him we would go and make one as big as that, and he should go home in it. He answered not one word, but looked very grave and sad. I asked him what was the matter with him. He asked me again thus, "Why you angry mad with Friday, what me done?" I asked him what he meant; I told him I was not angry with him at all. "No angry! No angry!" says he, repeating the words several times, "why send Friday home away to my nation?" "Why," says I, "Friday, did you not say you wished you were there?" "Yes, yes," says he, "wish we both there, no wish Friday there, no master there." In a word, he would not think of going there without me. "I go there! Friday," says I, "what shall I do there?" He turned very quick upon me at this: "You do great deal much good," says he, "you teach wild mans be good sober tame mans; you tell them know God, pray God, and live new life." "Alas! Friday," says I, "thou knowest not what thou sayest, I am but an ignorant man myself." "Yes, yes," says he, "you teachee me good, you teachee them good." "No, no, Friday," says I, "you shall go without me, leave me here to live by my self, as I did before." He looked confused again at that word, and running to one of the hatchets which he used to wear, he takes it up hastily, comes and gives it me. "What must I do with this?" says I to him. "You take, kill Friday," says he. "What must I kill you for?" said I again. He returns very quick, "What you send Friday away for? Take, kill Friday, no send Friday away?" This he spoke so earnestly, that I saw tears stand in his eyes. In a word, I so plainly discovered the utmost affection in him to me, and a firm resolution in him, that I told him then, and often after, that I would never send him away from me, if he was willing to stay with me. ❧

Signs of Friendship
PAUL TOURNIER

Paul Tournier, a Swiss physician, was greatly gifted both as a counselor and writer. Here we have examples of his skill in both fields, taken from his Reflections on Life's Most Crucial Questions.

In the life of each of us there are decisive hours that tell us more about the person than all the rest of our lives put together. Do I say hours? Minutes, seconds, rather; moments which are to determine the whole course of our lives thereafter.

Now, the cross-roads is this moment of true dialogue, of personal encounter with another person, which obliges us to take up a position with regard to him, to commit ourselves. Even to run away is to make some sort of decision, choosing a side-road in order to evade the dialogue. Most of the incessant fluctuations of our being and of our behavior, actions and words are, as in the animals, merely reflex responses to an external stimulus, manifestations of the personage. At the moment of true dialogue, of inner personal communion, we cannot avoid taking up a position, and in this genuine, responsible act the person is unveiled. That is why Sartre writes: "I cannot know myself except through the intermediary of another person."

The highest sign of friendship is that of giving another the privilege of sharing your inner thought. It is a personal gift in which there is self-commitment. ❧

Johnson on Friendship

JAMES BOSWELL

In which Boswell and Johnson, those inveterate talkers, discuss friendship and say some significant things on the subject (from Life of Johnson*).*

I have often thought, that as longevity is generally desired, and I believe, generally expected, it would be wise to be continually adding to the number of our friends, that the loss of some may be supplied by others. Friendship, "the wine of life," should like a well-stocked cellar, be thus continually renewed; and it is consolatory to think, that although we can seldom add what will equal the generous *first-growths* of our youth, yet friendship becomes insensibly old in much less time than is commonly imagined, and not many years are required to make it very mellow and pleasant. *Warmth* will, no doubt, make a considerable difference. Men of affectionate temper and bright fancy will coalesce a great deal sooner than those who are cold and dull.

The proposition which I have now endeavoured to illustrate was, at a subsequent period of his life, the opinion of Johnson himself. He said to Sir Joshua Reynolds, "If a man does not make new acquaintance as he advances through life, he will soon find himself left alone. A man, Sir, should keep his friendship *in constant repair.*"

On Saturday, April 24, I dined with him at Mr. Beauclerk's, with Sir Joshua Reynolds, Mr. Jones (afterwards Sir William), Mr. Langton, Mr. Stevens, Mr. Paradise, and Dr. Higgins. I mentioned that Mr. Wilkes had attacked Garrick to me, as a man who had no friend. "I believe he is right, Sir. . . . 'He had friends, but no friend.' Garrick was so diffused, he had no man to whom he wished to unbosom himself. He found people always ready to applaud him, and that always for the same thing: so he saw life with great uniformity." I took upon me, for once, to fight with Goliath's weapons, and play the sophist.—"Garrick did not need a friend, as he got from everybody all he wanted. What is a friend? One who supports you and comforts you, while others do not. Friendship, you know, Sir, is the cordial drop, 'to make the nauseous draught of life go down'; but if the draught be not nauseous, if it be all sweet, there is no occasion for that drop." JOHNSON. "Many men would not be content to live so. I hope I should not. They would wish to have an intimate friend, with whom they might compare minds, and cherish private virtues." 🏵

Thou Half of My Soul
ST. AUGUSTINE

In his Confessions, *Augustine of Hippo (354-430 A.D.) recounts the pain and pleasure of true friendship—a relationship he describes as "one soul in two bodies."*

In those years when I first began to teach rhetoric in my native town, I had made one my friend, but too dear to me from a community of pursuits, of mine own age, and, as myself, in the first opening flower of youth. He had grown up of a child with me, and we had been both school-fellows and play-fellows. But he was not yet my friend as afterwards, nor even then as true friendship is; for true it cannot be, unless in such as Thou cementest together, cleaving unto Thee, by that love which is shed abroad in our hearts by the Holy Ghost, which is given unto us. Yet was it but too sweet, ripened by the warmth of kindred studies: for, from the true faith (which he as a youth had not soundly and thoroughly imbibed), I had warped him also to those superstitious and pernicious fables for which my mother bewailed me. With me he now erred in mind, nor could my soul be without him. But behold Thou wert close on the steps of Thy fugitives, at once God of vengeance and Fountain of mercies, turning us to Thyself by wonderful means;

Thou tookest that man out of this life, when he had scarce filled up one whole year of my friendship, sweet to me above all sweetness of that my life.

"Who can recount all Thy praises," which he hath felt in his one self? What diddest Thou then, my God, and how unsearchable is the abyss of Thy judgments? For long, sore sick of a fever, he lay senseless in a death-sweat; and, his recovery being despaired of, he was baptized unknowing; myself meanwhile little regarding, and presuming that his soul would retain rather what it had received of me, not what was wrought on his unconscious body. But it proved far otherwise: for he was refreshed, and restored. Forthwith, as soon as I could speak with him (and I could, so soon as he was able, for I never left him, and we hung but too much upon each other), I essayed to jest with him, as though he would jest with me at that baptism which he had received when utterly absent in mind and feeling, but had now understood that he had received. But he so shrunk from me, as from an enemy; and with a wonderful and sudden freedom bade me, as I would continue his friend, forbear such language to him. I, all astonished and amazed, suppressed all my emotions till he should grow well, and his health were strong enough for me to deal with him as I would. But he was taken away from my phrensy, that with Thee he might be preserved for my comfort; a few days after, in my absence, he was attacked again by the fever, and so departed.

At this grief my heart was utterly darkened; and whatever I beheld was death. My native country was a torment to me, and my father's house a strange unhappiness; and whatever I had shared with him, wanting him, became a distracting torture. Mine eyes sought him everywhere, but he was not granted them; and I hated all places, for that they had not him; nor could they now tell me, "he is coming" as when he was alive and absent. I became a great riddle to myself, and I asked my soul, why she was so sad, and why she disquieted me sorely: but she knew not what to answer me.

And if I said, "Trust in God," she very rightly obeyed me not; because that most dear friend, whom she had lost, was, being man, both truer and better than that phantasm she was bid to trust in. Only tears were sweet to me, for they succeeded my friend in the dearest of my affections.

. . . Well said one of his friends, "Thou half of my soul": for I felt that my soul and his soul were "one soul in two bodies": and therefore was my life a horror to me, because I would not live halved. And therefore perchance I feared to die, lest he whom I had much loved should die wholly. ❧

A friend is a person with whom I may be sincere.
Before him, I may think aloud.
RALPH WALDO EMERSON

The ornament of a house is the friends who frequent it.
RALPH WALDO EMERSON

Honesty

A JOKE GOING THE ROUNDS of Washington some time ago suggested that while a certain president could not tell a lie, a well-known senator couldn't tell the truth, and another government official couldn't tell the difference. Good for a cynical laugh, I suppose, but too close to the common perception of politicians for comfort. And it isn't only politicians who dissemble when it suits their purposes. It is a strange fact that many people who regard themselves as honest, hardworking citizens do not hesitate to lie to a customs official about articles bought overseas or on a tax return concerning payments in cash for work done. One nationwide poll showed that there is not a lot of difference between Christians and unbelievers on these issues. Whatever happened to honesty?

Augustine, the bishop of Hippo, tabulated eight different kinds of lies. Mark Twain, in typical fashion, suggested that there were 869! Whatever the count might be, we are all familiar with the instinct for self-preservation that leads even a little child to lie. "Johnny did it" is a simple statement that may well be a barefaced lie. "The dog ate my homework" has probably been overdone as an explanation about the failure to submit a paper on time. But this type of untruth, if not handled in youth, may lead to a lifestyle of lying designed not only to protect one's hide, but also to gain the advantage over another. It's a practice that one suspects is becoming far too common in the workplace and the law courts, not to mention within the intimacy of the marital bond.

Children learn to lie when they fear the consequences of their actions. They need to be shown that lying only complicates matters further, generating even more unpleasant consequences. Once this is understood, painfully at times, it is helpful to reward a child for being truthful even when the consequences of truthfulness prove painful.

It also helps, of course, if parents are seen to be truthful in their dealings with their children's questions. What disillusionment and disappointment can set into a youngster's life when he discovers that he has been sold a bill of goods by the parents whose every word he trusted implicitly. Careful parents take great pains to answer youthful questions honestly and appropriately. A child does not need to know everything about sensitive matters and probably will be satisfied with a brief but honest response. But we must beware of producing confusion in a child's mind by less than straightforward statements. One little boy asked his friend, "Do you believe in the devil?" to which his friend replied, "Nah. It's like Santa Claus—it's your dad!" How do you think that confusion arose? 🐾

Ananias
JOHN KNAPP II

A brief word for Ananias, whose story is found in the Acts of the Apostles, chapter 5.

There once was a man Ananias,
    Who hid a most dishonest bias;
His gift to Saint Peter
    Proved him such a cheater,
He fell down stone-dead on the dais. 🦌

Max and the Big Fat Lie
MICHAEL P. WAITE

Max finds out that a lie is a big, ugly monster. At first it may be quite small, but as it grows, it gets more monsterish.

Max's friend Stevie had just got a movie,
    Slime Gobs from Space was its title.
"Get over here soon," Stevie phoned from his room.
    " 'Cause seeing this movie is vital!"
Max wanted badly to see this great movie.
    It was sure to be scary and loud.
But Mother and Dad would think it was bad
    For movies like this weren't allowed!
Max did his best to think up a plan.
    He thought 'til his eyeballs were sore.
And as he was thinking and painfully blinking
    Somebody knocked on the door.
Max quickly jumped to his feet in surprise
    For in through the door walked a fellow
Who was short as a stump, and equally plump—
    What's more, he was purple and yellow!

413

"Good day, my dear chap," said the short, purple creature.
      "You're caught in a fix, I'll agree.
I can see on your face that *Slime Gobs from Space*
      Is a movie you simply must see!"
"My name is Sir Fib and I think that you'll find
      My services tend to be handy.
Please do not question, just take my suggestion:
      A wee little fib would be dandy.
"Go tell your mother you're going to Stevie's,
      But change the show's title a bit—
Pokey the Cow is a flick she'll allow.
      Now go do your stuff—this is it!"
Of course, Max's mother was truly delighted—
      Pokey the Cow would be swell!
It sounded so good, that if Stevie's mom could
      The two moms might watch it as well.
This was a shocker to poor, little Max,
      He hurried upstairs nearly crying.
If Mom came along the whole plan would go wrong
      And Max would be punished for lying!
Sir Fib looked disturbed as he listened to Max.
      He said, "This one's too big for me!
But I have a friend for whom I can send.
      He'll know the answer, you'll see!"
So, he opened the door and he whistled a note.
      It just took a second, not more,
For a tall lanky guy with a dark, shifty eye
      To quickly slip through Max's door.
"Yo, Kid!" said the guy. "I'm Kleever Deceiver,
      And Fib here has told me your story.
I've got what you need, and I think you'll agree
      That deceiving should wipe out your worry!
"Go tell your ma that you just changed your mind

And you're gonna play baseball with Stevie.
She'll fall for the trick, then you go watch the flick.
 It works every time, Kid, believe me."
Max hurried off with his new, improved lie,
 Which Mother believed right away.
She showed not a doubt, but when Max turned about,
 She had something awful to say.
"Since you'll be playing with Stevie Malone,"
 Mom mentioned while feeding the cat,
"His mother and I could just visit awhile—
 I've been meaning to stop for a chat!"
Max felt quite ill as he slithered upstairs
 This was a problem indeed!
If Mother dropped by, he'd be caught in his lie
 (Which was growing as fast as a weed!).
Kleever Deceiver turned terrible pale
 When he heard about Mother's new plan.
"She's a foe I can't beat!" he cried in defeat.
 "But I know a fellow who can!"
He leaned out the door, and peering both ways,
 He called out "Hey yo! Big Fat Lie!"
And soon came a rumble, a thump, and a stumble
 That felt like a train rolling by!
The creature was giant, all green and red-spotted,
 It just barely squeezed through the door.
When it sat on the bed, the whole house shook instead,
 And the mattress sank down to the floor.
"So this is the kid with the problem?" it said.
 "A problem that I'll take away!
My name's Big Fat Lie, and I'll tell you why . . .
 It's because I know just what to say!"
"Go tell your mother that Mrs. Malone
 Has got the Mongolian Measles,

Their phone's disconnected, her toe is infected,
 And the house was just treated for weasels.
"Tell her you'd much rather pedal your bike
 Than have your mom give you a ride. . . .
Then she won't know where you boys really go—
 Watching the *Slime Gobs* inside!"
Plodding his way down the stairs Max recited,
 He practiced his new, big fat lie.
His kneecaps were shaking, his stomach was quaking,
 But he had to give it a try.
"Mother," he said as he tried to stay calm,
 "I fear that there's been complications. . . .
Mrs. Malone is no longer home,
 She's gone off to visit relations.
"Their phone's disconnected, their poodle got sick,
 And their house was attacked by a shark.
So, Stevie and I have just changed our minds—
 We're going to ride bikes in the park."

Stevie had already set up the movie
 By the time Max snuck up to his room.
They pulled down the shade and built a blockade,
 And the room was as dark as a tomb.
Each time he heard talking or someone's shoes walking,
 Max thought for sure he'd be caught.
He was in such a worry, the movie seemed blurry.
 It wasn't such fun as he'd thought.
Max thought he felt someone's breath on his neck,
 So he turned and he got a surprise.
It was Sir Fib and Kleever, that clever Deceiver,
 But the breath that he felt was the Lie's.
After a while he could take it no more,
 He jumped to his feet in a panic!

He raced his bike home, but he wasn't alone,
>For the weight on his bike was titanic!
On the back of his bike were Sir Fib and Deceiver
>And heavier still was the Lie.
"Whatever you do," said the Lie turning blue,
>"Don't look your mom in the eye!
"Tell her that you were attacked by a tiger
>And trapped in a telephone booth. . . .
The Martians invaded! The planet was raided!
>Just make sure you don't tell the truth!"
"Get lost!" shouted Max. "I don't need all your lies,
>The truth will work just fine for me.
I'm finished with lying and sneaking and spying—
>So you guys just might as well leave!"
At that very moment, in one mighty flash,
>The Lie and his friends disappeared.
Max felt more relieved than you could've believed . . .
>For now Max's conscience was cleared.
Max told his mom of the lies he'd made up,
>How he'd been sneaky and bad.
He said he was sorry, and she needn't worry—
>He learned from the lesson he'd had.
Mom never did let Max go see the *Slime Gobs*
>Though once in a while he still taunts her.
But Max doesn't lie, and we all know why—
>A lie's like a big, ugly monster! 🐾

One's mere word should be as trustworthy as a signed
agreement attested by legal witnesses.
CURTIS VAUGHAN

Monday Morning
MARK TWAIN

The young hero of The Adventures of Tom Sawyer *didn't like Monday mornings and he didn't like school. So when Monday morning came around, he pretended to be ill. He soon found himself in all kinds of trouble, and he learned the hard way that it's smart to be truthful.*

Monday morning found Tom Sawyer miserable. Monday morning always found him so—because it began another week's slow suffering in school. He generally began that day with wishing he had had no intervening holiday, it made the going into captivity and fetters again so much more odious.

Tom lay thinking. Presently it occurred to him that he wished he was sick; then he could stay home from school. Here was a vague possibility. He canvassed his system. No ailment was found, and he investigated again. This time, he thought he could detect colicky symptoms, and he began to encourage them with considerable hope. But they soon grew feeble, and presently died wholly away. He reflected further. Suddenly he discovered something. One of his upper front teeth was loose. This was lucky; he was about to begin to groan as a "starter," as he called it, when it occurred to him that if he came into court with that argument, his aunt would pull it out, and that would hurt. So he thought he would hold the tooth in reserve for the present, and seek further. Nothing offered for some little time, and then he remembered hearing the doctor tell about a certain thing that laid up a patient for two or three weeks and threatened to make him lose a finger. So the boy eagerly drew his sore toe from under the sheet and held it up for inspection. But now he did not know the necessary symptoms. However, it seemed well worthwhile to chance it, so he fell to groaning with considerable spirit. But Sid slept on unconscious.

Tom groaned louder and fancied that he began to feel pain in the toe.

No result from Sid.

Tom was panting with his exertions by this time. He took a rest and then swelled himself up and fetched a succession of admirable groans.

Sid snored on.

Tom was aggravated. He said, "Sid, Sid!" and shook him. This course worked well, and Tom began to groan again. Sid yawned, stretched, then brought himself up on his elbow with a snort, and began to stare at Tom. Tom went on groaning. Sid said:

"Tom! Say, Tom!" (No response.) "Here, Tom! Tom! What is the matter, Tom?" And he shook him and looked in his face anxiously.

Tom moaned out:

"Oh, don't Sid. Don't joggle me."

"Why, what's the matter, Tom? I must call Auntie."

"No—never mind. It'll be over by and by, maybe. Don't call anybody."

"But I must! Don't groan so, Tom, it's awful. How long you been this way?"

"Hours. Ouch! Oh, don't stir so, Sid, you'll kill me."

"Tom, why didn't you wake me sooner? Oh, Tom, don't! It makes my flesh crawl to hear you. Tom, what is the matter?"

"I forgive you everything, Sid. (Groan.) Everything you've ever done to me. When I'm gone—"

"Oh, Tom, you ain't dying are you? Don't, Tom—oh, don't. Maybe—"

"I forgive everybody, Sid. (Groan.) Tell 'em so, Sid. And, Sid, you give my window sash and my cat with one eye to that new girl that's come to town, and tell her—"

But Sid had snatched his clothes and gone. Tom was suffering in reality, now, so handsomely was his imagination working, and so his groans had gathered quite a genuine tone.

Sid flew downstairs and said:

"Oh, Aunt Polly, come! Tom's dying!"

"Dying!"

"Yes'm. Don't wait—come quick!"

"Rubbage! I don't believe it!"

But she fled upstairs, nevertheless, with Sid and Mary at her heels. And her face grew white, too, and her lip trembled. When she reached the bedside, she gasped out:

"You, Tom! Tom, what's the matter with you?"

"Oh, Auntie, I'm—"

"What's the matter with you, child?"

"Oh, Auntie, my sore toe's mortified!"

The old lady sank down into a chair and laughed a little, then cried a little, then did both together. This restored her, and she said:

"Tom, what a turn you did give me. Now you shut up that nonsense and climb out of this."

The groans ceased, and the pain vanished from the toe. The boy felt a little foolish, and he said:

"Aunt Polly, it *seemed* mortified, and it hurt so I never minded my tooth at all."

"Your tooth indeed! What's the matter with your tooth?"

"One of them's loose, and it aches perfectly awful."

"There, there, now, don't begin that groaning again. Open your mouth. Well—your tooth *is* loose, but you're not going to die about that. Mary, get me a silk thread, and a chunk of fire out of the kitchen."

Tom said:

"Oh, please, Auntie, don't pull it out. It don't hurt any more. I wish I may never stir if it does. Please don't, Auntie. *I* don't want to stay home from school."

"Oh, you don't, don't you? So all this row was because you thought you'd get to stay home from school and go a-fishing? Tom, Tom, I love you so, and you seem to try every way you can to break my old heart with your outrageousness." By this time, the dental instruments were ready. The old lady made one end of the silk thread fast to Tom's tooth with a loop and tied the other to the bedpost. Then she seized the chunk of fire and suddenly thrust it almost into the boy's face. The tooth hung dangling by the bedpost, now.

But all trials bring their compensations. As Tom wended to school after breakfast, he was the envy of every boy he met because the gap in his upper row of teeth enabled him to expectorate in a new and admirable way. He gathered quite a following of lads interested in the exhibition; and one that cut his finger and had been a center of fascination and homage up to this time now found himself suddenly without an adherent and shorn of his glory. His heart was heavy, and he said with a disdain which he did not feel, that it wasn't anything to spit like Tom Sawyer; but another boy said, "Sour grapes!" and he wandered away a dismantled hero. 🐿

You Are the Man
VIRGINIA MUIR

King David was very powerful, but he had done things that were wrong. A brave, honest man was needed to tell him the truth. Nathan stepped forward to do the job in II Samuel 12:1-7.

God was greatly displeased with David because he had coveted another man's wife and had committed adultery and murder. God sent a prophet named Nathan to talk to David about his sins.

Nathan told David this story: "Once two men were neighbors. One was very rich and had many sheep and cattle. The other was poor; he had only one little ewe lamb. The poor man's lamb was a beloved pet, almost like one of the family. Once the rich man had a guest. Instead of killing one of the sheep from his own large flock, he stole the poor man's lamb and cooked it for his guest's dinner."

David was terribly angry. He said, "Why, a selfish man like that should be killed, but first he must give the poor man four lambs to pay for the one he stole."

Nathan said, "David, you are that rich man. God has been good to you. He saved you from Saul and made you king over Israel and Judah. You have everything you need. Why have you done this great sin of stealing Uriah's wife [Bathsheba] and then murdering him? Now you shall always live in fear of war, and your family shall become rebellious."

David confessed that he had sinned against God. Nathan said that because he was sorry, he would not have to die, but Bathsheba's baby would die. In a few days the baby became very sick, and although David prayed for him, he died. ❧

The Shepherd's Boy and the Wolf
Aesop

A mischievous Shepherd's Boy used to amuse himself by calling, "Wolf, Wolf!" just to see the villagers run with their clubs and pitchforks to help him. After he had called this more than once for a joke and had laughed at them each time, they grew angry. One day a Wolf really did get among the sheep, and the Shepherd Boy called "Wolf, Wolf!" in vain. The villagers went on with their work, the Wolf killed what he wanted of the sheep, and the Shepherd Boy learned that liars are not believed, even when they do tell the truth. ❧

Dad, Did You Ever Cheat?

DANIEL TAYLOR

In Letters To My Children, *a father talks to his son honestly about honesty—a good idea for all parents and children.*

Dear Nate,

Yes. In fourth grade I copied the word *piano* off Janet Bowie's paper during a spelling test. I hadn't missed a spelling word all year and couldn't stand the thought of losing that gold star on my chart. I snapped under the pressure.

Then in eighth grade I couldn't remember what the outer ring of the sun is called. When my friend Tom Rauman whispered "corona" to someone else, I convinced myself I would have remembered it eventually anyway and wrote it down.

Is that all, you ask? Well, a few of my college term papers may have been footnoted more economically than was called for, but that was more out of ignorance than the desire to mislead anyone. And I used to be notoriously bad at calling shots in or out in tennis, but that was because I had a tendency to see the ball, well, optimistically. Besides, when I am running my eyes bounce and it's tough to make accurate calls with bouncing eyes.

Oh, do I ever cheat on anything now? Of course not. That is, not on important things. Well, perhaps I occasionally do some "creative estimating" on my taxes. That's when you're supposed to put down a figure for something which you haven't kept records on (and only a slave to organization ever would) so you have to guess. There's this powerful urge to guess in your own favor, and I may have once or twice suffered from too much creativity. But compared to most people I am a candidate for sainthood when it comes to taxes.

Hmmm. Looking over my answer, I see a disturbing pattern. The truth seems to be that I am quite willing to cheat if the situation calls for it, as long as I can convince myself that there's a reason for it, that it isn't "real cheating," and that I'm certainly no worse than and probably quite a bit better than most other people.

I stole the word *piano* because I had worked hard all year and thought I deserved my gold star. I allowed myself to use "corona" on the science test because I rationalized that I knew it anyway. I chalk my weak footnoting up to ignorance, but at times I was ignorant because I wanted to be. I keep money for myself that should go for the things we all share in this country because I convince myself that it's *mine* and that others cheat a lot more than I do.

I guess I try to distance myself from my actions. I create this space between an act that doesn't make me look good, and what I feel to be the real me. This real me insists on seeing itself as a good, even admirable person and certainly an honest one. For it to cohabit with this other person who cheats at times, it must create some wiggle room, some space from those deeds, so that it is not soiled. Do you see how this sort of splits me in two—one person to be a good fellow and the other to do the dirty work?

Nate, I am talking about integrity. Integrity means wholeness, unity. What is damaged every time I cheat is my integrity. I am no longer whole. I set one part of myself against another. I am made double—duplicitous.

And the truth is that cheating is only a superficial example of a loss of integrity. I become divided, become less, every time I choose to live my life at a lower level than God intended when he made me. And these choices, unlike spelling tests and tax returns, are offered me every day of my life.

When I was sixteen, I went to a Christian camp for boys. We had a speaker who, if I remember correctly, talked to us about sex, something of occasional interest to sixteen-year-old boys. He asked for questions at the end, and I remember working up my courage and asking if he thought it was sinful to look at "girlie" magazines—a nice distancing word.

He gave an answer which would perhaps not satisfy many moralists, but which had a great impact on me. He didn't say, as he rightfully could have, "Yes, it is a sin and God is not pleased if you do it, period!" Instead he said, "You need to decide at what plane you are going to live your life." He said more, but those are the words I remembered.

On what plane are you going to live your life? Are you going to make all the little daily compromises that most everyone else seems to make? Are you going to waver here, rationalize there, indulge yourself in this, temporarily suspend your convictions over that—until your life becomes characterized by fragmentations, half-heartedness and expedience?

The world as it is does not understand people who want to live their lives on a higher plane. They think they're either fools or saints (Mother Teresa), but either way they are out-of-touch with the so-called real world.

A trivial example: The first time I went to France, I walked out of my Paris hotel to buy a newspaper from a stand on the street. Having never used French money, I stared intently at my change as I walked away. Realizing the fellow had given me back ten francs too many, I returned immediately to the stand and tried to say he had given me too much. Thinking I was complaining about being shortchanged, the fellow adopted a surly tone (I couldn't tell what he was saying) until I simply held my hand of change out to him and he was able to see that he had given me too much. I handed him back the extra and walked away, but not before noting as great a look of incomprehension and amazement as I have seen. Nothing in the "real world," apparently, had prepared him for customers (much less Americans?) who returned excess change.

What I would suggest to you is that the real world is God's world, not the poor, perverted imitation world with which most people are satisfied. To live as fully as possible in that real world, you have to decide if you want to live on that high plane. That means being able to recognize as sin things like materialism, gossip, status-seeking and treating other people as objects (which both lust and manipulation do).

And after recognizing these and many other common actions and attitudes as sin, as things which fragment and distance you from the wholeness God intended, living in God's world means being able to say no to them. This does not mean that reading *Playboy* or lying or being unhappy until you have the latest pair of overpriced jeans or running down a friend behind her back will single-handedly destroy your life or your relationship to God. We will often do that which we hate. But I do hope that your goal, with God's help, will be to live on the highest possible plane. Life is so very short that it is a terrible waste to do anything less.

Besides, those gold stars? They're only paper.

Love,
Papa 🐾

A Secret Agony
FYODOR DOSTOEVSKY

Proverbs 28:13 says, "He who conceals his sins does not prosper, but whoever confesses and renounces them finds mercy." Dostoevsky's The Brothers Karamazov *illustrates this truth.*

At last, however, he began brooding over the past, and the strain of it was too much for him. Then he was attracted by a fine and intelligent girl and soon after married her, hoping that marriage would dispel his lonely depression, and that by entering on a new life and scrupulously doing his duty to his wife and children, he would escape from old memories altogether. But the very opposite of what he expected happened. He began, even in the first month of his marriage, to be continually fretted by the thought, "My wife loves me—but what if she knew?" When she first told him that she would soon bear him a child, he was troubled. "I am giving life, but I have taken life." Children came. "How dare I love them, teach and educate them, how can I talk to them of virtue? I have shed blood." They were splendid children, he longed to caress them; "and I can't look at their innocent candid faces, I am unworthy."

At last he began to be bitterly and ominously haunted by the blood of his murdered victim, by the young life he had destroyed, by the blood that cried out for vengeance. He had begun to have awful dreams. But, being a man of fortitude, he bore his suffering a long time, thinking: "I shall expiate everything by this secret agony." But that hope, too, was vain; the longer it went on, the more intense was his suffering.

He was respected in society for his active benevolence, though everyone was overawed by his stern and gloomy character. But the more he was respected, the more intolerable it was for him. He confessed to me that he had thoughts of killing himself. But he began to be haunted by another idea—an idea which he had as first regarded as impossible and unthinkable, though at last it got such a hold on his heart that he could not shake it off. He dreamed of rising up, going out and confessing in the face of all men that he had committed murder. For three years this dream had pursued him, haunting him in different forms. At last he believed with his whole heart that if he confessed his crime, he would heal his soul and would be at peace for ever. But this belief filled his heart with terror, for how could he carry it out? And then came what happened at my duel.

"Looking at you, I have made up my mind."

I looked at him. "Is it possible," I cried, clasping my hands, "that such a trivial incident could give rise to a resolution in you?"

"My resolution has been growing for the last three years," he answered, "and your story only gave the last touch to it. Looking at you, I reproached myself and envied you." He said this to me almost sullenly.

"But you won't be believed," I observed; "it's fourteen years ago."

"I have proofs, great proofs. I shall show them."

Then I cried and kissed him.

"Tell me one thing, one thing," he said (as though it all depended upon me), "my wife, my children! My wife may die of grief, and though my children won't lose their rank and property, they'll be a convict's children for ever! And what a memory, what a memory of me I shall leave in their hearts!"

I said nothing.

"And to part from them, to leave them for ever? It's for ever, you know, for ever!"

I sat still and repeated a silent prayer. I got up at last; I felt afraid.

"Well?" He looked at me.

"Go!" said I, "confess. Everything passes, only the truth remains. Your children will understand, when they grow up, the nobility of your resolution."

He left me that time as though he had made up his mind. Yet for more than a fortnight afterwards, he came to me every evening, still preparing himself, still unable to bring himself to the point. He made my heart ache. One day he would come determined and say fervently:

"I know it will be heaven for me, heaven, the moment I confess. Fourteen years I've been in hell. I want to suffer. I will take my punishment and begin to live. You can pass through the world doing wrong, but there's no turning back. Now I dare not love my neighbor nor even my own children. Good God, my children will understand, perhaps, what my punishment has cost me and will not condemn me! God is not in strength but in truth."

. . . I did not know that evening that the next day was his birthday. I had not been out for the last few days, so I had no chance of hearing it from anyone. On that day he always had a great gathering, everyone in the town went to it. It was the same this time. After dinner he walked into the middle of the room, with a paper in his hand—a formal declaration to the chief of his department who was present. This declaration he read aloud to the whole assembly. It contained a full account of the crime, in every detail.

"I cut myself off from men as a monster. God has visited me," he said in conclusion. "I want to suffer for my sin!"

Then he brought out and laid on the table all the things he had been keeping for fourteen years, that he thought would prove his crime, the jewels belonging to the murdered woman which he had stolen to divert suspicion, a cross and a locket taken from her neck with a portrait of her betrothed in the locket, her notebook and two letters; one from her betrothed, telling her that he would soon be with her, and her unfinished answer left on the table to be sent off next day. He carried off these two letters—what for? Why had he kept them for fourteen years afterwards instead of destroying them as evidence against him?

And this is what happened: everyone was amazed and horrified, everyone refused to believe it and thought that he was deranged, though all listened with intense curiosity. A few days later it was fully decided and agreed in every house that the unhappy man was mad. The legal authorities could not refuse to take the case up, but they too dropped it. Though the trinkets and letters made them ponder, they decided that even if they did turn out to be authentic, no charge could be based on those alone. Besides, she might have given him those things as a friend, or asked him to take care of them for her. I heard afterwards, however, that the genuineness of the things was proved by the friends and relations of the murdered woman, and that there was no doubt about them. Yet nothing was destined to come of it, after all.

Five days later, all had heard that he was ill and that his life was in danger. The nature of his illness I can't explain; they said it

429

was an affection of the heart. But it became known that the doctors had been induced by his wife to investigate his mental condition also, and had come to the conclusion that it was a case of insanity. I betrayed nothing, though people ran to question me. But when I wanted to visit him, I was for a long while forbidden to do so, above all by his wife.

"It's you who have caused his illness," she said to me; "he was always gloomy, but for the last year people noticed that he was peculiarly excited and did strange things, and now you have been the ruin of him. Your preaching has brought him to this; for the last month he was always with you."

Indeed, not only his wife but the whole town were down upon me and blamed me. "It's all your doing," they said. I was silent and indeed rejoiced at heart, for I was plainly God's mercy to the man who had turned against himself and punished himself. I could not believe in his insanity.

They let me see him at last; he insisted upon saying good-bye to me. I went in to him and saw at once, that not only his days, but his hours were numbered. He was weak, yellow, his hands trembled, he gasped for breath, but his face was full of tender and happy feeling.

"It's done!" he said. "I've long been yearning to see you. Why didn't you come?"

I did not tell him that they would not let me see him.

"God has had pity on me and is calling me to Himself. I know I am dying, but I feel joy and peace for the first time after so many years. There was heaven in my heart from the moment I had done what I had to do. Now I dare to love my children and to kiss them. Neither my wife nor the judges, nor anyone has believed it. My children will never believe it either. I see in that God's mercy to them. I shall die, and my name will be without a stain for them. And now I feel God near, my heart rejoices as in Heaven . . . I have done my duty." ❧

Kindness

IT IS QUITE POSSIBLE THAT JESUS made yokes for oxen when He was a carpenter in Nazareth. These yokes were heavy pieces of wood that served to hold a pair of oxen together while they united in their heavy work. If the yoke did not fit comfortably on the ox's shoulder, it would produce irritation and sores. This knowledge was probably what prompted Jesus to say to people who were being worn down by the heavy load of legalistic minutiae, "Come to me, all you who are weary and burdened, and I will give you rest. Take my yoke upon you and learn from me, for I am gentle and humble in heart, and you will find rest for your souls. For my yoke is easy and my burden is light."

The Greek word translated "easy" (*chrestos*) is usually translated "kind." An easy yoke was kind to a weary ox's shoulder, allowing the sores and irritations to heal more readily. So it was with the ministry of Jesus to hurting people. It was characterized by "kindness." This did not mean that He was prepared to overlook sin or tolerate unrighteousness. On the contrary, He still placed a yoke on His disciples, designed to keep them harmoniously on track. But it was not an arduous yoke; it was easy and kind—except for people who, like oxen, didn't want to go the way they ought. For them it rubbed.

Paul tells us that it is the "kindness of God" that leads people to repentance. In our efforts to encourage people to repent, we need to remember this, for there is often an understandable tendency to concentrate on the judgment of God as we try to lead people from their sin and into forgiveness. This is not to suggest that we should soft-pedal the judgment; it means, rather, that people are often more likely to be touched and moved by unde-served kindness than by anything else.

This holds true in all situations. A mother we know was struggling to discipline her teenage daughter. The issue in question was hardly earth-shattering, but Mother thought it was a matter of principle. Daughter thought it was a case of being picky. The issue: tidying up her room. Daily squabbles became normative until a wise soul suggested that instead of fighting, the mother should say nothing and simply clean up the room herself.

A couple of weeks passed, then one day the daughter called the mother on the phone and said, "Mom, I'm sorry I've been such a little beast! I'll pick up my room."

Mother was as surprised as she was elated and said, "What made you change your mind?"

The daughter answered, "It's your kindness, Mom. You're so kind."

How do we know this story? The teenager was our daughter.

Kindness works! Not every time, but more often than you'd think. And don't forget that kindness is one evidence of the fruit of the Spirit. &

Mary's Lamb

SARAH JOSEPHA HALE

Mary had a little lamb,
    Its fleece was white as snow;
And everywhere that Mary went,
    The lamb was sure to go.

He followed her to school one day,
    Which was against the rule;
It made the children laugh and play
    To see a lamb at school.

And so the teacher turned him out,
    But still he lingered near,
And waited patiently about
    Till Mary did appear.

Then he ran to her, and laid
    His head upon her arm,
As if he said, "I'm not afraid—
    You'll keep me from all harm."

"What makes the lamb love Mary so?"
    The eager children cried.
"Oh, Mary loves the lamb, you know,"
    The teacher quick replied.

And you each gentle animal
    In confidence may bind,
And make them follow at your will,
    If you are only kind. ❧

Androcles and the Lion
TRANSLATED FROM APION

You've heard of Christians being thrown to the lions in ancient Rome. But have you heard about the slave who was kind to a lion and how the lion responded? And what the emperor did?!

Androcles, a runaway slave, had fled to a forest for safety. He had not been there long when he saw a Lion who was groaning with pain. He started to flee, but when he realized that the Lion did not follow but only kept on groaning, Androcles turned and went to it. The Lion, instead of rushing at him, put out a torn and bloody paw. Androcles, seeing the poor beast was in pain and wanting to help it, went up, took its paw, and examined it. Discovering a large thorn, the man pulled it out and thus relieved the pain. The grateful Lion in return took Androcles to its cave and every day brought him food. Sometime later both were captured and taken to Rome. The slave was condemned to be killed by being thrown to the Lion, which had not had food for several days. Androcles was led into the arena in the presence of the Emperor and his court, and at the same time the Lion was loosed. It came headlong toward its prey, but when it came near Androcles, instead of pouncing upon him, it jumped up and fawned upon him like a friendly dog. The Emperor was much surprised and called to him Androcles who told his story. The Emperor freed both the slave and the Lion, for he thought such kindness and such gratitude were deserving of reward. 🍂

A New Home

ANNA SEWELL

Black Beauty (from the book by that name) is a lovely horse whose story about life's ups and downs shows how kindness makes life pleasant and cruelty makes it hard. In this section Black Beauty finds a kind owner and is very happy.

The next morning, [the coachman] took me into the yard and gave me a good grooming, and just as I was going into my box with my coat soft and bright, the Squire came in to look at me, and seemed pleased.

"John," he said, "I meant to have tried the new horse this morning, but I have other business. You may as well take him a round after breakfast; go by the common and the Highwood, and back by the watermill and the river, that will show his paces."

"I will, sir," said John. After breakfast, he came and fitted me with a bridle. He was very particular in letting out and taking in the straps, to fit my head comfortably; then he brought the saddle, that was not broad enough for my back; he saw it in a minute and went for another, which fitted nicely. He rode me first slowly, then a trot, then a canter, and when we were on the common, he gave me a light touch with his whip, and we had a splendid gallop.

"Ho, ho! my boy," he said, as he pulled me up, "you would like to follow the hounds, I think."

As we came back through the Park, we met the Squire and Mrs. Gordon walking; they stopped, and John jumped off.

"Well, John, how does he go?"

"First-rate, sir," answered John, "he is as fleet as a deer and has a fine spirit, too: but the lightest touch of the rein will guide him."

. . . John seemed very proud of me: he used to make my mane and tail almost as smooth as a lady's hair, and he would talk to me a great deal; of course, I did not understand all he said, but I learned more and more to know what he *meant*, and what he wanted me to

435

do. I grew very fond of him, he was so gentle and kind, he seemed to know just how a horse feels, and when he cleaned me, he knew the tender places, and the ticklish places; when he brushed my head, he went as carefully over my eyes as if they were his own, and never stirred up any ill-temper. . . .

I was quite happy in my new place and if there was one thing that I missed, it must not be thought that I was discontented; all who had to do with me were good, and I had a light airy stable and the best of food. What more could I want? Why, liberty! For three years and a half of my life, I had had all the liberty I could wish for; but now, week after week, month after month, and no doubt year after year, I must stand up in a stable night and day except when I am wanted, and then I must be just as steady and quiet as any old horse who has worked twenty years. Straps here and straps there, a bit in my mouth, and blinkers over my eyes. Now, I am not complaining, for I know it must be so. I only mean to say that for a young horse full of strength and spirits who has been used to some large field or plain, where he can fling up his head, and toss up his tail and gallop away at full speed, then round and back again with a snort to his companions—I say it is hard never to have a bit more liberty to do as you like. Sometimes, when I have had less exercise than usual, I have felt so full of life and spring, that when John takes me out to exercise, I really could not keep quiet; do what I would, it seemed as if I must jump, or dance, or prance, and many a good shake I know I must have given him, especially at the first; but he was always good and patient.

"Steady, steady, my boy," he would say; "wait a bit and we'll have a good swing, and soon get the tickle out of your feet." Then as soon as we were out of the village, he would give me a few miles at a spanking trot and then bring me back as fresh as before, only clear of the fidgets, as he called them. Spirited horses, when not enough exercised, are often called skittish, when it is only play;

and some grooms will punish them, but our John did not, he
it was only high spirits. Still, he had his own ways of making
understand by the tone of his voice or the touch of the rein.
was very serious and quite determined, I always knew it by hi
voice, and that had more power with me than anything else,
was very fond of him. 🐾

Entertaining Angels
MARILYN WOODY

Abraham and Sarah were very surprised when they discovered that some ordin
ing visitors were actually angels (Genesis 18:1-15). You never know whom yo
be meeting, so it's a good idea to be kind to everybody!

One day a man named Abraham saw three men coming tow:
tent-home. They had been traveling and were tired and hung
Abraham and his wife, Sarah, fixed them a picnic to eat und
trees.

Then one of the men said to Abraham, "Next year Sar:
have a son."

Abraham was amazed at this news. He was almost a hur
years old, and Sarah was ninety. Why, they were old enough
grandparents, not a new mom and dad!

"Is anything too hard for the Lord?" one of the men ask
Abraham.

Later, Abraham found out that the men were really ang
God had sent them to bring the happy announcement about
baby.

Perhaps you have seen an angel, too, and never even kı
When you and your family are kind to homeless, sick, or hur
people, you may be helping an angel. You never know! 🐾

The Wind and the Sun
AESOP

Once upon a time when everything could talk, the Wind and the Sun fell into an argument as to which was the stronger. Finally they decided to put the matter to a test; they would see which one could make a certain man, who was walking along the road, throw off his cape. The Wind tried first. He blew and he blew. The harder and colder he blew, the tighter the traveler wrapped his cape about him. The Wind finally gave up and told the Sun to try. The Sun began to smile and as it grew warmer and warmer, the traveler was comfortable once more. But the Sun shone brighter and brighter until the man grew so hot, the sweat poured out on his face, he became weary, and seating himself on a stone, he quickly threw his cape to the ground. You see, gentleness had accomplished what force could not. 🐝

Receive Him as Your Own
ELSIE E. EGERMEIER

Philemon had been kind to Paul. Paul was kind to Onesimus. Onesimus was kind to Paul. Paul asked Philemon to be kind to Onesimus. Now, there was a lot of kindness!

While in Rome, Paul met Onesimus, a runaway slave. Strangely enough Paul knew Onesimus' master, Philemon, a Christian who lived in Colosse.

Like many others Onesimus heard Paul tell about Jesus Christ, and he became a Christian. For a time he took care of Paul, and Paul taught him more about Jesus.

Paul would have liked to keep Onesimus, for he loved the young man. Also Onesimus made things easier and more comfortable for Paul. Yet according to the law the runaway slave still

belonged to Philemon. In those days many people owned slaves just as people today own animals. Onesimus would never feel right until he had made things right with Philemon. So he decided to go back.

Paul hated to see Onesimus leave. To make sure that Philemon would treat his runaway slave kindly, Paul sent a letter with Onesimus for his master.

In the letter Paul wrote, "I appeal to you for Onesimus who has been like a son to me while I am in prison. I have sent him back for you to receive as your own. I would have liked to keep him, but I could not do that. Receive him not as a servant but as a brother. Treat him as you would treat me. If he has wronged you or owes you anything, charge it to me and I will repay it." ❧

Words Children Like to Hear
RUTH A. TUCKER

Most parents would be surprised to know what words and phrases they most frequently use in speaking to their children. Too often they are words of criticism or demands to perform. Such words are indeed necessary at times, but so are words of assurance and praise and offers of kindness. Dolores Curran writes of this need in her book *Traits of a Healthy Family*.

"Recently, for my weekly newspaper column, I invited seventy-five fourth and fifth graders to submit the words they most like to hear from their mothers. Here are the five big winners, repeated over and over by almost all the kids:

I love you.

Yes.

Time to eat.

You can go.

You can stay up late. ❧

If I Can Stop One Heart from Breaking
EMILY DICKINSON

Emily Dickinson (1830-1886) rarely left her home in Amherst, but while she lived reclusively she did not isolate herself from need, neither did she lose her sense of compassion.

If I can stop one heart from breaking,
    I shall not live in vain;
If I can ease one life the aching,
    Or cool one pain,
Or help one fainting robin
    Unto his nest again,
I shall not live in vain. ❧

Prayer of St. Francis
ST. FRANCIS OF ASSISI

St. Francis's love of animals was legendary, but in his famous prayer, we see that his love for people was no less powerful.

Lord, make me an instrument of Thy peace; where there is hatred, let me sow love; where there is injury, pardon; where there is doubt, faith; where there is despair, hope; where there is darkness, light; where there is sadness, joy.

    O Divine Master, grant that I may not so much seek to be consoled as to console; to be understood as to understand; to be loved as to love. For it is in giving that we receive, it is in pardoning that we are pardoned, and it is in dying that we are born to eternal life. ❧

Part of the Family

E.B.R. HIRSH

David never forgot the kindness of Jonathan, and was delighted to be able to extend kindness in turn to Jonathan's crippled son. This story is from II Samuel 9.

One day David asked if there were any surviving children or grand-children of Saul's family. Because of his love and friendship for Jonathan, he sent messengers to find out.

An elderly servant of Saul's heard about the search and came before David, saying: "Jonathan had a son who is lame and he still lives. I have been caring for him."

David asked the servant to bring Jonathan's son to him. The boy arrived and bowed down before David.

"Do not be afraid," said the king. "I have called you here to show you kindness for your father's sake. He and I were as close as brothers and we made a covenant of friendship between us.

"I will restore to you the lands of your father. You and your faithful servant and his family will come to Jerusalem to live. Here you will never want for anything and you will become part of my household."

So Jonathan's lame son came to Jerusalem to live with King David as part of the royal household. 🐦

And be ye kind to one another, tenderhearted, forgiving one another, even as God for Christ's sake hath forgiven you.

EPHESIANS 4:32

The Grim Reaper
JANETTE OKE

Marty, the heroine of Janette Oke's novel Love Comes Softly, *was only nineteen years old when her husband was killed way out in the wild west. Surrounded by rough, unsophisticated pioneers, she found love and kindness in unexpected places and people.*

The morning sun shone brightly on the canvas of the covered wagon, promising an unseasonably warm day for mid-October. Marty fought for wakefulness, coming back slowly from a troubled and fitful sleep. Why did she feel so heavy and ill at ease—she who usually awoke with a bounce and a readiness for each new day's adventure? Then, as it all flooded over her, she fell back in a heap upon the blankets from which she had just emerged and let the sobs shake her slight body.

Clem was gone. The strong, boastful, boyish Clem who had so quickly and easily made her love him. Less than two short years ago she had seen him for the first time, self-assured, almost to the point of swaggering. Then in only fourteen months time, she was a married woman, out West, beginning a new and challenging adventure with the man she loved—until yesterday.

Yesterday her whole world had crumbled about her. The men who came told her that her Clem was dead. Killed outright. His horse had fallen. They'd had to destroy the horse. Did she want to come with them?

No, she'd stay.

Would she like his Missus to come over?

No, she'd be fine.

They'd care for the body. His Missus was right good at that. The neighbors would arrange for the buryin'. Lucky the parson was paying his visit through the area. Was to have moved on today but they were sure that he'd stay over. Sure she didn't want to come with them?

No, she'd be all right.

Hated to leave her alone.

She needed to be alone.

They'd see her on the morrow. Not to worry. They'd care for everything.

Thank ya—

And they had gone, taking her Clem with them, wrapped in one of her few blankets and tied on the back of the horse that the neighbor should have been riding but who was now led slowly, careful of its burden.

And now was the morrow and the sun was shining. Why was the sun shining? Didn't nature know that today should be as lifeless as she felt, with a cold wind blowing like the chill that gripped her heart?

"Oh, Clem! Clem!" she cried. "What am I gonna do now?"

The fact that she was way out West in the fall of the year, with no way back home, no one here that she knew and expecting Clem's baby besides, should have worried her. But for the moment the only thing that her mind could settle on and her heart understand was the pain of her great loss. . . .

There was kindness in all of them. She could feel it. It was not a piteous thing, but an understanding. This was the West. Things were hard out here. Most likely every neighbor there had had a similar time, but you didn't go under—you mustn't, you must go on. There was no time nor energy for pity here—not for self, not for one another. It took your whole being to face what must be faced. Death, too, must be accepted as part of life, and though it was hard, one carried on.

The visiting preacher spoke the words of commitment. He also spoke to the sorrowing, who in this case consisted of one lone, small person, the widow of the deceased; for one could hardly count the baby that she was carrying as one of the mourners, even if it was Clem's.

The preacher spoke words that were fitting for the occasion—

words of comfort and words of encouragement. The neighbors listened in silent sympathy to words similar to those that they had heard before. When the brief ceremony was over, Marty turned from the grave toward the wagon, and the four men with the shovels turned to the task of covering the stout wooden box that had kept some of the neighbor men up for most of the night to have it ready for this day. . . .

Her heavy feet carried her onto the wagon and her weighted hand lifted the canvas flap. She just wanted to crawl away, out of sight, and let the world cave in upon her.

It was hot in there in midday and the rush of torrid air sent her already dizzy head to spinning. She crawled back out through the entry and flopped down on the grass on the shady side of the wagon, propping herself up against the broken wheel. Her senses seemed to be playing tricks on her. She swam through unrealism into an intense feeling of loss. Round and round in her head it swept, making her wonder what truly was real and what imagined. She sat mentally groping for some sense to it all, when suddenly a male voice made her jump with its closeness.

"Ma'am."

She looked up—way up. A man stood before her, cap in hand, fingering it determinedly as he cleared his throat. She recognized him vaguely as one of the shovel bearers. He evidenced tall strength, and there was an oldness about his eyes that his youthful features declared a lie. Her eyes looked to him, but her lips refused to answer his address.

He seemed to draw courage from somewhere deep inside himself and spoke again.

"Ma'am, I know thet this be untimely—ya jest havin' buried yer husband an' all—but I'm afraid the matter can't wait none fer a proper-like time an' place."

He cleared his throat again and glanced up from the hat in his hands.

"My name be Clark Davis," he hurried on, "an' it peers to me thet you an' me be in need of one another."

At the sharp intake of breath on Marty's part, he raised a hand and hurried on.

"Now hold on a minute," he told her almost as a command. "It jest be a matter of common sense. Ya lost yer man, an' are here alone." He cast a glance at the broken wagon wheel.

"I reckon ya got no money to go to yer folks, iffen ya have folks to go back to. An' even if thet could be, ain't no wagon train fer the East will go through here 'til next spring. Me, now, I got me a need, too."

He stopped there and his eyes dropped. It was a minute before he raised them and was able to go on.

"I have a little 'un, not much more'n a mite—an' she be needin' a mama. Now as I see it, if we marries, you an' me—" he looked directly at her then, squatting down to put himself more on her level, "we could solve both of those problems. I would have waited but the preacher is only here fer today an' won't be back through agin 'til next April or May, so's it has to be today."

. . . He paused. "But she do be a needin' a woman's hand, my Missie. That's all I be askin' ya, Ma'am. Jest to be Missie's mama. Nothin' more. You an' Missie can share the bedroom. I'll take me the leanto. An'," he hesitated "I'll promise ya this, too. When the next wagon train goes through headin' east where ya can catch ya a stagecoach, iffen ya ain't happy here, I'll see to yer fare back home—on one condition: thet ya take my Missie along with ya. It jest don't be fair to the little mite not to have a mama."

He rose suddenly.

"I'll leave ya to be a thinkin' on it, Ma'am. We don't have much time."

He turned and strode away. The sag of his shoulders told her how much the words had cost him. Still, she thought angrily, what kind of a man could propose marriage to a woman who had just turned from her husband's grave—even this kind of a marriage? She felt despair well within her. I'd rather die, she told herself. I'd rather die. But what of Clem's baby? She didn't want death for him, for her sake or for Clem's. Frustration reigned within her. What a position to be in. No one, nothing, out in this God-forsaken west country. Family and friends were out of reach and she was completely alone. She knew that he was right. She needed him and she hated him for it.

"I hate this country! I hate it! I hate him, the cold miserable man! I hate him! I hate him!" But even as she stormed against him, she knew that she had no out.

She wiped her tears and got up from the shady grass. She wouldn't wait for him to come back in his lordly fashion for her decision, she thought stubbornly, and she went into the wagon and began to pack the few things that she called hers. ❧

Sharing the Harvest
DENNIS LARSON

Don Butcher was harvesting wheat in 1992 when his wife, Helen, fell ill. Preoccupied with looking after her, he asked others to store his wheat on his farm west of Othelle, Washington. After Helen died on Thanksgiving Day that year, Butcher came across a passage from Isaiah: "And if thou draw out thy soul to the hungry . . . then shall thy light rise in obscurity, and thy darkness be as the noon-day." It became his theme. "I'm going to feed the hungry," he said. Butcher decided to ship the wheat to the former Soviet Union as a memorial to his wife.

Large shipments of dried beans and wheat were sent to charities in the former Soviet Union for distribution. Another forty tons of wheat went to Belarus and Moldova. A federally funded program helps with the transportation, and Butcher pays the rest. He includes an address of an American family with each sack of flour so the recipients will have someone to write to and thank. "I want this grain to go to a family, from a family," Butcher says. "I want to say it's not bread alone, but sharing God's love that can make a world of difference." ❧

Every Soul That Touches Yours

GEORGE ELIOT

Novelist George Eliot's real name was Mary Ann Evans. She lived in England in the nineteenth century and was regarded as one of the leading intellectuals of her time.

Every soul that touches yours . . .
    Be it the slightest contact . . .
Gets therefrom some good;
    Some little grace; one kindly thought;
One aspiration yet unfelt;
    One bit of courage
For the darkening sky,
    One gleam of faith
To brave the thickening ills of life;
    One glimpse of brighter skies . . .
To make this life worth while
    And heaven a surer heritage. ❧

Kindness Is a Choice
STUART BRISCOE

A true story about a kind man we met years ago.

Shortly after I arrived in the United States, I was invited to speak at a banquet in one of the big Chicago hotels. My wife and I decided to drive down to the Windy City together and left ourselves plenty of time to find our way around. As we approached Chicago I noticed we were getting low on gas, but I knew there would be plenty of filling stations. When we suddenly came to a halt in the fast lane of the freeway, in the rush hour, with the rain pouring down, I realized my assumptions about filling stations were wrong as my tank was empty. I climbed out of my car, to be greeted by a chorus of horns expressing displeasure and expletives filling in the details. There was nothing I could do and less that anyone else was ready to do, so I stood in the rain, and like the sailors on Paul's sinking ship, I "wished for the day."

One particularly dilapidated car drew alongside; the driver rolled down his window. I braced myself for more verbal abuse but was relieved that his English was so bad I couldn't understand it. About fifteen minutes later the same car returned in the mass of traffic and pulled up in front of mine. The driver jumped out and without a word proceeded to fill my tank from a can. He had seen my plight, gone to a filling station off the freeway, borrowed a can, gotten back on the freeway, fought the traffic, and come to my rescue. When I tried to thank him, he shrugged and said, "You look kinda new around here. Me, I just come from Puerto Rico, Friday. Ain't nobody do nothing for nobody in this city," and with that he was gone. That was generosity, kindness in a rusty Chevy. 🦐

Love

PSYCHOLOGISTS TELL US that two of the greatest needs of humans are the ability to accept love and the willingness to express love. It doesn't sound difficult, but when we consider the number and variety of problems in human relationships, it's apparent that loving and being loved are not as easy as we think.

The initial human experience of love is perhaps the most selfless—mother love. While there are too many exceptions, of course, it is generally true that children born into the world are loved and cared for, nurtured and nourished. But despite this promising beginning, too often the family environment in which we are supposed to "learn love" has either been discarded, changed out of all recognition, or become such a scene of dysfunction that the possibilities of knowing how to love and be loved are severely jeopardized. Hence the vast number of fractured relationships and individuals tortured by relentless inner turmoil.

The problem is not helped by inadequate perceptions of love. "Falling in love," that ubiquitous happening that so often plunges normal, rational people into abnormal, irrational behavior, is the basis upon which many relationships flourish; sadly, falling out of love means the same relationships founder. We are told that love is "a feeling too deep for words." It is "never having to say you're sorry." Or perhaps "a sickness full of woes" or even, according to one sugary bumper sticker, "a warm puppy." One skeptic concluded, "Love is like the measles; everybody catches it sooner or later!"

So what is love? The biblical records show that in its fullest sense love is much more than a feeling. It is, surprisingly to modern ears, a decision—a decision to be primarily concerned with the well-being of the beloved, regardless of condition or reaction. The paramount example of this kind of love is, of course, the love of God for sinful humans. Despite our condition of fallenness and our attitude of indifference or rebellion, God, eager to draw us back to Himself, took an initiative that was immensely costly to Himself. "God so loved the world that He gave His only Son" is rightly the best-known verse of Scripture. But the point of God's love for us, which we should take great care not to miss, is that when we allow ourselves to be captured by it, His love is "shed abroad in our hearts by the Holy Spirit," with the result that we gradually discover a loving capacity to which we were formerly strangers.

The possibilities of loving God are immensely enlarged, a healthy love of self is engendered, and a corresponding love for neighbor becomes not only a concern, but a mission. The possibilities of love conquering all and even making the world go 'round become more than romantic sentiments—they can be spiritual dynamics that the world needs and deserves to witness. ᴥ

The Lamb

W<small>ILLIAM</small> B<small>LAKE</small>

How wonderful that He who made all things should come down to our world as a baby! And how wonderful that He allowed Himself to be nailed to a cross as meekly as a little lamb. This poem by William Blake (1757-1827) compares the lamb and the Lamb.

    Little Lamb, who made thee?
    Dost thou know who made thee?
Gave thee life & bid thee feed,
By the stream & o'er the mead;
Gave thee clothing of delight,
Softest clothing, wooly, bright;
Gave thee such a tender voice,
Making all the vales rejoice!
    Little Lamb, who made thee?
    Dost thou know who made thee?

    Little Lamb, I'll tell thee,
    Little Lamb, I'll tell thee!
He is callèd by thy name,
For he calls himself a Lamb.
He is meek & he is mild,
He became a little child:
I a child & thou a lamb,
We are callèd by his name.
    Little Lamb, God bless thee.
    Little Lamb, God bless thee.

A Country Wedding
HELEN NOORDEWIER

Katie called Benjy "a beautiful boy, outside and inside." Why do you think she said that to him? A sweet story from Helen Noordewier's Missy Doe.

Mama was usually in the kitchen when Benjy came home from school, but today the kitchen was empty, although it was filled with the smell of Swedish brown stew. "M-m-m," Benjy said. "It smells good here." Then he called, "Mama, where are you?"

"I am in the sewing room," Mama called back, and it was there that Benjy found her, half-hidden behind a pile of pure white material.

"What a mountain of cloth, Mama!" he said. "What are you making?"

"A wedding dress," Mama said.

"A wedding dress! A wedding dress for who?"

"For Katie, Carl's sister," Mama said.

"For Katie?" Benjy said. "But why are you making it?"

"To do something for Katie that her mother would be doing if she were still here," Mama said, "and because Charlie, the boy she is to marry, has been such a good helper for Papa at times."

"Will it be a beautiful dress?" Benjy asked.

"It has to be very beautiful," Mama said, "because there will be no other things at her wedding to make it beautiful. All the beauty must be in the dress. There will be no flowers."

"No flowers! Why not?" Benjy asked.

"For a very simple reason, Benjy," Mama said. "There is no money for flowers. Katie's father gave her a choice between flowers and refreshments and Katie thought it would be better to do with- out the flowers."

"I like Katie," Benjy said, "and I like Charlie, too. They said I could come to their wedding and that I could sit with Carl."

"That's nice," Mama said. "Now, do you think you could amuse Lisha for a little while? Then I can get some stitching done."

So Mama sewed and Benjy played games with Lisha until it was time for supper. The next days were much the same. Mama spent as much time as possible at the sewing machine, wondering all the while how she could manage flowers for Katie's wedding. But it was a problem she could not solve. It was early spring and there was not yet a flower in the garden. Mama put it out of her mind but Benjy kept talking about it.

"Couldn't we buy the wedding flowers?" he asked one day.

"Oh, no," Mama said. "The people from the flower shop would have to come all the way from the city and that would cost a lot of money. No, Benjy, we could not ask Papa to pay for them. He works very hard to buy what our own family needs. No, no, we must not even think of that."

The stitching went on and Katie came often for Mama to fit her dress. And then there was the dress for Laura, the bridesmaid. When the wedding dress was finished, Mama busied herself with the many yards of pale pink material for Laura's dress. "It is the color of a cloud when the setting sun is reflected in the sky," Mama said. Day after day Mama sewed.

The days passed by and the wedding day was very close. Both dresses had been finished and delivered. Mama's work was finished. She did not have to think about the food for the wedding. Many of the ladies from the church were working together. The tables had been set and everything was ready.

The day before the wedding Benjy ran home from the orchards as fast as his little legs would carry him. All out of breath, he swung the kitchen door open.

"Mama, Mama," he called. "The whole orchard is bursting. It looks like a giant flower garden."

"O my," Mama said. "The trees are blossoming early this year."

"But think, Mama! It could be wedding flowers for Katie. Apple blossoms for Katie's wedding."

Mama stopped what she was doing and stood still, just looking at Benjy. "You are right!" she finally said. "You are exactly right! That is just what it will be—wedding flowers for Katie!"

"But the wedding is tomorrow," Benjy said. "We'll have to hurry!"

"We will need Papa's help," Mama said. "He will want us to cut from certain trees, I am sure, and we must figure out where we are to put the flowers."

"Oh, I know," Benjy said. "There are two baskets in the corner of our Sunday-school room. They are made of reed and they look like giant ice cream cones. People use them for weddings."

"That is right. I have seen them," Mama said. "Look! Here comes Papa. We will ask him about the flowers."

Papa agreed. Benjy's idea was wonderful. "The trees are heavy with blossoms," he said, "A little thinning out will be good for them."

"But we must go to the church before we cut," Mama said, "and we must take a look at those baskets. And Benjy," she said, looking him straight in the eye, "we must make it a surprise, so keep the secret."

Benjy agreed and Papa drove them all to the church. Mama looked at the baskets carefully.

"They are thick with dust," she said. "Papa, I think we will take them home and introduce them to some soap and water."

In Mama's kitchen the baskets were scrubbed. "I'm sure they have not had a bath for many years," she said. And when they were dry they looked beautiful, fit for any wedding.

"Tomorrow is the wedding day," Mama said, "so we will not cut the blossoms until the morning. Apple blossoms do not last very long."

Long after everyone was asleep that night, Mama was busy.

She was measuring long satin ribbons and making little satin bows which she sewed onto the ribbons. These were the streamers for the two bouquets she would put together in the morning, one bouquet for the bride and one for the bridesmaid.

The morning dawned sunny and bright and Mama said a silent thank-you to God for sending such a beautiful day. Papa helped with the cutting, snipping branches that were long enough to extend high above the basket top.

"I think we have enough," Mama said at last. "I must now find two small branches that can easily be bent into circles. They will be the headpieces for the bride and her bridesmaid."

Benjy and his parents filled the tall baskets, put them in the back of the truck, and then took them to the church. Papa carried the baskets to their places on either side of the altar and they all stood back to look at their handiwork.

"Benjy," Papa said. "I think you should be a florist when you grow up. It was such a beautiful idea. And I think you had better hire your Mama to carry out your ideas."

Benjy was almost bubbling over and Mama was as excited as Mama could ever be.

"We must fill the baskets with water," she said. "Apple blossoms have thick stems and they are thirsty flowers."

"I wonder what Katie will say," Benjy said, and he kept repeating it over and over.

"We will go home now," Mama said, "and get ourselves ready. I am to meet Katie in the church basement just before four o'clock to help her with her dress. We will close the doors to the sanctuary and hope Katie will not see what we have done until she goes upstairs as a bride."

At home Mama got all the children dressed in their best clothes.

"Remember, I am going to sit in the front with Carl," Benjy said.

"I am remembering," Mama said. "But you must remember something, too. Don't talk together!"

"I know," Benjy said. "I know and I'll remember."

On the way to the church Mama carefully carried the precious bouquets and headpieces on her lap. But when they arrived she handed the flowers to Benjy. "Here," she said, "the apple blossoms thank you for seeing their beauty and they think you should be the one to give them away."

Benjy looked gratefully at Mama. "But you made the bouquets," he said.

"That is true," Mama answered. "But the idea grew in your little head and you deserve the joy of giving them."

When Benjy walked in with the flowers, Katie's face turned white. Her mouth fell open. After a long pause she said, "Flowers! Flowers! Wedding flowers! Benjy, are they real?"

"Oh, sure," Benjy said. "Smell them! Our whole orchard smells like them; it's just like a perfume factory."

Katie looked at Mama. "You did it!" she said.

"Yes," Mama said, "but it was Benjy's idea." She carefully put a circlet of flowers on Laura's head, and then Katie's circlet went on. Mama pinned both headpieces securely.

A few tears rolled down Katie's cheeks.

"Don't cry," Benjy said. "Everything's nice and it's your wedding day."

"Now you go upstairs," Mama said to Benjy. "Tell the usher you are supposed to sit next to Carl. I will stay with Katie."

Benjy was nicely seated and then the church bell began to ring, quietly and slowly, telling the whole neighborhood that it was wedding time.

"It is time to go up," Mama said to Katie. "I will follow and slip into the back seat with Papa and the children."

When Katie reached the top of the stairs she stopped. The beautiful surprise baskets were a little too much for her. She looked stunned, but Mama quickly said, "Smile, Katie, smile, and go down the aisle."

Mama quickly slipped into her place and she watched Katie slowly walk down the aisle. Katie's smile was big and wide and her cheeks were flushed with pink, almost the color of Laura's dress.

The ceremony was short and when the vows had been said, Katie turned to walk up the long aisle, holding on to Charlie's arm. For one short minute she stopped at the front pew where Benjy sat on the end next to Carl. She reached down and patted Benjy's head and then she bent down and whispered to him. "Benjy," she said, "you are a beautiful boy, outside and inside." 🦋

Ruth Finds a New Home

Naomi's two daughters-in-law both loved her, but one of them showed it more than the other (from the Book of Ruth, chapters 1 and 2).

People all over Judah were hungry. It had not rained for a long, long time. The fields were brown and dry. There was no food for anyone to eat.

"We will go to another country," said Elimelech. "We will go where we can raise food to eat." So Elimelech and his wife Naomi went to live in Moab. Their two sons, Mahlon and Chilion, went with them.

For a while Elimelech's family was very happy. They liked to live in Moab. Mahlon and Chilion married beautiful Moabite girls. Their names were Ruth and Orpah.

One day Elimelech died. Then Mahlon and Chilion died. Naomi was left alone with Ruth and Orpah. They were all very sad.

At last Naomi began to think of her home in Judah. "I want to go back," she said. "The people in Judah love God. They love the God I love. The Moabites love their idols."

Ruth and Orpah loved Naomi. "We will go back with you,"

they said. "No," said Naomi. "You must stay here. You must go back to your homes. Then you will be happy again."

So Orpah went back to her home. But Ruth did not go. "Do not ask me to leave you," she said. "I want to go where you go. I want to love your God. I want to live with you and your people."

Naomi was thrilled. "Then we will go together," she said happily. So Ruth and Naomi walked together. They went back to the land of Judah.

"Some of my family lives in Bethlehem," said Naomi. "We will go there." At last they came to Bethlehem. It was good to be home again. It was good to see grapevines. It was good to see fields of grain in the sun.

"Is that Naomi?" asked the people of Bethlehem. "We are glad you have come back. We are glad you brought Ruth. You will be happy living with us again."

The two women had arrived just as the barley harvest was beginning. And Naomi's relative, Boaz, welcomed Ruth to gather all the grain she needed from his fields. Naomi and Ruth were happy to be in Bethlehem. God had helped them find a new home. 🔖

Do you love me,
Or do you not?
I used to know,
But I forgot.
AUTHOR UNKNOWN

The Greatness of Love
I CORINTHIANS 13, MOFFATT

St. Paul's famous "hymn to love" was greatly needed in the church at Corinth. We all need to be reminded about true love too!

I may speak with the tongues of men and of angels, but if
    I have no love,
    I am a noisy gong or a clanging cymbal;
I may prophesy, fathom all mysteries and secret lore,
I may have such absolute faith that I can move hills
    from their place,
    but if I have no love,
    I count for nothing;
I may distribute all I possess in charity,
I may give up my body to be burnt,
    but if I have no love,
    I make nothing of it.
Love is very patient, very kind,
Love knows no jealousy;
Love makes no parade, gives itself no airs, is never
    rude, never selfish, never irritated, never resentful;
Love is never glad when others go wrong,
Love is gladdened by goodness, always slow to expose, always
    eager to believe the best, always hopeful, always patient.
Love never disappears.
As for prophesying, it will be superseded;
As for "tongues," they will cease;
As for knowledge, it will be superseded.
For we only know bit by bit, and we only prophesy bit by bit;
But when the perfect comes, the imperfect will be superseded.
When I was a child,
    I talked like a child,

I thought like a child,
I argued like a child;
Now that I am a man, I am done with childish ways.
At present we only see the baffling reflections in a mirror, but then
it will be face to face;
At present I am learning bit by bit,
But then I shall understand, as all along I have myself
been understood.
Thus "faith and hope and love last on, these three," but the
greatest of all is love. &

Promises Made
MADELEINE L'ENGLE

Marriage vows are often taken lightly, but for many people they are the staying power of the relationship. Madeleine L'Engle testifies to this in reflecting on her own marriage in these paragraphs from A Circle of Quiet.

When we were married we made promises, and we took them seriously. No relationship between two people which is worth anything is static. If a man and wife tell me they've never had a quarrel, I suspect that something is festering under the skin. There've been a number of times in my marriage when—if I hadn't made promises—I'd have quit. I'm sure this is equally true of Hugh; I'm not an easy person to live with.

I'm quite sure that Hugh and I would never have reached the relationship we have today if we hadn't made promises. Perhaps we made them youthfully, and blindly, not knowing all that was implied, but the very promises have been a saving grace. &

In-Spite-of Love
RUBY E. JOHNSON

Married love is much more than romanticism and sentimentalism; it involves commitment and sacrifice, concern and unselfishness. Ruby Johnson, in her book From the Heart of a Mother, *speaks from her own experience.*

After our honeymoon, we discovered traits in one another that disturbed us. Icebergs in our sea of matrimony began to surface, chilling our voyage. Not only that, but we realized that colliding with any one of them could have wrecked our precious craft and destroyed our cargo. A collision such as that must be avoided.

In answer to prayer, we learned how to change our course. We discovered that marriage needed another kind of love—*in-spite-of love*. That kind of love is unselfish.

Because love is selfish. It says: he is handsome, therefore he makes me feel proud; he is kind, therefore he will comfort me; he is reliable, therefore he will give me security.

In-spite-of love is different. It says: he is careless, therefore, even though it will make more work for me, I will try to compensate for his weakness and patiently endure; he is moody, and that disturbs my peace of mind, but I will do my best to help him cultivate a better mood; he is a spendthrift and that makes me feel insecure, but I will try to understand his generous spirit and charitable nature. 🦋

What Is Love?
LAURENCE STERNE

Love has been described a thousand ways. Laurence Sterne, in his book, Tristram Shandy, *offers us one of the most unusual!*

Love is certainly, at least alphabetically speaking, one of the most

A gitating

B ewitching

C onfounded

D evilish affairs of life—the most

E xtravagant

F utilitous

G alligaskinish

H andy-dandyish

I racundulous (there is no K to it) and

L yrical of all human passions: at the same time, the most

M isgiving

N innyhammering

O bstipating

P ragmatical

S tridulous

R idiculous—though by the bye the R should have gone first. &

Reverence for Motherhood

Elizabeth B. Custer

In this excerpt from the nineteenth-century work The Boy General, *we learn that everybody is capable of loving, even rough soldiers and tough buffalo.*

The reverence for motherhood is an instinct that is seldom absent from educated men. I know many instances in proof of the poet's words, "the bravest are the tenderest." Our officers taught the coarsest soldier, in time, to regard maternity as something sacred.

It was only by the merest chance that I heard something of the gentleness of one of our officers, whose brave heart ceased to beat on the battle-field of the Little Big Horn. In marching on a scouting expedition one day, Captain Yates went in advance a short distance with his sergeant, and when his ten men caught up with him he found that they had shot the mothers of some young antelopes. Captain Yates indignantly ordered the men to return to the young, and each take a baby antelope in his arms and care for it until they reached the post. For two days the men marched on, bearing the tender little things, cushioning them as best they could in their folded blouses. One man had twins to look out for, and as a baby antelope is all legs and head, this squirming collection of tiny hoofs and legs stuck out from all sides as the soldier guided his horse as best he could with one hand, the arm of which encircled the bleating little orphans. . . .

There were circles, perhaps fifteen feet in circumference, that I saw which were one of the mysteries of that strange land. When the officers told me that these circles were worn in the ground by the buffalo mother's walking round and round to protect her newly born and sleeping calf from the wolves at night, I listened, only to smile incredulously.

I had been so often "guyed" with ridiculous stories, that I did not believe the tale. In time, however, I found that it was true, and

I never came across these pathetic circles without a sentiment of deepest sympathy for the anxious mother whose vigilance kept up the ceaseless tramp during the long night. 🙠

On Love
St. Augustine

Love is so all embracing, a child can experience it and express it . . . and a theologian can expound it and explain it, as Augustine does in his Confessions.

Therefore the apostle says: "Now abideth faith, hope, charity, these three; but the greatest of these is charity"; because, when a man shall have reached the eternal world, while the other two graces will fail, love will remain greater and more assured."

. . . And, therefore, if a man fully understands that "the end of the commandment is charity, out of a pure heart, and of a good conscience, and of faith unfeigned," and is bent upon making all his understanding of Scripture to bear upon these three graces, he may come to the interpretation of these books with an easy mind. For while the apostle says "love," he adds "out of a pure heart," to provide against anything being loved but that which is worthy of love. And he joins with this "a good conscience," in reference to hope; for, if a man has the burthen of a bad conscience, he despairs of ever reaching that which he believes in and loves. And in the third place he says: "and of faith unfeigned." For if our faith is free from all hypocrisy, then we both abstain from loving what is unworthy of our love, and by living uprightly we are able to indulge the hope that our hope shall not be in vain. 🙠

The Parson's Tale

GEOFFREY CHAUCER

Of all Chaucer's pilgrims who told stories in The Canterbury Tales, *none had more to say than the parson! But none had more important things to say, either. That's what you expect from a preacher, isn't it?*

Now will I speak of the remedy for this foul sin of envy. First, is the love of God, and the love of one's neighbor as one's self; for indeed the one cannot be without the other. And trust well, that by the name of your neighbour you are to understand your brother; for certainly all of us have one fleshly father and one mother, that is to say, Adam and Eve; and even one spiritual father, and that is God in Heaven. Your neighbor you are bound to love and to wish all good things, and thereunto God says, "Love thy neighbor as thyself." That is to say, to the salvation both of life and soul. Moreover, you shall love him in word, and in benign admonition and in chastening; and comfort him in his vexations, and pray for him with all your heart. And you shall love him in deed and in such wise that you shall charitably do unto him as you would that it were done unto yourself. And therefore you shall do him no damage by wicked words, nor any harm in his body, nor in his goods, nor in his soul by the enticement of wicked example. You shall not covet his wife, nor any of his things. Understand also that in the word neighbors is included his enemy. Certainly man shall love his enemy, by the commandment of God; and truly, your friend shall you love in God. I say, you shall love your enemy for God's sake, and by His commandment. For if it were reasonable that a man should hate his enemies, then God would not receive us into His love, when we are His enemies. For three kinds of wrong that his enemy may do to a man, he shall do three things in return, thus: for hate and rancour, he shall love him in heart. For chiding and wicked words, he shall pray for his enemy. And for the wicked deed of his enemy, he shall do him kindness. For Christ says: "Love your enemies, bless them that curse you, do good to them that hate you, and pray for them which despitefully use you and persecute you." Lo, thus Our Lord Jesus Christ commands that we do to our enemies. For indeed, nature drives us to love our enemies, and faith, our enemies have more need for love than our friends; and they that have more need, truly to them men ought to do good; and truly, in the deed thereof have we remembrance of the love of Jesus Christ who died for His enemies. And in so much as that same love is the harder to feel and to show, in that much is the merit the greater; and therefore the loving of our enemy has confounded the venom of the Devil. For just as the Devil is discomfited by humility, so is he wounded to the death by love for our enemy. Certainly, then, love is the medicine that purges the heart of man of the poison of envy. &

I Never Knew a Night So Black
JOHN KENDRICK BANGS

I never knew a night so black
  Light failed to follow on its track.
I never knew a storm so gray
  It failed to have its clearing day.
I never knew such bleak despair
  That there was not a rift, somewhere.
I never knew an hour so drear
  Love could not fill it full of cheer! &

A Love for Children
JOHN POLLOCK

Despite the immense burden of the affairs of state, William Wilberforce, the champion of slaves, found time for children because he loved them and their company. This excerpt is from John Pollock's biography, Wilberforce.

Wilberforce was an indulgent Papa who loved to read aloud in their summer holidays and even play cricket, though a fast ball from William damaged his foot. Most men of the upper class, whether religious or not, kept well away from their smaller off-spring or else subscribed to the doctrine that children should be Seen and not Heard. In the House of Commons Wilberforce might rue "the bustle and turmoil . . . the vulgar and harsh contentions," but never the noise of the children playing and laughing and scrapping round his desk on a rainy day. A friend was with him at Kensington Gore as he hunted for a vital despatch until he looked vexed. At that moment came a din from the nursery above. The friend thought: "Now, for once, Wilberforce's temper will give way." But he turned, a seraphic smile on his face, all flurry forgotten. "What a blessing," he exclaimed, "to have these dear children! Only think what a relief, amidst other hurries, to hear their voices and know they are well." On the other hand, when they kept up an almost incessant din in a small house he confessed it a little wearing, and his relief at getting away for a quiet walk, or reading and talking after they had been put to bed.

For education he placed the boys at small private establishments because, like most of the Evangelicals, he regarded a Public School as a hot-bed of vice. He liked to broaden their minds in the holidays, sharing his love of literature and poetry and the wonders of nature. Charles Shore noticed that they naturally took boyish advantage of their father's playfulness: "On a visit . . . I observed him during a considerable time walking round the lawn followed by three of these striplings. Whilst he selected each in his turn as his companion, the other two amused themselves with practical jokes of which he was the victim. Repeatedly brought to bay, and remonstrating with his persecutors, each of whom in turn profited by his instructive converse, he passed much of his time fruitlessly on the defensive." Above all, Wilberforce liked to watch their progress in religion, "the grand concern of life." He desired from the bottom of his heart that they should not wait, as he had, until their mid-twenties before discovering the wonder of Christ's friendship. He did not expect or even welcome any sudden conversion but looked for signs of what he called "the great change," as each began to allow Christ to work on his character.

He held that parents "should labour to render religion as congenial as possible" but, again like most Evangelicals of the day, he could not leave their souls alone: "just as a gardener walks up again and again to examine his fruit trees," he wrote to nine-year-old Samuel, "and see if his peaches are set, if they are swelling and becoming larger, finally if they are becoming ripe and rosy. I would willingly walk barefoot from this place to Sandgate to see a clear proof of the *great change* being begun in my dear Saml at the end of the journey." ❦

When the Heart Is Full of Love
AUTHOR UNKNOWN

There is beauty in the forest
    When the trees are green and fair,
There is beauty in the meadow
    When wild flowers scent the air.
There is beauty in the sunlight
    And the soft blue beams above.
Oh, the world is full of beauty
    When the heart is full of love. ❦

Not Justice, But Love
Leo Tolstoy

It's not always easy to be a princess . . . especially if you're married to an unpleasant prince. But even princesses look to Christ for His example of love and draw on His power to be loving, as we read in these paragraphs from Tolstoy's War and Peace.

During that year after his son's departure, Prince Nicholas Bolkónski's health and temper became much worse. He grew still more irritable, and it was Princess Mary who generally bore the brunt of his frequent fits of unprovoked anger. He seemed carefully to seek out her tender spots so as to torture her mentally as harshly as possible. Princess Mary had two passions and consequently two joys—her nephew, little Nicholas, and religion—and these were the favorite subjects of the prince's attacks and ridicule. Whatever was spoken of he would bring round to the superstitiousness of old maids, or the petting and spoiling of children. "You want to make him"—little Nicholas—"into an old maid like yourself! A pity! Prince Andrew wants a son and not an old maid," he would say. Or, turning to Mademoiselle Bourienne, he would ask her in Princess Mary's presence how she liked our village priests and icons and would joke about them.

He continually hurt Princess Mary's feelings and tormented her, but it cost her no effort to forgive him. Could he be to blame toward her, or could her father, whom she knew loved her in spite of it all, be unjust? And what is justice? The princess never thought of that proud word "justice." All the complex laws of man centered for her in one clear and simple law—the law of love and self-sacrifice taught us by Him who lovingly suffered for mankind though He Himself was God. What had she to do with the justice or injustice of other people? She had to endure and love, and that she did. 🐾

Love Thyself Last
ELLA WHEELER WILCOX

Ella Wheeler Wilcox's poem, written a century ago, sounds a strikingly different and undoubtedly necessary note from the contemporary themes of self-love.

Love thyself last; look near, behold thy duty
    To those who walk beside thee down life's road;
Make glad their days by little acts of beauty,
    And help them bear the burden of earth's load.

Love thyself last; look far and find the stranger
    Who staggers 'neath his sin and his despair;
Go, lend a hand and lead him out of danger
    To heights where he may see the world is fair.

Love thyself last; the vastnesses above thee
    Are filled with spirit forces, strong and pure;
And fervently these faithful friends shall love thee,
    Keep thy watch over others and endure.

Love thyself last; and thou shalt grow in spirit
    To see, to hear, to know and understand;
The message of the stars, lo, thou shalt hear it,
    And all God's joys shall be at thy command. ❧

That best portion of a good man's life,
His little, nameless, unremembered acts
Of kindness and love.
WILLIAM WORDSWORTH

What Would Jesus Do?

CHARLES M. SHELDON

Charles M. Sheldon, pastor of Central Congregational Church, Topeka, Kansas, told a series of stories about a mythical church whose pastor challenged the congregation to ask themselves "What would Jesus do?" before taking any action. Mr. Sheldon's church was packed to the rafters, and his stories were published as In His Steps, *one of the world's top best sellers.*

"Hadn't we better take a policeman along?" said one of the girls with a nervous laugh. "It really isn't safe down there, you know."

"There's no danger," said Virginia briefly.

. . . The other girls were beginning to feel sober as the carriage turned into a street leading to the Rectangle. . . . As they entered farther into the district, the Rectangle seemed to stare as with one great, bleary, beer-soaked countenance at this fine carriage with its load of fashionably dressed young women. "Slumming" had never been a fad with Raymond society, and this was perhaps the first time that the two had come together in this way. The girls felt that instead of seeing the Rectangle they were being made the objects of curiosity. They were frightened and disgusted.

"Let's go back. I've seen enough," said the girl who was sitting with Virginia.

They were at that moment just opposite a notorious saloon and gambling house. The street was narrow and the sidewalk crowded. Suddenly, out of the door of this saloon a young woman reeled. She was singing in a broken, drunken sob that seemed to indicate that she partly realized her awful condition, "Just as I am, without one plea"—and as the carriage rolled past she leered at it, raising her face so that Virginia saw it very close to her own. It was the face of the girl who had kneeled sobbing, that night with Virginia kneeling beside her and praying for her.

"Stop!" cried Virginia, motioning to the driver who was

looking around. The carriage stopped, and in a moment she was out and had gone up to the girl and taken her by the arm. "Loreen!" she said, and that was all. The girl looked into her face, and her own changed into a look of utter horror. The girls in the carriage were smitten into helpless astonishment. The saloon keeper had come to the door of the saloon and was standing there looking on with his hands on his hips. And the Rectangle from its windows, its saloon steps, its filthy sidewalk, gutter and roadway, paused, and with undisguised wonder stared at the two girls. . . .

When Virginia left the carriage and went up to Loreen she had no definite idea as to what she would do or what the result of her action would be. She simply saw a soul that had tasted the joy of a better life slipping back again into its old hell of shame and death. And before she had touched the drunken girl's arm she had asked only one question, "What would Jesus do?" That question was becoming with her, as with many others, a habit of life.

She looked around now as she stood close by Loreen, and the whole scene was cruelly vivid to her. She thought first of the girls in the carriage.

"Drive on; don't wait for me. I am going to see my friend home," she said calmly enough.

The girl with the red parasol seemed to gasp at the word "friend," when Virginia spoke it. She did not say anything. The other girls seemed speechless.

"Go on. I cannot go back with you," said Virginia. One of the girls leaned a little out of the carriage.

"Can't we—that is—do you want our help? Couldn't you—"

"No, no!" cried Virginia. "You cannot be of any help to me."

The carriage moved on and Virginia was alone with her charge. She looked up and around. Many faces in the crowd were sympathetic. They were not all cruel or brutal. The Holy Spirit had softened a good deal of the Rectangle.

"Where does she live?" asked Virginia.

No one answered. . . . For the first time it flashed across her that the immortal being who was flung like wreckage upon the shore of this early hell called the saloon, had no place that could be called home. The girl suddenly wrenched her arm from Virginia's grasp. In doing so she nearly threw Virginia down.

"You shall not touch me! Leave me! Let me go to hell! That's where I belong! The devil is waiting for me. See him!" she exclaimed hoarsely. She turned and pointed with a shaking finger at the saloon keeper. The crowd laughed. Virginia stepped up to her and put her arm about her.

"Loreen," she said firmly, "come with me. You do not belong to hell. You belong to Jesus and He will save you. Come."

The girl suddenly burst into tears. She was only partly sobered by the shock of meeting Virginia.

Virginia looked around again. "Where does Mr. Gray live?" she asked. She knew that the evangelist boarded somewhere near the tent. A number of voices gave the direction.

"Come, Loreen, I want you to go with me to Mr. Gray's," she said, still keeping her hold of the swaying, trembling creature who now clung to her as firmly as before she had repulsed her.

So the two moved on through the Rectangle toward the evangelist's lodging place. The sight seemed to impress the Rectangle seriously. It never took itself seriously when it was drunk, but this was different. The fact that one of the richest, most beautifully dressed girls in all Raymond was taking care of one of the Rectangle's most noted characters, who reeled along under the influence of liquor, was a fact astounding enough to throw more or less dignity and importance about Loreen herself. The event of Loreen's stumbling through the gutter dead-drunk always made the Rectangle laugh and jest. But Loreen staggering along with a young lady from the society circles uptown supporting her, was another thing. The Rectangle viewed it with soberness and more or less wondering admiration. 🦜

Wilt Thou Love God?

JOHN DONNE

John Donne's advice to the soul that longs to love God more (and which pious soul does not?) is to engage in "wholesome meditation" on God's incredible love for us.

Wilt thou love God, as He thee? then digest,
    My soul, this wholesome meditation,
How God the Spirit, by angels waited on
    In heaven, doth make His Temple in thy breast.
The Father, having begot a Son most blest,
    And still begetting (for he ne'er begun),
Hath deigned to choose thee, by adoption,
    Coheir to His glory and sabbath's endless rest;
And as a robbed man which by search doth find
    His stol'n stuff sold must lose or buy it again,
The Son of glory came down, and was slain,
    Us whom He had made, and Satan stol'n, to unbind.
'Twas much that man was made like God before,
    But that God should be made like man, much more. 🍂

I believe that unarmed truth and unconditional love
will have the final word in reality.
MARTIN LUTHER KING, JR.

Unselfishness

ON THE ONE HAND, Christian teaching exhorts us to love our neighbors as ourselves. On the other, it admonishes us to deny ourselves. This has led some people to reason that before they can love their neighbors, they need to concentrate on loving themselves. This fits in well with what Daniel Yankelovich explained in his book *New Rules* as the modern tendency to prefer "duty to self" over the older tradition of "a sense of duty." So if loving ourselves and assuming that our first duty is to ourselves become the order of the day, where does denying ourselves fit in? Very often, unfortunately, it doesn't. But that clearly is not satisfactory, as the Scriptures teach both. Our responsibility is to find a balance, rather than suspect a contradiction.

Scripture assumes that there is a certain degree of self-love in all of us. We love ourselves so much that we instinctively prefer being warm to cold, safe rather than in jeopardy, liked rather than disliked, affirmed rather than demeaned, comfortable rather than uncomfortable. We have an innate sense that we have significance, and consequently some experiences are more appropriate for us than others. To love our neighbors as ourselves, then, means that we credit other people with having the same sensibilities and treat them accordingly.

But given that our innate self-interest is a fact—and apparently a necessary fact for our survival and well-being—we need to be aware that in our fallen state *everything* about us is fallen, including our self-interest. This can lead us to be more interested in self than in God, for example, which amounts to the deification of self—a most heinous sin. Or it can mean that our self-interest is so all-consuming that we fail to see the significance of others, to the point of using them for our own selfish purposes, rather than honoring them as significant, divinely created beings. Something has to be done about the fallen self which, while retaining aspects of the image of God that should be nurtured, is nevertheless shot through with the fallenness that leads to selfishness. It is not *selfhood* but *selfishness* that is to be denied.

The small child who throws a tantrum at his sister's birthday party because he hasn't got a present may be excused, but the superstar athlete who threatens to quit the team unless his contract is worth a dollar more than that of everyone else in the club has a major-league problem. So does the workman who strikes without genuine complaint, putting others' employment at risk, and the employer who shortchanges employees for the sake of profit. So does the man who doesn't want to be married anymore, and the wife who sacrifices her children to inadequate care so that she can feel fulfilled. There is no shortage of selfishness around. The cure is the denial of self. If we want an example, we need look no further than the Cross. For the energy to do it, we need look no further than the indwelling Spirit. It isn't easy, but nothing worthwhile ever is! 🦌

The Dog and His Shadow
AESOP

A Dog, carrying a piece of meat in his mouth, was crossing a stream on a narrow foot-bridge. He happened to look into the water and there he saw his Shadow, but he thought it another dog with a piece of meat larger than his. He made a grab for the other dog's meat; but in doing so, of course, he dropped his own; therefore he was without any, and thus learned that greediness may cause one to lose everything. 🐾

The Dog in the Manger
AESOP

A cross, selfish Dog went to rest one hot afternoon in a manger. When the tired Ox came in from the field and wanted to eat his hay, the Dog barked at him so that he dared not try it. "To keep others from having what they need," said the Ox to himself, "when you can't use it yourself, is the meanest selfishness I know." 🐾

Uncle Alphonso and the Greedy Green Dinosaurs
JACK PEARSON

Introducing a strange dinosaur, Greedogoldfuss, who has some lessons to teach us.

"I'm rich," sang Anna as she teetered on top of the retaining wall. "I've got twenty-one whole dollars in my bank account!"

Her twin brother, Nathan, didn't seem impressed. "Okay, so you've got twenty-one dollars. You need more than that to be rich."

477

"No, you don't," protested Anna with a toss of her head. "And I'm going to get even richer, too. When I get big, I'm going to make so much money I'll go swimming in it every day!"

"Yeah. You and the goldfish," Nathan snickered.

"Oooh, Nathan you're just jealous because you're not rich and I am," snapped Anna.

"Are not."

"Am too!"

"Are not!"

"Am too! I call 'no backs,' and besides, here we are at Uncle Alphonso's house. We'll ask him. He knows what rich is."

Nathan and Anna had stopped at the gate of a wonderful old house down the block from their house. Uncle Alphonso (who was actually the children's great-uncle) lived there with his old furniture, a cat named Teacup, and his study stacked to the ceiling with books and fossils.

Uncle Alphonso was one of Nathan's and Anna's favorite people. He had retired from teaching at the university, but still worked part-time down at the museum with the dinosaur exhibits. He was one of the world's leading dinosaur experts.

"Now you'll see," said Anna to her brother as she held open the screen door and clunked with the big door knocker.

A large, balding man answered. "Why, Nathan and Anna. Come in, come in! You must have smelled the cookies baking."

"No, but could we have one anyway?" asked Nathan.

"Of course," chuckled the old man, holding a plate within Nathan's eager reach. "And how about you, Anna?"

"Thank you very much," said Anna, remembering her manners. Then forgetting them again she mumbled with a mouthful of cookies. "Uncle Alph, I've got twenty-one whole dollars, but Nathan doesn't think I'm rich. I am rich, aren't I?"

"Well, well," replied the man thoughtfully. "That depends. But come up to the study. There's something I'd like to show you."

The children were excited because this meant that they would get to see Uncle Alphonso's amazing fossil collection. There was nothing they liked half as well. Their great-uncle was famous for finding funny fossils no one had ever heard of before. Up the stairs they went and into the study.

"Now then," began the old man as they all seated themselves. "Talk of money like this brings us smack up against one of the greatest fossil discoveries of my career." He opened a large box in the corner and took from it a large, odd-shaped stone.

"It looks like some kind of nest," said Nathan.

"Excellent! Excellent, my boy!" exclaimed Uncle Alphonso. "It is! The only known fossil nest of a rare dinosaur of the bone-head species: the Greedogoldfuss."

Teacup, the cat, jumped into his lap as he settled back into his chair.

Anna and Nathan settled in, too. They knew they were in for an interesting story.

"As you may have heard," began Uncle Alphonso, "I taught Boneheadology at the university for many years. The boneheads were a peculiar race of dinosaurs that died out for some very bone-headed reasons. Now take the Greedogoldfuss here. It was a rare type of winged lizard with real money problems!" He reached into the fossil nest and pulled out a round, yellow rock. "Do you kids know what this is?"

Anna and Nathan shook their heads slowly. "Gold," their great-uncle replied. "A solid-gold nest egg. The nest is full of them."

"That's why you call it the . . . the greedy-gold-foot?" asked Anna.

"Exactly, dear girl," replied Uncle Alphonso with a hearty laugh. "The Greedogoldfusses were in love with gold. And they did wear it on their feet, too. Legbands, toe rings, and also necklaces and bracelets. All made from gold they found in the bends of the river. What they couldn't wear, they made into these eggs for their nests."

"I'll bet they looked beautiful," said Anna, who was fond of jewelry.

"Oh, yes. Indeed," replied Uncle Alph. "But they also became terrible show-offs.

"By being greedy they lost most of their friends. The greediest of the Greedogoldfusses had to walk everywhere they went. They wore so much gold that they couldn't fly anymore, you see.

"These creatures may have been boneheads," Uncle Alphonso continued, "but they were quite intelligent in some ways, especially in how they built their nests. They were the first ones to think of making them in tree branches overhanging a river. It kept them safe from enemies, and also gave them a great view."

"I'll bet the gold got pretty heavy in those nests," said Nathan as he tested the weight of one of the eggs in his hand.

"It certainly did, Nathan," replied Uncle Alph. "With each passing year, the gold increased and the tree limbs began to sag under the weight of the Greedogoldfuss nests.

"One evening, a fierce windstorm swept through the river canyon. The trees all groaned and swayed. One by one the branches with the Greedogoldfuss nests in them cracked off and fell into the river far below. What a splash!"

"That's too bad about the nests, Uncle Alph," said Anna, "but what happened to the Greedogoldfusses themselves? Couldn't they live somewhere else?"

"Ah," said the old man with a sigh. "That's the saddest part of the story. The creatures might have survived if they hadn't all jumped into the river to save their nest eggs.

"They were so weighted down with their golden ornaments, they all promptly drowned, and that was the end of them."

The silence was broken only by Teacup's purring as Uncle Alphonso scratched her ears. Anna and Nathan stared at each other. Finally Nathan spoke. "Sounds like those Greedogoldfusses could have used some swimming lessons!"

"Or a lot less gold," added Anna.

"Or a little more faith!" said Uncle Alph. "That's what really made them boneheads, you know."

"What do you mean?" asked Anna.

"Well, God tells us we should love Him with everything we are, Anna. That's the only road to life. When money or anything else becomes more important than God, then we're headed in the wrong direction."

"I see what you mean," said Anna, glancing at the fossil nest. "Those Greedogoldfusses were like people who love gold more than God."

"Exactly."

After a brief pause Anna turned to her great-uncle. "I don't think I want to be rich, Uncle Alph."

The old man smiled. "I think twenty-one whole dollars is a lot of money, Anna. Use it wisely. But I also think that it's time for you two to get back to your own little nest. Boneheadology class dismissed!"

The children waved as they closed the gate in front of the house. They were part way down the block when Uncle Alphonso called out from the porch, "And say hello to your mother!" 🐾

Modesty and unselfishness—these are virtues
which men praise—and pass by.
ANDRÉ MAUROIS

481

We Give Thee but Thine Own
WILLIAM WALSHAM HOW

We give Thee but Thine own,
    Whate'er the gift may be:
All that we have is Thine alone,
    A trust, O Lord, from Thee.

May we Thy bounties thus
    As stewards true receive,
And gladly, as Thou blessest us,
    To Thee our first-fruits give.

To comfort and to bless,
    To find a balm for woe,
To tend the lone and fatherless,
    Is angels' work below.

The captive to release,
    To God the lost to bring,
To teach the way of life and peace,
    It is a Christ-like thing.

And we believe Thy word,
    Though dim our faith may be,
Whate'er for Thine we do, O Lord,
    We do it unto Thee.

The Poor Man and the Rich Man

AUTHOR UNKNOWN

The Bible says if we are kind to strangers, we might find out one of them is an angel. That would be wonderful, as the unselfish poor man discovered. The selfish rich man, on the other hand, had a very different experience!

In olden times angels often took the form of men and walked the earth. While one of these was wandering about, night came upon him before he had found shelter. At last he saw down the road ahead of him two houses standing opposite one another; one was large and handsome, while the other was miserably poor. The angel decided to ask for lodging in the large house, since it would be less burdensome for a rich man to entertain a guest. He knocked, and the rich man, peering out the window, asked the stranger what he sought.

The angel replied, "I seek a night's lodging."

Then the rich man looked scornfully at the stranger's ragged clothes and shook his head, saying, "I cannot take you in. If I sheltered everyone who knocks at my door, I might soon be a beggar myself! Find shelter in some other house."

And he banged the window shut and locked it. The good angel immediately turned his back upon the large house and went over to the little house. Here he had scarcely knocked when the door was opened. The poor man took one look at the stranger and said, "Come in. Come in. Stay here tonight; it is quite dark, and you can go no farther today."

This reception pleased the angel very much. The wife of the poor man also bade him welcome. Holding out her hand she said, "Make yourself at home, good sir. Though we do not have much, we will gladly share it with you." Then she put some potatoes in the coals, and while they roasted she milked her goat. When the

483

table was laid, the good angel sat down and ate with the poor couple. The coarse food tasted good, because such a warm welcome went with it. After they had finished eating, the wife called her husband aside and said, "Let us sleep on straw tonight and let this poor wanderer have our bed. He has been walking all day, and is doubtless tired."

The good angel at first refused to take the bed, but at last yielded to their entreaties and lay down on the soft feather mattress while they made a straw couch upon the floor.

The next morning the couple arose early and cooked their guest a breakfast of the best that they had. When the angel finished eating, he prepared to set out again. As he stood in the doorway, he turned around and said to his hosts, "Because you are so good and generous, you may wish three times and each time I will grant what you desire."

The poor man replied, "Ah, what more can I wish for than eternal happiness, and that we two, so long as we live, may have health, and strength, and our daily bread. For the third thing I do not know what to wish."

"Would you like a new house in place of this old one?"

"Oh, yes," said the man, "if I may keep it in this spot, it would be welcome."

The last wish was fulfilled at once, and the old house became a new red-brick cottage. Then giving the couple his blessing, the angel went along down the road.

Shortly thereafter the rich man arose. He looked out of his window and saw a handsome new house of red brick standing where the old hut had been.

"Come and look!" he called to his wife.

The wife was as curious as her husband and went across the road at once and asked the poor man what had happened. He told the story of the wanderer and the three wishes he had granted. When the man had finished his tale, the rich man's wife ran home and told her husband.

"Ah! Had I only known it!" he exclaimed. "The stranger came here first, but I sent him away."

"Hurry, then!" cried his wife. "Mount your horse, and perhaps you may overtake the man. Tell him you meant to let him stay. Then you may also ask three wishes for yourself."

The rich man followed this advice, and soon overtook the good angel. He begged him not to think ill of him, saying that he had gone to get the key for the door, and returned to find the wanderer gone. If only the angel would come back, he was welcome to stay. The angel promised that he would stop at the rich man's house on his return. Then the rich man asked if he might not have three wishes as his neighbor had.

"Yes," said the angel, "you may, but it will not be good for you, and it would be better if you did not wish."

But the rich man was sure he wanted the wishes. So the angel said, "Ride home, and your wishes will be granted."

The rich man was satisfied and as he rode homeward, he began to consider what he should wish. While he was thinking, he let his reins fall loose, and his horse stumbled so that the man nearly fell. "You dumb beast!" he cried out. "I wish you would break your neck!" He had no sooner said this than the horse fell to the ground and never moved again. Thus the rich man's first wish was fulfilled.

The rich man, being thrifty by nature, would not leave the saddle behind. He cut it off, slung it over his back, and traveled on by foot. "I still have two wishes," he thought to himself, and so was comforted.

As he walked slowly homeward, the sun became very hot. The saddle hurt his back, and besides, he had not yet decided what to wish for next. "Even if I should wish for all the riches in the world," he said to himself, "something else will occur to me later. I must manage to make a wish so that nothing at all shall remain for me to wish for."

As he walked along the sun grew hotter, and the saddle rubbed his back until it was as sore as a burn. Then he thought of how his wife sat comfortably at home in a cool room. This thought angered him, and without knowing it, he said aloud, "I wish she were sitting on this saddle, and couldn't get off."

As soon as he spoke these words, the saddle disappeared from his back, and he realized that his second wish had been fulfilled. Cursing himself for a fool, he hurried home determined to lock himself in his room to consider his last wish. But when he arrived home, he found his wife sitting on the saddle in mid-air, weeping and wailing because she could not get off.

"Stop your crying," he said to her. "I will wish for all the riches in the world, only keep sitting there."

But his wife only wailed the louder, saying, "Of what use are all the riches of the world if I have to sit on this saddle? You wished me on it, now you must wish me off."

She made so much racket that the man thought his ears would burst. "All right," he cried, "I wish you may get off!"

There went his third wish! His wife was free, but the rich man gained nothing from his wishes except worry, trouble, scolding, and a dead horse. But the poor couple lived contented and happy to the end of their lives. 🐎

Greater love has no one than this,
that he lay down his life for his friends.
JOHN 15:13

I Shall Not Pass Again This Way

ELLEN H. UNDERWOOD

The bread that bringeth strength I want to give,
    The water pure that bids the thirsty live;
I want to help the fainting day by day;
    I'm sure I shall not pass again this way.

I want to give the oil of joy for tears,
    The faith to conquer crowding doubts and fears,
Beauty for ashes may I give always;
    I'm sure I shall not pass again this way.

I want to give good measure running o'er
    And into angry hearts I want to pour
The answer soft that turneth wrath away;
    I'm sure I shall not pass again this way.

I want to give to others hope and faith;
    I want to do all that the Master saith;
I want to live aright from day to day;
    I'm sure I shall not pass again this way.

Love Your Life
HENRY DAVID THOREAU

In Walden, *Thoreau reminds us that internal attitudes are more important than external circumstances. The selfish person will be unhappy in a palace, the unselfish person contented in a poor house.*

However mean your life is, meet it and live it; do not shun it and call it hard names. It is not so bad as you are. It looks poorest when you are richest. The fault-finder will find faults even in paradise. Love your life, poor as it is. You may perhaps have some pleasant, thrilling, glorious hours, even in a poor-house. The setting sun is reflected from the windows of the alms-house as brightly as from the rich man's abode; the snow melts before its door as early in the spring. I do not see but a quiet mind may live as contentedly there, and have as cheering thoughts, as in a palace. The town's poor seem to me often to live the most independent lives of any. Maybe they are simply great enough to receive without misgiving. Most think that they are above being supported by the town; but it oftener happens that they are not above supporting themselves by dishonest means, which should be more disreputable. Cultivate poverty like a garden herb, like sage. Do not trouble yourself much to get new things, whether clothes or friends. Turn the old; return to them. Things do not change; we change. Sell your clothes and keep your thoughts. God will see that you do not want society. If I were confined to a corner of a garret all my days, like a spider, the world would be just as large to me while I had my thoughts about me. The philosopher said: "From an army of three divisions one can take away its general, and put it in disorder; from the man the most abject and vulgar one cannot take away his thought." Do not seek so anxiously to be developed, to subject yourself to many influences to be played on; it is all dissipation. Humility like darkness reveals the heavenly lights. The shadows of poverty and meanness gather around us, "and lo! creation widens to our view."

We are often reminded that if there were bestowed on us the wealth of Croesus, our aims must still be the same, and our means essentially the same. Moreover, if you are restricted in your range by poverty, if you cannot buy books and newspapers, for instance, you are but confined to the most significant and vital experiences; you are compelled to deal with the material which yields the most sugar and the most starch. It is life near the bone where it is sweetest. You are defended from being a trifler. No man loses ever on a lower level by magnanimity on a higher. Superfluous wealth can buy superfluities only. Money is not required to buy one necessary of the soul. 🍂

Lend A Hand
EDWARD EVERETT HALE

I am only one,
    But still I am one.
I cannot do everything,
    But still I can do something;
And because I cannot do everything
    I will not refuse to do the something that I can do. 🍂

Dr. Chestnut's Gift
RUTH A. TUCKER

Very few people have ever heard of Dr. Eleanor Chestnut, described in From Jerusalem to Irian Jaya, *but her lifelong commitment to helping people in dangerous and difficult circumstances wonderfully illustrates selflessness.*

During the years following the Boxer Uprising, China was anything but free from hostility toward foreigners. Missionaries were viewed with the deepest suspicion even though their work was largely humanitarian in nature. They were blamed for spreading a cholera epidemic that swept across the northern provinces in 1902, and as a result two [China Inland Mission] members were murdered by a mob. Another brutal attack against missionaries occurred near Hong Kong in 1905 and resulted in five deaths, including that of the greatly loved Dr. Eleanor Chestnut.

After coming to China in 1893 under the American Presbyterian Board, Dr. Chestnut built a hospital, using her own money to buy the bricks. Even before the hospital was completed she was performing surgery—in her own bathroom for want of a better place. One such operation involved the amputation of a coolie's leg. Complications arose and skin grafts were needed. Later the doctor was questioned about a leg problem from which she herself was suffering. "Oh, it's nothing," she answered, brushing off the inquiry. Later a nurse revealed that the graft for the "good-for-nothing coolie" had come from Dr. Chestnut's own leg while using only a local anesthetic.

During the Boxer Rebellion, Dr. Chestnut remained on her post longer than most missionaries, and she returned the following year. Then in 1905 while she was busy working at the hospital with four other missionaries, a mob stormed the building. Although she got away in time to alert authorities and in fact could have escaped, she instead returned to the scene to help rescue her colleagues. It was too late. Her colleagues had been slain. But there were others who needed her help. Her final act of service to the Chinese people whom she so loved was to rip a piece of material from her own dress to bandage the forehead of a child who had been wounded during the carnage. 🐾

The Sacrifice
STUART BRISCOE

Brilliant sunshine, blue skies and endless expanses of white sand. Sounds like paradise. Why haven't the developers seen the potential?

Well, it's the Sahara. There is no water, the sand isn't always white. In fact, the terrain in one part of the Sahara is made up of something resembling black cinders—as far as the eye can see.

When my wife, Jill, and I flew in to a missionary outpost in this incredibly inhospitable desert, we thought that we had never seen any place so desolate, so dry, so drab. Nothing grew, and nothing moved.

In the midst of this black expanse of nothingness, in the backyard of the missionary dwelling, we noticed a splash of green and a flash of orange. On closer inspection we found a tiny bush clinging tenaciously to life, proudly bearing a solitary rose. Beside the bush was a hole, a few feet deep, hacked out of the cinders and half filled with decaying vegetable matter from the kitchen.

The missionaries told us that the rose bush had been planted in a similar hole filled with vegetable matter. The missionaries, who had nurtured and nursed the plant into life and survival, proudly said, "This is the first flower we have produced in this desert!" There it bloomed—fragile and fragrant—a testimony to loving care, endless patience and sheer hard work.

Jill, exhausted from much travel, extended ministry and a chronic back problem that caused her constant pain, was promised breakfast in bed the next morning.

When breakfast arrived, lovingly prepared and meticulously arranged, there on the tray in a slender glass was the solitary orange rose. A handwritten card propped against the glass said simply, "Thank you for coming all this way." When Jill saw it, she cried. I, being a British male, swallowed hard. Our missionary hostess shyly explained, "We wanted to tell you how grateful we are that you came."

Many messages of appreciation have been showered on us through the years, but this one sticks in our memories. Why? Because the message of love was not just spoken or written; it was performed in a singular, gracious and sacrificial way.

Jesus gave us a message of love too. But he didn't just talk about love. He performed it, sacrificially.

This Valentine's Day I won't just send loving cards or speak grateful words. I will find my only "rose among the cinders," pluck it and give it to those I love, thanking them for coming all the way into my life.

Jesus will understand. He did it too. 🌹

Your attitude should be the same as that of Christ Jesus:
Who, being in very nature God,
did not consider equality with God something to be grasped,
but made himself nothing,
taking the very nature of a servant,
being made in human likeness.
PHILIPPIANS 2:5-7

Greater Love Hath No Man
CHARLES DICKENS

In the moving finale of Dickens's A Tale of Two Cities, *Sydney Carton takes the place of a condemned man—his rival. On the way to the guillotine, he befriends a terrified young woman and selflessly cares for her as he approaches his own death. In all English literature, there is no greater example of unselfishness.*

The door closed, and Carton was left alone. Straining his powers of listening to the utmost, he listened for any sound that might denote suspicion or alarm. There was none. Keys turned, doors clashed, footsteps passed along distant passages: no cry was raised, or hurry made, that seemed unusual. Breathing more freely in a little while, he sat down at the table, and listened again until the clock struck Two.

Sounds that he was not afraid of, for he divined their meaning, then began to be audible. Several doors were opened in succession and finally his own. A gaoler, with a list in his hand, looked in, merely saying, "Follow me, Evrémonde!" and he followed into a large dark room, at a distance. It was a dark winter day, and what with the shadows within, and what with the shadows without, he could but dimly discern the others who were brought there to have their arms bound. Some were standing; some seated. Some were lamenting and in restless motion; but these were few. The great majority were silent and still, looking fixedly at the ground.

As he stood by the wall in a dim corner, while some of the fifty-two were brought in after him, one man stopped in passing, to embrace him, as having a knowledge of him. It thrilled him with a great dread of discovery; but the man went on. A very few moments after that, a young woman, with a slight girlish form, a sweet spare face in which there was no vestige of colour, and large widely opened patient eyes, rose from the seat where he had observed her sitting, and came to speak to him.

"Citizen Evrémonde," she said, touching him with her cold

hand. "I am a poor little seamstress who was with you in La Force."

He murmured for answer: "True. I forget what you were accused of?"

"Plots. Though the just Heaven knows I am innocent of any. Is it likely? Who would think of plotting with a poor little weak creature like me?"

The forlorn smile with which she said it, so touched him, that tears started from his eyes.

"I am not afraid to die, Citizen Evrémonde, but I have done nothing. I am not unwilling to die, if the Republic which is to do so much good to us poor, will profit by my death; but I do not know how that can be, Citizen Evrémonde. Such a poor weak little creature!"

As the last thing on earth that his heart was to warm and soften to, it warmed and softened to this pitiable girl.

"I heard you were released, Citizen Evrémonde. I hoped it was true?"

"It was. But I was again taken and condemned."

"If I may ride with you, Citizen Evrémonde, will you let me hold your hand? I am not afraid, but I am little and weak, and it will give me more courage."

As the patient eyes were lifted to his face, he saw a sudden doubt in them, and then astonishment. He pressed the work-worn, hunger-worn young fingers, and touched his lips.

"Are you dying for him?" she whispered.

"And his wife and child. Hush! Yes."

"O you will let me hold your brave hand, stranger?"

"Hush! Yes, my poor sister; to the last." . . .

The supposed Evrémonde descends, and the seamstress is lifted out next after him. He has not relinquished her patient hand in getting out, but still holds it as he promised. He gently places her with her back to the crashing engine that constantly whirs up and falls, and she looks into his face and thanks him.

"But for you, dear stranger, I should not be so composed, for I am naturally a poor little thing, faint of heart; nor should I have been able to raise my thoughts to Him who was put to death, that we might have hope and comfort here to-day. I think you were sent to me by Heaven."

"Or you to me," says Sydney Carton. "Keep your eyes upon me, dear child, and mind no other object."

"I mind nothing while I hold your hand. I shall mind nothing when I let it go, if they are rapid."

"They will be rapid. Fear not!" . . .

"Brave and generous friend, will you let me ask you one last question? I am very ignorant, and it troubles me—just a little."

"Tell me what it is."

"I have a cousin, an only relative and an orphan, like myself, whom I love very dearly. She is five years younger than I, and she lives in a farmer's house in the south country. Poverty parted us, and she knows nothing of my fate—for I cannot write—and if I could, how should I tell her! It is better as it is."

"Yes, yes; better as it is."

"What I have been thinking as we came along, and what I am still thinking now, as I look into your kind strong face which gives me so much support, is this:—If the Republic really does good to the poor, and they come to be less hungry, and in all ways to suffer less, she may live a long time: she may even live to be old."

"What then, my gentle sister?"

"Do you think—" the uncomplaining eyes in which there is so much endurance, fill with tears, and the lips part a little more and tremble: "that it will seem long to me, while I wait for her in the better land where I trust both you and I will be mercifully sheltered?"

"It cannot be, my child; there is no time there, and no trouble there."

"You comfort me so much! I am so ignorant. Am I to kiss you

now? Is the moment come?"

"Yes."

She kisses his lips; he kisses hers; they solemnly bless each other. The spare hand does not tremble as he releases it; nothing worse than a sweet, bright constancy is in the patient face. She goes next before him—is gone. . . .

"I am the Resurrection and the Life, saith the Lord: he that believeth in me, though he were dead, yet shall he live: and whosoever liveth and believeth in me shall never die."

The murmuring of many voices, the upturning of many faces, the pressing on of many footsteps in the outskirts of the crowd, so that it swells forward in a mass, like one great heave of water, all flashes away. . . . 🙥

Acknowledgements

Efforts were made to trace the owners of all copyrighted material. If any questions of ownership arise, corrections will be made in subsequent printings. Thanks to all authors and publishers for permission to use the following material.

ABINGDON PRESS "Susanna Wesley's Rules of Order" and "Raising Responsible Children" taken From *Susanna—Mother of the Wesleys*, by Rebecca Lamar Harmon. Used by permission of Abingdon Press.

BAKER BOOK HOUSE COMPANY "The Middle Mile" taken from *In Tune With Heaven*, by Vance Havner. ©1990, pp. 38-39. "Tony the Pony" taken from *The Boola Pan*, by Helen Noordewier, pp. 17-27. "A Country Wedding" taken from *Missy Doe*, by Helen Noordewier, pp. 65-71. All used by permission of Baker Book House Company

BANTAM DOUBLEDAY DELL "To My Daughter" taken from *Thank You For Being a Friend*, by Jill Briscoe. ©1980 by Jill Briscoe. "Peter and the Angel," "Philip and the Ethiopian," and "A Rift in a Friendship" taken from *The Greatest Faith Ever Known*, by Fulton Oursler and April Oursler Armstrong. ©1953 by April Oursler Armstrong. All used by permission of Bantam Doubleday Dell.

BETHANY HOUSE PUBLISHERS "The Grim Reaper" taken from *Love Comes Softly*, by Janette Oke. ©1979, pp. 11-17. Used by permission of Bethany House Publishers.

BRISCOE, STUART "The Sacrifice," by Stuart Briscoe. Used by permission.

LARRY BURKETT "Restored," by Larry Burkett. ©1994 by Larry Burkett. Printed in *Decision* magazine November 1994; published by the Billy Graham Evangelistic Asssociation. Used by permission of Larry Burkett, founder and president of Christian Financial Concepts, Inc.

CHRISTIAN LITERATURE CRUSADE "No Is an Answer" taken from *Amy Carmichael of Dohnavur*, by Frank Houghton. Used by permission of Christian Literature Crusade.

CHARLES COLSON *Trouble in the Schoolyard*, by Charles Colson, Chariot Family Publishing. Used by permission of Charles Colson.

COLUMBIA INTERNATIONAL UNIVERSITY *Living By Vows*, by Robertson McQuilkin. Reprinted by permission of Columbia International University.

CONFRATERNITY OF CHRISTIAN DOCTRINE "Wise in Work" taken from the New American Bible. ©1970 by the Confraternity of Christian Doctrine, Washington, D.C. 20017. Used with permission. All rights reserved.

CONSTABLE PUBLISHERS "A Love for Children" taken from *Wilberforce*, by John Pollock, p. 232. Used by permission of Constable Publishers.

THE COPYRIGHT COMPANY "God's Giving" taken from *He Giveth More Grace*, by Annie Johnson Flint. © 1941, 1969 by Lillenas Publishing Company. Used by permission of The Copyright Company.

DAVID C. COOK PUBLISHING COMPANY "Ceiling Zero" taken from *The Gospel Blimp and Other Modern Parables*, by Joseph Bayly. ©1983 by Joseph Bayly. "Thoughts Before Surgery" taken from *Heaven* by Joseph Bayly. ©1977 by David C. Cook Publishing Company. "A Psalm of Minor Miracles" taken from *Psalms of My Life*, by Joseph Bayly. ©1987 by the Estate of Joseph Bayly. *Mrs. Rosey-Posey and the Chocolate Cherry Treat*, by Robin Jones Gunn. ©1991 by Robin Jones Gunn. *The*

True Princess, by Angela Elwell Hunt. ©1992 by Angela Elwell Hunt. *Adam Raccoon and the Flying Machine*, by Glen Keane. ©1989 by Glen Keane. "The Real Treasure" taken from *Apple Turnover Treasure*, by Nancy Simpson Levene. ©1992 by Nancy R. Simpson. "The Faithless Ranger" taken from *Tales of the Kingdom*, by David and Karen Mains. ©1983 by David and Karen Burton Mains. *Uncle Alphonso and the Greedy Green Dinosaurs*, by Jack Pearson. ©1992 by Jack Pearson. "Grandma's Prayer" taken from *In Grandma's Attic*, by Arleta Richardson. ©1974 by David C. Cook Publishing Co. "The Surprise Birthday Present" taken from *Still More Stories From Grandma's Attic*, by Arleta Richardson. ©1980 by David C. Cook Publishing Co. *Casey the Greedy Young Cowboy*, by Michael P. Waite. ©1988 by Michael P. Waite. *Max and the Big Fat Lie*, by Michael P. Waite. ©1988 by Michael P. Waite. "Entertaining Angels" taken from *A Child's Book of Angels*, by Marilyn J. Woody. ©1992 by Marilyn J. Woody.

ELISABETH ELLIOT "To Gain What He Cannot Lose" taken from *Shadow of the Almighty*, by Elisabeth Elliot. ©1958 by Elisabeth Elliot. Published by Zondervan Publishing House. Used by Permission of Elisabeth Elliot.

FABER AND FABER LTD. Excerpt from *Murder in the Cathedral*, by T.S. Eliot. Reprinted by permission of the publisher.

FARRAR, STRAUS & GIROUX "Five Finger Exercises" and "Promises Made" taken from *A Circle of Quiet*, by Madeleine L'Engle. ©1972 by Madeleine L'Engle Franklin. Reprinted by permission of Farrar, Straus & Giroux.

HARCOURT BRACE & COMPANY Excerpt from *Murder in the Cathedral*, by T.S. Eliot. ©1935 by Harcourt Brace & Company and renewed 1961 by T.S. Eliot. Reprinted by permission of the publisher. "The Apologist's Evening Prayer" taken from *Poems*, by C.S. Lewis, edited by Walter Hooper. ©1964 by the Executors of the Estate of C.S. Lewis and renewed 1992 by C.S. Lewis Pte., Ltd. Reprinted by permission of Harcourt Brace & Company.

HAROLD SHAW PUBLISHING COMPANY "Kicking a Habit" taken from *Transfroming the Daily Grind*, by Stuart Briscoe. "Kindness Is a Choice" taken from *The Fruit of the Spirit* by Stuart Briscoe. Both used by permission of Harold Shaw Publishing Company.

HARPERCOLLINS PUBLISHERS NEW YORK "Rise and Walk" taken from *Rise and Walk: The Trial and Triumph of Dennis Byrd*, by Dennis Byrd and Michael D'Orso. ©1993 by Dennis Byrd and Michael D'Orso. "Signs of Friendship" taken from *The Meaning of Persons* and *The Meaning of Gifts*, by Paul Tournier. ©1957 and ©1964 by SCM Press Ltd. "Words Children Like to Hear" taken from *The Christian Speaker's Treasury*, by Ruth A. Tucker. ©1989 by Ruth A. Tucker. All used by permission of HarperCollins Publishers.

HARPERCOLLINS PUBLISHERS LIMITED LONDON "Ninepence for a Baby" taken from *Girl Friday to Gladys Aylward*, by Vera Cowie, ©1976. "The Apologist's Evening Prayer" taken from *Poems*, by C.S. Lewis, edited by Walter Hooper. Both used by permission of HarperCollins Publishers Limited.

DAVID HIGHAM ASSOCIATES "To Labor Passionately" taken from *The Mind of the Maker*, by Dorothy Sayers. Used by permission of David Higham Associates.

INTERNATIONAL BIBLE SOCIETY All Scripture quotations marked NIV in this publication are from the Holy Bible, New International Version. ©1973, 1978, 1984, International Bible Society.

INTERVARSITY PRESS "Dad, Did You Ever Cheat?" taken from *Letters to My Children*, by Daniel Taylor. Used by permission of InterVarsity Press, P.O. Box 1400, Downers Grove, IL 60515.

JOHN KNAPP II "Aristarchus," "A Pillar of Pepper," "Ten Poor Lepers" and "Ananias" taken from *A Pillar of Pepper*, by John Knapp II. ©1982 by John Knapp II. Published by Chariot Family Publishing. Used by permission of John Knapp II.

JOHN LEAX "After the Stroke" taken from *Reaching Into Silence*, by John Leax. Published by Harold Shaw Publishers. Reprinted by permission of John Leax.

LESCHER & LESCHER, LTD. "Five-Finger Exercises" and "Promises Made" taken from *A Circle of Quiet* by Madeleine L'Engle. ©1972 by Madeleine L'Engle Franklin. Used by permission.

LION PUBLISHING PLC., OXFORD "Shout from the Pulpit", "The Squint-Eyed Preacher" and "The Courageous Preacher" taken from *George Whitefield and the Great Awakening*, by John Pollock, pp. 81-83, 219-220, ©1972. Reprinted by permission of Lion Publishing PLC.

THE LOCHMAN FOUNDATION All Scripture quotations marked NASB are from New American Standard Bible. © 1960, 1962, 1963, 1968, 1971, 1972, 1973, 1975, 1977 by The Lochman Foundation.

LONGMAN GROUP "The Doctor and the Street Children" taken from *Dr. Bernardo*, by Norman Wymer, ©1962. Published by Longman's, Green and Co, Ltd.

MCCRACKEN PRESS "The Secret of Joy" taken from *The Faithful Christian: An Anthology of Billy Graham*, by Billy Graham. Published by McCracken Press.

MOODY PRESS "In-Spite-of-Love" taken from *The Heart of a Mother*, by Ruby Johnson. ©1982 by Moody Press. Used by permission.

OTTENHEIMER "The Faithful Servant," "Part of the Family," and "Thunder on the Mountain" taken from *The Illustrated Children's Bible Storybook*, adapted by E.B.R. Hirsh. ©1988 by Ottenheimer Publishers. Published by Chariot Family Publishing.

OVERSEAS MISSIONARY FELLOWSHIP "Preparing For China" and "Lessons in Prayer" taken from *Hudson Taylor in Early Years*, by Dr. and Mrs. Howard Taylor, ©1911. Published by China Inland Mission. Reprinted by permission of Overseas Missionary Fellowship.

RANDOM HOUSE, INC. "An Unforgettable Day's Work" taken from *Koop: The Memoirs of America's Family Doctor*, by C. Everett Koop, M.D., ©1991. Reprinted by permission of Random House, Inc.

REED CONSUMER BOOKS "Freddy the Farm Horse" and "Silly to Fuss" taken from *366 Good Night Stories*, by Paul Hamlyn, ©1963. Published by Hamlyn Publishing Group Ltd. Reprinted by permission of Reed Consumer Books.

SCM PRESS, LTD. "Signs of Friendship" taken from *The Meaning of Persons* and *The Meaning of Gifts*, by Paul Tournier. ©1957 and © 1964 by SCM Press, Ltd. Used by permission.

SCRIPTURE UNION "The Good Samaritan" taken from *Ladybird New Testament*, by Jenny Robertson, ©1981. Reprinted by permission of Scripture Union.

THE SOCIETY FOR PROMOTING CHRISTIAN KNOWLEDGE "Prayer for the Children" taken from *Toward Jerusalem*, by Amy Carmichael. Published by The Society for Promoting Christian Knowledge in 1931. Used by permission of the Publishers.

TEAM HORIZONS "One Left Behind" taken from January/February 1994 *Team Horizons Magazine*. Used by permission of Team Horizons.

THOMAS NELSON INC. "Keeping Friends" taken from *Little House in the Ozarks*, by Laura Ingalls Wilder, ©1991. Published by Thomas Nelson Inc. Used by permission of the publishers.

THREE'S COMPANY *Mary Jones and Her Bible*, by Mig Holder. ©1992 by Three's Company. Published by British and Foreign Bible Society. Used by permission of Three's Company.

Index